Index to Characters in the Performing Arts

Part III - Ballets
A - Z and Symbols

compiled by
Harold S. Sharp
and
Marjorie Z. Sharp

The Scarecrow Press, Inc.
Metuchen, N. J.   1972

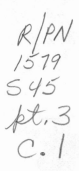
ii

Foreword

Following the publishing of Part II of Index to Characters in the Performing Arts in August of 1968, the compilers have been busy assembling and organizing the material for the present volume. Part I identifies characters in non-musical plays, Part II is concerned with characters in operas and other musical productions; and this volume, Part III of the series, deals with ballet characters. Part IV, radio and television characters, is in preparation.

Ballet is primarily a visual interpretation of music rather than a branch of drama. When a piece of music has program, the ballet has program, i.e., plot and characters. When the music is designed for mood and emotion, its ballet is motion rather than story. Consequently, the compilers of this volume have been limited, in listing ballet characters, to identifying those in "plot" ballets only.

Like the other volumes in this series, the purpose of this one is fourfold: to identify a character with the production in which he or she appears; to tell, in a few words, something about the character; to designate the individuals responsible for the creation of the production (composer, arranger, choreographer, librettist, décor designer, and original source of the plot or story, as applicable); and to indicate the date and place of the first performance.

This, like the previous volumes, is by no means a book of criticism. No attempt is made to analyze characters or evaluate the merits of the ballets in which they appear. It is essentially a finding list, and once the user has identified a character with the particular ballet concerned he may consult the production itself for additional information. It seeks only to answer the question, "In which ballet did such-and-such a character appear?" If it does this the compilers' objective has been achieved.

In terms of time, the coverage ranges from the ballets of the late 16th century to those of the present day. In all 818 ballets are covered, and approximately 3000 characters, both major and minor, are identified. No geographical or language limitations are imposed.

The book is divided into two sections. The first of these is an alphabetical listing of the characters covered. A sample entry is shown below:

```
ELEKTRA, avenges her father's murder
    ORESTES, her brother and ally
    AGAMEMNON, father of Elektra and Orestes
    CLYTEMNESTRA, wife of Agamemnon, mother of
    Elektra and Orestes; murders Agamemnon
    AEGISTHUS, Clytemnestra's lover and
    accomplice in the murder
    Elektra                                      ELEKT
```

Cross-references are made from "Orestes," "Agamemnon," "Clytemnestra" and "Aegisthus" to "Elektra." In addition, a five-letter citation symbol, in this case ELEKT, is shown.

The second section of the book, commencing on page 247, contains the key to the citation symbols, which are listed alphabetically. Reproduced below is the full citation to Elektra as it appears in the second section:

```
ELEKT  Elektra, ballet (1 act).  Music, Malcolm
    Arnold; choreography, Robert Helpmann; book,
    after the tragedies of Aeschylus, Sophocles
    and Euripides; décor, Arthur Boyd.  Royal
    Opera House, Covent Garden, London, March 26,
    1963.
```

The citation indicates, in order, the citation symbol ELEKT, the title of the ballet, the type of production, the number of acts, the composer of the music, the choreographer, the source of the book, the person responsible for the décor, and the place and date of the first production. Thus, if one wishes to identify the character Elektra only with a specific ballet, he may do this merely by consulting the first section. This applies also to the other characters in this ballet, who may be located by means of the cross-references. If one wishes additional information about the production, the second section will supply it. For further information the user is directed to the original production itself, as indicated above. It seemed best to divide the book into two sections rather than repeat the full bibliographic citation under each main entry as this would greatly increase the physical size of the volume.

During the compilation of this book many people were extremely helpful. Especially so were the reference staff members of the libraries of the University of California, Berkeley; the Oakland, Berkeley and San Francisco Public Libraries; the Gregg H. Sinclair Library, University of Hawaii; the Oahu Public Library of Honolulu; and the Cunningham Memorial Library, Indiana State University, Terre Haute, Indiana. The compilers wish to express their deep gratitude to all these willing helpers at this time.

Harold S. Sharp
Marjorie Z. Sharp

September 1971

Index to Ballet Characters

AASE, widow of John Gynt; peasant woman
PEER GYNT, her son
Peer Gynt   PEERG

AASE. See also:
Anitra
Ingrid
Solveig
Troll King, The

ABDERAM, a Saracen knight,
Raymonda   RAYMO

ABDERRAMAN. See: Caliph Abderraman

ABDURASSUL, BEY, wealthy, resolves to abduct Nozgulle and Zarragulle, daughters of Bobo-Safar; does so
THE OLD KADDISH, his servant
The Two Roses   TWORO

ABDURASSUL, BEY. See also:
Radzhab

ABEL. See: Cain

ABIGAIL, Michal's rival for the affections of David,
David   DAVID

ABIGAIL. See also: Jesse

ABINADAB. See: Jesse

ABISHAI, man to David, son of Jesse, David   DAVID

ABNER, captain of the Host,
David   DAVID

ABOUT TOWN, MAN. See:
Amazon Captain
Fashionable Lady

ABRAHAM. See:
Ibrahim
Lincoln, Abraham

ABU-BEKR, a notary, The Blood-Red Flower   BLOOD

ABU-SOLIMAN. See:
Caliph Abderraman
Hazdai-Ben-Shaprut

ACCORDION-PLAYER, AN, member of an artists' brigade, The Bright Stream   BRIGH

ACCUSED, THE (Lizzie Borden), convicted of murdering her father and stepmother with an ax; condemned to death on the gallows
HER MOTHER
HER FATHER
HER STEPMOTHER
Fall River Legend   FALLR

ACCUSED, THE. See also:
Pastor
Speaker for the Jury

ACE, playing card, participates in poker game, Card Game   CARDG

ACHILLES, apparition conjured up by Faust, Abraxas   ABRAX

ACHMET, oriental nobleman,

falls in love with the Peri,
La Péri   PERII

ACHMET. See also:
Jailer
Nourmahal
Roucem

ACROBAT, participant in
gypsy carnival
Aleko   ALEKO
Circus performer
Every Soul Is a Circus
                           EVERY

ACROBATS, members of troupe
of traveling players, Les
Forains   FORAI

ACROBATS, TWO, members
of group of performers,
Parade   PARAD

ACTAEON, hunter, sees Diana
bathing, turned by her
into a stag
Aubade   AUBAA
Aubade   AUBAB
Aubade   AUBAC
Aubade   AUBAD
Aubade   AUBAE

ACTION, personification,
Les Présages   PRESA

ACTRESS, AN (The One Who
Speaks), allegorical figure,
Letter to the World
                           LETTE

ADAGIO-BRIDE, THE
HER PARTNER AND HUS-
BAND, couple symbolic of
youthful love
The Widow in the Mirror
                           WIDOW

ADAH ISAACS MENKEN. See:
"Menken, The"

ADAM, the first man
EVE, his wife
The Creation of the World
                           CREAW

The first man
LILITH, his first wife
EVE, his second wife
STRANGER, enters Garden
of Eden
Embattled Garden   EMBAT

ADAM, PRINCE. See: Marie

ADAM ZERO. See:
Death
Principal Dancer, The
Stage Director, The

ADDA, Queen of the Elves,
confers life during the daytime on Stone Statue
(Sylvia), Les Elfes   ELFES

ADDIE. See: Bundren, Addie

ADÉLAÏDE, courtesan, expresses her moods through the
medium of flowers; attracts
Lorédan and the Duke,
Adêlaïde, or The Language
of the Flowers   ADELA

ADÉLAÏDE, See also: Count
Raoul de Créqui

ADMADEYA, a nymph, loved
by Pan and Boreas; appears
in ballet at the Serfs'
Theatre
HER FRIENDS
Katerina   KATER

ADMETUS. See: Alcestis

ADOLF, loved by Anna II, The
Seven Deadly Sins   SEVED

ADOLPHE, habitué at bar of
Folies-Bergère, Bar au
Folies-Bergère   BARAU

ADONCINO, CAPITANO, hand-
some cavalier, sought by
two Husband-Hunters,
The Lady and the Fool
                      LADYA

ADONIS, handsome young man,

loved by Venus
Adonis   ADONI
The Loves of Venus and
Adonis   LOVEV

ADONIS. See also: Advertising Adonis

ADRIAN. See:
Cronk, Reverend Adrian
Eleonore

ADRIANI. See: Lord Adriani

ADVENTURER, representation
of Jason, Cave of the
Heart   CAVEO

ADVENTURER. See also:
Victim

ADVERTISING ADONIS,
"headliner seeking refuge
from publicity," visiting
2222 Club, New York City,
Café Society   CAFES

AEGINA. See: Spartacus

AEGISTHUS, paramour, later
husband of Clytemnestra,
Clytemnestra   CLYTE

AEGISTHUS. See also: Elektra

AENEAS, Trojan warrior,
loved by Dido, Queen of
Carthage, Dido   DIDOO

AFRICAN, met by the Farm
Boy on his travels,
Yankee Clipper   YANKE

AFRICAN SLAVE, personification,
Concerto Brasileiro CONCB

AGALIA, a female smuggler,
Kalkabrino   KALKA

AGAMEMNON. See:
Clytemnestra
Elektra
Iphigenia

AGAMEMNON'S GHOST. See:
Clytemnestra

AGANIPPE, "innocent friend
of the Transgressor,"
Undertow   UNDER

AGANIPPE. See also: Nemesis

AGATHE, beautiful white cat,
temporarily changed into
human being; marries
Musician
MUSICIAN, her husband,
flute player
CAT BARON, her intended
husband
Les Demoiselles de la
Nuit   DEMOI

AGE, OLD. See: Poet, The

AGED WOMAN WITH GUITAR,
recalls the sad course of
her life, Shadow of the
Wind   SHADW

AGENT. See: Revenue Agent

AGENT, COMPANY'S. See:
Village Elder

AGLAË, young girl, instructed
by Cupid in the art of
dancing, Aglaë   AGLAE

AGLAË. See also:
Faun, The
Philemon
Youth, The

AGNES. See:
Cesarius
Selina

AGONISTES, SAMSON, "a man
blinded by his own strength
and reborn through his
vision"; betrayed by
Delilah
THE DEDICATED
THE DESTROYER
THE TEMPTER, "the three

aspects of Samson"
Samson Agonistes   SAMSO

AGRICULTURE. See: Genii
of Agriculture, The

AHIMELECH, priest, David
DAVID

AIDE-DE-CAMP, to the Prince,
The Prisoner in the Cau-
casus   PRISR

AIDE-DE-CAMP, HIS. See:
Peter I

AIMÉE. See: Robert

AIMÉE, LA BIEN. See:
Poet, The

AINA. See:
Anna
Sauldots
Sorceress, The
Tautvaldis

AIR. See: Queen of the Air,
The

AIR, DAUGHTER OF THE.
See: Queen of Shemakha

AIR, THE, personification,
Les Elements   ELEME

AIYA, a female slave, La
Bayadère   BAYAD

AJAX I
AJAX II, ordered by Cal-
chas to capture Paris' pet
lamb, Helen of Troy
HELEN

AJAX I. See also: Lamb

AKDAR, KING OF DELHI.
See: Damayanti

ALAIN. See:
Thomas
Ysaure

ALARIS, King of Bucharia, under
the name of Feramorz, the
poet; betrothed to Lalla
Rookh, daughter of The Emperor Aurungzebe, Emperor
of Hindustan
HIS AMBASSADOR
Lalla Rookh   LALLA

ALARIS. See also: Emperor
Aurungzebe, The, Emperor
of Hindustan

ALBA. See: Duke of Alba

ALBA, DUCHESS OF. See:
Duke of Alba

ALBERT OF HUNGARY, attracted
to Stone Statue (Sylvia) as
statue and as daytime maiden,
Les Elfes   ELFES

ALBERT OF HUNGARY. See
also: Princess Bathilde

ALBRECHT, Duke of Silesia, betrothed to Bathilde, daughter
of Prince of Courland; disguised as the peasant Loys,
in love with Giselle
Giselle   GISEE
Giselle   GISEL
Giselle   GISES

ALBRECHT. See also:
Giselle
Wilfrid

ALCESTIS, dies in place of her
husband, thereby saving his
life; brought back from Hades
by Hercules
ADMETUS, Argonaut and
King of Thessaly, her husband
Alcestis   ALCES

ALCHEMIST. See: Popoloni,
Alchemist

ALCHEMIST, THE, friend and
major-domo of the Contessa;
conjures up Rose, Violet and

5

Carnation, spirits of perfumed seduction, Quelques Fleurs   QUELQ

ALCHEMIST, THE. See also: Rose

ALCYONE, celestial star, Electra   ELECT

ALDONZA. See: Lorenzo, Aldonza

ALEKO, city youth, joins gypsy band; in love with Zemphira, spurned by her for Young Gypsy; stabs them both fatally, Aleko   ALEKO

ALEKO. See also:
Bat
Cat
Duke
Poet
Snake
Society Girls
Society Lady

ALEXANDER THE GREAT, conqueror, poisoned by the Queen of Babylon, Alexandre le Grand   ALEXA

ALEXANDER THE GREAT. See also: Zeus

ALEXANDROVITCH, SERGEI, impresario of Russian ballet company in which Junior appears, Slaughter on Tenth Avenue   SLAUG

ALFONSO. See: Alvarez

ALGERNON. See: Swinburne, Algernon C.

ALI, rich slave dealer, Namouna   NAMOU

ALI. See also: Iotis

ALI-BATYR. See: Suimbike

ALI-BEN-TAMARAT, an African chief, Zoraiya   ZORAI

ALIAS, accidentally shoots and kills mother of Billy the Kid; appears as sheriff, land agent, jailer and Indian guide, Billy the Kid   BILLY

ALICIA, friend of Young Tregennis, dances with him in haunted ballroom, The Haunted Ballroom   HAUNT

ALINE. See: Jailer

ALL-POWERFUL FATHER, THE, "symbol of a power that exists through His disciples," The Age of Anxiety AGEOE

ALLEGRETTO
ALLEGRO
LARGO
ANDANTE, musical terms, expressed in terms of the dance
Lyric Suite   LYRIC

ALLEN, BARBARA, loved by John and Marvin; killed by Marvin's knife during a fight
JOHN, stranger
MARVIN, native
Barbara Allen   BARBA

ALLEN, BARBARA. See also: Witches, Two Young

ALLEY SLOPER, representation of British publication, The Press   PRESS

ALMA. See:
Belfegor
Emazor

ALMAN, miner, loved by Rosida, Rosida   ROSID

ALMAN. See also: Queen of the Mines

ALOISA. See: Cinderella

ALOISE DE GONDELAURIER,
    MADAME. See: Fleur de
    Lys

ALONSO, DON. See: Duke of
    Medina-Celi, The

ALONZO. See: Don Alonzo

ALTAMIRANO. See: Don
    Altamirano

ALVA, in love
    ALVA'S SWEETHEART,
    daughter of a consul
    LIEUTENANT, in the Danish
    navy, Alva's rival
    Far From Denmark
                        FARFR

ALVAR. See:
    Danina
    Don Alvar
    Fernandez

ALVAREZ
    ARMANDO
    ANGELO, a page
    ALFONSO
    ORLANDO, lovers of Queen
    Clementine, wife of King
    Bobiche
    Bluebeard   BLUEB

ALYATAR, Moorish prince, La
    Fille de Marbre   FILLM

ALYOSHA. See: Popovich,
    Alyosha

AMADER OF GAUL, hero of
    chivalry, figment of Don
    Quixote's imagination,
    Don Quixote   DONQX

AMAGER COUPLE, performs
    dance for Cupid's approval,
    The Whims of Cupid and the
    Ballet Master   WHIMS

AMALIA. See: Don Alvar

AMAZON CAPTAIN, loves, wins
    the Bandit with the assistance
    of Amore (Cupid)
    TWO AMAZON LIEUTENANTS
    won by the Man About Town
    and the Sailor
    AMAZONS, followers of
    Amazon Captain
    Con Amore   CONAM

AMAZON LIEUTENANTS, TWO.
    See:
    Amazon Captain
    Fashionable Lady

AMAZONS, toys, Jeux d'Enfants
                        JEUXX

AMAZONS. See also: Amazon
    Captain

AMAZONS, QUEEN OF THE. See:
    Hippolyta
    Phaedra
    Queen of the Amazons, The

AMAZONS, THE, overcome by
    the Black Horses
    THEIR HORSES
    Le Massacre des Amazones
                        MASSA

AMBASSADOR. See: Egyptian
    Ambassador, An

AMBASSADOR, HIS. See:
    Alaris, King of Bucharia

AMBASSADOR OF ARROGANZA.
    See: Prince of Arroganza,
    The

AMBASSADOR, THE, wealthy
    representative of the Western
    World; offered hand of Chung-
    Yang in marriage by Man-
    darin, her father
    HIS TWO FRIENDS
    L'Épreuve d'Amour EPREU

AMBASSADORS. See: Murat's
    Ambassadors, Two

AMBROSIO, FRA, monk, helps
    reunite Teresina and Gen-
    naro,
    Napoli   NAPOL

AMELPHA, King Dondon's
    nurse, Le Coq d'Or
                        COQDO

AMERICAN. See: Young Stu-
    dent

AMERICAN, AN
    HIS FAMILY, customers at
    toy shop
    La Boutique Fantasque
                        BOUTI

AMERICAN GIRL, tourist in
    London, London Morning
                        LONDO

AMERICAN GIRL. See also:
    Little American Girl, The

AMERICAN GOOF. See: Great
    American Goof, The

AMERICAN PIONEER WOMAN,
    performs solo dance,
    Frontier   FRONT

AMINTA, shepherd youth,
    Sylvia   SYLVA

AMINTA. See also: Amyntas

AMOR, god of love, encourages
    Orpheus to bring his wife
    Eurydice back from the
    Underworld
    Orpheus and Eurydice
                        ORPHS
    God of love
    Orpheus and Eurydice
                        ORPHU
    "Mischievous god of love"
    Les Petits Reins PETIT

AMOR. See also:
    Amour
    Apollo
    Shepherdesses, Two

AMORE (CUPID), loved by the
    Timorous Student; reunites
    Fashionable Lady with her
    husband, Con Amore CONAM

AMORE (CUPID). See also:
    Bandit

AMOÛN, in love with Ta-Hor,
    fascinated by Cléopâtre,
    Queen of Egypt, Cléopâtre
                        CLEOP

AMOÛN. See also: High Priest
    of the Temple

AMOUR, an actress at the Court
    Theater, The Flames of
    Paris   FLAME

AMOUR. See also:
    Amor
    Bel-Amour

AMOUREUSE. See: Morte Amour-
    euse, La

AMPHITRITE, Goddess of the Sea
    TRITON, her son, a demigod
    The Beautiful Pearl BEAUT
    Queen of the Sea
    Flik and Flok   FLIKA

AMRAVATI, goddess of the heav-
    ly spirits
    NIRITI, her daughter
    The Talisman   TALIS

AMYNTAS (Aminta), shepherd,
    in love with Sylvia, Sylvia
                        SYLVI

ANAR, Genius of Good, protects
    Toniello against evil of
    Hertha, Queen of the El-
    frits, Fiorita et la Reine
    des Elfrides   FIORI

ANASTACHIUSKA. See: Princess
    Anastachiuska

ANCESTRESS, THE, allegorical
    figure, Letter to the World
                        LETTE

ANDANTE.   See: Allegretto

ANDREA, a nobleman
    ATLANTA, his mother
    CLARISSA, his sister
    Chronica   CHRON

ANDREI, Russian, Pages of
    Life   PAGEL

ANDREW.   See: King Andrew
    II, King of Hungary

ANDREY, betrothed to Ulinka
    THE GOVERNOR, his uncle
    Katerina   KATER

ANDREY.   See also:
    Bulba, Taras
    Odarka

ANDRIKÈS, Namouna's atten-
    dant, Namouna   NAMOU

ANGE, MADAME DE SAINT.
    See: Duc de Vendôme,
    The

ANGEL.   See:
    Dark Angel
    Grey Angel, The
    Guardian Angel

ANGEL OF DEATH.   See:
    Dark Angel
    Grey Angel, The

ANGEL OF INNOCENCE, per-
    sonification, Billy Sunday
                          BILLS

ANGELA.   See: Spada, Marco

ANGELIC APPARITION
    GUINEVERE
    LANCELOT, appear to
    Francesca (Francesca da
    Rimini) and Paolo Malatesta
    Francesca da Rimini
                          FRANC

ANGELICA, lady, figment of Don
    Quixote's imagination,

Don Quixote   DONQX

ANGELICA.   See also:
    Lugano, Marco
    Monster, A

ANGELO.   See: Alvarez

ANGELS, TWO, bar Five Foolish
    Virgins from the Bride's wed-
    ding, Les Vierges Folles
                          VIERG

ANGIOLA.   See: Massimo

ANGOT, MAM'ZELLE (Clairette),
    daughter of a market-woman,
    betrothed to the Barber, ne-
    glects him for the attentions
    of the Caricaturist, Mam'
    zelle Angot   MAMZE

ANGOT, MAM'ZELLE.   See also:
    Aristocrat, The

ANGUISH, personification,
    Anguish Sonata   ANGUI

ANGULO.   See: Moscatello,
    Sergeant

ANIMAL TRAINER, THE.   See:
    Young Girl, The

ANITRA, daughter of a Bedouin
    chief, steals everything from
    Peer Gynt, Peer Gynt
                          PEERG

ANITRA.   See also: Aase

ANN.   See:
    Anne
    Philemon

ANNA.   See:
    Aina
    Reuben, James

ANNA I
    ANNA II, sisters, represent-
    ing mankind's dual nature,
    mind and heart

THE FATHER
THE MOTHER, their parents
TWO SONS, their brothers
The Seven Deadly Sins
                              SEVED

ANNA I.   See also:
   Adolf
   Ballet-Master, The
   Demi-Monde, The
   Edward
   Film Star, The
   Manager, The
   Régisseur, The

ANNABEL.   See: Lee, Annabel

ANNE.   See:
   Ann
   Renoualle, Ysaure de

ANNE BOLEYN.   See: King
   Henry VIII, King of England

ANNE, SISTER.   See: Bluebeard

ANNOUNCER.   See: Radio
   Announcer

ANNUNZIATA.   See: Lugano,
   Marco

ANOTHER REFLECTION.   See:
   Lady With Him, The

ANSE.   See: Bundren, Addie

ANSELME, FATHER, priest,
   Le Violon du Diable
                              VIOLO

ANSELMI.   See: Count Anselmi

ANSWERS, representation of
   British publication, The
   Press   PRESS

ANTIGONE.   See: Oedipus

ANTOINE.   See: Mistral, Antoine

ANTOINETTE, QUEEN MARIE.
   See: King Louis XVI, King
   of France

ANTON.   See: Philemon

ANTONIA.   See: Rafael

ANTONINA, Bachelor Sampson
   Carrasco's servant, Don
   Quichotte   DONQU

ANTONY, Roman triumvir,
   friend of Julius Caesar
   Amor   AMORR
   Roman triumvir, seduced by
   Cleopatra
   OCTAVIA, his consort
   HER TWO CHILDREN, by
   Antony
   OCTAVIUS, Octavia's brother,
   Roman triumvir
   Les Amours d'Antoine et de
   Cléopâtre   AMOUR

ANTONY.   See also: Egyptian
   Ambassador, An

ANTS, inhabitants of the insect
   world, become victims of
   the Spider
   Le Festin de l'Araignée
                          FESTD
   Le Festin de l'Araignée
                          FESTI
   The Spider's Banquet SPIDE

ANUSUYA, friend of Sakuntala,
   Sakuntala   SAKUN

APHRODITE, goddess, imprisons
   the Dryad
   The Dryad   DRYAD
   Goddess, bribes Paris to
   declare her winner over
   Hera and Pallas Athena in
   beauty contest
   Helen of Troy   HELEN
   Goddess

Phaedra   PHAED

APHRODITE. See also:
  Cat, The
  King Menelaus, King of
    Sparta
  Mouse

APHRON, PRINCE. See: King
Dondon

APOLLO, Leader of the Muses;
son of Zeus
  LETO, his mother
  Apollo, Leader of the
  Muses   APOLL
  God
  Apollon Musagète APOLN
  Castor et Pollux CASTO
  The Creatures of Prome-
  theus   CREAU
  Orpheus   ORPHE
  Sylvia   SYLVA

APOLLO. See also:
  Amor
  Artemis
  Nymphs, Two

APPARITION. See: Angelic
Apparition

APPARITIONS, THREE. See:
Sleeper

APPRENTICE. See:
  Sorcerer's Apprentice
  Young Apprentice

APPRENTICE GARDENERS.
See: Student, The

APRIL, a young man, Twelve
for the Mail-Coach
          TWELV

AQUARIUM, represented by
three dancers, Carnival
of Animals   CARNV

ARBENIN, suspects his wife
of unfaithfulness, poisons
her

NINA, his wife, drops her
bracelet
PRINCE ZVEZDICH, finds
Nina's bracelet, mistakenly
thinks it the property of
Baroness Strahl
BARONESS STRAHL, ex-
changes costumes with Nina;
tells Arbenin truth concerning Nina's supposed unfaithfulness
Masquerade   MASQE

ARC, JOAN OF. See:
  d'Arc, Jeanne
  Saint Joan

ARCHANGEL, saves Joseph from
punishment by Potiphar's
Wife, La Légende de Joseph
          LEGEN

ARCHANGEL LUCIFER, apostate
angel, attempts to prevent
Bartolo and other shepherds
from reaching Bethlehem;
decides to wed Gila to Hermit, thwarted by Archangel
St. Michael, Pastorela
          PASTO

ARCHANGEL LUCIFER. See
also: Lucifer

ARCHANGEL ST. MICHAEL,
saves Bartolo and other
shepherds from the apostate
Archangel Lucifer, Pastorela
          PASTO

ARCHIMAGO, personification of
hypocrisy, The Quest
          QUEST

ARCHIPOSA, "the devil's splen-
did courtesan," Abraxas
          ABRAX

ARENA. See: Empress of the
Arena

ARGENTINA. See: Golfo

ARGENTINE, met by the Farm
    Boy on his travels, Yankee
    Clipper   YANKE

ARGOS, KING OF. See: Cly-
    temnestra.

ARIADNE, daughter of King
    Minos of Crete
    Bacchus and Ariadne
                               BACCU
    Helps Theseus conquer
    the Minotaur
    Labyrinth   LABYR
    The Minotaur   MINOT
    The Minotaur   MINOU
    Spectacle   SPECL
    Daughter of King Minos of
    Crete
    The Triumph of Bacchus
    and Ariadne   TRIUB

ARIADNE. See also:
    Minos, King of Crete
    Theseus

ARIANA. See: Bluebeard

ARICIA, loved by Hippolytus
    stepson of Phaedra
    Phaedra   PHAED
    Phèdre   PHEDR

ARICIA. See also: Phaedra

ARISTOCRAT, THE, old school
    friend of Mam'zelle Angot;
    attracts the Caricaturist,
    Mam'zelle Angot MAMZE

ARISTOCRAT, THE. See also:
    Chief of Police, The
    Government Official, A

ARMAND. See: Duval, Armand

ARMANDO. See: Alvarez

ARMEN, soldier, member of
    the Red army, eldest son
    of Gabo-bidza; in love with
    Cariné
    GABO-BIDZA, his father

HIS MOTHER
AZAT, his younger brother
Happiness   HAPPI

ARMEN. See also:
    Commandant of the Patrol
    at the Outpost
    Enemy Leader, The

ARMIDA, an enchantress,
    Rinaldo and Armida RINAL

ARMIDE, reincarnation of the
    Marquise Madeleine, seen in
    dream by Vicomte de Beau-
    gency
    FRIENDS OF ARMIDE
    SLAVE OF ARMIDE
    Le Pavillon d'Armide PAVIL

ARMIDE. See also: René

ARMY AND NAVY GAZETTE,
    THE, representation of Bri-
    tish newspaper, The Press
                            PRESS

ARMY OFFICERS. See: Cour-
    asche

ARROGANZA. See: Prince of
    Arroganza, The

ARROGANZA, AMBASSADOR OF.
    See: Prince of Arroganza,
    The

ART. See: Visions d'Art

ARTEMIS, Greek goddess, twin
    of Apollo
    Artémis Troublée   ARTEM
    Phaedra   PHAED

ARTHUR, page, in love with
    Ysaure de Renoualle, Barbe
    Bleue   BARBE

ARTHUR. See also: Saint-Léon,
    Arthur Michel

ARTIFICIAL NIGHTINGALE. See:
    Nightingale, Artificial

Nightingale, Mechanical
Nightingale, The

ARTIST, patron of fashionable
café, Offenbach in the
Underworld   OFFEN

ARTIST, THE, sketches the
First Hand, afterwards
loses her to the King of
the Dandies, Le Beau
Danube   BEAUD

ARTISTS. See: Trapeze
Artists, Two

ARTS. See: Spirits of Various Arts

ASAK, young Norwegian, falls
in love with Solveig, the
Ice Maiden
HIS FATHER
The Ice Maiden   ICEMA

ASH. See: Fairy of the
Mountain Ash, The

ASMODEUS, The Devil on Two
Sticks, released from im-
prisonment by Cleophas,
Le Diable Boiteux   DIABL

ASPICIA, Pharaoh's favorite
daughter, seen by Lord
Wilson in opium-induced
dream
PHARAOH, King of Egypt,
her father
La Fille du Pharaon
                      FILLP

ASPICIA. See also:
High Priest
King of Nubia, The
King of the Nile
Monkey, A
Mummy of Pharaoh's
  Daughter
Ramseya

ASPIRANT, THE, understudy
of La Gloire (The Star);

hopes to achieve similar
fame, La Gloire   GLOIR

ASSAY OFFICER, determines
value of gold in Sierra min-
ing town, Ghost Town
                      GHOST

ASSISTANT. See: Hypnotist

ASSISTANT COOKS. See: Jeanne

ASSISTANT, HIS. See:
Barman
Burgomaster
Shopkeeper, The

ASSOL. See: Longren

ASTOLFO, bandit, Rinaldo's
lieutenant, La Prima Ballerina   PRIMA

ASTROLOGER, THE, presents
Golden Cockerel (Le Coq
d'Or) to King Dondon, Le
Coq d'Or   COQDO

ASTRONOMY, a muse, Sylvia
                      SYLVA

ATALANTA, mythological figure,
Spectacle   SPECL

ATALANTA. See also: Atlanta

ATE, "sensually disgusting,"
temporarily attracts the
Transgressor, Undertow
                      UNDER

ATHENA, goddess, I, Odysseus
                      IODYS

ATHENA. See also: Pallas
Athena

ATHENS, DUKE OF. See:
Theseus

ATHLETE, THE (The Strong
Man), participates in street
dance with the Street Dancer,

Le Beau Danube   BEAUD

ATHLETE, THE. See also:
    Manager, The

ATLANTA. See:
    Andrea
    Atalanta

ATTENDANT. See: Hérodiade

ATTENDANT CAVALIERS TO
    THE RUSSIAN BALLE-
    RINA. See: Queen of the
    Dance

ATTENDANT SPIRIT. See:
    Comus

ATTENDANTS, HER. See:
    Christian Girl

ATTENDANTS, HER FOUR.
    See: Oriane

ATTORNEY. See:
    Defending Attorney, A
    Prosecuting Attorney, A

AUGUST, an old woman,
    Twelve for the Mail-
    Coach   TWELV

AUGUSTE, a page, Les Pages
    du Duc de Vendôme
                     PAGES

AUNT, THE STOUT. See:
    Daughter, The

AUNT, THE THIN. See:
    Daughter, The

AURORA, the dawn, The
    Stars   STARS

AURORA. See also: Princess
    Aurora, The

AURUNGZEBE. See: Emperor
    Aurungzebe, The

AUSTRIA. See: Emperor of
    Austria, The

AUTUMN, personification, Les
    Quatre Saisons   QUATR

AUTUMN, THE FAIRY. See:
    Fairy Spring, The

AUTUMN WIND, THE, uproots
    Chrysanthemum which dies
    despite efforts of Young Poet
    to save her, Autumn Leaves
                     AUTUM

AVETTE, "a joker," Happiness
                     HAPPI

AWAKENER, THE. See: Delilah

AZALEA, chief odalisque, charac-
    ter in ballet "Azalea, or the
    Odalisque," The Débutante
                     DEBUT

AZAT. See: Armen

AZUCENA, gypsy girl, avenges
    her mother's death by kid-
    napping Manrico, son of
    Count di Luna
    HER MOTHER, executed by
    order of Count di Luna
    Revanche   REVAN

B

BABA-YAGA, ogress, lives in
    magic house, Contes Russes
                     CONTE

BABETTE, Mathurin's housekeep-
    er, Les Papillons   PAPIO

BABETTE (ROSINE). See:
    Pedrillo

BABY. See: Jazz-Baby, The

BABY STORK, brought up by
    Soviet children
    BABY STORK'S MOTHER,
    killed by Vasia
    Baby Stork   BABYS

BABY STORK. See also: Negro,
    A

BABYLON. See: Queen of
Babylon, The

BACCHANTES. See: Leader
of the Bacchantes

BACCHANTES, THREE,
"three harridans of the
lowest class," Undertow
                    UNDER

BACCHANTES, TWO, partici-
pants in the bacchanale,
Bacchanale   BACCH

BACCHUS, Greek god of wine
Bacchus and Ariadne
                    BACCU
The Creatures of Prome-
theus   CREAU
The Triumph of Bacchus
and Ariadne   TRIUB

BACCHUS. See also:
Ceres
Comus
Jaseion
Persephone
Pluto

BACHELOR. See: Carrasco,
Bachelor Sampson

BACKED. See: Hump-Backed
Horse, The

BAD PUPIL, THE. See:
Felicita

BADOUIN, landowner, neighbor
of Count Raoul de Créqui;
seizes the latter's lands
and attempts to seize his
wife, Raoul de Créqui
                    RAOUL

BADOUIN. See also: Hum-
bert

BAILIFF. See: Danila

BAKER, THE, loved by the
Young Girl, La Nuit NUITT

BAKHMETIEV, Armenian officer,
rival of the Prince for the
affections of the Princess
Nina; afterwards prisoner,
loved by the Circassian
Maid, The Prisoner in the
Caucasus   PRISR

BAKHMETIEV. See also: Leader of the Band

BALBI, JACOPPO. See: Petrucio

BALDA, gay, carefree tramp,
becomes handyman for the
priest Pop, The Fairy-Tale
of the Priest and His Workman Balda   FAIRY

BALDA. See also:
Little Hare, The First
Old Devil, The

BALINESE, met by the Farm Boy
on his travels, Yankee Clipper   YANKE

BALL. See: Lost Ball

BALL DRESS. See: Woman in
Ball Dress, The

BALLAD SINGER, THE, prostitute in London brothel, The
Rake's Progress   RAKES

BALLERINA, loved by Handyman,
plays part of Princess in the
ballet "The Captive Princess
and Her Hero," On Stage!
                    ONSTA

BALLERINA. See also:
Ballerina, The
Death
Master of Ceremonies
Prima Ballerina
Tall Ballerina

BALLERINA, ATTENDANT CAVA-
LIERS TO THE RUSSIAN.
See: Queen of the Dance

BALLERINA, CAVALIER TO
THE FRENCH. See:
Queen of the Dance

BALLERINA, CAVALIER TO
THE ITALIAN. See:
Queen of the Dance

BALLERINA, THE, in love
with the Cavalier
THE CAVALIER, her
lover
Ballet Imperial   BALLE
Enacts plot indicated by
musical score with Premi-
er Danseur
PREMIER DANSEUR, her
partner
Danses Concertantes
DANSE

BALLERINA, THE. See also:
Ballerina
Principal Dancer, The
(Adam Zero)
Soloist

BALLERINAS, TWO FORMER,
apparently mad; tenants
of ramshackle old house
YOUNG GIRL, their dance
pupil, thought by the Thief
to be a ghost
The Thief Who Loved a
Ghost   THIEF

BALLESTRIGA, witch, induces
Faust to sign compact with
Hell; accompanies him in
several guises, Abraxas
ABRAX

BALLESTRIGA. See also:
Satan
Serpent, The
Tiger, The

BALLET. See: Maître de
Ballet

BALLET MASTER, conducts
dancing school
PUPILS, studying dancing

at the school
Ballet School   BALLS
At Grand Opéra, Paris
Foyer de la Danse   FOYER

BALLET MASTER, THE, at the
Theatre Royal, Madrid
Le Diable Boiteux   DIABL
Met by Anna I and Anna II
The Seven Deadly Sins
SEVED

BALLOON-VENDOR, falls into
huge cake, The Three Fat
Men   THREE

BAMBO, Queen of the Demons,
Faust   FAUST

BANANA. See: King Banana

BAND. See: Leader of the Band

BANDIT, won by Amazon Captain
with the assistance of Amore
(Cupid), Con Amore CONAM

BANDITS, THREE, accomplices
of Carmen; help Don José
rob guard of his gold,
Carmen   CARME

BANTAM, bird, Carnival of
Animals   CARNV

BANU. See: Queen Mehmene-
Banu

BAPTIST. See: John the
Baptist

BAR. See: Fille au Bar, La

BARBARA, Countess Gemma's
maid, Gemma   GEMMA

BARBARA. See also: Allen,
Barbara

BARBAROSSA, invades the town
of Susa, Amor   AMORR

BARBER, THE, friend of Don

Quixote
Don Quixote   DONQX
In love with Mam'zelle An-
got, jilted by her for the
Caricaturist
Mam'zelle Angot   MAMZE

BARBER, THE TRAVELING,
deprived of his basin by
Don Quixote, Don Quixote
                   DONQX

BAREBACK RIDERS. See:
Jinx
Ringmaster

BARGAIN SEEKERS. See:
Floorwalker

BARMAN, observes contest
between Classic and Jazz,
Rhapsody in Blue   RHAPS

BARMAN. See also: Bar-
tender

BARMAN, THE
HIS ASSISTANT, employed
at the Big Tent, dance
hall and gambling resort
Union Pacific   UNION

BARON BLUEBEARD, much-
married nobleman
HELOISE
ELEANORE
ROSALINDE
BLANCHE
ISAURE, his first five
wives, thought by him to
be dead
BOULOTTE, his sixth wife
Bluebeard   BLUEB

BARON BLUEBEARD. See
also:
Bluebeard
Popoloni, Alchemist

BARON, CAT. See: Agathe

BARON DE GRINDBERG, nobleman

BARONESS DE GRINDBERG,
his wife
La Vivandière   VIVAN

BARON DE GUEBRIANT, THE
Vert-Vert   VERTV

BARON DE SAINT IBARS, THE,
nobleman, Le Violon du
Diable   VIOLO

BARON DE SANS-SOUS, THE.
See: Cinderella

BARON HAAGER, nobleman
BARONESS HAAGER, his
wife
Vienna- 1814   VIENN

BARON POPOFF. See: Sonia

BARON SALOMON, patron of the
ballet, sponsor of Mademoi-
selle Delphine Duvet, the
Débutante
RAFAEL, his son
The Débutante   DEBUT

BARON, THE, falls in love with
Glove-Seller at Paris café
Gaîte Parisienne   GAITE
THE HOST, aristocratic
gentleman, greets his guests
at masked ball; jealous of attention shown the Coquette by
the Poet; kills him
THE SLEEPWALKER, his
wife, appears at masked
ball; attracts the Poet, incurs jealousy of the Coquette,
killed by the Baron (the Host)
Night Shadow   NIGHT

BARON, THE. See also:
Coquette, The
Harlequin
Poet, The

BARON WILLIBALD, nobleman,
seeks wife, proposes to
Fleur-des-Champs; is re-
jected, La Fille du Danube
                   FILLD

BARON WILLIBALD. See
   also: Rudolph

BARONESS DE GRINDBERG.
   See: Baron de Grindberg

BARONESS HAAGER. See:
   Baron Haager

BARONESS STRAHL. See:
   Arbenin

BARROSO, BOI. See: Nunes,
   Blau

BARTENDER, proprietor of
   Paris bistro
   La Croqueuse de Diamants
                         CROQU
   Officiates at New York
   side street bar
   Fancy Free   FANCY
   Informs Frankie of John-
   ny's infidelity
   Frankie and Johnny
                         FRANK

BARTENDER. See also: Barman

BARTOLO
   CUCHARON
   PARADO
   DORISTO
   BATO
   TULIO, shepherds, jour-
   ney to Bethlehem to wor-
   ship the Child God; dream
   of Archangel Lucifer and
   Archangel St. Michael
   Pastorela   PASTO

BASHMIRSKAYA, PANNI, pro-
   prietress of the estate
   MAKAR, her estate manager
   The Nightingale   NIGHI

BASIL, barber, in love with
   Kitri, Don Quichotte
                        DONQU

BASMACH, LEADER OF THE.

See: Radzhab

BASTOÑERAS, LAS. See:
   Niña del Oro, La

BAT, creature of Aleko's delirium, Aleko   ALEKO

BATH CHAIR. See: Gentleman
   in the Bath Chair

BATHERS, three girls, members
   of gypsy band, Aleko
                         ALEKO

BATHILDE. See:
   Batilde
   Prince of Courland, The
   Princess Bathilde

BATHING BELLE, THE. See:
   Young Man, The

BATHING-GIRL FROM TROU-
   VILLE, THE, appears at
   Eiffel Tower, Les Mariés
   de la Tour Eiffel   MARIE

BATHSHEBA, Biblical figure,
   wife of Uriah the Hittite,
   Billy Sunday   BILLS

BATILDE, dancer, Vert-Vert
                          VERTV

BATILDE. See also: Bathilde

BATO. See: Bartolo

BATTISTA, betrothed to Pasquina, Les Femmes de Bonne
   Humeur   FEMME

BATYR, ALI. See: Suimbike

BAUCIS. See: Philemon

BAUDIN. See: Christophe

BAVARIA, KING LUDWIG OF.
   See: King Louis II

BAYADÈRE SORCERESS, A, in

love with Tamaragua, The
Dance Dream   DANCE

BEAR, participant in gypsy
carnival, Aleko   ALEKO

BEAR-LEADER
BEAR, participate in carni-
val celebrating Butter Week
Petrouchka   PETRO

BEARDED LADY. See:
Jinx
Ringmaster

BEARDED OLD MAN, "a boy
of fourteen discovering
Poetry"
GIRL DANCING, "his fever"
The Great American Goof
GREAT

BEARERS. See: Pall Bearers, Four

BEAST, THE. See: Beauty

BEATRICE, in love with
Florindo
FEDERIGO RASPONI, her
brother, wealthy resident
of Turin; once betrothed
to Clarice; killed by Flor-
indo in duel
The False Bridegroom
FALSE
Friend of Young Tregennis,
dances with him in haunt-
ed ballroom
The Haunted Ballroom
HAUNT

BEATRICE. See also:
Clarice
Truffaldino

BEATRIX, governess to Hé-
lène de Vardeck, Le Vio-
lon du Diable   VIOLO

BEATRIX. See also:
Cesarius
Comte de Vardeck, The

BEATRIX'S WAITING-MAID.
See: Cesarius

BEAU. See: Gosse, Beau

BEAUGENCY. See: Vicomte
de Beaugency

BEAUREGARD. See: Marquis
Costa de Beauregard, The

BEAUTIFUL. See: Tsarevna,
The Beautiful

BEAUTIFUL GIRL IN THE
WORLD, THE MOST. See:
Young Man

BEAUTY, meets the Beast in
the forest; at first frightened,
afterwards falls in love with
him
THE BEAST, falls in love
with Beauty, afterwards
transformed into a handsome
young man
Beauty and the Beast
BEAUB
Character in woman's dream
of her childhood
THE BEAST, character in
the dream
Mother Goose Suite   MOTHE

BEAUTY. See also:
Florentine Beauty, A
Poet

BEAUTY, FADED. See: Hypnotist

BEAUTY, THE SLEEPING. See:
Princess Aurora, The
Sleeping Beauty, The

BEAUVOIR, DUC DE. See:
Clairemonde

BEAUVOIR, GASTON DE. See:
Clairemonde
Marguerite

BEE. See: Queen Bee, The

BEELZEBUB, Lord of Evil,
    buys Count Frédéric's
    soul, Le Diable Amoureux
                              DIABE

BEELZEBUB. See also:
    Belzebu
    Devil, The
    Satan
    Urielle

BEETLE. See: Stag Beetle

BEETLES, inhabitants of the
    insect world
    Le Festin de l'Araignée
                              FESTD
    Le Festin de l'Araignée
                              FESTI
    The Spider's Banquet
                              SPIDE

BEGGAR, A, resident of the
    Gorbals, slum quarter in
    Glasgow, Miracle in the
    Gorbals   MIRAC

BEGGAR, THE, interrupts
    wedding of the Hussar and
    his new bride, The Widow
    in the Mirror   WIDOW

BEGGAR, THE. See also:
    Gypsy Girl, The
    Old Lord, The

BEKR. See: Abu-Bekr

BEL-AMOUR, gentleman-in-
    waiting, Cinderella
                              CINDA

BELAYE, CAPTAIN, British
    naval officer, commander
    of H. M. S. "Hot Cross
    Bun, " in love with
    Blanche; marries her,
    Pineapple Poll   PINEA

BELAYE, CAPTAIN. See
    also: Pineapple Poll

BELERMA, THE LADY. See:

Durandarte

BELFEGOR, Genius of Evil,
    creates Alma from rock
    ALMA, created by Belfegor;
    "if she yields to love she
    turns again to stone"; loved
    by Emazor
    Alma   ALMAO

BELFEGOR. See also: Bel-
    phegor

BELL-RINGER, resident of small
    European village,
    Coppélia   COPPE

BELLASPADA, CAPTAIN. See:
    Doña Dorotea

BELLE. See: Princess Belle
    Epine

BELLE FLORENCE, LA, pur-
    sued by Don Juan, Juan de
    Zarissa   JUAND

BELLE ROSE, PRINCESS. See:
    Princess Belle Epine

BELLE, THE BATHING. See:
    Young Man, The

BELLS, THE, personifications,
    L'Homme et son Désir
                              HOMME

BELOVED. See: Man

BELOVED, DARK. See: Sisters,
    Three

BELOVED, HIS. See: Fisher-
    man

BELOVED, POETIC. See: Sis-
    ters, Three

BELOVED, POET'S. See: Poet

BELOVED, THE. See: Young
    Musician, A

BELPHEGOR, leader of the
Salamanders, La Fille
de Marbre   FILLM

BELPHEGOR. See also:
Belfegor

BELZEBU, a devil, Pastorela
PASTO

BELZEBU. See also: Beelzebub

BEN, the Stranger, becomes
enmeshed with Rose and
Martha, daughters of
Father, Ballad   BALLD

BEN. See also:
Ali-Ben-Tamarat
Father
Hazdai-Ben-Shaprut
Kyram, Ben

BENEDICT. See: Cesarius

"BENICIA BOY." See: Hee-
nan, "Benicia Boy"

BENNO, Prince Siegfried's
friend
Swan Lane   SWANA
Swan Lake   SWANE
Swan Lake   SWANK
Swan Lake   SWANL

BENVOLIO, friend of Romeo
Romeo and Juliet   ROMEA
Romeo and Juliet   ROMEJ

BENVOLIO. See also:
Montague

BEPPO. See: Marietta

BERANGER, companion of
Fleur de Lys
La Esmeralda   ESMER
A troubadour
Raymonda   RAYMO

BERGER, hunter, friend of
Ehrick, Electra   ELECT

BERGERAC, CYRANO DE, long-
nosed poet, swordsman and
soldier; in love with Roxane,
woos her by proxy for
Christian
ROXANE, his cousin, mar-
ries Christian
CHRISTIAN, Roxane's inartic-
ulate lover and husband;
killed in battle
Cyrano de Bergerac CYRAN

BERNADONE, FRANCESCO (St.
Francis), becomes monk,
founds Franciscan order
PIETRO BERNADONE, his
father, wealthy shopkeeper
HIS THREE COMPANIONS
become monks
Saint Francis   SAINT

BERNADONE, FRANCESCO.
See also:
Knight, The
Poor Man, The
Poverty
Wolf, The

BERNARD. See: Ventadour,
Bernard de

BERTA. See: Marguerite

BERTHA. See: Duke, The

BERTHE, Ysaure's nurse
La Filleule des Fées
FILLU
A dancer
Vert-Vert   VERTV

BERTHE. See also:
Giselle
Ondine
Palemon

BETRAYED GIRL, THE, the
Rake's maid, in love with and
seduced by him
HER MOTHER, an old harridan.
The Rake's Progress RAKES

BETRAYER, THE. See: Delilah

21   BETROTHED

BETROTHED, HIS. See:
   Rotislav

BETT. See: Van Bett

BETTEMBERG, a farmer on
   Lord Rewena's estate
   CHARLOTTE, his wife
   HENRIETTE, his eldest
   daughter, engaged to Karll
   NATHALIE, his youngest
   daughter
   Nathalie   NATHA

BETTY. See: Coop

BEY. See: Abdurassul, Bey

BEY, ISMAIL. See:
   Farfalla
   Prince Djalma

BIANCA, studying dancing
   under Rigadon, Scuola di
   Ballo   SCUOL

BIBERMANN. See: Kathi

BIDGI, negro cabin boy on
   ship commanded by Mon-
   sieur de Bougainville,
   Ozaï   OZAII

BIDZA, GABO. See: Armen

BIEN-AIMÉE, LA. See:
   Poet, The

BIG BOSS. See: Strip Teaser

BILBY, American sea captain;
   befriends Doll, takes her
   into his Salem home
   HANNAH, his wife, jealous of Doll
   A Mirror for Witches
                     MIRRO

BILBY. See also: Titus

BILL WHITE. See: Duras,
   Manos

BILLY. See: Sunday,
   Billy

BILLY THE KID, American des-
   perado and frontier gunman
   HIS MOTHER, accidentally
   shot and killed by Alias
   HIS MEXICAN SWEETHEART
   Billy the Kid   BILLY

BILLY THE KID. See also:
   Alias
   Cowboy in Red
   Garrett, Pat

BIONDELLO, TRANIO, harbor-
   master, The Blood-Red
   Flower   BLOOD

BIRBANTO, a pirate, Conrad's
   lieutenant, Le Corsaire
                     CORSA

BIRD, friend of Peter, helps
   him capture Wolf
   Peter and the Wolf PETER
   Peter and the Wolf PETEW

BIRD. See also: Blue Bird, The

BIRD-CATCHER, THE, attendant
   to the Prince; presents the
   Princess a songbird, The
   Hundred Kisses   HUNDR

BIRD GIRL, character in Woman's
   dream, ensnares Hop o' My
   Thumb, Mother Goose Suite
                     MOTHE

BIRD OF FIRE, THE. See:
   Firebird

BIRD OF WINTER, THE, sym-
   bolic figure, The Ice Maiden
                     ICEMA

BIRD OF WINTER, THE. See
   also: Winter

BIRD WOMAN, transforms women of village into birds

LOVERS, overcome Bird
Woman, free village wom-
en from her power
The House of Birds
                          HOUSE

BIRDS, accompany Spring
Les Saisons   SAISO
Personifications
The Seventh Symphony
                          SEVEN

BIRDS. See also:
Fairy of the Humming
   Birds, The
Fairy of the Song Birds,
   The
Girl With Birds

BIRTHE, MISS, heiress to
the manor-house
SQUIRE OVE, her cousin
and fiance
MRS. KIRSTINE, their
aunt
A Folk Tale   FOLKT

BISHOP. See: Poet

BISHOPS. See: Red Bishops

BITS. See: Tid-Bits

BLACK AND WHITE, repre-
sentation of British publication,
The Press   PRESS

BLACK CASTLES, chessmen,
Checkmate   CHECK

BLACK FAIRY, THE, with-
holds gifts to Ysaure until
the latter's fifteenth year,
La Filleule des Fées
                          FILLU

BLACK GROUP. See: Des-
tiny

BLACK GROUP, LEADER OF.
See: Destiny

BLACK HORSES, THE, companions of the White Horse,
overcome the Amazons, Le
Massacre des Amazones
                          MASSA

BLACK HOURS, THE, personifications, L'Homme et son
Désir
                          HOMME

BLACK KING, King of Cannibals,
marries, eats Young Girl
HIS CHAMBERLAINS
HIS CHAUFFEUR
HIS WITCH-DOCTOR
Bonne Bouche   BONNE

BLACK KNIGHTS, chessmen,
Checkmate   CHECK

BLACK PAWNS, chessmen,
Checkmate   CHECK

BLACK PEARLS. See: White
Pearl, The

BLACK QUEEN, THE, chessman,
Checkmate   CHECK

BLACKAMOOR, THE, puppet,
brought to life by the Old
Charlatan, kills Petrouchka,
Petrouchka   PETRO

BLACKSMITH, THE. See:
Leader of the Convicts

BLANCHE, loved by Captain
Belaye, becomes his bride
MRS. DIMPLE, her busybody
aunt
Pineapple Poll   PINEA
The Queen's maid of honor,
makes Vert-Vert pet
Vert-Vert   VERTV

BLANCHE. See also:
Baron Bluebeard
de Bois, Blanche

BLAU. See: Nunes, Blau

BLEU, P'TIT, a milkman,
    Cinderella   CINDA

BLIND GIRL, pursues the
    Woman (the Prostitute)
    The Miraculous Mandarin
                        MIRAR
    The Miraculous Mandarin
                        MIRAU

BLIND OLD MAN, magician,
    turns Mazourka into the
    Countess and the Countess
    into Mazourka, Le Diable
    à Quatre   DIABQ

BLINVAL. See:
    Governor of the Province,
    The
    Nina

BLONDELAINE, captivated
    by the music of Scara-
    mouche's violin
    LEILO, her husband
    Scaramouche   SCARA

BLONDELAINE. See also:
    Eleonore
    Gigolo
    Juliette
    Mezzetinto

BLONDINE. See: Cinderella

BLOSSOM. See: Cherry
    Blossom Fairy, The

BLUE. See: Girl in Blue

BLUE BIRD, THE, fairy tale
    character, The Sleeping
    Beauty   SLEEP

BLUE GROUP. See: Leader
    of Blue Group

BLUE ROSE, travels from
    hand to hand, A Blue
    Rose   BLUER

BLUEBEARD, much-married
    nobleman, becomes husband

of Ysaure de Renoualle, attempts to kill her after she
opens forbidden door; killed
by her brother Ebremard
Barbe-Bleue   BARBE
Fairy tale character
ARIANA, his wife
SISTER ANNE, Ariana's sister, also fairy tale characters
The Sleeping Beauty SLEEP

BLUEBEARD. See also: Baron
    Bluebeard

BOATSWAIN. See: Chief Boat-
    swain

BOBICHE. See: King Bobiche

BOBO-SAFAR, Russian peasant
    NOZGULLE (Golden Rose),
    his daughter, betrothed to
    Zamon
    ZARRAGULLE (White Rose),
    his daughter, betrothed to
    Sanghine
    The Two Roses   TWORO

BOBO-SAFAR. See also:
    Abdurassul, Bey
    Sanghine
    Zamon

BODYGUARD, caricature of car-
    toon character, The New
    Yorker   NEWYO

BOGEY MAN, THE, seen by the
    Princess in her dream, A
    Spring Tale   SPRIN

BOI. See also: Boy

BOI BARROSO. See: Nunes,
    Blau

BOLERO, personification of
    dance, Soirée Musicale
                        SOIRE

BOLERO, LA, "engaging in an
    Edwardian romp at a French

plage, " Les Sirènes
SIREN

BOLEYN, ANNE. See: King
Henry VIII, King of Eng-
land

BONANZA KING. See: Com-
stock, Bonanza King

BONAVENTURI, ZENOBIO,
young man of fashion,
loved by the Contessa;
indifferent to her, Quelques
Fleurs   QUELQ

BONAVENTURI, ZENOBIO.
See also: Rose

BONDURA PLAYER, partici-
pant in gypsy carnival,
Aleko   ALEKO

BONIFACCIO, a peasant,
Gemma   GEMMA

BONNE. See: Fée, La Bonne

BOOTBLACKS, working at
metropolitan railroad
terminal,
Terminal   TERMI

BOOTFACE, a clown, The Lady
and the Fool   LADYA

BOOTMAKER, THE, proprietor
of shop in Paris market,
Mam'zelle Angot   MAMZE

BOOTS. See: Puss in Boots

BOOTS, LITTLE JOHNNY IN
TOP. See: Csizmás
Janko

BORDEN, LIZZIE. See:
Accused, The

BOREAS, a north wind, in
love with Admadeya; ap-
pears in ballet at the
Serf's Theatre,

Katerina   KATER

BORIA, Soviet schoolboy, Baby
Stork   BABYS

BORIS. See: Vodka, Boris

BORN UNDER MARS. See:
Mortal Born Under Mars

BORN UNDER MERCURY. See:
Mortal Born Under Mercury

BORN UNDER NEPTUNE. See:
Mortal Born Under Neptune

BORN UNDER VENUS. See:
Mortals, Two, Born Under
Venus

BORROMEO, FRA, lay brother,
treasurer of the convent,
Marco Spada   MARCO

BOSS, BIG. See: Strip Teaser

BOTHWELL. See: Mary, Queen
of Scots

BOTTOM, a weaver
The Dream   DREAM
A Midsummer Night's Dream
                      MIDSU

BOUGAINVILLE, MONSIEUR DE,
ship captain
MADAME DE BOUGAINVILLE,
his wife
MADEMOISELLE DE BOU-
GAINVILLE, his daughter,
in love with Monsieur de
Surville
MONSIEUR DE SURVILLE,
his nephew, naval officer,
sole survivor of shipwreck,
declares Ozaï "his wife in
the sight of heaven"
Ozaï   OZAII

BOUGAINVILLE, MONSIEUR DE.
See also:
Bidgi
Guimard, La

King of France
Ozai

BOULOTTE. See: Baron
Bluebeard

BOVA. See: Korolevich, Bova

BOWERS, SANDY. See:
Orum, Eilley

BOXER. See:
Negro Boxer
White Boxer

BOY, caricature of cartoon
character, The New Yorker
NEWYO

BOY. See also:
Boi
Call-Boy, The
Chaperones
Delivery Boy
Farm Boy, The
Girl
Heenan, "Benicia Boy"
Host
Praying Boy
Rich Boy, The
Street Boy, A
Telegraph Boy
Witch Boy

BOY, A. See: Scaramouche

BOY-FRIENDS, HER THREE.
See: Debutante

BOY IN GREY, friend of
Flower Vendor in Green,
Voices of Spring   VOICE

BOY HIKER
GIRL HIKER, meet Old
Prospector at Sierra
ghost town
Ghost Town   GHOST

BOY IN GREEN, demonstrates
his skating virtuosity, Les
Patineurs   PATIN

BOY SWIMMER. See: Nearly

Drowned Girl

BOY, THE
THE GIRL, students, engage
in classroom flirtation
Un et Un Font Deux UNETU

BOY, THE. See also:
Girl, The
Young Man, The

BOY, THE FISHER. See:
Spirit of the Sea, The

BOY WITH A FEVER OF 105,
"one of the living, " The Great
American Goof   GREAT

BRABANZIO. See: Otello

BRACACCIO, pirate chief, sells
Lilia and Phoebe to the
Grand Vizier, Le Diable
Amoureux   DIABE

BRAMA, THE GOD. See: Un-
known, The

BRANGAENE. See: Maid
(Brangaene)

BRASS. See: Woodwinds

BRAVO, THE, friend of the Rake;
The Rake's Progress RAKES

BREILLE. See: Marquis de Breille

BRIAREUS, giant, I Titani TITAN

BRIDE, attracts Toby
BRIDEGROOM, newly married
Antic Spring   ANTIS
Participates in wedding
GROOM
SYLPHIDE
BRIDESMAIDS
MINISTER, also participate
in wedding
Highland Fling   HIGHL
Participates in wedding
BRIDEGROOM
PARENTS
MATCHMAKERS, also par-

ticipate in wedding
Les Noces   NOCEE
About to be married
BRIDEGROOM, to be married
The Wise Virgins   WISEV

BRIDE. See also:
Adagio-Bride, The
Wise Virgins
Young Bride

BRIDE, A
GROOM, A, witnesses in
murder case
Hear Ye! Hear Ye! HEARY

BRIDE, THE, wrongfully com-
mitted to an asylum, be-
comes insane as a result
THE HUSBAND, commits
the Bride to an asylum
Eaters of Darkness EATER
Members of wedding party
at which Csizmás Janko
meets Ildikó
THE BRIDEGROOM, mem-
ber of same wedding party
Little Johnny in Top-Boots
                     LITTL
Member of wedding party
at the Eiffel Tower
THE BRIDEGROOM
THE MOTHER-IN-LAW
THE FATHER-IN-LAW
FIRST BRIDESMAID
SECOND BRIDESMAID
FIRST BRIDESMAN
SECOND BRIDESMAN
THE GENERAL, also mem-
bers of the wedding party
Les Mariés de la Tour
Eiffel   MARIE
Russian peasant girl, about
to marry the Bridegroom
HER FATHER
HER MOTHER
HER FRIENDS
Les Noces   NOCES
About to be married
THE BRIDEGROOM, also
about to be married
Les Vierges   VIERG

BRIDE, THE. See also:

Angels, Two
Bridegroom
Bridegroom, The
Foolish Virgins, Five
Older Married Couple, An
Wise Virgins, Five

BRIDEGROOM, young man, betrothed to the Bride, claimed
as husband by the Ice Maiden
THE BRIDE, his fiancée,
daughter of the village miller
HIS MOTHER, perishes in
snow storm
THE ICE MAIDEN (FAIRY),
supernatural being, casts
spell over the Bridegroom
Le Baiser de la Fée BAISE
At wedding
Peer Gynt   PEERG

BRIDEGROOM. See also:
Bride
Wise Virgins

BRIDEGROOM, THE, lured
away from the Bride by
the King of the Ghouls
THE BRIDE
The Bells   BELLS
Yela's suitor, favored by
her family
The Devil in the Village
                     DEVIV
Russian peasant, about to
marry the Bride
HIS FATHER
HIS MOTHER
HIS FRIENDS
Les Noces   NOCES
About to be married
THE BRIDE, to be married
A Wedding Bouquet   WEDDI

BRIDEGROOM, THE. See also:
Bride, The
Julia
Matchmaker, The
Older Married Couple, An
Wife, The

BRIDESMAID, FIRST. See:
Bride, The

BRIDESMAID, SECOND. See:
    Bride, The

BRIDESMAIDS. See: Bride

BRIDESMAN, FIRST. See:
    Bride, The

BRIDESMAN, SECOND. See:
    Bride, The

BRIDOUX, a French sergeant,
    courting Dona Marianna,
    Diavolina's cousin
    Diavolina   DIAVO
    A recruiting sergeant
    Pâquerette   PAQUE

BRIENNE, JEAN DE, be-
    trothed to Raymonda,
    Raymonda   RAYMO

BRITAIN, KING OF. See:
    Lear

BRITISH GOVERNOR, THE,
    guest at the Maharajah's
    ball,
    Ilga   ILGAA

BRONTË SISTERS. See:
    Sisters, Three

BROOM. See: Sorcerer's
    Apprentice

BROTHER. See: Girl, The

BROTHER, HIS. See:
    Young Man

BROTHER, THE. See:
    Selina

BROTHERS, HIS TWO. See:
    Innocent Ivan

BROTHERS, THE LADY'S
    TWO. See: Comus

BROTHER, THE SHAH'S. See:
    Scheherazade

BROWN, ISIDOR, engaged to
    Miss Harrison, Gaucho
                         GAUCH

BROWN, W., journalist, visits
    fairyland, sawed in half by
    King of the Ogres, The Tri-
    umph of Neptune   TRIUM

BROWN, W. See also: Jour-
    nalists, Two

BRUNETTE. See: Cinderella

BRUTUS, Roman, enemy of Ju-
    lius Caesar, Amor AMORR

BRYAXIS, pirate chief, abducts
    Chloë, Daphnis et Chloë
                         DAPHN

BUBBLES. See: Soap Bubbles

BUCHARIA. See: Princess of
    the Court of Bucharia

BUCHARIA, KING OF. See:
    Aliris

BUFFOON, THE, victimizes
    seven other buffoons by sell-
    ing them a "magic" whip
    BUFFOON'S WIFE, his part-
    ner in the victimization
    Chout   CHOUT

BULBA, TARAS, Ukrainian peas-
    sant, former Cossack
    OSTAP, his son, in love
    with Oksana
    ANDREY, his son, in love
    with Odarka, the Pannochka
    Taras Bulba   TARAS

BULBA, TARAS. See also:
    Odarka
    Oksana

BULL, JOHN, later Passifont,
    Lord Wilson's servant, La
    Fille du Pharaon   FILLP

BULL, THE. See: Taurus

BUMPPO, NATTY, "the Deer'
slayer," American fron-
tiersman,
Les Mohicans   MOHIC

BUNDREN, ADDIE, a dying
old woman
ANSE, her husband,
farmer
DARL
CASH
JEWEL
VARDAMAN, their sons
DEWEY DELL, their
daughter
LAFE, father of Dewey
Dell's unborn illegitimate
child
As I Lay Dying   ASILA

BURGOMASTER, of small
European village
HIS ASSISTANT
Coppélia   COPPE

BURLEIGH. See: Lord
Burleigh

BUSINESSMEN, passing
through metropolitan
railroad terminal,
Terminal   TERMI

BUSTAMENTE. See: Don
Bustamente

BUTCHER, THE, proprietor
of stall in Paris market,
Mam'zelle Angot   MAMZE

BUTLER, HIS. See: Rich
Old Neighbor, A

BUTLER, THE, grotesque
attendant of the Princess,
A Spring Tale   SPRIN

BUTTERFLIES. See: Tor-
toise Shell Butterflies

BUTTERFLY, participant in gypsy revelry, Aleko   ALEKO

BUTTERFLY HUNTERS, pursue
butterflies, Piège de Lumière
PIEGE

BUTTERFLY LAND, QUEEN OF.
See: Imperialis, Vanessa

BUTTERFLY, THE, annoys
Mandarin
L'Épreuve d'Amour   EPREU
Inhabitant of the insect
world, victim of the Spider
Le Festin de l'Araignée
FESTD
Le Festin de l'Araignée
FESTI
The Spider's Banquet SPIDE

BUZA, in love with Osöd, The
Holy Torch   HOLYT

BUZA. See also: Guardian
Angel

C

CABOCLO. See: Mancenilha

CADAVAL, Satan in disguise,
La Fille de Marbre FILLM

CADET. See:
Edward, Cadet
Paul, Cadet

CADETS, JUNIOR. See:
Leader of the Junior Cadets

CADETS, TWO, meet the Flirt
at Belvedere Gardens,
Vienna, Voices of Spring
VOICE

CADMO, a Lusitanian youth,
Holerut's slave, Sieba
SIEBA

CAESAR. See also: Cesare

CAESAR, JULIUS, Roman em-
peror, enemy of Brutus
CALPURNIA, his wife

29   CAESAR

Amor   AMORR

CAESAR, JULIUS. See also:
Antony

CAIN, Biblical character
ABEL, his brother, killed
by him
Cain and Abel   CAINA

CALAMITY. See: Night

CALCHAS, priest, covets
Paris' pet lamb, Helen
of Troy   HELEN

CALCHAS. See also:
Ajax I
Lamb

CALIPH. See also: Kalaf

CALIPH ABDERRAMAN,
Moorish ruler in Spain
ZORAIYA, his daughter
ABU-SOLIMAN, his adop-
ted son, pupil of Hazai-
Ben-Shaprut
Zoraiya   ZORAI

CALIPH ABDERRAMAN. See
also:
Governess of the Harem,
The
Hazdai-Ben-Shaprut
Tisbah

CALL-BOY, THE, at the
Theatre Royal, Madrid,
Le Diable Boiteux
                    DIABL

CALLER, calls figures to be
performed by square dan-
cers
SQUARE DANCERS, per-
form dance
Square Dance   SQUAR

CALLER, THE, officiates at
square dance at Burnt
Ranch,
Rodeo   RODEO

CALLIOPE, muse, "personifying
poetry and its rhythm"
Apollo, Leader of the Muses
                    APOLL
Muse
Apollon Musagète   APOLN

CALPURNIA. See: Caesar,
Julius

CALYPSO, sea nymph, captor of
Ulysses (Odysseus)
I, Odysseus   IODYS
Télémaque dans l'Ile de
Calypso   TELEM

CAMARGO, French gentleman
MARIE
MADELEINE, his daughters,
loved by Comte de Melun
Camargo   CAMAR

CAMELLIAS, THE LADY OF THE.
See: Gautier, Marguerite

CAMERAMAN, THE, takes pic-
tures of completion of con-
struction of the Union Pacific Railroad, Union Pacific
                    UNION

CAMILLE, woman of Paris,
Camille   CAMIL

CAMPBELL. See: Lord Campbell

CANARDOT, a poulterer,
Cinderella   CINDA

CANCAN DANCERS, two mechanical toys, perform at toy
shop, La Boutique Fantasque
                    BOUTI

CANCAN GIRLS, performers at
2222 Club, New York City,
Café Society   CAFES

CANCAN GIRLS. See also:
Dance Master

CANCAN GIRLS, LEADER OF

THE. See: Dance Master

CANDAULES, King of Lydia, consults the oracle Pythia NISIA, his wife
Le Roi Candaule   ROICA

CANDELAS, young gypsy girl, haunted by ghost of a former lover; loved by Carmelo
GHOST OF CANDELAS' FORMER LOVER, attracted to Lucia
El Amor Brujo   AMORB

CANDIDE. See: Vert-Vert

CANDY GIRL, sells her wares at fair, The Fair at Sorochinsk   FAIRA

CANGACEIRA, female bandit, Cangaceira   CANGA

CANNIBALS, KING OF. See: Black King

CANTALBUTTE, Master of the Ceremonies at court of King Florestan XXIV, The Sleeping Beauty
SLEEP

CANTALBUTTE. See also: Princess Aurora, The

CANZONETTA, personification of dance, Soirée Musicale   SOIRE

CAPITALISM, PERSONIFICATIONS OF. See: Fat Men, The Three

CAPITALISTS, THE, financiers of the Union Pacific Railroad, Union Pacific   UNION

CAPITANO. See: Adoncino, Capitano

Captain

CAPRICCIOSA, LA, a beauty, guest of Signor Nidas
FOOTMAN
COACHMAN, her servants
The Lady and the Fool
LADYA

CAPTAIN of a Danish frigate
Loin du Danemark   LOIND
Character portrayed by strolling player
Le Marché des Innocents
MARCH
Young sea captain, shipwrecked, saved by Océanide
OCÉANIDE, Queen of the Sea, attracted to, spurned by Captain, casts him into sea to drown
FIANCÉE of Captain, taken to bottom of sea by spectre of Captain there to be married to him
Les Noces Fantastiques
NOCEF

CAPTAIN. See also:
Amazon Captain
Belaye, Captain
Capitano
Faloppa, Captain
Lieutenant
Vavasour, Captain

CAPTAIN BELLASPADA. See: Doña Dorotea

CAPTAIN CARTUCCIA, prospective husband of Rosetta, selected for her by her father, Tartaglia,
Salade   SALAD

CAPTAIN JOHN SMITH. See: Rolfe, John

CAPTAIN OF A SOVIET STEAMER, unloading at treaty-port in China, The Red Poppy   REDPO

CAPTAIN OF HUSSARS, offi-
cer, member of troop
passing through small
Austrian village, Halte de
Cavalerie   HALTE

CAPTAIN OF SOVIET FOOT-
BALL TEAM, attracts
Deva
SOVIET FOOTBALL TEAM,
players
The Golden Age   GOLDE

CAPTAIN OF THE GARDES-
FRANÇAISES, one of
Cydalise's lovers, Cyda-
lise et le Chèvre-pied
                   CYDAL

CAPTAIN OF THE GLOW-
WORM PATROL, resident
of Butterfly Land, Les
Papillons   PAPIO

CAPTAIN OF THE GUARD,
follower of Olifour
Le Dieu et la Bayadère
                   DIEUE
Officer
La Gypsy   GYPSY

CAPTAIN OF THE GUARD.
See also: Hassan

CAPULET, head of a house
at variance with the house
of Montague
LADY CAPULET, his wife
Romeo and Juliet ROMEO
Head of a house at vari-
ance with the house of
Montagu
Romeo and Juliet ROMEJ
JULIET, his daughter, in
love with, marries Romeo
TYBALT, nephew of Lady
Capulet, kills Mercutio,
killed by Romeo
Romeo and Juliet ROMEJ
Romeo and Juliet ROMEO

CAPULET.   See also:

Laurence, Friar
Mercutio
Nurse
Old Capulet
Old Montague
Paris
Romeo

CAPULET, LADY.   See:
Capulet
Old Capulet

CARABOSSE, wicked fairy,
places the Princess Aurora
under spell causing her to
sleep for 100 years
HER TWO PAGES
HER FOUR RATS
The Sleeping Beauty SLEEP

CARDS.   See: Small Cards,
Four

CARELIS.   See: Eleonore

CARETAKER (MERLIN).   See:
Husband (King Mark)

CARICATURIST, THE, attracts
Mam'zelle Angot away from
the Barber, transfers his at-
tentions to the Aristocrat,
Mam'zelle Angot   MAMZE

CARINÉ, in love with Armen
HER TWO FRIENDS
Happiness   HAPPI

Carl. See:
Karl
Karll

CARLINO, a puppet-master
Napoli   NAPOL
Studying dancing under Riga-
don
Scuola di Ballo   SCUOL

CARLOTTA GRISI.   See:
Grisi, Carlotta
Taglioni, Marie

CARMELO, handsome village
boy, wins Candelas with
the help of Lucia, El
Amor Brujo   AMORB

CARMEN, beautiful Spanish
factory girl, seduces Don
José; attracted to the To-
reader, stabbed by José
Carmen   CARME
Gypsy dancer, rival of
Micaela for the affections
of José; falls in love with
Escamillo
Guns and Castanets
                  GUNSA

CARMEN. See also: Bandits,
Three

CARNATION. See:
Alchemist, The
Rose

CARNATION FAIRY, THE,
fairy godmother of the
Princess Aurora
HER PAGE
The Sleeping Beauty
                  SLEEP

CAROLINE, the bride-to-be,
about to enter into a marriage of convenience
HER LOVER, whom she
really loves
THE MAN SHE MUST
MARRY, her fiance, with
whom she is not in love
AN EPISODE IN HIS PAST,
former mistress of Caro-
line's fiance, still in love
with him
Jardin aux Lilas   JARDI

CAROLINE. See also:
Philemon

CARRAOLANA. See: Mos-
catello, Sergeant

CARRASCO, BACHELOR
SAMPSON, friend of Don

Quixote, appears as Knight
of the Silver Moon, Don
Quichotte   DONQU

CARRASCO, BACHELOR SAMP-
SON. See also: Antonina

CARRIAGE TRADE. See:
Queen of the Carriage Trade

CARTER, A, enemy of William
Targett; kills him, The
Sailor's Return   SAILO

CARTER, A. See also: Tulip

CARTHAGE, QUEEN OF. See:
Dido

CARTUCCIA. See: Captain
Cartuccia

CASANOVA, GIOVANNI, Italian
adventurer, Casanova
                  CASAN

CASH. See: Bundren, Addie

CASSANDRA, daughter of King
Priam and Hecuba
Cassandre   CASSA
Clytemnestra   CLYTE

CASSANDRE. See: Colombine

CASSIO, Otello's lieutenant,
Otello   OTELL

CASTLEREAGH. See: Lord
Castlereagh

CASTLEREAGH, LADY. See:
Lord Castlereagh

CASTLES. See:
Black Castles
Red Castles

CASTOR
POLLUX, brothers; twin
sons of Leda
Castor and Pollux   CASTR

CASTOR. See also: Leda

CASTRO. See:
    Count de Castro
    Doña Ines de Castro

CAT, creature of Aleko's
    delirium
    Aleko   ALEKO
    Friend of Peter, helps
    him capture Wolf
    Peter and the Wolf
                             PETER
    Peter and the Wolf
                             PETEW
    Friend of Rooster
    Le Renard   RENAR

CAT. See also:
    Cat, The
    White Cat, The

CAT BARON. See: Agathe

CAT, THE, resident of
    Soviet garden
    Baby Stork   BABYS
    Loved by the Young Man;
    changed by Aphrodite
    into a girl, reverts to
    original form when temp-
    ted by Mouse
    THE YOUNG MAN, her
    lover
    La Chatte   CHATT
    Cinderella's pet, unties
    her slipper, by which
    the Prince identifies her
    Cinderella   CINDR
    Participant in orgy on
    Bald Mountain
    The Fair at Sorochinsk
                             FAIRA

CAT, THE. See also:
    Cat
    Kikimora

CATALINA. See: Don
    Alvar

CATARINA, youthful leader
    of band of robbers; cap-
tures and captivates Salvator Rosa, Catarina CATAR

CATARINA. See also: Diavo-
    lino

CATCHER. See: Bird-Catcher,
    The

CATHARINA, a farmer
    LOUISELLE, her daughter
    Stella   STELL

CATHERINE, first cantinière
    MARTHE, second cantinière
    MARIE, third cantinière
    Pâquerette   PAQUE

CATHERINE. See also:
    Guérin, Georges-Emile
    Tsarina Catherine II, Tsar-
    ina of Russia

CATHERINE OF PORTUGAL,
    PRINCESS. See: Prince
    Charles

CATHRINE, an old housekeeper,
    formerly a nurse, A Folk
    Tale   FOLKT

CAUGHT. See: Woman Who
    Was Caught, The

CAVALIER, HER SHORT. See:
    Tall Ballerina

CAVALIER PIGNEROLLE, THE
    HENRIETTA, his wife
    THEIR DAUGHTERS, guests
    at Prince Charming's ball
    Cinderella   CINDL

CAVALIER, THE. See:
    Ballerina, The
    Niña del Oro, La

CAVALIER TO THE FRENCH
    BALLERINA. See: Queen
    of the Dance

CAVALIER TO THE ITALIAN
    BALLERINA. See: Queen

of the Dance

CAVALIERS TO THE RUSSIAN
BALLERINA, ATTENDANT.
See: Queen of the Dance

CAVALLINES. See: Don
José Cavallines

CAVALLINES, JOVITA. See:
Don Alvar
Don José Cavallines

CAVIELLO, in love with Rosetta, Pulcinella   PULCI

CAXTON, WILLIAM, "father
of English printing," The
Press   PRESS

CELADON, gentleman-in-
waiting, Cinderella CINDA

CELENO, celestial star,
Electra   ELECT

CELESTINE. See: Pirouette,
Monsieur

CELI. See: Duke of Medina-
Celi, The

CEREMONIES. See:
Master of Ceremonies
Mistress of Ceremonies,
The

CERES, attends feast of
Bacchus, Sylvia SYLVA

CERITO, FANNY. See:
Taglioni, Marie

CESARE, Roman emperor,
Cesare in Egitto CESAR

CESARE. See also: Caesar

CESARIUS, wealthy goldsmith
of Ghent
BEATRIX, his daughter, betrothed to Benedict
AGNES, his younger

daughter
BENEDICT, his nephew, be-
trothed to Beatrix
JULIA, cousin to Beatrix
and Agnes
BEATRIX'S WAITING-MAID
La Jolie Fille de Gand
JOLIE

CHAIN STORE NYMPH, "head-
liner seeking refuge from
publicity," visiting 2222
Club, New York City, Café
Society   CAFES

CHAIR. See: Gentleman in the
Bath Chair

CHAMBERLAIN at Prince Charming's court, Cinderella
CINDL

CHAMBERLAIN. See also:
Court Chamberlain

CHAMBERLAIN, THE, official
at the court of the Prince,
Cinderella   CINDR

CHAMBERLAINS, HIS. See:
Black King

CHAMP, THE, pugilist, visiting
2222 Club, New York City
CHORINE, his platinum
blonde date
HIS MANAGER
HIS HANDLERS, all also
visiting the Club
Café Society   CAFES

CHAMPAGNE, drink served at
2222 Club, New York City,
Café Society   CAFES

CHAMPION. See: Tennis
Champion

CHAMPION ROPER, THE, com-
petes with the Head Wrangler
for the Rancher's Daughter;
wins the Cowgirl, Rodeo
RODEO

CHAMPS. See: Fleur-des-
Champs

CHANCE, GODDESS OF. See:
Fortuna

CHANCELLOR, official, orders
Doctor Gaspard to repair
Prince Tutti's doll, The
Three Fat Men   THREE

CHAO-KANG, Chinese, Chao-
Kang   CHAOK

CHAPERONES, choose Boy to
dance with Young Girl
BOY
YOUNG GIRL
Arcade   ARCAD

CHARACTER DANCERS, THE.
See: Principal Dancer,
The (Adam Zero)

CHARACTERS, FOUR, three
men and a girl, strangers,
"show the life of Man from
birth to death in a set of
seven variations," The
Age of Anxiety   AGEOE

CHARLATAN. See: Old
Charlatan, The

CHARLES. See: Prince
Charles

CHARLES II, KING, King of
England. See:
Lord Campbell
Prince Charles

CHARLIE. See: Ney, Char-
lie

CHARLOTTE. See: Bettem-
berg

CHARMIAN, friend and con-
fidante of Cleopatra,
Queen of Egypt, Les
Amours d'Antoine et de
Cléopâtre   AMOUR

CHARMING, PRINCE. See:
Chamberlain
Gallison
Master of Ceremonies
Prince Charming
Prince Fleur-de-Lys
Prince, The
Princess Aurora, The

CHARTREUSE, MADEMOISELLE
MARIANNE, a liqueur, Schlagobers   SCHLA

CHASE, GODDESS OF THE.
See: Diana

CHASSE, LA, a Negro, The
Three Fat Men   THREE

CHASTELARD, poet, follower of
and in love with Mary, Queen
of Scots, Episodes   EPISO

CHASTITY, personification,
Saint Francis   SAINT

CHATEAUPERS, PHOEBUS DE,
officer, loved by La Es-
meralda, betrothed to Fleur
de Lys, La Esmeralda
                          ESMER

CHATELAINE, THE YOUNG.
See; Julien

CHAUFFEUR, caricature of
cartoon character
The New Yorker   NEWYO
Servant of Husband (King
Mark)
Picnic at Tintagel   PICNI

CHAUFFEUR, HIS. See: Black
King

CHECK. See: Hat-Check Girl

CHEEKY. See: Hetyke

CHEFS, THREE, prepare chickens for roasting oven in
kitchen representing Hell,
L'Oeuf à la Coque   OEUFA

CHEFS, THREE. See also:
    Chickens, Four
    Egg

CHERRY BLOSSOM FAIRY,
    THE, fairy godmother of
    the Princess Aurora
    HER PAGE
    The Sleeping Beauty
                        SLEEP

CHESS-PLAYERS, TWO, Love
    and Death, play game of
    chess won by Death,
    Checkmate   CHECK

CHEVALET, first violin in
    orchestra at the opera
    house,
    The Débutante   DEBUT

CHIARA, nurse to Francesca
    (Francesca da Rimini),
    Francesda da Rimini
                        FRANC

CHIARINA, loved by Eusebius,
    Le Carnaval   CARNA

CHICHILLO. See: Don
    Chichillo

CHICKENS, FOUR, being
    prepared for roasting by
    Chefs in kitchen repre-
    senting Hell, L'Oeuf à la
    Coque   OEUFA

CHICKENS, FOUR. See also:
    Chefs, Three
    Egg

CHIEF. See:
    Cossack Chief, The
    Enemy Chief
    Fury, The Chief
    Jester, The Chief

CHIEF BOATSWAIN, of the
    Danish navy, Loin du
    Danemark   LOIND

CHIEF EUNUCH of Seyd's

harem
SECOND EUNUCH
    Le Corsaire   CORSA
    In charge of Shahryar's
    harem
    Schéhérazade   SCHEH

CHIEF NURSEMAID, THE
    NURSEMAIDS, participate in
    carnival celebrating Butter
    Week
    Petrouchka   PETRO

CHIEF OF POLICE, THE, a
    Fascist
    The Golden Age   GOLDE
    Guest at the Aristocrat's
    ball
    Mam'zelle Angot   MAMZE

CHIEF OF THE GYPSIES. See:
    Parembo
    Zarifi

CHIEF OF THE LETTS. See:
    Tautvaldis

CHIEF OF THE PORT, official
    at treaty-port in China,
    The Red Poppy   REDPO

CHIEF OF THE SLAVES, servant
    of Olifour, Le Dieu et la
    Bayadère   DIEUE

CHIEF, POLOVETSIAN. See:
    Polovetsian Girl

CHIEF SUPERVISOR OVER
    COOLIES unloading vessel
    in Chinese treaty-port
    COOLIES, unloading vessel
    The Red Poppy   REDPO

CHILD, personification
    Day on Earth   DAYON
    Participates in Punch and
    Judy show; associates char-
    acters of the show with
    people around her
    Punch and the Child PUNCH

CHILD. See also:

Constable
Fishwife
Husband
Judy
Punch
Puppeteer

CHILD GOD. See: Bartolo

CHILD, HIS. See: Count
    Rackozski

CHILD, THE, enjoys toys
    animated by the Spirits
    who Govern the Toys
    Jeux d'Enfants   JEUXX
    Appears at Eiffel Tower
    Les Mariés de la Tour
    Eiffel   MARIE
    Passer-by on Paris street
    La Nuit   NUITT
    "About whom everyday
    objects are transformed
    by magic into animated
    figures"
    The Spellbound Child
                        SPELL

CHILD, THE. See also:
    Traveler, The

CHILD, THEIR. See:
    Motorist, The

CHILDREN, of city slums,
    play games improvised
    to street songs
    Games   GAMES
    Residents of a big city
    MOTHERS, also residents
    of a big city
    Impressions of a Big
    City   IMPRE

CHILDREN. See also:
    Destiny
    Loving Children

CHILDREN, HIS. See:
    Officer, An

CHILDREN, HUSBAND'S. See:
    Lady, The

CHILDREN OF DARKNESS, em-
    bodiment of the forces of
    evil,
    Dante Sonata   DANTE

CHILDREN OF LIGHT, embodi-
    ment of the forces of good,
    Dante Sonata   DANTE

CHILDREN, THEIR TWO. See:
    Medea

CHIMERA OF ISOLDE. See:
    Isolde

CHINA, EMPEROR OF. See:
    Emperor of China
    Nightingale, Mechanical
    Nightingale, The

CHINA, KING OF INDIA AND.
    See: Shahryar

CHINESE CONJURER, THE,
    member of group of per-
    formers,
    Parade   PARAD

CHINESE CREW, SURVEYOR OF
    THE. See: Surveyor of
    Irish Crew

CHINESE POET. See: Old
    Chinese Poet

CHINESE PRINCE, character
    in Woman's dreams of her
    childhood, Mother Goose
    Suite   MOTHE

CHLOE, in love with Daphnis
    Daphnis and Chloe   DAPHC
    Daphnis and Chloe   DAPHI
    Daphnis et Chloë   DAPHN
    Daphnis and Chloe   DAPHS

CHLOE. See also:
    Bryaxis
    Dorkon
    Pan

CHLORIS. See: Flora (Chloris)

CHOLERIC VARIATION. See:
Melancholic Variation

CHOREOGRAPHER, THE, re-
hearses ballet under emo-
tional difficulties
Conflicts   CONFL
Creates new dance
La Création   CREAI

CHOREOGRAPHER, THE. See
also:
Idea
Ideal
Principal Dancer, The
(Adam Zero)
Temptation
Uncertainty

CHORINE. See: Champ, The

CHORUS, traditional perform-
er(s) in Greek drama,
Cave of the Heart CAVEO

CHORUS GIRL, A, defendant
in murder case, Hear Ye!
Hear Ye!   HEARY

CHOSEN ONE, THE (The
Chosen Maiden), beauti-
ful virgin, selected as
tribal sacrifice to insure
well-being of her people
Le Sacré du Printemps
                       SACRD
Le Sacré du Printemps
                       SACRE

CHOSEN ONE, THE. See
also:
Sage
Witch

CHOTA. See: Roustaveli,
Chota

CHOUB, would-be lover of
Solaxa, Christmas Eve
                       CHRIS

CHRIST. See: Traitor

CHRISTIAN. See: Bergerac,
Cyrano de

CHRISTIAN GIRL, A, restores
Young Man's faith in God
HER ATTENDANTS
El Greco   GRECO

CHRISTMAS NUMBER, THE, representation of British publication, The Press   PRESS

CHRISTOPHE, escaped prisoner,
killed by Baudin
BAUDIN, his companion,
also escaped prisoner
CHRISTOPHE'S WIFE, falls
in love with Baudin, per-
suades him to kill her husband
The Prisoners   PRISS

CHRYSANTHÈME, MADAME,
Japanese courtesan, enters
into temporary union with
Pierre
MONSIEUR TRÈS-PROPRE,
her father
MADAME RENONCULE, her
mother
MADEMOISELLE PURETÉ
MADEMOISELLE PRUNE,
her cousins
Madame Chrysanthème
                       MADAM

CHRYSANTHÈME, MADAME.
See also: Dignitary, A

CHRYSANTHEMUM, A, uprooted
by the Autumn Wind, dies
despite efforts of Young Poet
to save her, Autumn Leaves
                       AUTUM

CHRYSORIS, chief officer of the
royal dragonfly guard,
Les Papillons   PAPIO

CHUNG-YANG. See:
Ambassador, The
Mandarin

CHURCHMEN, FOUR. See:
  Martyr, The

CIGALA, a female smuggler,
  loves Kalkabrino, jealous
  of Marietta, <u>Kalkabrino</u>
                  KALKA

CIGARETTE GIRL, at 2222
  Club, New York City,
  <u>Café Society</u>   CAFES

CINDERELLA, slavey, attends
  ball, loses slipper, loved
  by Prince Fleur-de-Lys
  THE BARON DE SANS-
  SOUS, her father
  FI-FI, the Baroness,
  second wife of the Baron
  BRUNETTE
  BLONDINE, Fi-Fi's
  daughters, Cinderella's
  step-sisters
  FORTUNEE, Cinderella's
  fairy godmother, helps
  her attend ball
  <u>Cinderella</u>   CINDA
  Slavey, attends ball,
  loses slipper; falls in love
  with the Prince
  HER FATHER
  HER TWO UGLY STEP-
  SISTERS
  THE RAGGED FAIRY GOD-
  MOTHER, helps her attend
  ball
  <u>Cinderella</u>   CINDE
  Slavey, attends Prince
  Charming's ball, loses
  slipper
  ODETTE
  ALOISA, her half-sisters
  THEIR PARENTS
  THE GOOD FAIRY, Cinder-
  ella's fairy godmother,
  helps her attend ball
  <u>Cinderella</u>   CINDL
  Made a slavey by her sis-
  ters; goes to ball, loses
  slipper; identified by the
  Prince who falls in love
  with her
  THE TWO UGLY SISTERS,

  her sisters
  THE GOOD FAIRY, her
  fairy godmother, helps her
  gain her proper place in
  society
  <u>Cinderella</u>   CINDR

CINDERELLA. See also:
  Cat, The
  Sambo

CINEMATIC CIRCE, "headliner
  seeking refuge from publicity," visiting 2222 Club,
  New York City, <u>Café Society</u>
                         CAFES

CINZIO, Isabella's sweetheart
  THE DOCTOR, his father,
  Isabella's tutor
  <u>Salade</u>   SALAD

CIRCASSIAN MAID, THE, in
  love with Bakhmetiev, frees
  him from his chains
  CIRCASSIAN'S FIANCÉ
  CIRCASSIAN'S FATHER
  <u>The Prisoner in the Caucasus</u>
                         PRISR

CIRCE, enchantress
  <u>Ballet Comique de la Reine</u>
  <u>Enchantress, tempts Ulysses</u>
  <u>Circe</u>   CIRCE
  <u>I, Odysseus</u>   IODYS

CIRCE. See also:
  Cinematic Circe
  Comus
  Deer
  Goat
  Helmsman
  Lion
  Snake

CIRCUS DANCER. See: Girl,
  The

CITY SLICKER, THE. See:
  Light Lady, The

CIVILIZATION, personification,
  <u>Excelsior</u>   EXCEL

CIVILIZATION. See also:
Genii of Civilization, The

CLAIREMONDE, betrothed to
Count de Castro
DUC DE BEAUVOIR, her
father
GASTON DE BEAUVOIR,
her brother, betrothed to
Marguerite
The Stars   STARS

CLAIREMONDE. See also:
Marguerite

CLAIRETTE. See: Angot,
Mam'zelle

CLARA, forester's daughter,
attracts Jean, Miss Julie
MISSJ

CLARA. See also:
Julie, Miss
King of the Mice
Lady Clara
Nutcracker
President
Sugarplum Fairy

CLARENCE. See: Duke of
Clarence, The

CLARICE, formerly betrothed
to Federigo Rasponi,
brother of Beatrice; later
betrothed to Silvio
PANTALONE, her father
The False Bridegroom
FALSE

CLARINETIST, plays for dancers on bare stage, The
Pied Piper   PIEDP

CLARISSA. See: Andrea

CLASSIC, representation of
classical music, engages
in contest for supremacy
with Jazz, Rhapsody in
Blue   RHAPS

CLASSIC. See also: Barman

CLAUDE. See: Frollo, Claude

CLAUDIUS, friend of Decius,
son of Licinius Murena,
La Vestale   VESTA

CLAUDIUS. See also:
Hamlet, Prince of Denmark
Philemon

CLAUS. See: Prince Santa
Claus

CLEANER, STREET. See:
Constable

CLEMENCE, friend of Raymonda,
Raymonda   RAYMO

CLEMENTINE, QUEEN. See:
Alvarez
King Bobiche

CLEONISA, nymph, flirts with
Zephyrus, Flore et Zéphire
FLORE

CLEONTE. See: Jourdain,
Monsieur

CLEOPATRA, Queen of Egypt,
falls in love with, seduces
Antony
Les Amours d'Antoine et de
Cléopâtre   AMOUR
Queen of Egypt
Cesare in Egitto   CESAR
Cleopatra   CLEOR
Spectacle   SPECL

CLEOPATRA. See also:
Charmian
Iras

CLÉOPÂTRE, Queen of Egypt,
fascinates Amoûn, Cléopâtre
CLEOP

CLÉOPÂTRE. See also: High
Priest of the Temple

CLEOPHAS, a student of Al-
    cala; frees Asmodeus from
    imprisonment in bottle,
    Le Diable Boiteux
                        DIABL

CLEOPHAS. See also:
    Doña Dorotea
    Florinda
    Paquita

CLERK, THE, would-be lover
    of Solaxa, Christmas Eve
                        CHRIS

CLOPIN. See: Trouillefou,
    Clopin

CLORINDA. See: Tancred

CLORINDE, SIGNORA. See:
    Omepatico, Doctor

CLOWN, participant in gypsy
    carnival
    Aleko   ALEKO
    Member of a troupe of
    traveling players
    Les Forains   FORAI

CLOWNS, "perform merry
    antics," One in Five
                        ONEIN

CLOWNS, SEVEN, victimized
    by the Buffoon
    THEIR SEVEN WIVES,
    killed by them
    THEIR SEVEN DAUGHTERS,
    rejected in marriage by
    Rich Merchant
    SEVEN SOLDIERS, arrest
    the Seven Clowns
    Chout   CHOUT

CLUB. See: Night-Club
    Hostess, A

CLUBS. See:
    Knave of Clubs
    Queen of Clubs, The

CLYTEMNESTRA, wife, later

widow of Agamemnon; looks
    backward at her life follow-
    ing her death
    AGAMEMNON, King of Argos,
    her husband; murdered
    AGAMEMNON'S GHOST, ap-
    parition
    IPHIGENIA
    ELECTRA, their daughters
    ORESTES, their son
    Clytemnestra   CLYTE

CLYTEMNESTRA. See also:
    Aegisthus
    Electra

CLYTIA, betrothed to Gyges,
    Le Roi Candaule   ROICA

COACHMAN. See:
    Capricciosa, La
    Head Coachman, The

COACHMEN. See: Head Coach-
    man, The

COAT. See: Red Coat

COBRAS, serpents, The Cobras
                        COBRA

COCK, THE, resident of Soviet
    garden, Baby Stork BABYS

COCKEREL. See: Golden
    Cockerel, The

COCOA. See: Prince Cocoa

COFFEE. See: Prince Coffee

COLIN (COLAS), lover of Lisette
    (Lise), daughter of Mother
    Simone
    La Fille Mal Gardée FILLE
    La Fille Mal Gardée FILLG

COLLECTOR, THE, appears at
    Eiffel Tower, Les Mariés
    de la Tour Eiffel   MARIE

COLLEGE STAGS. See: Debu-
    tante

COLOMBINE, sought by Lean-
dre, loved by Harlequin
CASSANDRE, her father
Harlequinade   HARLI

COLOMBINE. See also:
Columbine
Fée, La Bonne

COLOMBUS, Vert-Vert's tu-
tor, Vert-Vert   VERTV

COLONEL, caricature of cartoon character, The New
Yorker   NEWYO

COLONEL OF HUSSARS, A,
guest at ball
Carnival at Pest   CARNI
Commands troops passing
through small Austrian
village
Halte de Cavalerie
                    HALTE

COLORED GENTLEMAN, THE,
American type, seen by
the Immigrant, Within the
Quota   WITHI

COLUMBINE, traditional
pantomime figure
Ballade   BALLA
The Bronze Horseman
                    BRONZ
Traditional pantomime fig-
ure, loved by Harlequin
Le Carnaval   CARNA
Harlequin in April
                    HARLE
Clockwork toy
The Nutcracker   NUTCA
The Nutcracker   NUTCK
The Nutcracker   NUTCR
Traditional pantomime fig-
ure
The Sleeping Beauty
                    SLEEP
Vert-Vert   VERTV

COLUMBINE. See also:
Colombine

COLUMBINES, TWO, traditional
pantomime figures, Veneziana
                    VENEZ

COLUMBUS. See: Colombus

COLUMNIST, visiting 2222 Club,
New York City, Café Society
                    CAFES

COLUMNIST. See also: Gossip
Columnist

COMEDY, a muse, Sylvia
                    SYLVA

COMET, A, celestial body, The
Stars   STARS

COMFORTERS, THREE, creatures
of Satan, attempt to insinuate
themselves into Job's confi-
dence, Job   JOBBB

COMIC STRIPS, personification,
Metropolitan Daily   METRO

COMMANDANT, Red army offi-
cer
HIS WIFE
Happiness   HAPPI

COMMANDANT OF THE PATROL
AT THE OUTPOST, Armen's
commanding officer
HIS WIFE
Happiness   HAPPI

COMMANDANT, THE. See:
Lauva, Lieutenant

COMMANDER, THE. See:
Don Juan
Donna Elvira

COMMENDATORE. See:
Laurencia

COMMISSARS, personifications,
Le Pas d'Acier   PASDA

COMMUNICANT. See: Young
Communicant, The

COMMUNIST GIRL. See:
Young Communist Girl, A

COMMUNIST YOUTH. See:
Woman of Soviet Commu-
nist Youth

COMPANIONS, HER TWO.
See: Venus

COMPANIONS, HIS THREE.
See: Bernadone, Frances-
co

COMPANIONS OF THE PRODI-
GAL SON. See: Prodi-
gal Son, The

COMPANY AGENT. See:
Village Elder

COMPOSER, of opera presented
at the Grand Opera, Paris,
Foyer de la Danse
FOYER

COMSTOCK, BONANZA KING,
prospector and mine own-
er; friend of Eilley Orum,
Ghost Town   GHOST

COMTE. See also: Count

COMTE DE MELUN, French
nobleman and violinist,
in love first with Made-
leine, then with Marie
Camargo, Camargo,
CAMAR

COMTE DE MELUN. See
also: Don Hernandez

COMTE DE MONTBAZON,
THE, nobleman, Vert-
Vert   VERTV

COMTE DE N--, LE, MON-
SIEUR, Marguerite
Gautier's lover
Lady of the Camellias
LADYB

The Lady of the Camellias
LADYC

COMTE DE VARDECK, THE,
nobleman
HÉLÈNE DE VARDECK, his
daughter
Le Violon du Diable VIOLO

COMTE DE VARDECK, THE.
See also: Beatrix

COMTE D'HERVILLY, THE,
French general
LUCIEN D'HERVILLY, his
son, in love with Paquita
THE COMTESSE, his mother
DONA SERAPHINA, his sis-
ter
Paquita   PAQUI
Paquita   PAQUT

COMTE D'HERVILLY, THE.
See also: Paquita

COMTE GEOFFROY. See:
Marquis Costa de Beaure-
gard, The

COMTE, THE. See:
Georges
Nina

COMTESSE. See also:
Contessa
Countess

COMTESSE, THE. See:
Comte d'Hervilly, The

COMUS, son of Circe and
Bacchus; disguised as
countryman, casts spell
over the Lady
THE LADY, victim of
Comus' spell
THE LADY'S TWO BROTH-
ERS, drive Comus from his
castle
ATTENDANT SPIRIT, inform
the Lady's brothers of her
danger

SABRINA, nymph, undoes Comus' spell
Comus   COMUS

CONCORD. See: Genii of Concord, The

CONCUBINES, HIS. See: Orion

CONDUCTOR, conducts orchestra at the ballet, Gala Performance   GALAP

CONGO, personification of river, La Fille du Pharaon
FILLP

CONJUGAL FAITH, personification, Spectacle SPECL

CONJURER, performs in bar located in treaty-port in China, The Red Poppy
REDPO

CONJURER. See also: Chinese Conjurer, The

CONQUERED INDIAN, personification, Concerto Brasileiro   CONCB

CONRAD, a pirate, Le Corsaire   CORSA

CONRAD. See also: Birbanto

CONSORT, HER. See:
Queen of the Air, The
Queen of the Earth, The
Queen of the Fire, The
Queen of the Waters, The

CONSTABLE, character in Punch and Judy show
STREET CLEANER, becomes associated with Constable in Child's mind
Punch and the Child
PUNCH

CONSTANZA, betrothed to the Count Rinaldo
THE MARQUISE SILVESTRA, her aged aunt
Les Femmes de Bonne Humeur   FEMME

CONSTANZA. See also:
Dorotea
Felicita
Mariuccia
Pasquina

CONTESSA. See also:
Comtesse
Countess

CONTESSA, THE, in love with Zenobio Bonaventuri; resorts to perfumes as a decoy, Quelques Fleurs   QUELQ

CONTESSA, THE. See also:
Alchemist, The
Rose

CONVICT, THE YOUNG. See: Leader of the Convicts

CONVICTS See: Leader of the Convicts

COOKS, ASSISTANT. See: Jeanne

COOLIES. See: Chief Supervisor over Coolies

COOP, old sailor, proprietor of the Grand Admiral Inn
BETTY, his daughter
Betty   BETTY

COPPELIA, mechanical doll constructed by Coppelius; thought by Swanilda to be loved by Frantz
Coppélia   COPPE
Coppélia   COPPI

COPPELIUS, village toy maker; constructs Coppélia and

other mechanical dolls
Coppélia   COPPE
Coppélia   COPPI

COPPER MOUNTAIN, MIS-
TRESS OF THE. See:
Danila

COQ D'OR, LE. See: Golden
Cockerel, The

COQUETRY, personification,
Fiammetta   FIAMM

COQUETTE, THE, inmate of
the Logéat Mental Hospital,
Les Algues   ALGUE
Guest at the Baron's
masked ball; attracted to
the Poet, jealous of the
Sleepwalker, wife of the
Baron
Night Shadow   NIGHT
Attends gas-attack precau-
tions course
Perhaps Tomorrow!
                        PERHA

CORALIA, daughter of Trois-
ondin, adopted by Ulrich;
loves and marries Sir
Hildebrand
TROISONDIN, King of the
Waters, her father
ULRICH, fisherman, her
foster-father
Coralia   CORAL

CORALINE, character por-
trayed by strolling player,
Le Marché des Innocents
                        MARCH

CORALLA. See: Golfo

CORALS. See: King of the
Corals

CORD. See:
Cords
First Golden Cord, The

CORDELIA. See: Lear, King

of Britain

CORDOBA, PEDRO, a gypsy
HIS WIFE
THEIR TWO LITTLE
DAUGHTERS
Zoraiya   ZORAI

CORDS. See also: Cord

CORDS, THE GOLDEN. See:
First Golden Cord, The

CORINTH, KING OF. See: Sisyphus

CORK, MRS. See: Tebrick, Mr.

CORN. See: Spirit of the Corn

CORNET OF LANCERS, soldier,
member of troop passing
through small Austrian village, Halte de Cavalerie
                        HALTE

CORREGIDOR, THE, "a dodder-
ing old fool," attracted to
the Miller's Wife
THE CORREGIDOR'S WIFE
Le Tricorne   TRICO

CORSAIRE, LE, pirate, Le
Corsaire   CORSI

CORTEZ. See: Malinche

COS, PASHA OF THE ISLE OF.
See: Seyd

COSSACK CHIEF, THE
THE COSSACK GIRL
FIVE COSSACK SOLDIERS,
mechanical dolls, perform
in toy shop
La Boutique Fantasque
                        BOUTI

COSTA. See: Marquis Costa
de Beauregard, The

COTTYS, giant, I Titani TITAN

COULISSE, callboy at the opera

house, The Débutante
DEBUT

COUNCILLOR, THE, official
at court of King of Portugal, wishes Don Pedro to
marry the Infanta of Nav-
arre, Doña Ines de Castro
DONAI

COUNCILLOR, THE. See
also: Doña Ines de Castro

COUNT. See also:
Comte
Countess

COUNT ANSELMI, nobleman,
in love with Josephina,
Scuola di Ballo   SCUOL

COUNT DANDINI, THE, secretary to Prince Fleur-de-
Lys, Cinderella   CINDA

COUNT DE CASTRO, be-
trothed to Clairemonde,
The Stars   STARS

COUNT DE CASTRO. See
also:
Doctor
Master of Ceremonies
Morning Star

COUNT DI LUNA, Italian
nobleman, orders death
of mother of Azucena
COUNT DI LUNA, his son,
in love with Leonora
MANRICO, his son, kid-
napped by Azucena, in
love with Leonora
Revanche   REVAN

COUNT DI LUNA. See also:
Azucena
Leonora

COUNT FRÉDÉRIC, Phoebe's
lover, later flees with
Lilia as his bride; sells his
soul to Beelzebub, Le Diable

Amoureux   DIABE

COUNT FRÉDÉRIC. See also:
Hortensius, Doctor
Janetta
Urielle

COUNT FREDERICK, a Pala-
tine nobleman, falls in
love with Stone Statue, Les
Elfes   ELFES

COUNT FRIEDRICH STERNHOLD,
dissipated nobleman, wishes
to marry Ragonda for the
money of her mother, Princess Millefleurs, Fiametta
FIAMM

COUNT FRIEDRICH STERNHOLD.
See also:
Fiametta
Martini
Molari

COUNT LEONARDO, nobleman,
La Jolie Fille de Gand
JOLIE

COUNT OF SAN-SEVERINO.
See: Countess Gemma

COUNT OSCAR, King Bobiche's
Chancellor, Bluebeard BLUEB

COUNT PEPINELLI, the Mar-
chesa Sampietri's cecisbeo;
captain of dragoons, Marco
Spada   MARCO

COUNT PEPINELLI. See also:
Prince Osorio, Governor of
Rome

COUNT POLINSKI, THE, nobleman
THE COUNTESS, his bad-
tempered wife, changed by
Blind Old Man into Mazourka for a day
Le Diable à Quatre DIABQ

COUNT POLINSKI, THE. See

also:
Blind Old Man
Yelva
Yvan

COUNT RACKOZSKI, former
soldier, subject to arrest
for lèse majesté; par-
doned by the Emperor of
Austria
HIS WIFE
HIS CHILD
The Hungarian Hut
                                    HUNGA

COUNT RACKOZSKI. See also:
Sergeant
Veteran Soldier, A

COUNT RAOUL DE CRÉQUI,
returns from Crusades,
finds his lands seized by
Badouin who also desires
de Créqui's wife
ADELAIDE, his wife
RAOUL DE CRÉQUI, his
elder son
CRAON, aged seven, his
younger son
Raoul de Crêqui   RAOUL

COUNT RAOUL DE CRÉQUI.
See also:
Jailer
Knight Renshi, The
Morlaque
Peter
Warder

COUNT RASUMOVSKY, noble-
man, Vienna-1814 VIENN

COUNT RINALDO, THE, be-
trothed to Constanza, Les
Femmes de Bonne Hu-
meur   FEMME

COUNT, THE. See:
Julie, Miss
Kristin

COUNTESS, noblewoman
COUNT, nobleman

The Unicorn, The Gorgon
and the Manticore   UNICO

COUNTESS. See also:
Comtesse
Contessa

COUNTESS GEMMA, in love with
Massimo; almost victim of
Marquis de Santa-Croce,
mesmerist
COUNT OF SAN-SEVERINO,
her guardian
Gemma   GEMMA

COUNTESS GEMMA. See also:
Barbara
Giacomo

COUNTESS KITTY, "engaging in
an Edwardian romp at a
French plage, " Les Sirènes
                          SIREN

COUNTESS SYBILLE, THE. See:
Raymonda

COUNTESS, THE. See:
Blind Old Man
Count Polinski, The
Yelva

COUNTRY. See: Leader of
Yellow Group (Country)

COUNTRY GIRL. See: Silly
Country Girl

COUNTRY YOUTH, A, celebrating St. John's Eve, Nuit de
Saint-Jean   NUITD

COUPLE. See:
Amager Couple
French Couple
Greek Couple
Negro Couple
Norwegian Couple
Older Married Couple, An
Quaker Couple
Styrian Couple

COUPLES, TWO FLIRTATIOUS.

See: Umbrella

COURASCHE, carries out daring thievery and liberations
during Thirty Years War
SPRINGINSFELD, her
friend, assists in her ex-
ploits
ARMY OFFICERS
GUARDS
VILLAGE MAGISTRATE
MERRY WIDOW
SHOPKEEPERS, fooled
and swindled by Courasche
and Springinsfeld
The Gay Swindles of Cour-
asche   GAYSW

COURLAND. See: Prince of
Courland, The

COURT CHAMBERLAIN, offi-
cial in Butterfly Land,
Les Papillons   PAPIO

COURT OF BUCHARIA. See:
Princess of the Court of
Bucharia

COURTESAN, mistress of
the Prince
THE PRINCE, lover of
Courtesan
FIORA
MADDELENA, sisters of
the Prince, jealous of
his love for Courtesan
SEBASTIAN, Moorish
slave belonging to Fiora
and Maddelena, killed by
them while protecting
Courtesan from their
witchcraft
Sebastian   SEBAS

COURTESAN, TYRANT'S.
See: Tyrant

COURTIER, A, at the court
of Dushmata, King of
India, Sakuntala   SAKUN

COUSIN, GIRL'S. See:

Girl, The

COUSIN, THE PRINCESS'S. See:
Princess Nina, The

COUSINS, THEIR. See: President

COVIELLO, servant to Tartaglia, father of Rosetta,
Salade   SALAD

COWBOY IN RED, member of
Billy the Kid's gang, Billy
the Kid   BILLY

COWBOY, THE, American type,
seen by the Immigrant,
Within the Quota   WITHI

COWGIRL, THE, hoyden, rival
of the Rancher's Daughter;
attracted to the Head Wrangler, won by the Champion
Roper, Rodeo   RODEO

CRAKENTORP, NARCISSE DE. See:
Lord Campbell

CRAON. See: Count Raoul de
Créqui

CREATION. See: Spirit of
Creation, The

CREATION, THE LORD OF.
See: Man

CREATURE OF FEAR, inhabi-
tant of "the maze of the
heart's darkness"
WOMAN, makes "psycholo-
gical exploration of the
maze, overcomes the
Creature of Fear"
Errand into the Maze
                   ERRAT

CREOLE, THE, native, A Day
in a Southern Port DAYIN

CREON, usurping King of Thebes,
forbids honorable burial to

sons of Oedipus who were
killed in battle
HAEMON, his son
Antigone   ANTIG

CRÉQUL   See: Count Raoul de
Créqui

CRÉQUI, RAOUL DE.   See:
Count Raoul de Créqui

CRETE, KING OF.   See:
Minos, King of Crete

CRETE, QUEEN OF.   See:
Minos, King of Crete

CREUSA, loved by Jason,
husband of Medea; killed
by the latter by means of
a poisoned robe, Medea
                       MEDEA

CREW.   See: Surveyor of the
Irish Crew

CREW, SURVEYER OF THE
CHINESE.   See: Surveyor
of the Irish Crew

CRIME, personification
La Douairière de Bille-
bahaut   DOUAI
Metropolitan Daily   METRO

CRISTOBAL.   See: Moscatello, Sergeant

CROCE, MARQUIS DE SANTA.
See: Marquis de Santa
Croce

CROCODILE, THE, consumes
Planter, Baby Stork
                       BABYS

CRONE, THE OLD.   See:
Kwahu

CRONK, REVEREND ADRIAN,
minister, The Sailor's
Return   SAILO

CROONER, passing through
metropolitan railroad
terminal "on his way to
new triumphs"
HIS WIFE
Terminal   TERMI

CROQUEUSE, LA (The Dia-
mond Cruncher), young
girl, has insatiable appe-
tite for diamonds which she
steals and eats as food,
La Croqueuse de Diamants
                       CROQU

CROSS KNIGHT, THE RED.
See: Sir Lancelot

CRUNCHER, THE DIAMOND.
See: Croqueuse, La

CRUTCHES.   See: Man on
Crutches, The

CRY.   See: War Cry, The

CRYSTAL, "the little glass
slipper fairy, " Cinderella
                       CINDA

CRYSTAL GAZER, circus performer, The Incredible
Flutist   INCRE

CSIZMÁS JANKO (Little Johnny
in Top-Boots), shepherd
boy, falls in love with Ildikó; has ambition to own
a pair of boots, Little Johnny in Top-Boots   LITTL

CSIZMÁS JANKO.   See also:
Bride, The
Fairy Queen, The
Seppi
Witch, The

CUCHARON.   See: Bartolo

CUCKOO, bird, Carnival of
Animals   CARNV

CUNIGONDA.   See: Valentine

The Holy Torch   HOLYT

DADJE, the Khan's favorite,
La Source   SOURC

DAHOMEY, KING OF.   See:
Tulip

DAHOMEY, PRINCESS GUNDE-
MEY OF.   See: Tulip

DAILY MAIL, THE, representation of British newspaper,
The Press   PRESS

DAILY TELEGRAPH, THE, representation of British newspaper, The Press   PRESS

DAÏTA, PRINCESS.   See:
Izuna
Jamato
Kwannon

DAÏTA'S NURSE, PRINCESS.
See: Jamato

DAMAYANTI, betrothed to
Noureddin, Maharajah of
Lahore
AKDAR, King of Delhi,
her father
The Talisman   TALIS

DAMIS.   See: Marquis Damis

DAN.   See: McGrew, Dan

DANAË, wooed by Jupiter in
the form of a shower of
gold, Les Amours de
Jupiter   AMOUJ

DANAË   See also:
Jailers, Three
Shower of Gold

DANCE.   See: Queen of the
Dance

DANCE, GODESS OF THE.
See: Queen of the Dance

DANCE MASTER
LEADER OF THE CAN-
CAN GIRLS
CANCAN GIRLS, perform
at Paris café
Gaîté Parisienne   GAITE

DANCE, PERSONIFICATION
OF. See:
Bolero
Ganzonetta
Tarantella
Tirolese

DANCE, THE, a muse, Sylvia
SYLVA

DANCER. See:
Danseur
Dégas Dancer
Drum-Dancer, The
Female Dancer, A
Jazz Dancer
Principal Dancer, The (Adam
Zero)
Snake Dancer
Street Dancer, The
Tambourine Dancer

DANCER, A MALE. See: Fe-
male Dancer, A

DANCER, CIRCUS. See: Girl, The

DANCER, THE, puppet, brought
to life by the Old Charlatan,
Petrouchka   PETRO

DANCER, THE GYPSY. See:
Young Girl, The

DANCERS. See:
Cancan Dancers
Street Dancers, The
Tarantella Dancers

DANCERS, SQUARE. See:
Caller

DANCERS, THE CHARACTER.
See: Principal Dancer, The
(Adam Zero)

DANCES. See: One Who Dances, The

DANCING, GIRL. See: Bearded Old Man

DANCING MASTER, THE, helps Cinderella's two ugly stepsisters prepare for ball
Cinderella   CINDE
Hopes to profit from the Rake's recently inherited wealth
The Rake's Progress RAKES

DANCING POODLES, two mechanical toys, perform at toy shop, La Boutique Fantasque   BOUTI

DANDIES. See: King of the Dandies, The Vaudeville Dandies, Two

DANDINI. See: Count Dandini, The

DANDY. See: Poet

DANDY, THE, chased away by the Miller after being attracted to the latter's wife
Le Tricorne   TRICO
Seduces Tom Tug's wife
The Triumph of Neptune
                               TRIUM

DANDY, THE. See also: Miller's Wife, The

DANILA, stonecutter, working on creation of stone flower
KATERINA, in love with and loved by Danila
BAILIFF, attempts to carry Katerina away
MISTRESS OF THE COPPER MOUNTAIN, causes the earth to swallow Bailiff
Stone Flower   STONE

DANILO. See: Petr

DANILO, PRINCE. See: Sonia

DANINA, Brazilian girl, slave of Don Alonzo, secretly married, saves Joko from venomous snake
ALVAR, her husband, commander of Portuguese fleet
SABI, their five-year-old son, rescued by Joko from Jeafre's kidnap attempt
Danina   DANIN

DANSUER. See also: Dancer

DANSEUR, PREMIER. See: Ballerina, The Premier Danseur

DANUBE. See: Nymph of the Danube, The Spirit of the Danube, The

DANUBE, THE DAUGHTER OF THE. See: Fleur-des-Champs

DAPHNIS, handsome shepherd, in love with Chloe
Daphnis and Chloe   DAPHC
Daphnis and Chloe   DAPHI
Daphnis et Chloë   DAPHN
Daphnis and Chloe   DAPHS

DAPHNIS. See also: Lykanion Pan

DAR. See: Tchop-Dar, The

D'ARC, JEANNE (Joan of Arc), French heroine, burned at the stake
LIONEL, English officer, loved by Jeanne; killed by her after he offers her freedom in return for betraying her people
Jeanne d'Arc   JEANN

DAREDJAN, NESTAN, Princess,

loved by Tariel, Chota
Roustaveli   CHOTA

DA RIMINI, FRANCESCA. See:
Francesca

DARK ANGEL, the Angel of
Death, accompanies Orpheus
to the Underworld, Orpheus
                   ORPHE

DARK BELOVED. See: Sisters,
Three

DARKLING, THE, girl, transformed through love,
"moves from shadow into
light"
DARKLING'S LOVER
The Darkling   DARKL

DARKNESS. See:
Children of Darkness
Spirit of Darkness, The

DARL. See: Bundren, Addie

DARNLEY. See: Mary,
Queen of Scots

D'ART. See: Visions d'Art

DAUGHTER. See:
Mummy of the Pharaoh's
Daughter
Rancher's Daughter, The

DAUGHTER, HER. See:
Frickes, Mrs.

DAUGHTER, HIS. See: Old
Lord, The

DAUGHTER, HUSBAND'S. See:
Husband, The

DAUGHTER, NEPTUNE'S. See:
Neptune
Tug, Tom

DAUGHTER OF TERPSICHORE.

See: Queen of the Dance

DAUGHTER OF THE AIR.
See: Queen of Shemakha

DAUGHTER OF THE DANUBE,
THE. See: Fleur-des-
Champs

DAUGHTER, THE, engaged to
the Hussar
HER SISTER
THE FATHER
THE MOTHER, her family
Le Beau Danube   BEAUD
In love with the Kuruc
Lieutenant
THE FATHER
THE MOTHER
THE STOUT AUNT
THE THIN AUNT
THE UNCLE, her family,
insist that she marry the
Labanc Suitor
Kuruc Fairy Tale   KURUC

DAUGHTER, THE. See also:
Nurse, The

DAUGHTER, THEIR. See:
Farmer, A

DAUGHTER, VILLAGE ELDER'S.
See: Village Elder

DAUGHTERS, HER THREE. See:
Patroness, The

DAUGHTERS, HER TWO. See:
Mother

DAUGHTERS, HIS THREE. See:
Job

DAUGHTERS, HIS TWO. See:
Veteran Soldier, A

DAUGHTERS OF PAI-DO-MATO.
See: Zuimaaluti

DAUGHTERS OF THE NIGHT.
See: Shadow, The

DAUGHTERS' SWEETHEARTS,
   HIS. See: Veteran Soldier, A

DAUGHTERS, THEIR. See:
   Cavalier Pignerolle, The

DAUGHTERS, THEIR SEVEN.
   See: Clowns, Seven

DAUGHTERS, THEIR TWO
   LITTLE. See: Cordoba,
   Pedro

DAVID, shepherd, son of
   Jesse, kills Goliath; loved
   by Melchola, daughter of
   King Saul, King of the
   Israelites, David Triom-
   phant   DAVIT

DAVID. See also:
   Abigail
   Abishai
   Jesse
   Rizzio, David

D'AVRIL, MADEMOISELLE
   PLUIE, a courtesan,
   Madame Chrysanthème
                           MADAM

DAWN, personification, Ardent
   Song   ARDEN

DAWN, THE. See: Aurora

DAY. See:
   Hours of Day, Six
   Queen of the Day, The

DEACON, THE, attends vil-
   lage barn dance, Barn
   Dance   BARND

DEAD GIRL, THE
   THE WIDOWER, her hus-
   band, attempts to bring her
   back to life
   Caprichos   CAPRH

DEADLY SINS, THE SEVEN.
   See:

Seven Deadly Sins, The
Seven Sins, The
Young Girl

DEALER. See:
   Picture-Dealer, The
   Slave-Dealer, A

DEATH, claims the Principal
   Dancer (Adam Zero)
   Adam Zero   ADAMZ
   Takes Annabel Lee and her
   lover
   Annabel Lee   ANNAB
   Personification
   Canticle for Innocent Come-
   dians   CANTI
   Makes pact with Donald
   Donald of the Burthens
                            DONAL
   Personification
   The Five Gifts   FIVEG
   The Green Table   GREEN
   Assumes guise of beautiful
   woman, fascinates Young
   Man, leads him to self-de-
   struction
   YOUNG MAN, hangs himself
   Le Jeune Homme et la Mort
                            JEUNE
   Personification
   Oriane et le Prince d'Amour
                            ORIAN
   Takes Lieutenant Kije
   Russian Soldier   RUSSI
   Comes for Emperor of China;
   persuaded by the Nightingale
   to permit him to live
   Song of the Nightingale
                            SONGO
   Impersonated by Tyl Ulen-
   spiegel
   Tyl Ulenspiegel   TYLUL
   Dances waltz with Ballerina
   BALLERINA, dances waltz
   with Death and with her
   Partner; dies
   HER PARTNER, dances with
   Ballerina
   Le Valse   VALSS

DEATH. See also:
   Chess-Players, Two

Knight of Death
Maiden, The
Matador
Messenger of Death
Morte Amoureuse, La
Night
Old Mother, The
Thanatos
Young Soldier, The

DEATH, ANGEL OF. See:
    Dark Angel
    Grey Angel, The

DE BEAUGENCY. See:
    Vicomte de Beaugency

DE BEAUREGARD. See:
    Marquis Costa de Beaure-
        gard, The

DE BEAUVOIR, DUC. See:
    Clairemonde

DE BEAUVOIR, GASTON.
    See:
    Clairemonde
    Marguerite

DE BERGERAC. See: Ber-
    gerac, Cyrano de

DE BOUGAINVILLE, MADAME.
    See: Bougainville, Mon-
        sieur de

DE BOUGAINVILLE, MA-
    DAMOISELLE. See:
    Bougainville, Monsieur de
    Guimard, La

DE BOUGAINVILLE, MON-
    SIEUR. See: Bougain-
        ville, Monsieur de

DE BREILLE. See: Marquis
    de Breille

DE BRIENNE. See: Brienne,
    Jean de

DEBUTANTE
    COLLEGE STAGS, her es-

corts, all visiting 2222 Club,
New York City
Café Society   CAFES
Caricature of cartoon charac-
ter
HER THREE BOY-FRIENDS,
also caricatures of cartoon
characters
The New Yorker   NEWYO
Patron of fashionable café
Offenbach in the Underworld
                      OFFEN

DEBUTANTE. See also: Gigolo

DEBUTANTE, THE. See:
    Baron Salomon
    Dubet, Mademoiselle Del-
        phine

DEBUTANTES, attending ball
    tendered by Prince Metter-
    nich, Vienna- 1814   VIENN

DE CASTRO. See:
    Count de Castro
    Doña Ines de Castro

DECEIT. See: Night

DECEMBER, an old woman,
    Twelve for the Mail-Coach
                      TWELV

DE CHATEAUPERS. See:
    Chateaupers, Phoebus de

DECIUS. See:
    Claudius
    Murena, Licinius

DE CRAKENTORP, NARCISSE.
    See: Lord Campbell

DE CRÉQUI. See: Count Raoul
    de Créqui

DE CRÉQUI, RAOUL. See:
    Count Raoul de Créqui

DEDALUS. See: Icare

DEDICATED, THE. See:

Agonistes, Samson

DEER, one of Ulysses' sail-
ors, transformed by Circe
Circe   CIRCE
Personifications
The Seventh Symphony
                          SEVEN

DEER, THE, seen by Young
Musician in his dream,
Symphonie Fantastique
                          SYMPH

DEERSLAYER, THE. See:
Bumppo, Natty

DEFENDANT, A
VICTIM, THE, night-club
dance team, involved in
murder case
Hear Ye! Hear Ye!
                          HEARY

DEFENDING ATTORNEY, A,
defends in murder case,
Hear Ye! Hear Ye!
                          HEARY

DE FIERBOIS. See: Marquis
de Fierbois

DEFORMITY, personification,
La Douairière de Billeba-
haut   DOUAI

DÉGAS DANCER, portrait
hanging in the Louvre,
comes to life between two
rounds of the night watchman
NIGHT WATCHMAN, on
guard at the Louvre
Entre Deux Rondes
                          ENTRE

DE GONDELAURIER, MADAME
ALOISE. See: Fleur-de-
Lys

D'ÉGOUT, GRILLE, can-can
dancer, Bar aux Folies-
Bergère   BARAU

DE GRINDBERG. See: Baron
de Grindberg

DE GRINDBERG, BARONESS.
See: Baron de Grindberg

DE GUÉBRIANT. See: Baron
de Guébriant, The

DE LA MARTINIÈRE, MONSIEUR,
governor of the island, Les
Deux Créoles   DEUXC

DELHI, KING OF. See: Damayanti

DE LIGNE. See: Prince de
Ligne

DELILAH, Biblical figure, be-
trayer of Samson
Billy Sunday   BILLS
Betrayer of Samson Agonis-
tes
THE AWAKENER
THE BETRAYER
THE SEDUCER, "the three
aspects of Delilah"
Samson Agonistes   SAMSO

DELIVERY BOY, delivers couch
to Paris bistro, La Cro-
queuse de Diamants CROQU

DELL, DEWEY. See: Bundren,
Addie

DELLA, young wife, cuts off
and sells her hair to pur-
chase chain for husband's
watch as Christmas present
JIM, her husband, sells
watch to buy comb for wife's
hair as Christmas present
Gift of the Magi   GIFTO

DEL ORO. See: Niña del Oro,
La

DELPHINE. See: Duvet, Mademoiselle Delphine

DEL SATO, ORSINO, fiancé of

one of Marco Lugano's
elder daughters, The Blood-
Red Flower   BLOOD

DE LUZY. See: Marquis de
Luzy, The

DE LYS. See:
Fleur-de-Lys
Prince Fleur-de-Lys

DE MAYENNE. See: Duc de
Mayenne

DE MELUN. See: Comte de
Melun

DE MENDOZA. See: Don
Lopez de Mendoza

DEMETER. See: Perse-
phone, Queen of Hades

DEMETRIUS, in love with
Hermia
The Dream   DREAM
A Midsummer Night's
Dream   MIDSU

DEMETRIUS. See also:
Helena

DEMI-MONDE, THE, met by
Anna I and Anna II, The
Seven Deadly Sins SEVED

DEMONS, QUEEN OF THE.
See: Bambo

DE MONTBAZON. See:
Comte de Montbazon, The

DEMURE. See: Szelid

DE N---. See: Comte de
N---, Le, Monsieur

DEN. See: Proprietor of
an Opium Den

DE NAVAILLES. See:
Navailles, Madame de

DENISE, Lindor's mistress, Le
Marché des Innocents
                      MARCH

DENMARK, KING OF. See:
Hamlet, Prince of Denmark
Lodbrok, Regnar

DENMARK, PRINCE OF. See:
Hamlet, Prince of Denmark

DENMARK, QUEEN OF. See:
Hamlet, Prince of Denmark

DE PERIGORD. See: Perigord,
Madame de

DE POITIERS. See: Poitiers,
Mireille de

DE PROVENCE. See: Prince
Hugues de Provence

DE RENOUALLE, YSAURE. See:
Arthur
Renoualle, Ysaure de
Spirit of Curiosity, The

DE SAGAN. See: Sagan,
Madame de

DE SAINT-ANGE, MADAME.
See: Duc de Vendôme, The

DE SAINT IBARS. See: Baron
de Saint Ibars, The

DE SAINT-RAMBERT. See:
Saint-Rambert, Monsieur de

DE SAN LUCAR. See: Marquis
de San Lucar, The

DE SANS-SOUS, THE BARON.
See: Cinderella

DE SANTA-CROCE, MARQUIS.
See: Marquis de Santa-
Croce

DES-CHAMPS. See: Fleur-
des-Champs

DESDEMONA. See:
   Emilia
   Otello
   Othello

DE SÉNANGE, MADAME.
   See: Théodore

DESIGNER, THE. See:
   Principal Dancer, The
   (Adam Zero)

DESTINIES, personifications,
   Les Présages   PRESA

DESTINY, causes death of
   Young Man after the latter
   finds his ideal
   Le Rendez-Vous   RENDE
   Leader of Black Group
   BLACK GROUP, personi-
   fications of evil forces
   Rouge et Noir   ROUGE
   Personification
   CHILDREN, obey the call
   of Destiny, "return later
   in search of their lost
   innocence"
   The Scarecrow   SCARE

DESTINY. See also: Spirit
   of Destiny

DESTROYER, THE. See:
   Agonistes, Samson

DE SURVILLE, MONSIEUR.
   See:
   Bougainville, Monsieur de
   Ozaï

DETECTIVE, attempts to ap-
   prehend the Thief, The
   Thief Who Loved a Ghost
                 THIEF

DEVA, celebrated Fascist
   performer, attracted to
   Captain of Soviet Football
   Team, The Golden Age
                 GOLDE

DE VARDECK. See: Comte

de Vardeck, The

DE VARDECK, HÉLÈNE. See:
   Beatrix
   Comte de Vardeck, The

DE VENDÔME. See: Duc de
   Vendôme, The

DE VANTADOUR. See: Ventadour, Bernard de

DEVIL, A, disguised as a beggar, tempts and overcomes
   the Three Virgins, Three
   Virgins and a Devil THREV

DEVIL, A. See also: Priggish
   Virgin

DEVIL ON TWO STICKS, THE.
   See: Asmodeus

DEVIL, THE, personification
   Billy Sunday   BILLS
   Friend of the witch Solaxa
   Christmas Eve   CHRIS
   Amuses himself by meddling
   in the affairs of humans
   Devil's Holiday   DEVIL
   Temporarily possesses
   Mirko
   THE DEVIL'S MISTRESS,
   tempts Mirko
   The Devil in the Village
                 DEVIV
   Personification
   La Fiancée du Diable
                 FIANC
   The Stranger, involved by
   Doll, appears as man dressed
   in green, seduces her
   A Mirror for Witches
                 MIRRO

DEVIL, THE. See also:
   Archiposa
   Beelzebub
   Belzebu
   Gypsy Girl, The
   Joseph
   Mephistopheles
   Old Devil, The

Old Lord, The
Puppeteer
Red Coat
Satan
Yela

DEVIL, THE SHE. See: Old
Devil, The

DEVILKIN, THE. See: Old
Devil, The

DEWEY DELL. See: Bund-
ren, Addie

D'HERVILLY. See: Comte
d'Hervilly, The

D'HERVILLY, LUCIEN. See:
Comte d'Hervilly, The
Paquita

D'HOTEL. See: Maître d'
Hotel

DIABLE. See: Trousse-
Diable

DIAMOND CRUNCHER, THE.
See:
Croqueuse, La

DIAMOND FAIRY, The. See:
Fairy Hamza, The

DIAMONDS. See:
Knave of Diamonds
Queen of Diamonds

DIAMONDS, THE KING OF.
See: Queen of Clubs, The

DIANA, seen bathing by Ac-
taeon, turns him into a
stag
Aubade   AUBAA
Aubade   AUBAB
Aubade   AUBAC
Aubade   AUBAD
Aubade   AUBAE
Première danseuse at the
Fanice Theatre
La Jolie de Gand JOLIE

Goddess of the hunt
Spectacle   SPECL
The Stars   STARS
Sylvia   SYLVA
Goddess of the chase
Sylvia   SYLVI

DIANA. See also:
Endymion
Sylvia

DIANE, compansion of Fleur-
de-Lys, La Esmeralda
                ESMER

DIAVOLINA, a wealthy peasant
girl, about to be married
to Gennariello
DONA MARIANNA, her cou-
sin
DON PEPPINO, her guardian
VZULA, Don Peppino's niece
Diavolina   DIAVO

DIAVOLINA. See also:
Bridoux
Don Chicillo
Don Fortunato

DIAVOLINO, Catarina's lieutenant, in love with her,
Catarina   CATAR

DICTATORSHIP, PERSONIFICA-
TION OF. See: Leader, The

DIDELOT, MONSIEUR, premier
danseur at the King's Theatre, London, The Prospect
Before Us   PROSP

DIDERIK. See: Muri

DIDO, Queen of Carthage, in
love with Aeneas, Dido
                DIDOO

DIGGER. See: Grave Digger

DIGNITARY, A, performs "wedding" ceremony for Pierre
and Madame Chrysanthème,
Madame Chrysanthème

MADAM

DI LUCA. See: Marquis di
Luca, The

DI LUNA. See: Count di
Luna

DI MALASPINA. See: Mar-
quis Obizzo di Malaspina

DIMPLE, MRS. See: Blanche

DIONYSUS, god of wine and
the drama
Dionysus   DIONY
The Minotaur   MINOU

DIPLOMATS, visiting 2222
Club, New York City
Café Society   CAFES
Negotiate at "green table"
The Green Table GREEN

DIRECTOR, dignitary at exhib-
it, The Golden Age GOLDE

DIRECTOR. See also:
Stage Director, The

DIRECTOR OF AN INDUSTRIAL
EXHIBITION called "The
Golden Age" in a large
capitalistic city, The Gold-
en Age   GOLDE

DIRECTOR OF THE OPERA
at Grand Opera, Paris,
Foyer de la Danse
                    FOYER

DISCORD. See: Night

DIVERSION, personification,
Wind in the Mountains
                    WINDI

DIVINE GENIUS, THE, in-
spires the violinist Paganini, Paganini   PAGAN

DIVORCEES, passing through
metropolitan railroad

terminal, Terminal TERMI

DJALMA. See: Prince Djalma

DJARDJE, rebel leader, loved by
Manije; takes up arms against
Moyravi, Prince of Eristav,
her father, The Heart of the
Hills   HEART

DJARDJE. See also: Zyrab

DJÉMIL, a hunter
La Source   SOURC
Bodyguard to Noureddin,
Maharajah of Lahore
The Talisman   TALIS

DLUGOSZEWSKI, LUCIA, com-
poser, participates in ballet
by playing hand-made instruments, 8 Clear Places
                     EIGHT

DO-MATO, DAUGHTERS OF PAL
See: Zuimaaluti

DO-MATO, PAL. See: Zuimaaluti

DOBRYNA. See: Nikitytch,
Dobryna

DOCTOR, treats Count de Castro,
The Stars   STARS

DOCTOR. See also:
Dottore
Faust, Doctor
Gaspard, Doctor
Hortensius, Doctor
Matheus, Doctor
Omeopatico, Doctor
Wife

DOCTOR, HIS WITCH. See:
Black King

DOCTOR LOMBARD. See:
Silvio

DOCTOR, THE, called to attend
Florinda

Le Diable Boiteux
DIABL
Attends the Young Communi-
cant
Schlagobers   SCHLA

DOCTOR, THE.   See also:
Cinzio

DOG.   See: Tractor-Driver

DOG, THE, resident of Soviet
garden, Baby Stork
BABYS

DOGE, THE, Venetian ruler,
Otello   OTELL

DOLL, daughter of Witch, be-
friended by Bilby, taken
into his home in Salem;
loved by Titus, seduced
by the Devil, condemned
as a witch
WITCH, her mother,
burned at the stake
A Mirror for Witches
MIRRO

DOLL, FEMALE.   See:
Puppet, Mister

DOLLS, come to life at night
in toyshop where they are
displayed, Die Puppenfee
PUPPE

DOM SANDOVAL, Spanish
nobleman, La Fille de
Marbre   FILLM

DOMINGUO, servant of Théodore, Les Deux Créoles
DEUXC

DON ALONSO.   See: Duke of
Medina-Celi, The

DON ALONZO, wealthy Portuguese landowner, master
of the slave girl Danina,
Danina   DANIN

DON ALONZO.   See also: Jeafre

DON ALTAMIRANO, naval officer, Jovita   JOVIT

DON ALVAR, friend of Jovita
Cavallines
AMALIA
INES
CATALINA, his sisters,
also friends of Jovita
Cavallines
Jovita   JOVIT

DON ALVAR.   See also: Don
José Cavallines

DON BUSTAMENTE, Spaniard,
friend of The Marquis de
San Lucar, La Jolie Fille
de Gand   JOLIE

DON CHICHILLO, a wealthy citi-
zen, clowns at wedding of
Diavolina and Gennariello,
Diavolina   DIAVO

DON FORTUNATO, a rich citizen
of Caserta, to be witness at
wedding of Diavolina and
Gennariello
FRANCESCA, his wife
Diavolina   DIAVO

DON GIL, Spanish nobleman,
aspires to the hand of Doña
Dorotea, Le Diable Boiteux
DIABL

DON HERNANDEZ, Spanish nobleman
DONNA HERNANDEZ, his
wife, attracts Comte de
Melun, Camargo   CAMAR

DON JOSÉ, soldier, attracted to,
seduced by, Carmen; stabs
her, Carmen   CARME

DON JOSÉ.   See also:
Bandits, Three
José

DON JOSÉ CAVALLINES, own-
er of plantation in Mexico
JOVITA CAVALLINES, his
daughter, friend of Don Alvar
Jovita   JOVIT

DON JOSÉ CAVALLINES. See
also: Don Alvar

DON JUAN
Pursues many women, ac-
tually in love with La
Morte Amoureuse (Death)
Don Juan   DONJA
Spanish nobleman and rake
Don Juan   DONJN
Spanish roué, courts Donna
Elvira, afterwards for-
sakes her; kills the Com-
mander, her father, in
duel
Don Juan   DONJU
Spanish nobleman and rake
Joan von Zarissa   JOANV
Juan de Zarissa   JUAND

DON JUAN. See also:
Belle Florence, La
Fury, The Chief
Isabeau
Sganarelle
Young Wife, The

DON LOLLO, wealthy farmer,
owner of oil jar repaired
by Zi'Dima
NELA, his daughter
A YOUTH, friend of Nela
La Jarre   JARRE
La Jarre   JARRR

DON LOPEZ DE MENDOZA,
Spanish governor of the
province,
Paquita   PAQUI
Paquita   PAQUT

DON MANUEL, the governor,
challenged to duel by
Don Rodrigo, recognizes
Graziosa as girl who
broke up duel, orders

Pietro freed,
Graziosa   GRAZI

DON OTTAVIO, wins Namouna
from Lord Adriani in game
of chance, Namouna NAMOU

DON OTTAVIO. See also:
Hélène

DON PEDRO. See:
Councillor, The
Doña Ines de Castro
Infanta of Navarre, The

DON PEDRO RICCO, in love
with the gypsy Manuela,
Gaucho   GAUCH

DON PEPPINO. See: Diavolina

DON QUIXOTE, impoverished,
demented Spanish nobleman,
imagines himself a knight-
errant
Don Quixote   DONQI
Don Quixote   DONQO
Don Quixote   DONQT
Don Quichotte   DONQU
Don Quichotte   DONQV
Don Quixote   DONQX
JUANA, his niece
Don Quichotte   DONQU

DON QUIXOTE. See also:
Amader of Gaul
Angelica
Barber, The
Barber, The Traveling
Carrasco, Bachelor Sampson
Durandarte
Furioso, Orlando (Roland)
Galley-Slaves
Housekeeper, The
Innkeeper, An
Kitri
Lorenzo, Aldonza
Oriana
Palmeris of England
Panza, Sancho
Priest, A
Rosinante
Rozinante

Shepherd
Urganda
Windmills

DON RODRIGO, cavalier,
challenges Don Manuel to
duel, Graziosa   GRAZI

DON RODRIGO. See also:
Graziosa
Pietro

DON SUGURO, found in pastry-
shop, Schlagobers SCHLA

DOÑA. See also: Donna

DOÑA DOROTEA, a young
widow, flirted with by
Cleophas
CAPTAIN BELLASPADA,
her brother
Le Diable Boiteux DIABL

DOÑA INES DE CASTRO, mis-
tress of Don Pedro; stab-
bed
DON PEDRO, in love with
Doña Ines, betrothed to
The Infanta of Navarre
THE KING OF PORTUGAL,
Don Pedro's father
Doña Ines de Castro
DONAI

DOÑA INES DE CASTRO.
See also: Nymphs of
Mondego

DOÑA MARIANNA. See:
Bridoux
Diavolina

DOÑA SERAPHINA. See:
Comte d'Hervilly, The

DONALD, young woodcutter,
makes pact with Death,
becomes great doctor,
saves King from Death,
Donald of the Burthens
DONAL

DONALD. See also: Goat Men,
Three

DONDON. See: King Dondon

DONNA. See also Doña

DONNA ELVIRA, courted by
Don Juan, later forsaken by
him
THE COMMANDER, her
father, killed by Don Juan
in duel, later reappears as
ghost
Don Juan   DONJU

DONNA ELVIRA. See also:
Duenna, The

DONNA HERNANDEZ. See:
Don Hernandez

DOORMAN, caricature of cartoon character, The New
Yorker   NEWYO

D'OR, LE COQ. See: Golden
Cockerel, The

DORI, "a beautiful girl," I
Titani   TITAN

DORISTO. See: Bartolo

DORIVAL, a planter, Marie's
owner, Les Deux Créoles
DEUXC

DORKON, shepherd, Chloë's
would-be lover, Daphnis et
Chloë   DAPHN

DOROTEA, friend of Constanza,
Les Femmes de Bonne
Humeur   FEMME

DOROTEA. See also: Doña
Dorotea

DORTHE, a lady's maid, A Folk
Tale   FOLKT

DOTTORE. See also: Doctor

DOTTORE, IL. See: Pru-
denza

DOUBLE STARS, celestial
bodies, The Stars STARS

DOVE. See: Nightingale

DOWAGER, THE, caricature
of cartoon character, The
New Yorker   NEWYO

DRAGINIATZA, female devil,
assumes likeness of
Marietta, overcomes Kal-
kabrino, Kalkabrino
KALKA

DRAGON. See: Lover, The

DRAGONFLY, THE, inhabi-
tant of the insect world
Le Festin de l'Araignée
FESTD
Le Festin de l'Araignée
FESTI
The Spider's Banquet
SPIDE

DRESS. See:
Manager in Evening Dress,
The
Woman in Ball Dress, The

DRESSER. See: Hair-Dres-
ser, The

DRESSER, A, at the ballet,
Gala Performance GALAP

DRESSER, THE. See: Prin-
cipal Dancer, The (Adam
Zero)

DRESSING UP, danced by
three female dancers,
Street Games   STREE

DRESSMAKERS, TWO, help
Cinderella's two ugly stepsisters prepare for ball,

Cinderella   CINDE

DRIVER. See: Tractor-Driver,
A

DROSSELMEYER. See:
Nutcracker
President

DROWNED GIRL. See: Nearly
Drowned Girl

DRUM-DANCER, THE, primitive
medicine man, Qarrtsiluni
QARRT

DRUNKARD, turned into a goose
by Red Coat
The Fair at Sorochinsk
FAIRA
"A religious man"
The Great American Goof
GREAT
Caricature of cartoon charac-
ter
The New Yorker   NEWYO

DRUZHKO, young Norwegian,
village boy, The Ice Maiden
ICEMA

DRYAD, THE, imprisoned in
tree by Aphrodite, hopes to
be liberated by the Shepherd
who proves unfaithful, The
Dryad   DRYAD

DRYAD, THE. See also: Eoline

DRYADS, supernatural beings,
Ballet Comique de la Reine
BALLC

DRYAS, a shepherd, appears in
ballet at the Serfs' Theatre,
Katerina   KATER

DU BOIS, BLANCHE, penniless,
widowed, fading Southern
aristocrat, visits her sister
in New Orleans
STELLA KOWALSKI, her
sister

STANLEY KOWALSKI,
Stella's husband, attacks
Blanche
MITCH, friend of Stanley
Kowalski, becomes inter-
ested in Blanche
A Streetcar Named Desire
                    STRET

DUC. See also:
    Duke
    Duke, The

DUC DE BEAUVOIR. See:
    Clairemonde

DUC DE MAYENNE, French
    nobleman, Camargo
                    CAMAR

DUC DE VENDÔME, THE,
    nobleman
    MADAME DE SAINT-
    ANGE, his sister
    ELISE, Madame de Saint-
    Ange's niece
    Les Pages du Duc de
    Vendôme   PAGES

DUCHESS LUCINDE, THE.
    See: Isabelle

DUCHESS OF ALBA. See:
    Duke of Alba

DUCHESS, THE, flirts with
    the Torero, falls in love
    with him
    THE DUKE, her husband,
    orders the Torero killed
    THE DUKE'S SERVANTS,
    two men, stab and kill the
    Torero
    Del Amor y de la Muerte
                    AMORY
    Dreams of the past and
    of her dead lover
    THE GHOST OF HER
    LOVER, reappears
    HER DAUGHTER, newly
    betrothed
    HER DAUGHTER'S FIANCE
    L'Ange Gris   ANGEG

DUCHESS, THE. See also:
    Duke of Medina-Celi, The
    Grey Angel, The

DUCHIC, MONSIEUR, couturier,
    stabs himself with his scis-
    sors "when his masterpiece
    did not please his richest
    client"
    ORCHIDÉE, his richest
    client
    TWO MODELS, employees
    of Monsieur Duchic
    A Tragedy of Fashion
                    TRAGF

DUCK, friend of Peter, eaten
    by Wolf; disgorged unharmed,
    Peter and the Wolf PETER
    Peter and the Wolf PETEW

DUEL, danced by two male dan-
    cers, Street Games STREE

DUENNA, THE, Donna Elvira's
    companion, Don Juan
                    DONJU

DUENNA, YOUNG GIRL'S. See:
    Young Girl

DUESSA, personification of false-
    hood, The Quest   QUEST

DUGMANTA. See: Rajah Dug-
    manta, The

DUKE, creature of Aleko's de-
    lirious fantasy, Aleko
                    ALEKO

DUKE. See also:
    Duc
    Duke, The

DUKE OF ALBA, lieutenant of
    Prince Philip of Spain; in-
    vading Flanders, overcome
    by Tyl Ulenspiegel
    DUCHESS OF ALBA, his
    wife
    Tyl Ulenspiegel   TYLUL

DUKE OF ATHENS. See:
Theseus

DUKE OF CLARENCE, THE,
nobleman, The Press
                           PRESS

DUKE OF GLOSTER. See:
Richard, Duke of Gloster

DUKE OF MEDINA-CELI, THE,
nobleman
THE DUCHESS, his wife
LAURETTA, their daughter,
kidnapped as child by Pa-
rembo, chief of gypsies
DON ALONSO, their son
La Gitana   GITAN

DUKE OF MEDINA-CELI, THE.
See also:
Perez
Smouroff

DUKE OF ROCHESTER, THE,
nobleman, Betty BETTY

DUKE OF SACRAMENTO, THE,
allegorical figure, The
Duke of Sacramento
                           DUKEO

DUKE OF SILESIA. See:
Albrecht

DUKE OF YORK, THE,
nobleman, The Press
                           PRESS

DUKE, THE, attracted to
Adélaïde
Adélaïde, or The Language
of the Flowers   ADELA
Hunter, pursues the Fox
DUKE'S FRIEND, also a
hunter
The Chase   CHASE
Nobleman, gives tourna-
ment in which Sir Hilde-
brand appears
BERTHA, his adopted
daughter, attracted to Sir
Hildebrand

Coralia   CORAL
Nobleman, escorts La Lionne
to Paris café
Gaîté Parisienne   GAITE

DUKE, THE. See also:
Duc
Duchess, The
Duke
Eoline

DUKE'S FRIEND. See: Duke,
The

DUKE'S SERVANTS, THE. See:
Duchess, The

DULCINEA, THE LADY. See:
Kitri
Lorenzo, Aldonza

DUMMY, THE, "tradition and the
ordinary," The Great American Goof   GREAT

DURANDARTE, legendary French
hero
MONTESINOS, his cousin,
French soldier
THE LADY BELERMA, his
beloved; all met by Don
Quixote, Don Quixote
                           DONQX

DURAS, MANOS, a wandering
gaucho
BILL WHITE, "his mate"
Gaucho   GAUCH

DURFORT, SERGEANT, rapacious
creditor of Martin, father of
François
JOB, his son, "a lanky
booby"
Pâquerette   PAQUE

DURWASA, a fakir, Sakuntala
                           SAKUN

DUSHMATA, King of India, in
love with Sakuntala,
Sakuntala   SAKUN

DUSHMATA. See also:
Courtier, A
Fisherman
Hamsati
Madhava

DUTCH LEGATION, attending
ball tendered by Prince
Metternich, Vienna-1814
VIENN

DUTCH MERCHANT, arrives
at St. Petersburg, The
Bronze Horseman   BRONZ

DUVAL, ARMAND, young
Frenchman, attracted
to Marguerite Gautier
MONSIEUR DUVAL, his
father, disapproves of
Armand's interest in
Marguerite
Lady of the Camellias
LADYB
The Lady of the Camellias
LADYC
DUVET, MADEMOISELLE DEL-
PHINE, The Débutante,
dancer, protégée of Baron
Solomon
MADAME DUVET, her
mother
The Débutante   DEBUT

DWARF, member of the court,
Prince of the Pagodas
PRINO

DWARF. See also: Infanta
of Spain

DWARFS, servants of Gian-
ciotto Malatesta, Francesca
da Rimini   FRANC

DWARFS. See also: Fran-
cesca (Francesca da
Rimini)

DWARFS, THE SEVEN, adopt
Snow-White, Blanche-
Neige   BLANC

DWELLER, A, "middle-aged,
in a country bungalow"
HIS WIFE, "anxious to ap-
pear younger than she is"
The Bright Stream   BRIGH

DYING. See:
Immigrant, Dying
Old Woman, Dying

DYNAMOS. See: Principal
Dynamos, Two

E

EAGLE, THE, form assumed by
Jupiter when he carries
Ganymede away, Les Amours
de Jupiter   AMOUJ

EAGLE, THE. See also: Kwahu

EARS. See: Personage With
Long Ears

EARTH. See:
Genie of the Earth
Queen of the Earth, The
Spirits of the Earth

EARTH, THE, personification
Canticle for Innocent Come-
dians   CANTI
Les Eléments   ELEME
The Seventh Symphony
SEVEN

EAST GOTHLAND, LORD OF.
See: Thora

EAST INDIAN PRINCE
EAST INDIAN PRINCESS,
visiting nobility at 2222 Club,
New York City
Café Society   CAFES

EBBA, peasant, Miss Julie
MISSJ

EBREMARD. See: Renoualle,
Ysaure de

ECHO, nymph, in love with,
  dies for Narcissus,
  Narcissus and Echo
                    NARCE

ECHO FIGURE, personification,
  Narkissos   NARKI

EDDA, Norwegian village
  maiden, betrothed to
  Ehrick
  JENNY, her cousin
  Electra   ELECT

EDGAR, betrothed to Eoline,
  Eoline   EOLIN

EDGAR. See also: Rübezahl

EDMOND, wealthy farmer, betrothed to Thérèse, La
  Somnambule   SOMNA

EDMOND. See also: Notary,
  A

EDWARD, page to Prince
  Charles
  Betty   BETTY
  Anna II's rich lover
  The Seven Deadly Sins
                     SEVED

EDWARD. See also: King
  Edward IV, King of Eng-
  land

EDWARD, CADET, of the
  Danish navy, Loin du
  Danemark   LOIND

EDWARD ELGAR, SIR. See:
  Theme and First Variation

EDWARD, PRINCE OF WALES,
  heir-apparent to the English throne, The Press
                     PRESS

EFFIE. See:
  Old Madge
  Reuben, James

EGEUS. See: Hermia

EGG, laid by chicken being pre-
  pared for roasting by chefs
  in kitchen representing Hell;
  hatches into chicken, L'Oeuf
  à la Coque   OEUFA

EGG. See also:
  Chefs, Three
  Chickens, Four

EGL. See: Longren

EGYPT, KING OF. See:
  Aspicia

EGYPT, QUEEN OF. See:
  Cleopatra
  Cléopâtre

EGYPTIAN AMBASSADOR, AN,
  attempts to make treaty with
  Antony, Les Amours d'
  Antoine et de Cléopâtre
                     AMOUR

EHRICK, Norwegian hunter, betrothed to Edda, deserts her
  for Electra, Electra ELECT

EHRICK. See also:
  Berger
  Stenbock

EIFFEL TOWER. See: Manager
  of the Eiffel Tower, The

EIGHT. See: Satyrs, Eight

EIGHTH VARIATION. See:
  Theme and First Variation

EILLEY. See: Orum, Eilley

EL INDIO. See: Malinche

ELDER. See: Village Elder

ELDER'S DAUGHTER, VILLAGE.
  See: Village Elder

ELDER'S HEIR, VILLAGE.
   See: Village Elder

ELDEST SISTER. See: Hagar

ELEANORE. See:
   Baron Bluebeard
   Eleonore

ELECTOR, THE GRAND.
   See: Princess Bathilde

ELECTRA, "a bright particular
   star," loved by Ehrick,
   leaves the firmament, becomes village maiden,
   <u>Electra</u>   ELECT

ELECTRA. See also: Cly-
   temnestra

ELEKTRA, avenges her fa-
   ther's murder
   ORESTES, her brother
   and ally
   AGAMEMNON, father of
   Elektra and Orestes
   CLYTEMNESTRA, wife of
   Agamemnon, mother of
   Elektra and Orestes;
   murders Agamemnon
   AEGISTHUS, Clytemnestra's
   lover and accomplice in
   the murder
   <u>Elektra</u>   ELEKT

ELEMENTS, THE, personifi-
   cations
   Amor   AMORR
   <u>Canticle for Innocent</u>
   <u>Comedians</u>   CANTI

ELEONORE, saved by Carelis
   and his two brothers from
   being kidnapped; won by him
   MIREWELT, her father, alchemist
   CARELIS, rewarded by Mirewelt with a magic fiddle
   GEERT, Carelis' brother,
   rewarded by Mirewelt with
   a magic ring
   ADRIAN, Carelis' brother,

rewarded by Mirewelt with
a magic sword
<u>The Kermis in Bruges</u>
                  KERMI
Friend of Blondelaine
<u>Scaramouche</u>   SCARA

ELEONORE. See also: Eleanore

ELEVENTH VARIATION. See:
   Theme and First Variation

ELFRITS, QUEEN OF THE. See:
   Hertha

ELGAR, SIR EDWARD. See:
   Theme and First Variation

ELIAB. See: Jesse

ELIHU, indicates to Job his er-
   ror in accusing God of in-
   justice, <u>Job</u>   JOBBB

ELISE. See: Duc de Vendôme,
   The

ELIZABETH, in love with Peter
   I, Tsar of Russia
   SHUKANIN, her father, commander of the Streletsy
   <u>Gli Strelizzi</u>   STREL

ELIZABETH. See also:
   Queen Elizabeth I, Queen of
      England
   Queen Elizabeth Woodville

ELORA, bashful nymph, taught
   by Cupid how to dance
   YOUTH, in love with her
   FAUN, jealous of the Youth
   <u>Romantic Age</u>   ROMAN

ELSE, a pantrymaid, <u>A Folk</u>
   <u>Tale</u>   FOLKT

ELVES, QUEEN OF THE. See:
   Adda

ELVIRA. See: Donna Elvira

ELYSE, Nina's governess, <u>Nina</u>

NINAO

EMAZOR, Moorish prince exiled from Granada, falls in love with Alma, the creation of Belfegor,
Alma   ALMAO

EMAZOR. See also: Lara

EMERALD, a fairy, The Triumph of Neptune   TRIUM

EMERALD, FLOWER VENDOR IN. See:
Flower Vendor in Green Lieutenant

ÉMILE. See: Guérin, Georges-Émile

EMILIA, confidential maid to Desdemona, wife of Otello
Otello   OTELL
Vestal virgin
La Vestale   VESTA

EMPEROR. See: Little Emperor

EMPEROR AURUNGZEBE, THE, Emperor of Hindustan
LALLA ROOKH, his daughter, betrothed to Alaris, King of Bucharia
Lalla Rookh   LALLA

EMPEROR AURUNGZEBE, THE. See also: Alaris, King of Bucharia

EMPEROR JONES, self-made emperor-dictator in Caribbean; pursued and captured by his recent victims
WHITE MAN, aids in Jones' downfall
Emperor Jones   EMPER

EMPEROR OF AUSTRIA, THE, pardons Count Rackozski, The Hungarian Hut HUNGA

EMPEROR OF CHINA, ruler, fascinated by song of the Nightingale; saved from Death by her song, Song of the Nightingale   SONGO

EMPEROR OF CHINA. See also: Nightingale, Mechanical Nightingale, The

EMPEROR OF HINDUSTAN. See: Emperor Aurungzebe, The

EMPEROR OF JAPAN. See: Nightingale, Mechanical Nightingale, The

EMPEROR OF RUSSIA. See: Emperor Paul I, Emperor of Russia

EMPEROR OF THE MIDDLE KINGDOM. See: Princess Belle Épine

EMPEROR OF THE TOLTECS. See: Tepancaltzin

EMPEROR PAUL I, Emperor of Russia, visits coffin of non-existent Lieutenant Kije, finds coffin empty, Lieutenant Kije   LIEUT

EMPIRE. See: Lord Empire

EMPIRE, LADY. See: Lord Empire

EMPRESS OF THE ARENA, circus performer, Every Soul Is a Circus   EVERY

ENCHANTED PRINCESS, THE, fairy tale character, The Sleeping Beauty   SLEEP

END MEN, two female dancers at minstrel show, Cakewalk
                        CAKEW

ENDYMION, shepherd youth

Ballet de la Nuit BALLN
Shepherd youth, loved by
Selene
SELENE, goddess of the
moon, caresses Endymion
while he sleeps
Endymion   ENDYM
Shepherd, one-time lover
of Diana
Sylvia   SYLVI

ENEMY CHIEF, leader of band
overcome by Tariel, Chota
Roustaveli   CHOTA

ENEMY LEADER, THE, sol-
dier, wounds Armen,
Happiness   HAPPI

ENGLAND. See: Palmeris
of England

ENGLAND, KING OF. See:
King Edward IV, King of
England
King Henry VIII, King of
England
Lord Campbell
Prince Charles

ENGLAND, QUEEN OF. See:
Queen Elizabeth I

ENGLISH PRINCE, THE,
seeks hand of the Princess
Aurora in marriage, The
Sleeping Beauty   SLEEP

ENGLISH PRINTING, THE
FATHER OF. See:
Caxton, William

ENGLISH SLAVE, AN, pro-
perty of Seyd, Le Cor-
saire   CORSA

ENVY, personification, spectator at Paganini's concert,
Paganini   PAGAN

EOLINDA, friend of Ragonda,
daughter of Princess Millefleurs, Fiametta   FIAMM

EOLINE, "The Dryad," betrothed
to Edgar, may live as long
as her oak does
THE DUKE, her brother
Eoline   EOLIN

EOLINE. See also: Rübezahl

EONE, "a beautiful girl," I
Titani   TĪTAN

EPIC POETRY, a muse, Sylvia
                     SYLVA

EPINARD, a greengrocer, Cinderella   CĪNDA

ÉPINE. See: Princess Belle
Épine

EPISODE IN HIS PAST, AN.
See: Caroline

EQUESTRIENNE, circus performer, Carte Blanche   CARTE

ERESHKIGAL. See: Ishtar

ERIC. See: Ehrick

ERIK. See: Ehrick

ERISTAV, PRINCE OF. See:
Djardje
Manije

ERNEST, young man, pursued
by Violet, A Wedding Bouquet
                     WEDDI

EROS, god of love, appears in
ballet at the Serfs' Theatre
Katerina   KATER
God of love
Sylvia   SYLVA
God of love, represented by
statue, later appears in
various guises
Sylvia   SYLVI

ERÖSZAKOS (Violent), shepherd
The Holy Torch   HOLYT

EROTIC POETRY, a muse,
Sylvia   SYLVA

EROTOMANIACS, THE, in-
mates of the Logéat Men-
tal Hospital, Les Algues
ALGUE

ERRANT.   See: Knight-Errant,
The

ESCALUS, Prince of Verona,
Romeo and Juliet ROMEJ

ESCAMILLO, Rebel aviator,
rival of José for the love
of Carmen, Guns and
Castanets   GUNSA

ESCAMILLO. See also:
Toreador, The

ESCORT, OPERETTA STAR'S.
See: Operetta Star

ESCORT SERVICE MEN, paid
gigolos working at 2222
Club, New York City,
Café Society   CAFES

ESMERALDA, LA, gypsy
street dancer, sought by
Claude Frollo, in love
with Phoebus de Chateau-
pers; loved by Quasimodo,
marries Pierre Gringoire,
La Esmeralda   ESMER

ESPADA. See: Spanish Espada

ESTRELLA, "ambitious and
flirtatious," loved by
Florestan, Le Carnaval
CARNA

ETIOCLES. See: Oedipus

ETOILE. See: l'Etoile

EUGENE, in love with Parasha
The Bronze Horseman
BRONZ

A page
Les Pages du Duc de Ven-
dôme   PAGES

EULENSPIEGEL, TIL, "merry
peasant and rogue," loves
Nell
NELL, "the one girl Til
Eulenspiegel loves"
Til Eulenspiegel   TILEU

EULENSPIEGEL, TIL. See also:
Eulenspiegel, Tyl
Ulenspiegel, Tyl

EULENSPIEGEL, TYL, "merry
prankster"
NELL, his wife
Tyl Eulenspiegel   TYLEU

EULENSPIEGEL, TYL. See also:
Eulenspiegel, Til
Ulenspiegel, Tyl

EUNUCH. See: Chief Eunuch

EUNUCH, SECOND. See: Chief
Eunuch

EUPHÉMIE, dancer, Vert-Vert
VERTV

EUPHROSINE. See: Philemon

EUROPA, raped by Jupiter
Abraxas   ABRAX
Wooed by Jupiter in the
form of Taurus, the Bull
Les Amours de Jupiter
AMOUJ

EUROPA. See also: Taurus

EURYDICE. See:
Amor
Orfeo
Orphée
Orpheus

EURYSTÉE, village girl, loved
by Nautéos, Nautéos
NAUTE

EUSEBIUS, romantic poet, in
  love with Chiarina, Le
  Carnaval   CARNA

EUSTACE. See: Tilley,
  Eustace

EUTERPE, muse of music,
  The Creatures of Prome-
  theus   CREAU

EVE. See: Adam

EVENING DRESS. See:
  Manager in Evening Dress,
  The

EVERITT, MRS. , a bee-keep-
  er, The Sailor's Return
                       SAILO

EVERYWOMAN, PERSONIFI-
  CATION OF. See: Héro-
  diade

EVIL. See: Spirit of Evil,
  The

EVIL FAIRIES. See: Queen
  of the Evil Fairies

EVIL FORCES, PERSONIFICA-
  TIONS OF. See:
  Destiny
  Leader of Blue Group
  Leader of Red Group
    (Town)
  Leader of Yellow Group
    (Country)

EVIL, GENIUS OF. See:
  Belfegor

EVIL GENIUS OF THE MINES,
  THE. See: Torbern

EVIL, LORD OF. See:
  Beelzebub

EVIL MAGICIAN, THE. See:
  St. George

EVIL, PERSONIFICATION OF.

See: Serpent

EXECUTIONER, ordered to do
  away with Sakuntala, Sakuntala   SAKUN

EXHIBITION. See: Director of
  an Industrial Exhibition

EXILE. See: Portuguese Exile

EXPERIENCE, LOVERS-IN. See:
  Lovers-in-Innocence

F

FABIANI, LUCENTIO, fiance of
  one of Marco Lugano's elder
  daughters, The Blood-Red
  Flower   BLOOD

FABRIZIO, an impresario,
  Scuola di Ballo   SCUOL

FABRIZIO. See also: Notary,
  The

FADED BEAUTY. See: Hypnotist

FADETTE, young, poor peasant
  girl, in love with son of
  rich peasant
  FADETTE'S GRANDMOTHER,
  thought to be a witch
  RICH PEASANT, opposes
  his son's wish to marry
  Fadette
  RICH PEASANT'S SON, loves,
  marries Fadette
  Fadetta   FADET

FADLADEEN, grand vizier,
  Lalla Rookh   LALLA

FAIRIES. See: Queen of the
  Evil Fairies

FAIRIES, KING OF THE. See:
  Oberon

FAIRIES, QUEEN OF THE. See:
  Titania

Bridegroom

FAIRY, THE PEARL. See:
Fairy Hamza, The

FAITH. See: Conjugal Faith

FALOPPA, CAPTAIN, officer,
Les Femmes de Bonne
Humeur   FEMME

FALSEHOOD, PERSONIFICA-
TION OF. See: Duessa

FAME, personification
The Five Gifts   FIVEG
Le Nuit et le Jour
                   NUITE

FAME. See also: Genii of
Fame, The

FAMILY, HIS. See:
American, An
Russian Merchant, A

FAMINE, personification,
Job   JOBBB

FANNY, betrothed to Valentine
WILLIAM, her father, a
farmer
Excelsior   EXCEL

FANNY CERITO. See: Tag-
lioni, Marie

FANTASY, personification,
Anguish Sonata   ANGUI

FARFALLA, maid to the
Fairy Hamza; long-lost
daughter of Ismail Bey,
uncle of Prince Djalma;
turned into butterfly, Le
Papillon   PAPIL

FARFALLA. See also:
Leila
Zaidée

FARM BOY, THE, goes to sea,
becomes sailor, visits many

new lands
THE QUAKER GIRL, his
sweetheart, deserted by him
for the sea
SAILORS, his mates aboard
ship
Yankee Clipper   YANKE

FARM BOY, THE. See also:
African
Argentine
Japanese
Tahitian

FARM GIRL. See: Young Farm
Girl

FARMER. See: Young Farmer

FARMER, A
HIS WIFE
THEIR DAUGHTER, family,
celebrating St. John's Eve
Nuit de Saint-Jean   NUITD

FARMER-GENERAL, THE, one
of Cydalise's lovers, Cydalise et le Chèvre-pied
                   CYDAL

FASHION, representation of
British publication, The Press
                   PRESS

FASHIONABLE LADY, has sev-
eral lovers
HER HUSBAND, reunited to
her by Amore (Cupid)
MAN ABOUT TOWN, one of
her lovers, won by Amazon
Lieutenant
SAILOR, one of her lovers,
won by other Amazon Lieu-
tenant
TIMOROUS STUDENT, one
of her lovers, won by Amore
(Cupid)
Con Amore   CONAM

FAT MEN, THE THREE, per-
sonifications of capitalism,
The Three Fat Men THREE

FATE, personification
   Fate's Rebellion   FATES
   Les Présages   PRESA

FATE. See also: Night

FATE, PERSONIFICATION OF.
   See: Nemesis Figure

FATES, THE THREE. See:
   Parcae

FATHER, head of Western
   farm family
   MOTHER, his wife
   ROSE
   MARTHA, their two
   daughters, "become en-
   meshed with Ben, the
   Stranger"
   Ballad   BALLD
   Cobbler, head of family,
   dies of starvation
   MOTHER, his wife
   SON, their child
   Inquest   INQUE

FATHER. See also:
   All-Powerful Father, The
   Anselme, Father
   Narrator
   Punch

FATHER, CIRCASSIAN'S. See:
   Circassian Maid, The

FATHER, GHOST OF HAM-
   LET'S. See: Hamlet,
   Prince of Denmark

FATHER, HER. See:
   Accused, The (Lizzie Bor-
     den)
   Bride, The
   Cinderella
   Javotte
   Lise
   Ulinka
   Yedda
   Zoshka

FATHER, HER LOVER'S. See:
   Fifi, Mademoiselle

FATHER, HIS. See:
   Asak
   Bridegroom, The
   Rotislav

FATHER-IN-LAW, THE. See:
   Bride, The

FATHER OF ENGLISH PRINTING,
   THE. See: Caxton, William

FATHER OF THE PRODIGAL
   SON. See: Prodigal Son,
   The

FATHER OF THE WOODS. See:
   Zuimaaluti

FATHER OF XOCHITL, THE.
   See: Tepancaltzin

FATHER, THE, grief-stricken
   at the death of his children
   THE MOTHER, his wife
   Dark Elegies   DARKE

FATHER, THE. See also:
   Anna I
   Daughter, The

FATHER, THE PRINCESS'S. See:
   Princess Nina, The

FATHER TIMES, representation
   of British newspaper, The
   Press   PRESS

FATHER, ZEMPHIRA'S. See:
   Zemphira

FATMA, marble statue created
   by Manasses; brought to life,
   La Fille de Marbre FILLM

FATME. See: Zoloe

FAUN. See:
   Elora
   Old Faun, The

FAUN, THE, boy-animal, fascinated by the Nymph, obtains
   her scarf

The Afternoon of a Faun
                        AFTEN
The Afternoon of a Faun
                        AFTER
Becomes enamoured of Ag-
laë
Aglaë   AGLAE
Participant in the baccha-
nale
Bacchanale   BACCH
Pet of the ladies at the
court of Sparta
Helen of Troy   HELEN

FAUST, medieval necromancer,
aging; temporarily restored
to youth by signing com-
pact with the witch Ballestriga
Abraxas   ABRAX
Medieval necromancer,
under the power of Mephistopheles (Mephisto); se-
duces, later abandons
Marguerite
Mephisto Valse   MEPHI
Mephisto Valse   MEPHS
Vision of Marguerite
                        VISIO

FAUST. See also:
Achilles
Hector
Helen
Marguerite

FAUST, DOCTOR, alchemist,
sells his soul to Mephis-
topheles, seduces Mar-
guerite, kills Valentine,
Faust   FAUST

FAUST, DOCTOR. See also:
Wolger

FAVORITA, LA, dancer, ad-
mired by many cavaliers,
Veneziana   VENEZ

FAVORITE SLAVE, ZOBEDIA'S.
See: Shahryar, King of
India and China

FAVORITE WIFE, HIS. See:
Khan, The

FAVORITE WIFE, SECOND.
See: Gierey

FEAR. See: Creature of Fear

FEBRUARY, a director, Twelve
for the Mail-Coach TWELV

FEDERICI. See: Prince Osorio,
Governor of Rome

FEDERIGO RASPONI. See:
Beatrice
Clarice

FÉE, LA BONNE, The Good
Fairy, bestows millions on
Harlequin, thus making him
an acceptable suitor to Colombine, Harlequinade
                        HARLI

FÉLÉNK (Timid), shepherd, The
Holy Torch   HOLYT

FELICE. See: Robert

FELICITA, friend of Constanza
LEONARDO, her husband
Les Femmes de Bonne
Humeur   FEMME
"The bad pupil," studying
dancing under Rigadon
Scuola di Ballo   SCUOL

FEMALE DANCER, A, old
friend of Zina; member of
an artists' brigade
A MALE DANCER, her part-
ner, also member of art-
ists' brigade
The Bright Stream   BRIGH

FEMALE DOLL. See: Puppet,
Mister

FEMALE SABIÁ. See: Gavião

FEMALE SERVANT. See: Una

FEMALE SLAVES, FOUR.
　See: Slave-Dealer, A

FEMINA, Queen of the Tribes;
　personification of Woman,
　overcome by the Spirit of
　Vanity, Femina   FEMIN

FEMINA.　See also:
　High Priest, The
　Spanish Espada

FENCING MASTER, THE, hopes
　to profit from the Rake's
　recently inherited wealth,
　The Rake's Progress
　　　　　　　　　　RAKES

FERAMORZ.　See: Aliris,
　King of Bucharia

FERHAD.　See: Queen
　Mehmene-Banu

FERNANDEZ, a consul
　ROSITA, his daughter
　ALVAR, her suitor
　Loin de Danemark LOIND

FERRONE, a condottiere,
　Chronica   CHRON

FERTILITY, GODDESS OF
　LOVE AND.　See: Ishtar

FERTILITY, GODDESS OF
　MOTHERHOOD AND.　See:
　Isis

FEVER.　See: Boy With a
　Fever of 105

FI-FI.　See: Cinderella

FIAMETTA, "girl of surpassing
　beauty," conjured up and
　ordered by Cupid to fasci-
　nate Count Friedrich Stern-
　hold, Fiametta   FIAMM

FIANCE, CIRCASSIAN'S.　See:
　Circassian Maid, The

FIANCE, THE.　See: Old Lord,
　The

FIANCEE.　See: Captain

FIANCEE, LETIKA'S.　See:
　Letika

FIDDLER, THE, allegorical fig-
　ure, Sea Gallows   SEAGA

FIERBOIS.　See: Marquis de
　Fierbois

FIFI, MADEMOISELLE, famous
　French soubrette star
　HER LOVER
　HER LOVER'S FATHER,
　disapproves his son's attach-
　ment, falls in love with her
　himself
　Mademoiselle Fifi   MADEM

FIFTH TELEGRAM.　See: First
　Telegram

FIFTH VARIATION.　See: Theme
　and First Variation

FIGURE.　See:
　Echo Figure
　Nemesis Figure

FIGURE OF GRIEF, personifica-
　tion, Lamentation   LAMET

FILIPPO, a clerk, Chronica
　　　　　　　　　　CHRON

FILIPPO.　See also:
　Philip
　Philippe

FILIPUCCIO, an innkeeper,
　Catarina   CATAR

FILLE AU BAR, LA, barmaid at
　bar of Folies-Bergère, Bar
　aux Folies-Bergère BARAU

FILLY, THE, appears in Stable-
　boy's dream, The Filly
　　　　　　　　　　FILLY

FILM STAR, THE, elopes with
    Telegraph Boy
    Pastorale   PASTE
    Cowboy actor, met by Anna
    I and Anna II
    The Seven Deadly Sins
                         SEVED

FINANCIAL NEWS, THE, rep-
    resentation of British news-
    paper, The Press PRESS

FINANCIAL TIMES, THE, rep-
    resentation of British news-
    paper, The Press PRESS

FINANCIER, A, gives Ozaï
    beautiful ring as gift,
    Ozaï   OZAII

FIORA. See: Courtesan

FIORITA, betrothed to Toniello,
    Fiorita et la Reine des El-
    frides   FIORI

FIRE, personification
    Les Éléments   ELEME
    Prince of the Pagodas
                         PRINO

FIRE. See also:
    Queen of Fire, The
    Spirit of Fire

FIREBIRD (The Bird of Fire),
    part magical bird, part
    beautiful woman, meets
    Prince Ivan, gives him
    magic feather to summon
    her.
    Firebird   FIREB
    Firebird   FIRED
    Also gives him magic
    sword with which to over-
    come Kostchei
    Firebird   FIREI

FIREMAN. See: Weidman,
    Fireman

FIRST. See: Little Hare, The
    First

FIRST BRIDESMAID. See:
    Bride, The

FIRST BRIDESMAN. See:
    Bride, The

FIRST GOLDEN CORD, THE,
    personification
    GOLDEN CORDS, THE,
    personifications L'Homme
    et son Désir   HOMME

FIRST HAND, THE, Viennese
    girl, sketched by the Artist,
    later taken from him by the
    King of the Dandies
    Le Beau Danube   BEAUD

FIRST HUNTER
    SIX HUNTERS, take Wolf to
    Zoo after Peter captures
    him
    Peter and the Wolf PETER
    Peter and the Wolf PETEW

FIRST INTRUDER, man, killed
    by the Novice
    SECOND INTRUDER, man,
    loved by the Novice; ulti-
    mately killed by her
    The Cage   CAGEE

FIRST LIEUTENANT, of the Dan-
    ish navy, Loin du Danemark
                        LOIND

FIRST PHONOGRAPH
    SECOND PHONOGRAPH, in-
    troduce characters of ballet
    to the audience
    Les Mariés de la Tour Eiffel
                        MARIE

FIRST RED KNIGHT
    SECOND RED KNIGHT, chess-
    men
    Checkmate   CHECK

FIRST SAILOR
    SECOND SAILOR
    THIRD SAILOR, friends of
    the Young Girl, one of whom
    becomes engaged to her

Les Matelots   MATEL

FIRST SAILOR.   See also:
    Young Girl, The

FIRST TELEGRAM
    SECOND TELEGRAM
    THIRD TELEGRAM
    FOURTH TELEGRAM
    FIFTH TELEGRAM, de-
    livered at Eiffel Tower
    Les Mariés de la Tour
    Eiffel   MARIE

FIRST VARIATION.   See:
    Theme and First Variation

FISH, personification, The
    Seventh Symphony SEVEN

FISHER-BOY, THE.   See:
    Spirit of the Sea, The

FISHERMAN, Soviet, ship-
    wrecked on foreign shore,
    withstands trials and re-
    turns home
    HIS BELOVED, helps him
    through his trials
    Coast of Hope   COAST
    "Attempts to rid himself
    of his Soul that he may con-
    summate his love for Mer-
    maid"
    MERMAID, loved by Fisher-
    man
    WITCH, provides solution
    for Fisherman's problem
    The Fisherman and His
    Soul   FISHE
    Finds ring belonging to
    Dushmata, King of India
    Sakuntala   SAKUN

FISHWIFE, proprietress of
    stall in Paris market
    Mam'zelle Angot   MAMZE
    Character in Punch and
    Judy show
    POLLY, becomes associated
    with Fishwife in Child's mind
    Punch and the Child
                      PUNCH

FIVE.   See:
    Foolish Virgins, Five
    Wise Virgins, Five

FIVE COSSACK SOLDIERS.   See:
    Cossack Chief, The

FIVE MEN.   See: Woman, The

FIVE WIVES, HIS.   See: Hyde,
    Orson

FLAMINIA.   See: Lugano, Marco

FLAPPER, personification, H. P.
                      HPPPP

FLAUTIST (The Stranger Player),
    apparition, plays for ghosts
    and for the Master of Tre-
    gennis, The Haunted Ballroom
                      HAUNT

FLAUTIST, See also: Flutist

FLEUR DE LYS,
    betrothed to Phoebus de
    Chateaupers
    MADAME ALOISE DE GON-
    DELAURIER, her mother
    La Esmeralda   ESMER

FLEUR DE LYS.   See also:
    Beranger
    Diane
    Prince Fleur-de-Lys

FLEUR-DES-CHAMPS, the
    Daughter of the Danube,
    orphan girl, loved by Ru-
    dolph, rejects Baron Willi-
    bald
    IRMENGARDE, her foster
    mother
    La Fille du Danube FILLD

FLEUR-DES-CHAMPS.   See
    also:
    Nymph of the Danube, The
    Spirit of the Danube, The

FLIK, alchemist's son, has ad-
    venture with Flok

MARTA, his grandmother
NELLA, Marta's god-
daughter
Flik and Flok   FLIKA

FLIK. See also:
King of the Gnomes, The
Van Bett

FLIRT, THE, attracted to the
Lamplighter at Belvedere
Gardens, Vienna, Voices
of Spring   VOICE

FLIRT, THE. See also:
Cadets, Two

FLIRTATIOUS COUPLES,
TWO. See: Umbrella

FLOK, a street musician,
friend of Flik, Flik and
Flok   FLIKA

FLOK. See also: King of
the Gnomes, The

FLOORWALKER in store,
unable to cope with hordes
of bargain seekers
BARGAIN SEEKERS, cus-
tomers of department store
Atavisms   ATAVI

FLOOZIE, member of farm
community of the Great
Plain, Grasslands GRASS

FLORA (CHLORIS), nymph,
loved by Zephyrus
Flore et Zéphire FLORE
Loved by Zephyr
Zephyr and Flora ZEPHY

FLORA (CHLORIS). See also:
Cupid

FLORENCE. See: Belle
Florence, La

FLORENCIJA. See: Maharajah,
The

FLORENTINE BEAUTY, A, dances to Paganini's music
A FLORENTINE YOUTH, her
lover and dance partner
Paganini   PAGAN

FLORESTAN, in love with Estrella, Le Carnaval CARNA

FLORESTAN XXIV, KING. See:
Cantalbutte
Princess Aurora, The

FLORETTA (PRINCESS HERMI-
LIA). See: King Bobiche

FLORIDA, young Spanish widow,
betrothed to Salvator Rosa,
Catarina   CATAR

FLORINDA, a dancer, flirted
with by Cleophas
HER MAID
Le Diable Boiteux   DIABL

FLORINDA. See also:
Doctor, The
Hairdresser, The

FLORINDO, in love with Beatrice;
kills her brother Federigo
Rasponi in duel
The False Bridegroom
                      FALSE
In love with Prudenza
Pulcinella   PULCI

FLORINDO. See also: Truffaldino

FLORIST, THE, proprietress of
shop in Paris market,
Mam'zelle Angot   MAMZE

FLORITA, MADEMOISELLE,
principal dancer at the
opera, The Débutante
                      DEBUT

FLOWER FAIRY, THE, brings
Thea and Prince Hussein
together, Thea   THEAO

FLOWER FAIRY, THE.   See
    also: Fairy Hamza, The

FLOWER GIRL, sells flowers
    at Paris café, Gaîté Pari-
    sienne   GAITE

FLOWER-SELLER, Paris
    street vendor, Le Rendez-
    Vous   RENDE

FLOWER SELLERS, participate
    in gaiety at Seville café,
    Cuadro Flamenco CUADR

FLOWER, THE (XOCHITL).
    See: Tepancaltzin

FLOWER VENDOR IN EMERALD.
    See:
    Flower Vendor in Green
    Lieutenant

FLOWER VENDOR IN GREEN
    FLOWER VENDOR IN
    EMERALD, business rivals
    in Belvedere Gardens,
    Vienna
    Voices of Spring VOICE

FLOWER VENDOR IN GREEN.
    See also:
    Boy in Grey
    Lieutenant

FLOWERS, accompany Spring,
    Les Saisons   SALSO

FLOWERS. See also: Toby

FLUTIST (The Incredible
    Flutist), star performer
    of circus, is able to charm
    circus animals with his
    playing; saves Wealthy
    Widow
    GIRL OF THE TOWN,
    dated by Flutist
    The Incredible Flutist
                        INCRE

FLUTIST. See also: Flautist

FLY WHEEL, representation of
    machinery, Iron Foundry
                          IRONF

FOAL, THE, appears in Stable-
    boy's dream, The Filly
                          FILLY

FOOL, THE. See: Lear, King
    of Britain

FOOLISH VIRGINS. See: Wise
    Virgins

FOOLISH VIRGINS, FIVE, atten-
    dants of the Bride, fail to
    trim their lamps, Les Vier-
    ges Folles   VIERG

FOOLISH VIRGINS, FIVE. See
    also: Angels, Two

FOOTBALL TEAM. See: Cap-
    tain of Soviet Football Team

FOOTMAN, servant of Husband
    (King Mark), Picnic at Tin-
    tagel   PICNI

FOOTMAN. See also: Capric-
    ciosa, La

FORCE. See: Genii of Force,
    The

FORCES, PERSONIFICATIONS OF
    EVIL. See:
    Destiny
    Leader of Blue Group
    Leader of Red Group (Town)
    Leader of Yellow Group
      (Country)

FORESTER. See: Head Forester

FORMER BALLERINAS. See:
    Two Former Ballerinas

FORMER LOVER, GHOST OF
    CANDELAS'. See: Candelas

FORTUNA, blind goddess of

chance, <u>Fortuna</u>   FORTU

FORTUNATO, a stranger,
<u>Chronica</u>   CHRON

FORTUNATO. See also: Don
Fortunato

FORTUNE. See: Spirit of
Fortune

FORTUNE TELLER, gypsy,
foretells Young Gypsy's
death, <u>Aleko</u>   ALEKO

FORTUNE TELLER. See also:
Gypsy Fortune Teller

FORTUNÉE. See: Cinderella

FOUETTÉ. See: Prince Tutti

FOUR. See:
Characters, Four
Chickens, Four
Hepiales, The Four
Pall Bearers, Four
Seal Hunters, Four
Small Cards, Four
Virtues, Four

FOUR ATTENDANTS, HER.
See: Oriane

FOUR CHURCHMEN. See:
Martyr, The

FOUR FEMALE SLAVES. See:
Slave-Dealer, A

FOUR FRIENDS, THE PRINCE'S.
See: Prince, The

FOUR LADIES, HER. See:
Princess Teaflower

FOUR LITTLE PULCINELLAS
See: Pulcinella

FOUR RATS, HER. See:
Carabosse

FOUR TEMPERAMENTS, THE.

See: Melancholic Variation

FOUR YOUNGER SONS. See:
Jesse

FOURBO, friend of Pulcinella,
<u>Pulcinella</u>   PULCI

FOURTEENTH VARIATION. See:
Theme and First Variation

FOURTH TELEGRAM. See:
First Telegram

FOURTH VARIATION. See:
Theme and First Variation

FOX, THE, pursued by the Duke,
the Duke's Friend and other
hunters
<u>The Chase</u>   CHASE
<u>Le Renard</u>, outwitted by
Rooster
<u>Le Renard</u>   RENAR

FRA. See:
Ambrosio, Fra
Borroemo, Fra

FRANCA-TRIPPA, a gypsy
<u>Les Deux Pigéons</u>   DEUXN
<u>Les Deux Pigéons</u>   DEUXP

FRANÇAISES. See: Captain of
the Gardes-Françaises

FRANCE, KING OF. See:
King Louis XIV
King Louis XVI
King of France

FRANCESCA (Francesca da Rimini), married by proxy to
Gianciotto Malatesta
GIANCIOTTO MALATESTA,
ugly and deformed
PAOLO MALATESTA, Gian-
ciotto's younger brother,
loves and loved by Fran-
cesca
<u>Francesca da Rimini</u> FRANC
<u>Francesca da Rimini</u> FRANE

FRANCESCA. See also:
Angelic Apparition
Chiara
Don Fortunato
Dwarfs
Girolamo

FRANCESCO. See: Berna-
done, Francesco

FRANCIS, SAINT. See:
Bernadone, Francesco

FRANÇOIS, in love with
Pâquerette
MARTIN, his father, in
debt to Sergeant Durfort
Pâquerette   PAQUE

FRANKIE, prostitute, in love
with Johnny; kills him for
being untrue to her with
Nellie, Frankie and John-
ny   FRANK

FRANKIE. See also: Bar-
tender

FRANTZ, village boy, be-
trothed to Swanilda who
thinks him in love with
Coppélia
Coppélia   COPPE
Coppélia   COPPI

FRÉDÉRIC. See:
Count Frédéric
Frederich
Frederick
Friedrich

FREDERICH. See:
Frédéric
Frederick
Friedrich
von Gentz, Frederich

FREDERICK. See:
Count Frederick
Frédéric
Frederich
Friedrich

FREEBEE, performer at minstrel show, Cakewalk
                    CAKEW

FRENCH BALLERINA, CAVALIER
TO THE. See: Queen of
the Dance

FRENCH COUPLE, performs
dance for Cupid's approval,
The Whims of Cupid and the
Ballet Master   WHIMS

FRENCH SLAVE, A, property of
Seyd, Le Corsaire   CORSA

FRENCH WIFE. See: Young
Student

FRIAR. See: Laurence, Friar

FRICKES, MRS. , a modiste
A MOTHER
HER DAUGHTER, apprenticed
to Mrs. Frickes
The Sailor's Return SAILO

FRIEDRICH. See:
Count Friedrich Sternhold
Frédéric
Frederich
Frederick

FRIEND, DUKE'S. See: Duke,
The

FRIEND, HER. See: Young
Girl, The

FRIEND, MOOR'S. See: Moor,
The

FRIEND, PERSONAGE'S LADY.
See: Personage, A

FRIEND, THE, of Hagar and her
family; attracted to Youngest
Sister, Pillar of Fire
                    PILLA

FRIENDS, HER. See:
Admadeya
Bride, The

FRIENDS, HER THREE BOY.
See: Debutante

FRIENDS, HER TWO.   See:
Carine

FRIENDS, HIS.   See: Bridegroom, The

FRIENDS, HIS TWO.   See:
Ambassador, The

FRIENDS OF ARMIDE.   See:
Armide

FRIENDS, THE PRINCE'S
FOUR.   See: Prince, The

FRIENDS, THEIR.   See:
President

FRIEND'S WIFE, MOOR'S.
See: Moor, The

FRITZ, a boatman, Excelsior
EXCEL

FRITZ.   See also: President

FRIVOLITY, personification,
Les Présages   PRESA

FROLLO, CLAUDE, churchman,
loves, abducts La Esmeralda,
La Esmeralda   ESMER

FROMAGE, LA MÔME, can-
can dancer, Bar aux Folies-
Bergère   BARAU

FRONDOZO.   See: Laurencia

FROST.   See: Hoar-Frost

FRUIT.   See: Seller of Fruit,
The

FRY.   See: Small Fry

FU.   See: Li-Shan-Fu

FUN, representation of British
publication, The Press

PRESS

FURIES.   See:
Fury, The Chief
Leader of the Furies

FURIOSO, ORLANDO (ROLAND),
hero of chivalry, figment of
Don Quixote's imagination,
Don Quixote   DONQX

FURY, THE CHIEF
FURIES, drag Don Juan to
his fate
Don Juan   DONJU

G

GABO-BIDZA.   See: Armen

GAIETY.   See: Visions of
Gaiety

GAILIS, an adjutant, Ilga ILGAA

GALATEA.   See:
Pigmalion
Pygmalion

GALERIUS, Roman emperor,
Amor   AMORR

GALIYA, a schoolgirl, The
Bright Stream   BRIGH

GALLEY-SLAVES, liberated by
Don Quixote
TWO OVERSEERS, their
guards
Don Quixote   DONQX

GALLISON, tutor to Prince
Charming, The Sleeping
Beauty   SLEEP

GALYA.   See: Ismailova, Galya

GAMACHE, rich nobleman, in
love with Kitri, Don Quichotte
DONQU

GAMSATTI.   See:
Nikia

Rajah Dugmanta, The
Solor

GANDOLFO, Rinaldo's com-
panion, Rinaldo and Ar-
mida   RINAL

GANGSTER, THE, attempts to
hold up Mac's filling station, Filling Station
                            FILLI

GANGSTERS. See: Strip
Teaser

GANGSTERS, THREE. See:
Prostitute, The

GANYMEDE, young shepherd,
carried off by Jupiter who
assumes the form of an
eagle, Les Amours de
Jupiter   AMOUJ

GANYMEDE. See also: Eagle,
The

GARATUJA, O., young, imagina-
tive boy, "delights in using
his talent for drawing what-
ever he sees in the streets
(mainly to play practical
jokes); falls in love with a
nice girl, has to reform to
please her parents"
YOUNG GIRL, loved by O.
Garatuja
YOUNG GIRL'S PARENTS
O. Garatuja   OGARA

GARDENER, THE, employed
in public garden in Vienna
Le Beau Danube   BEAUD
Attendant to the Prince,
presents the Princess with
a rose
The Hundred Kisses
                            HUNDR

GARDENER, THE. See also:
Student, The

GARDENERS, APPRENTICE.

See: Student, The

GARDES-FRANÇAISES. See:
Captain of the Gardes-
Françaises

GARRETT, PAT, sheriff;
friend of Billy the Kid,
Billy the Kid   BILLY

GASPARD, French peasant
JEANNE, his daughter
PIERRE, his son, revolu-
tionaries of Marseille
The Flames of Paris FLAME
A notary
Les Papillons   PAPIO

GASPARD, DOCTOR, observer
of the passing scene, The
Three Fat Men   THREE

GASPARD, DOCTOR. See also:
Chancellor

GASTON DE BEAUVOIR. See:
Clairemonde
Marguerite

GAUL. See: Amader of Gaul

GAUTAMI, superintendent of the
young priestesses, Sakuntala
                        SAKUN

GAUTIER, MARGUERITE, "The
Lady of the Camellias,"
loved by Monsieur Le Comte
de N--, attracted to Armand
Duval; dies of tuberculosis
Lady of the Camellias
                        LADYB
The Lady of the Camellias
                        LADYC

GAVIÃO, tropical bird of prey,
attacks other birds, killed
by them
MALE SABIÁ, killed by
Gavião
FEMALE SABIÁ, victim of
unsuccessful abduction attempt by Gavião

Death of a Bird   DEATB

GAVRILICH, a shock-worker,
The Bright Stream
BRIGH

GAVRILO. See: Petr

GAY. See: Lady Gay, The

GAY MERCHANT, THE, par-
ticipates in carnival celebrating Butter Week,
Petrouchka   PETRO

GAYNE, industrious, straight-
forward member of collec-
tive farm near Kolkhoz,
southern Armenia; loves
Kozakov
GIKO, her husband, drinks
and consorts with crimi-
nals; denounced by Gayne
to the workers; exiled
RIPSIK, their child, held
as hostage by Giko
Gayne   GAYNE

GAZER. See: Crystal Gazer

GAZETTE. See: Army and
Navy Gazette, The

GEARS, representations of
machinery, Iron Foundry
IRONF

GEERT. See: Eleonore

GEMINI, signs of the Zodiac,
Horoscope   HOROS

GEMINI. See also:
Young Man, The
Young Woman, The

GEMMA. See: Countess Gemma

GENARIO, Roman bandit,
follower of Marco Spada,
Marco Spada   MARCO

GENARIO. See also: Genarro

GENERAL. See:
Farmer-General, The
Lieutenant
Old General, The
Polkan, General

GENERAL, THE. See: Bride, The

GENII OF AGRICULTURE, THE,
personification, Excelsior
EXCEL

GENII OF CIVILIZATION, THE,
personification, Excelsior
EXCEL

GENII OF CONCORD, THE, personification, Excelsior
EXCEL

GENII OF FAME, THE, personification, Excelsior   EXCEL

GENII OF FORCE, THE, personification, Excelsior   EXCEL

GENII OF GLORY, THE, personification, Excelsior   EXCEL

GENII OF INDUSTRY, THE,
personification, Excelsior
EXCEL

GENII OF INVENTION, THE,
personification, Excelsior
EXCEL

GENII OF PERSEVERANCE, THE,
personification, Excelsior
EXCEL

GENII OF SCIENCE, THE, personification, Excelsior
EXCEL

GENII OF THE EARTH, THE,
engages in combat with King
of the Corals for the White
Pearl; wins, The Beautiful
Pearl   BEAUT

GENII OF UNION, THE, personi-

fication, Excelsior
                      EXCEL

GENII OF VALOR, THE, per-
    sonification, Excelsior
                      EXCEL

GENIUS.   See: Divine Genius,
    The

GENIUS-HUSBAND, engrossed
    in his books
    WIFE, attempts to arouse
    her husband's jealousy by
    responding to attentions of
    Prince
    PRINCE, attracted to Wife
    Tally-Ho, or The Frail
    Quarry   TALLY

GENIUS OF EVIL. See: Bel-
    fegor

GENIUS OF GOOD. See: Anar

GENIUS OF THE MINES, EVIL.
    See: Torbern

GENNARIELLO, a fisherman,
    about to be married to
    Diavolina, Diavolina
                      DIAVO

GENNARIELLO. See also:
    Don Chichillo
    Don Fortunato

GENNARO, fisherman, in love
    with and loved by Tere-
    sina; becomes her be-
    trothed, Napoli   NAPOL

GENNARO. See also:
    Ambrosio, Fra
    Genario
    Giovanina
    Vitelli

GENNARO, VASIANO, a mer-
    chant, The Blood-Red
    Flower   BLOOD

GENTLEMAN. See:
    Colored Gentleman, The
    Intoxicated Gentleman

GENTLEMAN, A. See: Lady, A

GENTLEMAN FROM VIENNA, A,
    guest at ball, Carnival at
    Pest   CARNI

GENTLEMAN IN THE BATH
    CHAIR, visiting London,
    London Morning   LONDO

GENTLEMAN WITH A ROPE, THE,
    madman in London madhouse,
    The Rake's Progress RAKES

GENTLEMAN WITH HER, THE.
    See:
    Lady With Him, The
    She Wore a Perfume
    Who Was She?

GENTZ. See: von Gentz,
    Frederich

GEOFFROY, COMTE. See:
    Marquis Costa de Beaure-
    gard, The

GEORGE. See:
    Georges
    Georgi
    Saint George
    Valentine

GEORGES, steward to the Comte,
    Nina's father
    GEORGETTE, his daughter,
    loved by Victor
    Nina   NINAO

GEORGES. See also:
    George
    Georgi
    Victor

GEORGES-ÉMILE. See: Guérin,
    Georges-Émile

GEORGETTE. See:

Georges
Victor

GEORGI, Russian, Pages of
Life   PAGEL

GEORGI. See also:
George
Georges

GEORGIA, QUEEN OF. See:
Thamar

GEORGIAN PRINCE, THE,
passing through metropolitan railroad terminal,
Terminal   TERMI

GERMEUIL, in love with Nina,
Nina   NINAO

GERTRUDE. See: Hamlet,
Prince of Denmark

GERTRUDE, MADAME, a
young widow and inn-keep-
er, La Somnambule
                   SOMNA

GERTRUDE, MADAME. See
also: Marcelline

GERTRUDE (MIKALIA). See:
Gourouli

GESSLER. See: Tell, Wil-
liam

GHOST, AGAMEMNON'S. See:
Clytemnestra

GHOST OF CANDELAS' FORM-
ER LOVER. See: Can-
delas

GHOST OF DUCHESS' LOVER,
THE. See: Duchess, The

GHOST OF HAMLET'S FATHER.
See: Hamlet, Prince of
Denmark

GHOST, ROSE. See: Rose Spirit

GHOULS. See: King of the
Ghouls, The

GIACOMO, major-domo to Count-
ess Gemma, tries to protect
her from Marquis de Santa-
Croce
Gemma   GEMMA
Proprietor of a macaroni
stall, in love with Teresina
Napoli   NAPOL

GIANCIOTTO MALATESTA. See:
Dwarfs
Francesca (Francesca da
Rimini)
Girolamo

GIANNINA, orphan, betrothed to
Matteo, Ondine   ONDIN

GIEREY, a Khan, falls in love
with Marie
ZAREMA, his Georgian wife
and favorite
SECOND FAVORITE WIFE
The Fountain of Bakhchisarai
                   FOUNT

GIGOLO
DEBUTANTE, perform tango
Facade   FACAD
Friend of Blondelaine
Scaramouche   SCARA

GIKO. See: Gayne

GIL, a buccaneer, Jovita JOVIT

GIL. See also: Don Gil

GILA, cook, intended as bride
for Hermit by Archangel
Lucifer, Pastorela PASTO

GILBERT, resident of Marseille,
French revolutionist, The
Flames of Paris   FLAME

GILGAMESH. See: Ishtar

GIN, drink served at 2222 Club,
New York City, Café Society

CAFES

GIOVANINA, one of Gennaro's
customers, Napoli
NAPOL

GIOVANNI. See:
Casanova, Giovanni
Podesta, Giovanni

GIPSIES. See: Gypsies

GIPSY. See: Gypsy

GIRL, prostitute, used by
Three Thugs to entice
clients whom they rob and
kill
BOY, night repair hand,
loved by Girl, killed by
Thugs
THREE THUGS, accom-
plices of Girl
The Night City   NIGHY

GIRL. See also:
American Girl
Bathing-Girl from Trou-
ville, The
Betrayed Girl, The
Bird Girl
Blind Girl
Candy Girl
Chorus Girl, A
Christian Girl, A
Cigarette Girl
Dead Girl, The
Flower Girl
Gypsy Girl, The
Hat-Check Girl
Host
Little American Girl, The
Little Girl
Little Girl, A
Lonely Girl
Mysterious Girl
Nearly Drowned Girl
Peasant Girl, The
Polovetsian Girl
Poor Girl, A
Rich Girl, A
Silly Country Girl
Witch Boy

Young Communist Girl, A
Young Farm Girl
Young Girl
Young Girl, The
Young Man
Youth

GIRL, A YOUNG. See: Youth, A

GIRL, AMERICAN. See: Little
American Girl, The

GIRL DANCING. See: Bearded
Old Man

GIRL HIKER. See: Boy Hiker

GIRL IN BLUE, ballet dancer,
becomes member of company,
On Stage!   ONSTA

GIRL IN PINK, aspiring ballet
dancer, helped by Handyman,
On Stage!   ONSTA

GIRL IN THE WORLD, THE MOST
BEAUTIFUL. See: Young Man

GIRL OF THE TOWN. See:
Flutist

GIRL, PEASANT. See: Mexican
Peon

GIRL, POOR. See: Hypnotist

GIRL-REINDEER, in love with
Nilas, spurned by him, seeks
help of Sorcerer
NILAS, kills Girl-Reindeer
SORCERER, requires Girl-
Reindeer to assume shape of
reindeer and lure hunters to
their deaths
The Moon Reindeer   MOONR

GIRL, THE, seduced by the
Husband
GIRL'S COUSIN, seduces
the Wife
THE WIFE
THE HUSBAND
The Invitation   INVIT

"Caught up in the feverish
gaiety of a carnival"
THE BOY, her friend
CIRCUS DANCER
THE PUGILIST, partici-
pants in the carnival
Mardi Gras   MARDI
Caricature of a cartoon
character
The New Yorker   NEWYO
Loved by Young Man
YOUNG MAN, killed by
Brother in a fight
BROTHER, younger brother
of Young Man, jealous of
his happiness with the Girl
Two Brothers   TWOBR

GIRL, THE. See also:
    Boy, The
    Officer, The
    Tennis Player, The

GIRL, THE COSSACK. See:
    Cossack Chief, The

GIRL, THE QUAKER. See:
    Farm Boy, The

GIRL, THE RICH. See:
    Rich Boy, The

GIRL, THE YOUNG. See:
    Young Man, The

GIRL WITH BIRDS, central
    figure, Carnival of Ani-
    mals   CARNV

GIRL, YOUNG. See:
    Ballerinas, Two Former
    Chaperones
    Garatuja, O.
    Lover, The
    Officer, An
    Rich Old Neighbor, A
    Rose Spirit
    Young Workman

GIRLS. See:
    Lepidopterist
    Society Girls

GIRLS, CANCAN. See:
    Cancan Girls
    Dance Master

GIRL'S COUSIN. See: Girl, The

GIRL'S DUENNA, YOUNG. See:
    Young Girl

GIRLS, JUNIOR. See: Leader
    of the Junior Girls

GIRLS, LEADER OF THE CAN-
    CAN. See: Dance Master

GIRL'S LOVER, YOUNG. See:
    Young Girl

GIRL'S PARENTS, YOUNG. See:
    Garatuja, O.

GIRLS, TWO, "foul girls with
    stools, bored and slightly
    amused by disaster,"
    Caprichos   CAPRH

GIRLS, TWO. See also: Tennis
    Player

GIRLS WITH GLOVED HANDS,
    THREE, symbolic figures,
    The Widow in the Mirror
                        WIDOW

GIROLAMO, Gianciotto Malatesta's
    spy, Francesca da Rimini
                        FRANC

GIROLAMO. See also: Fran-
    cesca (Francesca da Rimini)

GISELLE, village girl, loved by
    Albrecht, Duke of Silesia
    and by Hilarion; in love with
    Albrecht
    BERTHE, her mother
    Giselle   GISEE
    Giselle   GISEL
    Giselle   GISES
    Lures Albrecht into her
    coffin, nails him there
    ALBRECHT, Giselle's victim

Giselle's Revenge   GISER

GITANA, LA, gypsy, La
Gitana   GITAA

GLOIRE. See also: Glory

GLOIRE, LA (The Star), great
actress, portrays Lucre-
tia, Phaedra and Hamlet,
La Gloire   GLOIR

GLOIRE, LA. See also:
Aspirant, The
Ophelia
Tarquinius, Sextus

GLORIETTE, milliner, loved
by Simon, Le Marché des
Innocents   MARCH

GLORIETTE. See also: Lindor

GLORY. See:
Genii of Glory, The
Gloire

GLOSTER. See: Richard,
Duke of Gloster

GLOVE-SELLER, sells gloves
at Paris café, falls in
love with the Baron, Gaîté
Parisienne   GAITE

GLOVED HANDS. See: Girls
With Gloved Hands, Three

GLOW-WORM PATROL. See:
Captain of the Glow-Worm
Patrol

GNOME, THE. See: Rübezahl

GNOMES. See: King of the
Gnomes, The

GNOMES, THE, inmates of the
Logéat Mental Hospital,
Les Algues   ALGUE

GOAT, one of Ulysses' sailors,
transformed by Circe, Circe
                       CIRCE

GOAT MEN, THREE, demented
men, believe themselves to
be goats, cured by Donald,
Donald of the Burthens
                       DONAL

GOATS, TWO, attend feast of
Bacchus, Sylvia   SYLVA

GOD. See:
Elihu
Stranger, The

GOD BRAMA, THE. See: Unknown, The

GOD, CHILD. See: Bartolo

GOD OF LOVE. See:
Amor
Cupid
Cupidon
Eros

GOD OF MARRIAGE. See:
Hymen

GOD OF THE SEA. See:
Neptune
Poseidon

GOD OF THE UNDERWORLD.
See: Pluto

GOD OF THE WIND. See:
Vayou

GOD OF WAR. See: Mars

GOD OF WINE. See: Bacchus

GODDESS OF CHANCE. See:
Fortuna

GODDESS OF LOVE. See: Venus

GODDESS OF LOVE AND FERTIL-

ITY. See: Ishtar

GODDESS OF MOTHERHOOD
AND FERTILITY, See:
Isis

GODDESS OF NIGHT, THE,
supernatural being, The
Stars   STARS

GODDESS OF THE CHASE.
See: Diana

GODDESS OF THE DANCE.
See: Queen of the Dance

GODDESS OF THE HEAVENLY
SPIRITS. See: Amravati

GODDESS OF THE HUNT.
See: Diana

GODDESS OF THE MOON.
See: Endymion

GODDESS OF THE SEA. See:
Amphitrite

GODFATHER, HIS. See:
Young Communicant, The

GODMOTHER to Ysaure, La
Filleule des Fées FILLU

GODMOTHER, FAIRY. See:
Cinderella

GODMOTHER, THE RAGGED
FAIRY. See: Cinderella

GODS OF THE SEA, bring
appropriate fish dishes to
banquet, Spectacle SPECL

GODS, THE, punish sinners
for their transgressions,
The Seventh Symphony
                        SEVEN

GOLD, SHOWER OF. See:
Danaë
Shower of Gold

GOLDEN COCKEREL, THE, Le
Coq d'Or, magic bird given
King Dondon by the Astrolo-
ger to warn the King of the
approach of his enemies,
Le Coq d'Or   COQDO

GOLDEN CORD. See: First
Golden Cord, The

GOLDEN CORDS, THE. See:
First Golden Cord, The

GOLDEN PENNY, THE, repre-
sentation of British newspaper, The Press   PRESS

GOLDEN ROSE. See: Bobo-
Safar

GOLF PLAYER, appears on
beach, Le Train Bleu
                         BLEU

GOLFO, a sea-sprite, turns
Teresina into a naiad
CORALLA
ARGENTINA, his naiads
Napoli   NAPOL

GOLIATH. See:
David
Jesse

GOLOVA, mayor of Russian village, Christmas Eve CHRIS

GONDELAURIER, MADAME
ALOISE DE. See: Fleur-
de-Lys

GONERIL. See: Lear, King of
Britain

GOOD FAIRY, THE. See:
Cinderella
Fée, La Bonne
Prince

GOOD, GENIUS OF. See: Anar

GOOF. See: Great American
Goof, The

GORGON. See: Poet, The

GORILLA, THE, protects son
of Negro from Planter,
Baby Stork   BABYS

GOSSE, BEAU, appears on
beach, Le Train Bleu
                    TRAIN

GOSSIP, personification, spectator at Paganini's con-
cert, Paganini   PAGAN

GOSSIP COLUMNIST, caricature
of cartoon character, The
New Yorker   NEWYO

GOSSIPING TOWNSWOMEN.
See: Weidman, Fireman

GOTHLAND, LORD OF EAST.
See: Thora

GOUANDI, bloodthirsty idol
seen by Tai-Hoa in her
dream, The Red Poppy
                    REDPO

GOUDAL. See: Prince Goudal

GOUDAL'S WIFE, PRINCE.
See: Prince Goudal

GOULAD, finds Mélisande in
forest; becomes her husband
PELLEAS, his brother
Pelléas et Mélisande
                    PELLE

GOULUE, LA, star of the Folies-Bergère, Bar aux Fo-
lies-Bergère   BARAU

GOUROULI, betrothed to Pepio
MIKALIA (GERTRUDE), her
aged mother
Les Deux Pigéons DEUXN
Les Deux Pigéons DEUXP

GOUROULI. See also: Zarifi

GOVERNESS OF THE HAREM,
THE, at the court of Caliph
Abderraman, Zoraiya
                    ZORAI

GOVERNESS OF THE NYMPHS,
THE, supernatural being,
Cydalise et le Chèvre-pied
                    CYDAL

GOVERNMENT OFFICIAL, A,
guest at the Aristocrat's
ball, Mam'zelle Angot
                    MAMZE

GOVERNOR. See: British
Governor, The

GOVERNOR OF NIJNI NOVGOROD.
See: Smouroff

GOVERNOR OF ROME. See:
Prince Osorio

GOVERNOR OF SEVILLE, THE,
official, Le Fille de Marbre
                    FILLM

GOVERNOR OF THE ISLAND.
See: de la Martinière,
Monsieur

GOVERNOR OF THE PROVINCE,
THE, official
BLINVAL, his son, in love
with Nina
Nina   NINAO

GOVERNOR, THE. See: Andrey

GOVINE. See: Morlaque

GRACES, THE THREE, tradition-
al figures, "faceless, with
strange protuberances"
Bacchanale   BACCH
Perform dance with Venus at
the minstrel show
Cakewalk   CAKEW
Traditional figures
Fiametta   FIAMM

Le Jugement de Paris
                            JUGEM

GRACIOSO, a notary, Stella
                            STELL

GRACIOSO. See also:
    Graziosa
    Grazioso

GRAHN, LUCILE. See: Tag-
    lioni, Marie

GRANADA, KING OF. See:
    Mahomet

GRAND ELECTOR, THE. See:
    Princess Bathilde

GRAND VIZIER, THE, pur-
    chases Lilia and Phoebe
    from Bracaccio, Le Diable
    Amoureux   DIABE

GRANDFATHER. See: Peter

GRANDMOTHER, FADETTE'S.
    See: Fadette

GRAPHIC, THE, representation
    of British newspaper, The
    Press   PRESS

GRASSHOPPER, master of the
    revels, Les Papillons
                            PAPIO

GRAVE DIGGER, clown, Ham-
    let   HAMLE

GRAY. See: Grey

GRAZIOSA, young Neapolitan
    girl, in love with Pietro;
    breaks up duel between
    Don Rodrigo and Don
    Manuel, Graziosa GRAZI

GRAZIOSA. See also:
    Gracioso
    Grazioso
    Nunziata

GRAZIOSO, gypsy chief's
    daughter, Don Quichotte
                            DONQU

GRAZIOSO. See also:
    Gracioso
    Graziosa

GREAT. See: Alexander the
    Great

GREAT AMERICAN GOOF, THE,
    "the naïve white hope of the
    human race," The Great
    American Goof   GREAT

GREEDY VIRGIN. See: Priggish
    Virgin

GREEK COUPLE, perform dance
    for Cupid's approval, The
    Whims of Cupid and the
    Ballet Master   WHIMS

GREEN. See: Boy in Green

GREEN, FLOWER VENDOR IN.
    See:
    Boy in Grey
    Flower Vendor in Green
    Lieutenant

GREEN ONE, THE, supernatural
    being, Peer Gynt   PEERG

GRETEL. See: Hansel

GREY, ship captain, Red Sails
                            REDSA

GREY. See also:
    Boy in Grey
    Letika

GREY ANGEL, THE, angel of
    death, claims the Duchess,
    L'Ange Gris   ANGEG

GREY MOTHS, residents of But-
    terfly Land, Les Papillons
                            PAPIO

GRIEF. See: Figure of Grief

GRILLE. See: d'Égout, Grille

GRINDBERG. See: Baron de Grindberg

GRINDBERG, BARONESS DE. See: Baron de Grindberg

GRINGOIRE, PIERRE, poet, marries La Esmeralda, La Esmeralda ESMER

GRISI, CARLOTTA, famous nineteenth century ballerina, La Grisi GRISI

GRISI, CARLOTTA. See also: Taglioni, Marie

GRITZKO, Parassia's lover, The Fair at Sorochinsk FAIRA

GRITZKO. See also: Khivria

GROOM. See: Bride

GROOM, A. See: Bride, A

GROUND. See: She of the Ground

GROUP, BLACK. See: Destiny

GROUP, BLUE. See: Leader of Blue Group

GROUP, LEADER OF BLACK. See: Destiny

GROUP, RED. See: Leader of Red Group (Town)

GROUP, YELLOW. See: Leader of Yellow Group (Country)

GRUBS, inhabitants of the insect world Le Festin de l'Araignée

FESTD
Le Festin de l'Araignée
FESTI
The Spider's Banquet
SPIDE

GUADALQUIVIR, personification of river, La Fille du Pharaon FILLP

GUARD, CAPTAIN OF THE. See: Captain of the Guard Hassan

GUARDIAN ANGEL, Buza's protectress, The Holy Torch HOLYT

GUARDS. See: Courasche

GUEBRIANT. See: Baron de Guebriant, The

GUÉRIN, GEORGES-ÉMILE, sane inmate of the Logéat Mental Hospital CATHERINE, his sweetheart, insane inmate of the Hospital Les Algues ALGUE

GUÉRIN, GEORGES-ÉMILE. See also: Notary, The

GUESTS, HER. See: Hostess, The

GUIABLESSE, LA, she-devil of Martinique folklore, tempts men to cast themselves from pinnacles, La Guiablesse GUIAB

GUIDON, PRINCE. See: King Dondon

GUIGNOL. See: Pandora

GUILE, personification, spectator at Paganini's concert, Paganini PAGAN

GUILLAUME. See: Ysaure

GUIMARD, LA, gives Made-
    moiselle de Bougainville
    dancing lesson, Ozaï
                        OZAII

GUIMARD, LA. See also:
    Bougainville, Monsieur de

GUINEVERE. See: Angelic
    Apparition

GUITAR. See: Aged Woman
    With Guitar

GULNARE, slave belonging to
    Seyd, Le Corsaire
                        CORSA

GUNDEMEY OF DAHOMEY,
    PRINCESS. See: Tulip

GURN. See: Reuben, James

GUSTAVE, habitué at bar of
    Folies-Bergère, Bar au
    Folies-Bergère   BARAU

GYGES, shepherd, betrothed
    to Clytia
    Le Roi Candaule ROICA
    Giant
    I Titani   TITAN

GYNT, JOHN. See: Aase

GYNT, PEER. See:
    Aase
    Anitra
    Ingrid
    Solveig
    Troll King, The

GYPSIES, CHIEF OF THE.
    See:
    Parembo
    Zarifi

GYPSIES, QUEEN OF THE.
    See:
    Mab
    Queen of the Gypsies

GYPSIES, THE, two participants

in carnival celebrating Butter
    Week, Petrouchka   PETRO

GYPSIES, THREE, drive Peddler
    from fair, The Fair at
    Sorochinsk   FAIRA

GYPSY. See: Young Gypsy

GYPSY DANCER, THE. See:
    Young Girl, The

GYPSY FORTUNE TELLER
    HER PARTNER, participants
    in festival in small Spanish
    town
    Capriccio Espagnol CAPRI

GYPSY FORTUNE TELLER. See
    also: Fortune Teller

GYPSY GIRL, THE, participant
    in festival in small Spanish
    town
    Capriccio Espagnol CAPRI
    Conjured up by the Devil;
    temporarily causes the Beg-
    gar to forget Daughter of
    the Old Lord
    Devil's Holiday   DEVIL

GYPSY, THE, merrymaker, Don
    Juan   DONJU

GYPSY YOUTH, THE, participant
    in festival in small Spanish
    town, Capriccio Espagnol
                        CAPRI

GYULYANAK. See: Kahn, The

                    H

H. P. , personification of modern
    man, H. P.   HPPPP

HAAGER. See: Baron Haager

HAAGER, BARONESS. See:
    Baron Haager

HADES. See: King Hades

HADES, KING OF. See:
Persephone, Queen of
Hades

HADES, QUEEN OF. See:
Persephone, Queen of
Hades

HAEMON. See: Creon

HAGAR, attracted by the
Friend, seduced by the
Young Man From the
House Opposite
ELDEST SISTER, her sis-
ter, old-maidish and cold
YOUNGEST SISTER, her
sister, grasping and mali-
cious; attracts the Friend
Pillar of Fire   PILLA

HAIL, personification, Les
Saisons   SAISO

HAIR. See: Hare

HAIRDRESSER, THE, helps
Cinderella's two ugly step-
sisters prepare for ball
Cinderella   CINDE
Attends Florinda
Le Diable Boiteux
                    DIABL

HAMILTON, MARY, seduced
by the Suitor; drowns her
child, hanged
THE MISTRESS, her em-
ployer
THE SUITOR, to the Mis-
tress
The Four Marys   FOURM

HAMLET, Prince of Denmark,
dying, looks back over his
life
Hamlet   HAMLE
Prince of Denmark
GERTRUDE, Queen of Den-
mark, his mother, widow of
Hamlet's father; now married
to Claudius

CLAUDIUS, his uncle, pres-
ent King of Denmark, brother
of Hamlet's father whom he
has murdered
GHOST OF HAMLET'S FA-
THER, apparition of former
King of Denmark
Hamlet   HAMLE
Hamlet   HAMLL
Hamlet   HAMLS
Hamlet   HAMLT

HAMLET. See also:
Gloire, La
Ophelia
Pall Bearers, Four
Polonius

HAMLET'S MOTHER. See:
Ophelia

HAMLET'S STEPFATHER. See:
Ophelia

HAMSATI, favorite of Dushmata,
King of India, Sakuntala
                    SAKUN

HAMZA, THE FAIRY. See:
Fairy Hamza, The
Farfalla
Patimate

HAND. See:
First Hand, The
Hands
Hans

HANDLERS, HIS. See: Champ,
The

HANDMAIDENS, THREE. See:
Sphinx, The

HANDS. See:
Girls With Gloved Hands,
Three
Hand
Hans

HANDSOME INDIAN. See:
Uirapurú

HANDYMAN at ballet theater,
vaguely in love with the
Ballerina; helps Girl in
Pink to dance, On Stage!
ONSTA

HANNAH. See: Bilby

HANS. See:
Hand
Hands
Kathi

HANSEL
GRETEL, his sister, lost
in the woods
WITCH, owner of ginger-
bread house
Hansel and Gretel HANSE

HARE. See: Little Hare, The
First

HARE, THE SECOND LITTLE.
See: Little Hare, The First

HAREM. See: Governess of
the Harem, The

HARLEQUIN, traditional panto-
mime figure, portrayed by
girl dancer
Ballade   BALLA
Traditional pantomime fig-
ure
The Bronze Horseman
BRONZ
Traditional pantomime fig-
ure, in love with Colum-
bine
Le Carnaval   CARNA
Traditional pantomime fig-
ure
Harlequin in April HARLE
Suitor to Columbine, out-
wits Leandre, made rich
by La Bonne Fée
Harlequinade   HARLI
Traditional pantomime fig-
ure
Harlequinade   HARLJ
Harlequinade   HARLN
Harlequin for President

HARLQ
Harlequin in the Street
HARLS
Harlequinade Pas de Deux
HARLX
Entertains at masked ball
given by the Baron
Night Shadow   NIGHT
Passer-by on Paris street
La Nuit   NUITT
Clockwork toy
The Nutcracker   NUTCA
The Nutcracker   NUTCK
The Nutcracker   NUTCR
Traditional pantomime figure
The Sleeping Beauty SLEEP
Vert-Vert   VERTV

HARLEQUINS, TWO, traditional
pantomime figures, Veneziana
VENEZ

HARMODIUS. See: Spartacus

HAROLD, King of Thule, falls
in love with Sieba, Sieba
SIEBA

HAROLD. See also:
Kafur
Wotan

HAROLDE (THE POET), performs
dance at minstrel show with
Hortense, Queen of the Swamp
Lilies, Cakewalk   CAKEW

HARRISON, MR., a wealthy
American
MISS HARRISON, his
daughter, engaged to Isidor
Brown, Gaucho   GAUCH

HARRY TARGETT. See: Tulip

HARVEST FAIRY, THE. See:
Fairy Hamza, The

HASSAN, Captain of the Guard;
character in the ballet
"Azalea, or the Odalisque,"
The Débutante   DEBUT

HAT-CHECK GIRL, at 2222
Club, New York City,
Café Society   CAFES

HAT SELLER, THE, creditor
of The Old Lord, Devil's
Holiday   DEVIL

HAVAI, a Negro, The Three
Fat Men   THREE

HAWKER. See: Melon Hawk-
er, The

HAZDAI-BEN-SHAPRUT, vizier
and famous doctor at the
court of Caliph Abderra-
man; tutor to Abu-Soliman,
the caliph's adopted son,
Zoraiya   ZORAI

HE, black stallion, friend of
the white mare She; tem-
porarily deserted for The
Other, circus horse,
Idylle   IDYLL
Dances waltz at ball with
She
SHE, his partner
La Valse   VALSE

HE WHO SUMMONS, allegori-
cal figure, Dark Meadow
                      DARKM

HE WORE A WHITE TIE, man
of the world, recalled as
a memory by The Lady
With Him, Dim Lustre
                      DIMLU

HEAD COACHMAN, THE
COACHMEN, participate
in carnival celebrating Butter Week
Petrouchka   PETRO

HEAD FORESTER, woodsman,
Cinderella   CINDA

HEAD MISTRESS, THE, of
fashionable girls' school
in Vienna, Graduation Ball

HEAD WRANGLER, THE, com-
petes with the Champion
Roper for the Rancher's
Daughter, Rodeo   RODEO

HEAD WRANGLER, THE. See
also: Cowgirl, The

HEADMAN OF THE VILLAGE.
See: Marie

HEART. See: King Heart

HEARTS. See:
Knave of Hearts
Queen of Hearts

HEARTS, THE QUEEN OF. See:
Queen of Clubs, The

HEAVENLY SPIRITS, GODDESS
OF THE. See: Amravati

HEBE, cupbearer to the gods,
spills nectar, banished to
Earth by Jupiter where she
meets and is wooed by Her-
cules
The Descent of Hebe DESCE
Cupbearer to the gods
Spectacle   SPECL

HECTOR, apparition conjured up
by Faust, Abraxas   ABRAX

HECUBA. See: Cassandra

HEENAN, "BENICIA BOY,"
American prize fighter, one-
time husband of "The Men-
ken" (Adah Isaacs Menken),
Ghost Town   GHOST

HEIR, VILLAGE ELDER'S. See:
Village Elder

HELEN, gives Faust refuge in
the Elysian Fields
Abraxas   ABRAX
Wife of Menelaus, kidnapped
by Paris

Clytemnestra   CLYTE
"Most beautiful of women, "
wife of Menelaus, kid-
napped by Paris
Spectacle   SPECL

HELEN. See also: Paris

HELEN OF TROY. See:
King Menelaus, King of
Sparta
Orestes

HELENA, in love with Deme-
trius
The Dream   DREAM
A Midsummer Night's
Dream   MIDSU

HÉLÈNE, "the beloved of Don
Ottavio, " Namouna NAMOU

HÉLÈNE DE VARDECK. See:
Beatrix
Comte de Vardeck, The

HELIOS. See: Hyperion

HELMSMAN, on Ulysses'
ship, succeeds in drawing
Ulysses away from Circe,
Circe   CIRCE

HELOISE. See: Baron Bluebeard

HEN. See: Nightingale

HEN, THE, bird, Carnival of
Animals   CARNV

HENRIETTA. See: Cavalier
Pignerolle, The

HENRIETTE, friend of Ray-
monda, Raymonda RAYMO

HENRIETTE. See also:
Bettemberg
Karll

HENRY. See: King Henry
VIII, King of England

HÉPIALES, THE FOUR, butterflies, Piège de Lumière
PIEGE

HERA, goddess, competes with
Aphrodite and Pallas Athena
in beauty contest judged by
Paris, Helen of Troy
HELEN

HERA. See also:
Hymen
King Menelaus, King of
Sparta
Zeus

HERCULES, titan, rescues Al-
cestis from Hades
Alcestis   ALCES
Titan, meets, woos Hebe
The Descent of Hebe DESCE

HERMANN. See: Philemon

HERMES, god, appoints Paris
judge in beauty contest
Helen of Troy   HELEN
God
I, Odysseus   IODYS

HERMIA, in love with Lysander
EGEUS, her father
The Dream   DREAM
A Midsummer Night's Dream
MIDSU

HERMIA. See also: Demetrius

HERMILIA, PRINCESS (FLORET-
TA). See: King Bobiche

HERMIT, seeking the New Mes-
siah, intended as husband of
Gila by Archangel Lucifer,
Pastorela   PASTO

HERMIT, THE WONDROUS, helps
unite the Prince and the
Princess, A Spring Tale
SPRIN

HERNANDEZ. See: Don Hernandez

HERNANDEZ, DONNA. See:
Don Hernandez

HERO, performer in ballet
"The Captive Princess and
Her Hero, " On Stage!
ONSTA

HERO, THE, personification
of Man, Les Présages
PRESA

HEROD, KING. See:
John the Baptist
Salomé

HÉRODIADE, personification of
Everywoman "gazing into a
mirror which pitilessly reveals to her both her present and future"
ATTENDANT, to Hérodiade
Hérodiade   HEROD

HÉRODIAS, QUEEN. See:
Salomé

HEROTH. See: Thora

HERSELF, dancer, performs
before city workers, Sky-
scrapers   SKYSC

HERTHA, Queen of the Elfrits
(Evil Elves), falls in love
with Toniello, Fiorita et
la Reine des Elfrides
FIORI

HERTHA. See also: Anar

HERVE, young farmer, en-
gaged to Yvonne, daughter
of Mathurin, Les Papillons
PAPIO

HETYKE (Cheeky), shepherdess,
The Holy Torch   HOLYT

HIGH PRIEST, Egyptian church-
man, attempts to discern
Aspicia's fate, La Fille du
Pharaon   FILLP

HIGH PRIEST OF THE TEMPLE,
gives Amoûn cup of poison
on orders of Cléopâtre,
Cléopâtre   CLEOP

HIGH PRIEST OF THE TEMPLE
OF PEACE, churchman, Les
Amours d'Antoine et de
Cléopâtre   AMOUR

HIGH PRIEST, THE, enamored of
Femina as priestess in an-
cient Assyria, Femina
FEMIN

HIKER. See: Boy Hiker

HIKER, GIRL. See: Boy Hiker

HILARION, gamekeeper, in love
with Giselle
Giselle   GISEE
Giselle   GISEL
Giselle   GISES

HILDA, a mountain girl, A Folk
Tale   FOLKT

HILDEBRAND. See: Sir Hildebrand

HINDUSTAN, EMPEROR OF. See:
Emperor Aurungzebe, The

HIPPOLYTA, Queen of the Ama-
zons, betrothed to Theseus,
A Midsummer Night's Dream
MIDSU

HIPPOLYTE. See: Phaedra

HIPPOLYTUS. See:
Aricia
Phaedra
Poseidon

HIPS. See: Sir Hips

HIRONDELLE, cancan dancer,
Bar aux Folies-Bergère
BARAU

HISTORY, a muse, Sylvia

SYLVA

HITTITE, URIAH THE. See:
Bathsheba

HIU (Vain), shepherd, The
Holy Torch   HOLYT

HOA. See: Tai-Hoa

HOAR. See also: Hor

HOAR-FROST, personification,
Les Saisons   SAISO

HOKINSON LADY, caricature
of clubwoman depicted in
cartoons, The New Yorker
NEWYO

HOLERUT, chief of the Danish
pirates, Sieba   SIEBA

HOLERUT. See also: Cadmo

HOLINESS, PERSONIFICATION
OF. See: St. George

HOLOFERNES. See: Judith

HONOR, HER MAIDS OF. See:
Princess, The

HONOR, QUEEN'S MAID OF.
See: Blanche

HONOR, QUEEN'S MAIDS OF.
See:
Blanche
Navailles, Madame de
Vert-Vert

HOOD. See: Red Riding Hood

HOODLUMS. See: Street Boy,
A

HOP O' MY THUMB, fairy
tale character in Woman's
dream; ensnared by Bird
Girl, Mother Goose Suite
MOTHE

HOPAK LEADER, dancer, The
Fair at Sorochinsk   FAIRA

HOPE, personification, The Triumph of Hope   TRIUH

HOPSCOTCH, danced by four female dancers, Street Games
STREE

HOR. See also: Hoar

HOR, TA. See:
Lord Wilson
Ta-Hor

HORSE, participant in gypsy
carnival, Aleko   ALEKO

HORSE. See also: Hump-Backed
Horse, The

HORSE, HIS. See: Manager on
Horseback, The

HORSE, THE WHITE. See:
Black Horses, The
Queen of the Amazons, The

HORSEBACK. See: Manager on
Horseback, The

HORSES. See:
Black Horses, The
Wooden Rocking Horses, The

HORSES, THEIR. See: Amazons,
The

HORTENSE, Queen of the Swamp
Lilies, performs dance at
minstrel show with Harolde
(The Poet), Cakewalk
CAKEW

HORTENSIUS, DOCTOR, Count
Frédéric's tutor, Le Diable
Amoureux   DIABE

HOST, at ball in which two
groups participate
BOY, member of one group,

falls in love with Girl
GIRL, member of other
group, falls in love with
Boy
The Guests   GUEST

HOST, THE. See: Baron, The

HOSTESS. See: Night-Club
Hostess, A

HOSTESS, THE, at house
party, eager to recapture
her youth
HER GUESTS, young men
and women
Les Biches   BICHE

HOUAN. See: Pantoka, Houan

HOURS. See:
Black Hours, The
White Hours, The

HOURS OF DAY, SIX, personifications, La Nuit et le
Jour   NUITE

HOURS OF NIGHT, TWELVE,
personifications, La Nuit
et le Jour   NUITE

HOUSE OPPOSITE. See:
Young Man From the
House Opposite

HOUSEKEEPER, THE, servant
of Don Quixote
HER NIECE
Don Quixote   DONQX

HUGUES. See: Prince Hugues
de Provence

HUMBERT, Badouin's squire,
Raoul de Créqui   RAOUL

HUMMING BIRDS. See: Fairy
of the Humming Birds, The

HUMP-BACKED HORSE, THE,
captured by Petr's son Ivanoushka, purchased by the

Khan
The Hump-Backed Horse
                       HUMPB
The Hump-Backed Horse
                       HUMPH

HUNCHBACK, Parisian, Le Rendez-Vous   RENDE

HUNGARY. See: Albert of
Hungary

HUNGARY, KING OF. See:
King Andrew II, King of
Hungary

HUNT. See: Master of the Hunt

HUNT, GODESS OF THE. See:
Diana

HUNTER. See: First Hunter

HUNTERS. See:
Butterfly Hunters
Husband-Hunters, Two
Seal Hunters, Four

HUNTERS, SIX. See: First
Hunter

HUNTRESS. See: Uirapurú

HUNTSMAN, THE, instructed by
the Queen to kill Snow-White;
spares her, Blanche-Neige
                       BLANC

HUNTSMAN, THE. See also:
Prince, The

HUSBAND
WIFE, engage in war of the
sexes
CHILD, reconciles his par-
ents
The War Between Men and
Women   WARBE

HUSBAND. See also:
Genius-Husband
Husband, The
Wife

Young Husband

HUSBAND, HER. See:
  Fashionable Lady
  Patroness, The
  Young Bride

HUSBAND, HER PARTNER
  AND. See: Adagio-Bride,
  The

HUSBAND-HUNTERS, TWO,
  seek to win Capitano Adoncino, The Lady and the
  Fool   LADYA

HUSBAND (KING MARK),
  cuckolded by his wife and
  her lover
  WIFE (ISEULT), having affair with Lover (Tristram);
  stabbed by Husband (King
  Mark)
  LOVER (TRISTRAM), having
  affair with Wife (Iseult);
  killed in duel by Husband
  (King Mark)
  CARETAKER (MERLIN),
  takes Husband, Wife and
  Lover back to sixth century
  where they become King
  Mark, Iseult and Tristram
  Picnic at Tintagel PICNI

HUSBAND (KING MARK). See
  also:
  Chauffeur
  Footman
  Knights, Two
  Maid (Brangaene)

HUSBAND, THE
  HUSBAND'S WIFE
  HUSBAND'S DAUGHTER,
  family, overcome terrible
  obstacles, raise cross for
  religious festival in South
  American village
  Hazaña   HAZAN

HUSBAND, THE. See also:
  Bride, The
  Girl, The

Husband
Lady, The
Wife, The

HUSBAND'S CHILDREN. See:
  Lady, The

HUSSAR, THE, apparition; hand-
  some swashbuckler, rival of
  the Poet for the Woman in
  Ball Dress,
  Apparitions   APPAR
  Former lover of the Street
  Dancer, now engaged to the
  Daughter
  Le Beau Danube   BEAUD
  Newly married
  HIS WIFE
  The Widow in the Mirror
                           WIDOW

HUSSAR, THE. See also: Beggar, The

HUSSARS. See:
  Captain of Hussars
  Colonel of Hussars, A

HYDE, ORSON, Mormon apostle
  HIS FIVE WIVES
  Ghost Town   GHOST

HYDRAO. See: King Hydrao

HYDROLA. See: Ondine

HYMEN, god of marriage
  Le Jugement de Paris
                           JUGEM
  Spectacle   SPECL
  Groom
  HERA, bride, suggest to the
  Transgressor "the true powers
  of love"
  Undertow   UNDER

HYMNS. See: Sublime Hymns

HYPERION, father of the family
  THEIA, his wife
  HELIOS, their son
  SELENE, their daughter
  I Titani   TITAN

HYPNOTIST, performer at
theater, puts members of
the audience under his
hypnotic spell
ASSISTANT, terrified by
Hypnotist's performance
FADED BEAUTY
POOR GIRL
RICH MAN
SOLDIER, members of
audience, placed under
Hypnotist's spell, express
their suppressed longings
Noctambules   NOCTA

HYPOCRISY, PERSONIFICATION
OF.   See: Archimago

                I

IAGO, Otello's officer and
enemy
Otello   OTELL
Othello's officer and
enemy
Othello   OTHEL

IAGO. See also: Jago (Iago)

IBARS. See: Baron de Saint
Ibars, The

IBRAHIM, a Russian, The
Bronze Horseman BRONZ

IBRAHIM. See also: Abraham

ICARE (Icarus), attempts to
fly, approaches too near
the sun, plummets to earth
DEDALUS, his father, de-
signer of wings used by his
son
Icare   ICARE

ICAROS, personification of
modern man in space,
Icaros   ICARO

ICE, personification, Les Saisons
SAISO

ICE MAIDEN, THE. See: Solveig

ICE MAIDEN, THE (FAIRY).
See: Bridegroom

IDA, betrothed to Karl
HER PARENTS
Les Métamorphoses METAM

IDEA for new dance, aids the
Choreographer, La Création
CREAI

IDEAL, sought by the Choreographer, La Création
CREAI

IGNACIO. See: Mejias, Ignacio
Sanchez

ILDIKÓ, member of wedding-
party, loved by Csizmás
Janko and Seppi, Little Johnny in Top-Boots   LITTL

ILDIKÓ. See also: Bride, The

IL DOTTORE. See: Prudenza

ILGA, Latvian refugee, falls in
love with Lieutenant
Lauva
HER MOTHER
Ilga   ILGAA

ILKO, young Russian, in love
with Svetlana, Svetlana
SVETL

ILLUSIONIST. See: Louis the
Illusionist

ILLUSTRATED LONDON NEWS,
THE, representation of Bri-
tish newspaper, The Press
PRESS

IMMIGRANT, DYING, "one of
the living," The Great
American Goof   GREAT

IMMIGRANT, THE, lands in
America, sees American
types previously observed
in the cinema, Within the
Quota   WITHI

IMMIGRANT, THE. See also:
Colored Gentleman, The
Cowboy, The
Jazz-Baby, The
Millionairess, The
Puritan, The
Revenue Agent
Sheriff
Social Reformer
Uplifter
World's Sweetheart, The

IMMORTAL, THE. See:
Kostchei

IMPERIALIS, VANESSA, Queen
of Butterfly Land, Les
Papillons   PAPIO

INCREDIBLE FLUTIST, THE.
See: Flutist

INDIA AND CHINA, KING OF.
See: Shahryar

INDIA, KING OF. See: Dushmata

INDIAN, "races the homage of
his people to the Messiah, "
Pastorela   PASTO

INDIAN. See also: Conquered
Indian

INDIAN, HANDSOME. See:
Uirapurú

INDIAN PRINCE. See: East
Indian Prince

INDIAN PRINCE, THE, seeks
hand of the Princess
Aurora in marriage,
The Sleeping Beauty
                         SLEEP

INDIAN PRINCESS, EAST. See:
East Indian Prince

INDIAN, UGLY. See: Uirapurú

INDIANS, American aborigines,
Les Mohicans   MOHIC

INDIANS. See also: Princess
Pocahontas

INDIO, EL. See: Malinche

INDUSTRIAL EXHIBITION. See:
Director of an Industrial
Exhibition

INDUSTRY, See: Genii of
Industry, The

INES. See:
Don Alvar
Doña Ines de Castro

INFANTA OF NAVARRE, THE,
intended bride of Don Pedro,
Doña Ines de Castro DONAI

INFANTA OF NAVARRE, THE.
See also:
Councillor, The
Doña Ines de Castro

INFANTA OF SPAIN, having
birthday, gives Dwarf white
rose
DWARF, dances to amuse Infanta; images himself handsome young man; repulsed by
Infanta; dies
VISION, seen by Dwarf
The White Rose   WHITE

INGRID, daughter of owner of the
Haegstad Farm, seduced by
Peer Gynt, Peer Gynt
                         PEERG

INGRID. See also: Aase

INIGO, chief of a band of gypsies
Paquita   PAQUI

Paquita   PAQUT

INNKEEPER, AN, knights Don
Quixote, Don Quixote
                           DONQX

INNKEEPER, THE, proprietor
of inn where performance
given, Vert-Vert VERTV

INNOCENCE. See:
Angel of Innocence
Lovers-in-Innocence

INNOCENT IVAN
HIS TWO BROTHERS, per-
form Russian dance
The Sleeping Beauty
                           SLEEP

INNOCENT, THE, personification, The Seventh Symphony
                           SEVEN

INTERLOCUTOR, conducts pro-
ceedings at minstrel show;
also appears as Louis the
Illusionist, Cakewalk
                           CAKEW

INTOXICATED GENTLEMAN,
visiting 2222 Club, New
York City, Café Society
                           CAFES

INTRUDER, FIRST. See:
First Intruder

INTRUDER, SECOND. See:
First Intruder

INVENTION. See: Genii of
Invention, The

IOTIS, slave belonging to Ali,
Namouna   NAMOU

IPHIAS, THE, butterfly, Piège
de Lumière   PIEGE

IPHIGENIA, daughter of Agamemnon, Iphigénie en
Aulide   IPHIG

IPHIGENIA. See also: Clytemnestra

IRAS, attendant of Cleopatra,
Queen of Egypt, Les Amours
d'Antoine et de Cléopâtre
                           AMOUR

IRATE SQUIRE, AN. See: Silly
Country Girl

IRIS, goddess, Les Amours de
Jupiter   AMOUJ

IRISH CREW. See: Surveyor of
the Irish Crew

IRMENGARDE. See: Fleur-des-
Champs

ISAAC. See: Lanquedem, Isaac

ISAACS MENKEN, ADAH. See:
"Menken, The"

ISABEAU, pursued by Don Juan
Joan von Zarissa   JOANV
Juan de Zarissa   JUAND

ISABELLA, sweetheart of Cinzio,
Salade   SALAD

ISABELLE, engaged to the Marquis Damis
THE DUCHESS LUCINDE, her
mother
Ruses d'Amour   RUSES

ISABELLE. See also: Marinette

ISAURE. See: Baron Bluebeard

ISCARIOT, JUDAS. See: Traitor

ISEAULT (WIFE). See:
Husband (King Mark)
Knights, Two
Maid (Brangaene)

ISHTAR, Babylonian goddess of
love and fertility
TAMMUZ, her brother and
husband

ERESHKIGAL, Queen of the Underworld
GILGAMESH, Babylonian hero, spurns Ishtar
Ishtar of the Seven Gates
                                    ISHTA

ISIDOR. See: Brown, Isidor

ISIDORE. See: Pirouette, Monsieur

ISIS, Egyptian goddess of motherhood and fertility, Egypta
                                    EGYPT

ISKENDER. See: Péri, The

ISLAND, GOVERNOR OF THE. See: de la Martinière, Monsieur

ISLAND OF TOKYO, KING OF THE. See: Jamato

ISLE OF COS, PASHA OF THE. See: Seyd

ISMAËL, commander of the army; betrothed to Zulma, La Révolte au Sérail
                                    RÉVOL

ISMAIL BEY. See:
Farfalla
Prince Djalma

ISMAILOVA, GALYA, famous ballerina, depicts an incident in her life, Ballerina
                                    BALLX

ISOLDE, Irish princess, loved by Tristan
CHIMERA OF ISOLDE, apparition
Mad Tristan   MADTR

ISRAELITES, KING OF THE. See:
King Saul
Saul

IT WAS SPRING, recalled as a memory by The Lady With Him, Dim Lustre   DIMLU

ITALIAN BALLERINA, CAVALIER TO THE. See: Queen of the Dance

ITALIAN PRINCE, THE, seeks hand of the Princess Aurora in marriage, The Sleeping Beauty   SLEEP

ITALIAN SLAVE, AN, property of Seyd, Le Corsaire
                                    CORSA

IVAN. See:
Innocent Ivan
Prince Ivan
Smouroff
Yvan

IVAN TSAREVICH. See:
Prince Ivan

IVANOUSHKA. See:
Hump-Backed Horse, The
Petr
Tsar-Maiden, The

IZUNA, friend of Princess Daïta, daughter of Jamato, King of the Island of Tokyo, Daïta
                                    DAITA

J

JACK. See: Salt, Jack

JACK OF CLUBS. See: Knave of Clubs

JACK OF DIAMONDS. See: Knave of Diamonds

JACK OF HEARTS. See: Knave of Hearts

JACK OF SPADES. See: Knave of Spades

JACKDAW
  PIGEONS, birds
  The Jackdaw and the Pigeons
                        JACKD

JACOB, a postilion, La Vivandière   VIVAN

JACOPPO BALBI. See:
  Petrucio

JAGO (IAGO), Othello's ensign
  or standard bearer; plots
  against him, The Moor of
  Venice   MOORO

JAGO (IAGO). See also: Iago

JAILER, guards Achmet in
  prison
  La Péri   PERII
  Guards Count Raoul de
  Créqui's imprisoned family
  ALINE, his son
  Raoul de Créqui   RAOUL

JAILER, THE, seen by Young
  Musician in his dream,
  Symphonie Fantastique
                        SYMPH

JAILERS, THREE, imprison
  Danaë Les Amours de
  Jupiter   AMOUJ

JAMATO, King of the Island of
  Tokyo
  PRINCESS DAÏTA, his
  daughter, charmed by reed
  pipe music of Nao-Shiko
  PRINCESS DAÏTA's NURSE
  Daïta   DAITA

JAMATO. See also:
  Izuna
  Kwannon

JAMES. See: Reuben, James

JANETTA, servant to Count
  Frédéric; Simplice's sweetheart, Le Diable Amoureux
                        DIABL

JANIK, a beggar-boy, La Korrigane   KORRI

JANKO. See: Csizmás Janko

JANUARY, a merchant, Twelve
  for the Mail-Coach   TWELV

JAPAN, EMPEROR OF. See:
  Nightingale, Mechanical
  Nightingale, The

JAPAN, RULER OF. See:
  Mikado, The

JAPANESE, met by the Farm
  Boy on his travels, Yankee
  Clipper   YANKE

JASEION, attends feast of Bacchus,
  Sylvia   SYLVA

JASEION. See also: Jason

JASMIN, officer of the guard,
  Cinderella   CINDA

JASON, a colored servant
  Loin du Danemark   LOIND
  Argonaut, loved by Médée,
  jilts her
  Médée et Jason   MEDEE
  Argonaut
  Spectacle   SPECL

JASON. See also:
  Adventurer
  Creusa
  Jaseion
  Medea
  Médée
  Victim

JASPER, potboy at "The Steam
  Packet," Portsmouth, Eng-
  land; in love with Pineapple
  Poll, Pineapple Poll PINEA

JAVOTTE, peasant girl, in love
  with Jean
  HER FATHER
  HER MOTHER
  Javotte   JAVOT

JAZZ, representation of jazz
music, engages in contest
for supremacy with Clas-
sic, Rhapsody in Blue
                        RHAPS

JAZZ.   See also: Barman

JAZZ-BABY, THE, American
type, seen by The Immi-
grant, Within the Quota
                        WITHI

JAZZ DANCER, performs
"lyrical jazz journey
danced to whistled accom-
paniment, " Ballad in a
Popular Style   BALLP

JEAFRE, overseer of Don
Alonzo's plantation, in
love with Danina; attempts
to kidnap Sabi, her five-
year-old son, foiled by
Joko, Danina   DANIN

JEAN, a peasant, in love with
Javotte
Javotte   JAVOT
A smuggler
Kalkabrino   KALKA

JEAN.   See also:
Brienne, Jean de
Clara
Julie, Miss

JEAN, PETIT. See: Mathurin

JEANNE, a cook
ASSISTANT COOKS
Cinderella   CINDL

JEANNE. See also:
d'Arc, Jeanne
Gaspard

JENNY. See:
Edda
Lind, Jenny

JEROME, resident of Marseille;
French revolutionist, The

Flames of Paris   FLAME

JESSE, Israelite
ELIAB
ABINADAB
SHAMMAH, his son
DAVID, his son, kills Go-
liath
FOUR YOUNGER SONS
David   DAVID

JESSE. See also:
Abishai
David

JESTER, THE, to the Prince
Cinderella   CINDE
Clown
Juan de Zarissa   JUAND
Reads Oriane's future with
cards
Oriane et le Prince d'Amour
                     ORIAN

JESTER, THE CHIEF
JESTERS, participate in
merrymaking
Don Juan   DONJU

JEWEL. See: Bundren, Addie

JEWELLER, A, helps Cinderella's
two ugly stepsisters prepare
for ball, Cinderella CINDE

JIM. See: Della

JINX, circus performer, thought
by other performers to bring
bad luck, Jinx   JINXX

JINX. See also: Ringmaster

JOAN OF ARC. See:
d'Arc, Jeanne
Saint Joan

JOB, Biblical character, tested
by Satan
HIS WIFE
HIS THREE DAUGHTERS
HIS SEVEN SONS
HIS SPIRITUAL SELF

<u>Job</u>   JOBBB

JOB. See also:
    Durfort, Sergeant
    Elihu

JOBIN, a seneschal, <u>La
    Filleule des Fées</u> FILLU

JOCASTA. See: Oedipus

JOCKEY, THE, hopes to profit
    from the Rake's recently
    inherited wealth, <u>The Rake's
    Progress   RAKES</u>

JOHN. See:
    Allen Barbara
    Bull, John
    Paul
    Philemon
    Rolfe, John
    Witches, Two Young

JOHN GYNT. See: Aase

JOHN SMITH, CAPTAIN. See:
    Rolfe, John

JOHN THE BAPTIST, "comes
    to purge the sin-ridden
    palace of King Herod," be-
    headed at the request of
    Salomé
    Salomé   SALOM
    <u>La Tragédie de Salomé</u>
                          TRAGD
    <u>La Tragédie de Salomé</u>
                          TRAGE
    <u>La Tragédie de Salomé</u>
                          TRAGG
    <u>La Tragédie de Salomé</u>
                          TRAGH
    <u>La Tragédie de Salomé</u>
                          TRAGI

JOHNNY, Frankie's sweetheart,
    killed by her for making
    love to Nellie, <u>Frankie and
    Johnny   FRANK</u>

JOHNNY. See also: Bartender

JOHNNY IN TOP-BOOTS, LITTLE.
    See: Csizmás Janko

JOKER, wild playing card, par-
    ticipates in poker game,
    <u>Card Game</u>   CARDG

JOKO, Brazilian ape, saves Sabi,
    five-year-old son of Danina,
    from kidnap attempt by
    Jeafre, <u>Danina</u>   DANIN

JONATHAN. See: Saul, King
    of the Israelites

JONES. See: Emperor Jones

JONGLEUR, THE, sings song
    celebrating Oriane's dance,
    <u>Oriane et le Prince d'Amour</u>
                          ORIAN

JOSÉ, Loyalist officer, loves and
    loved by Micaela, attracted
    to Carmen; Escamillo's rival
    for Carmen, <u>Guns and Cas-
    tanets   GUNSA</u>

JOSÉ. See also:
    Don José
    Don José Cavallines

JOSEPH, Biblical character
    MARIA (MARY), his wife,
    mother of Christ
    <u>Bibliska Bilder</u>   BIBLI
    Illiterate soldier, gives up
    his violin, "the instrument
    that speaks like his own
    heart," to the Devil
    THE DEVIL, appears in
    several disguises, persuades
    Joseph to trade his violin
    for "a book of great value"
    THE PRINCESS, cured of
    illness by Joseph
    <u>L'Histoire du Soldat</u> HISTO
    Shepherd boy, falsely ac-
    cused of attempting to se-
    duce Potiphar's wife
    <u>Josephslegende</u>   JOSEL
    <u>Joseph the Beautiful</u> JOSEP

Purchased from Sheik by
Potiphar; attracts the lat-
ter's wife, saved by Arch-
angel
La Legende de Joseph
LEGEN

JOSEPH. See also: Potiphar

JOSEPHINA, favorite pupil of
Rigadon; loved by Count
Anselmi, Scuola di Ballo
SCUOL

JOSEPHINE, gate crasher at
the wedding; friend of
Julia; gets drunk, A Wed-
ding Bouquet   WEDDI

JOSEPHINE. See also:
Julia
Paul

JOURDAIN, MONSIEUR, newly
rich member of middle
classes, ashamed of his
origin; wishes his daughter
to marry a nobleman
LUCILE, his daughter, has
no pretensions of grandeur;
in love with Cléonte
CLÉONTE, young man, in
love with Lucile
Le Bourgeois Gentilhomme
BOURE
Le Bourgeois Gentilhomme
BOURG

JOURNALISTS, passing through
metropolitan railroad
terminal, Terminal
TERMI

JOURNALISTS, TWO, compete
for news concerning Tom
Tug and W. Brown, The
Triumph of Neptune
TRIUM

JOVITA CAVALLINES. See:
Don Alvar
Don José Cavallines

JUAN. See: Don Juan

JUANA. See: Don Quixote

JUDAS ISCARIOT. See: Traitor

JUDGE, THE, sitting on murder
case
Hear Ye! Hear Ye! HEARY
Sentences Luc to death,
forced to dance through
power of magic flute
The Magic Flute   MAGIC

JUDITH, Israelite girl, delivers
her people by killing Holofernes
YOUNG JUDITH, Judith at
an earlier age
HOLOFERNES, general of
invading army
Legend of Judith   LEGEJ

JUDY, character in Punch and
Judy show
MOTHER of Child, becomes
associated with Judy in
Child's mind
Punch and the Child PUNCH
Traditional comic puppet fig-
ure
Punch and the Judy PUNCJ

JUGGLERS, circus performers,
The Incredible Flutist
INCRE

JULIA, forlorn young lady,
abandoned by the Bride-
groom; friend of Josephine,
A Wedding Bouquet WEDDI

JULIA. See also:
Cesarius
Josephine
Pépé

JULIAS. See:
Julies, Miss
Julius

JULIE, MISS, young girl, rest-

less, seduced by Jean; sui-
cide
THE COUNT, her father
JULIAS, her fiance, se-
lected for her by her father
JEAN, butler to the Count
Miss Julie   MISSJ

JULIE, MISS. See also:
Clara
Kristin

JULIEN, a country boy, meets
the Young Chatelaine, falls
in love with her
THE YOUNG CHATELAINE,
noblewoman, betrothed to
the Young Nobleman
THE YOUNG NOBLEMAN,
her fiance
La Fête Étrange   FETEE

JULIET. See:
Capulet
Laurence, Friar
Nurse
Old Capulet
Paris
Romeo

JULIETTE, friend of Blondelaine, Scaramouche
                  SCARA

JULIUS. See:
Caesar, Julius
Julias
Silanus, Julius

JULY. See: June

JUNE, a young woman and her
sweetheart
JULY, her brother
Twelve for the Mail-Coach
                  TWELV

JUNIOR, American vaudeville
dancer, finds himself
member of Russian ballet
company managed by Sergei
Alexandrovitch; falls in
love with Strip Teaser,

Slaughter on Tenth Avenue
                  SLAUG

JUNIOR CADETS. See: Leader
of the Junior Cadets

JUNIOR GIRLS. See: Leader of
the Junior Girls

JUNO, goddess, wife of Jupiter
Les Amours de Jupiter
                  AMOUJ
Aging entertainer, dances
for Paris in boîte de nuit,
afterwards picks his pockets
The Judgment of Paris
                  JUDGM

JUPITER, god, rapes Europa
Abraxas   ABRAX
God, woos Europa, Leda and
Danaë, carries Ganymede
away
Les Amours de Jupiter
                  AMOUJ
God
Ballet Comique de la Reine
                  BALLC
God, banishes Hebe to Earth
The Descent of Hebe DESCE
Celestial body
The Stars   STARS
God
I Titani   TITAN

JUPITER. See also:
Eagle, The
Juno
Leda
Shower of Gold
Swan
Taurus
Titans

JURY. See: Speaker for the
Jury

K

KADDISH, THE OLD. See:
Abdurassul, Bey

KADOOR. See: Nal

KAFUR, Prime Minister of
Thule; friend of Meuhor,
enemy of Harold, King of
Thule, Sieba   SIEBA

KALAF. See:
Caliph
Princess Turandot

KALKABRINO, a smuggler,
loved by Cigala, infatuated
by Marietta, overcome by
Draginiatza, Kalkabrino
KALKA

KALKABRINO. See also:
Monk, A

KANGAROO, animal, Carnival
of Animals   CARNV

KANGAROU, MR., marriage-
broker, Madame Chrysan-
thème   MADAM

KANU. See: Sakuntala

KARL, student, betrothed to
Ida, "passes the bounds
of hallowed knowledge,"
tricked by The Sprite
HIS PARENTS
Les Métamorphoses
METAM

KARL MARX. See: Student
of Karl Marx, A

KARLL, fiance of Bettemberg's
daughter Henriette,
Nathalie   NATHA

KATERINA, parlor-maid and
première danseuse of the
Serfs' Theatre; friend of
Vladimir, Katerina
KATER

KATERINA. See also: Danila

KATHI, a vivandière
BIBERMANN, her guardian,
a tavern-keeper

HANS, Bibermann's son
La Vivandière   VIVAN

KATUSHA. See: Zoshka

KEEPER OF THE PYRAMIDS,
shows Lord Wilson mummy
of the Pharaoh's daughter,
La Fille du Pharaon FILLP

KEEPER OF THE PYRAMIDS.
See also: Mummy of the
Pharaoh's Daughter

KEEPERS. See: Telescope
Keepers

KHADRA, "a child of the East,"
learns of the beauties of the
outside world
TWO LOVERS, seen by
Khadra in the outside world
Khadra   KHADR

KHAÏNITZA, Moorish slave, captivates Kitzos, Namouna
NAMOU

KHAN, THE, purchases the Hump-
Backed Horse
HIS FAVORITE WIFE
The Hump-Backed Horse
HUMPB
The Hump-Backed Horse
HUMPH
Despot, banishes his wife
and daughter from his palace
HIS WIFE
GYULYANAK, his daughter
The Maiden's Tower MAIDE
Oriental potentate, taken
with Nouredda, dismisses
his harem
La Source   SOURC

KHAN, THE. See also:
Dadje
Kzelkia
Nouredda
Sindjar
Tsar-Maiden, The

KHIVRIA, witch, lover of Red

Coat
PARASSIA, her step-
daughter, in love with
Gritzko
The Fair at Sorochinsk
                                    FAIRA

KHIVRIA. See also:
Mayor of Sorochinsk
Sexton

KID, BILLY THE. See:
Alias
Billy the Kid
Cowboy in Red
Garrett, Pat

KID, THE, Negro street ur-
chin, loses his kite
THE PARROT, The Kid's
kite, returns to him transformed
Papagaio do Moleque
                                    PAPAG

KIJE, LIEUTENANT, Russian
soldier, created when army
clerk enters his name on
orders by mistake
Lieutenant Kije   LIEUT
Russian soldier, dying on
battlefield
Russian Soldier   RUSSI

KIJE, LIEUTENANT. See also:
Death
Emperor Paul I, Emperor
of Russia

KIKIMORA, a witch; embodiment
of wickedness
THE CAT, her protector
Contes Russes   CONTE

KING, playing card, participates in poker game, Card
Game   CARDG

KING. See also:
Black King
Comstock, Bonanza King
King, The
Little King, The

Péri, The
Poet
Red King, The
Sun King, The
Troll King, The

KING ANDREW II, King of Hungary, Raymonda   RAYMO

KING BANANA, personification,
H. P.   HPPPP

KING BOBICHE, ruler of a
mythical kingdom, disposes
of new new-born daughter
because she is not a boy
QUEEN CLEMENTINE, his
fickle wife
FLORETTA (PRINCESS HER-
MILIA), his daughter, falls
in love with Prince Sapphire
Bluebeard   BLUEB

KING BOBICHE. See also:
Alvarez
Count Oscar

KING CHARLES II, King of Eng-
land. See:
Lord Campbell
Prince Charles

KING DONDON, fat, foolish king,
given the Golden Cockerel
(Le Coq d'Or) by the Astrolo-
ger; marries Queen of She-
makha
PRINCE GUIDON
PRINCE APHRON, his sons
Le Coq d'Or   COQDO

KING DONSON. See also:
Amelpha
Golden Cockerel, The
Polkan, General

KING EDWARD IV, King of England, The Press   PRESS

KING FLORESTAN XXIV. See:
Cantalbutte
Princess Aurora, The

KING HADES, King of the Underworld, Clytemnestra
CLYTE

KING HADES. See also: King
of Hades

KING HEART, "engaging in an
Edwardian romp at a
French plage, " Les Sirènes
SIREN

KING HENRY VIII, King of
England
ANNE BOLEYN, his wife
Henry VIII   HENRY

KING HEROD. See:
John the Baptist
Salomé

KING HYDRAO, seen by Vis-
count de Beaugency in
dream, Le Pavillon d'
Armide   PAVIL

KING LEAR. See: Lear

KING LOUIS II, representation
of the mad King Ludwig of
Bavaria, Bacchanale
BACCH

KING LOUIS XIV, King of
France, Camargo CAMAR

KING LOUIS XVI, King of
France
QUEEN MARIE ANTOINETTE,
his wife
The Flames of Paris
FLAME

KING LUDWIG OF BAVARIA.
See: King Louis II

KING MARK. See: Husband
(King Mark)

KING MENELAUS, King of
Sparta, fat and senile
HELEN (Helen of Troy),
his young and beautiful

wife; given to Paris by Aphrodite in return for Paris' de-
claring her winner in beauty
contest over Hera and Pallas
Athena
Helen of Troy   HELEN

KING MENELAUS. See also:
Orestes

KING MIDAS, King of Phrygia;
"all that he touched turned
to gold"
Midas   MIDAS
The Triumph of Bacchus
and Ariadne   TRIUB

KING MINOS. See: Ariadne

KING OF ARGOS. See: Clytemnestra

KING OF BRITAIN. See: Lear

KING OF BUCHARIA. See:
Aliris

KING OF CANNIBALS. See:
Black King

KING OF CORINTH. See: Sisyphus

KING OF CRETE. See: Minos

KING OF DAHOMEY. See: Tulip

KING OF DELHI. See: Dama-
yanti

KING OF DENMARK. See:
Hamlet, Prince of Denmark
Lodbrok, Regnar

KING OF DIAMONDS, THE.
See: Queen of Clubs, The

KING OF EGYPT. See: Aspicia

KING OF ENGLAND. See:
King Edward IV, King of
England
King Henry VIII, King of

England
Lord Campbell
Prince Charles

KING OF FRANCE, appoints
Monsieur de Bougainville
to command expedition to
South Seas, Ozaï OZAII

KING OF FRANCE. See also:
King Louis XIV
King Louis XVI

KING OF GRANADA. See:
Mahomet

KING OF HADES. See:
King Hades
Persephone, Queen of
Hades

KING OF HUNGARY. See:
King Andrew II

KING OF INDIA. See: Dushmata

KING OF INDIA AND CHINA.
See: Shahryar

KING OF LYDIA. See: Candaules

KING OF NUBIA, THE, at-
tracted to Aspicia, wishes
to marry her, La Fille
du Pharaon   FILLP

KING OF PHRYGIA. See:
King Midas

KING OF PORTUGAL, THE.
See: Doña Ines de Castro

KING OF SNOW
QUEEN OF SNOW, rulers
of the Kingdom of Sweets
The Nutcracker   NUTCA
The Nutcracker   NUTCK
The Nutcracker   NUTCR

KING OF SPADES, THE.
See: Queen of Clubs, The

KING OF SPAIN, THE, ruler,
La Fille de Marbre FILLM

KING OF SPARTA. See: King
Menelaus

KING OF THE CORALS, engages
in combat with the Genii of
the Earth for the White Pearl;
loses, The Beautiful Pearl
BEAUT

KING OF THE DANDIES, THE,
wins the First Hand from the
Artist, Le Beau Danube
BEAUD

KING OF THE FAIRIES. See:
Oberon

KING OF THE GHOULS, THE,
lures the Bridegroom away
from the Bride, The Bells
BELLS

KING OF THE GNOMES, THE,
ruler
THE QUEEN, his wife
TOPAZZA, their daughter,
discovered by Flik and Flok
Flik and Flok   FLIKA

KING OF THE ISLAND OF TOKYO.
See: Jamato

KING OF THE ISRAELITES. See:
King Saul
Saul

KING OF THE MICE, engages
Nutcracker and his troops in
battle, killed by Clara
(Masha)
The Nutcracker   NUTCA
The Nutcracker   NUTCK
The Nutcracker   NUTCR

KING OF THE MICE. See also:
President

KING OF THE NILE, restores
Aspicia to life, La Fille du
Pharaon   FILLP

KING OF THE OGRES, super-
   natural being, saws W.
   Brown in half, The Triumph
   of Neptune   TRIUM

KING OF THE SEA.   See:
   Poseidon

KING OF THE SNAKE PIT, inmate of the Logéat Mental
   Hospital, Les Algues
                ALGUE

KING OF THE UNDERWORLD.
   See: King Hades

KING OF THE WATERS.   See:
   Coralia
   Tirrenio

KING OF THEBES.   See:
   Creon
   Oedipus

KING OF THESSALY.   See:
   Alcestis

KING OF THULE.   See:
   Harold

KING POWHATAN.   See:
   Princess Pocahontas

KING PRIAM.   See: Cassandra

KING SAUL, King of the Israelites
   MELCHOLA, his daughter,
   in love with David
   David Triomphant DAVIT

KING SAUL.   See also:
   Saul, King of the Israelites
   Sorceress, The

KING, THE, saved from Death
   by Donald
   Donald of the Burthens
              DONAL
   Madman in a London mad-
   house
   The Rake's Progress
              RAKES

   Wears suit of invisible
   clothes made for him by
   the Three Tailors
   THE QUEEN, his wife
   THE QUEEN'S LOVER
   Le Roi Nu   ROINU
   Le Roi Nu   ROINV

KING, THE.   See also:
   King
   Ladies in Waiting
   Ministers, The Three
   Prince Charming
   Princess, The
   Tailors, The Three

KING, THE FAIRY.   See: Fairy
   Queen, The

KING, THE TROLL.   See: Troll
   King, The

KINGDOM, EMPEROR OF THE
   MIDDLE.   See: Princess
   Belle Épine

KIRSTINE, MRS.   See: Birthe,
   Miss

KITRI, in love with Basil, thought
   by Don Quixote to be the Lady
   Dulcinea; loved by Gamache
   LORENZO, her father, an
   innkeeper
   Don Quichotte   DONQU

KITRI.   See also: Lorenzo, Aldonza

KITTY.   See: Countess Kitty

KITZOS, soldier, captivated by
   the Moorish slave Khaïnitza,
   Namouna   NAMOU

KNAVE OF CLUBS, playing card,
   participates in poker game,
   Card Game   CARDG

KNAVE OF DIAMONDS, playing
   card, participates in poker
   game, Card Game   CARDG

KNAVE OF HEARTS, playing
card, participates in poker
game, Card Game CARDG

KNAVE OF SPADES, playing
card, participates in poker
game, Card Game CARDG

KNIGHT. See:
First Red Knight
Knight, The

KNIGHT-ERRANT, THE, meets
the Princess; later wins
joust, wins Princess' hand,
Le Chevalier et la Damoi-
selle   CHEVA

KNIGHT OF DEATH, "a large,
black, perambulating um-
brella"
HIS SUITE, "two men
wrapped in opposite ends
of a winding sheet"
Bacchanale   BACCH

KNIGHT OF THE SILVER
MOON. See: Carrasco,
Bachelor Sampson

KNIGHT RENSHI, THE, comes
to the aid of Count Raoul
de Crêqui, Raoul de Crêqui
                    RAOUL

KNIGHT, SECOND RED. See:
First Red Knight

KNIGHT, THE
HIS TWO SQUIRES, en-
counter Francesco Berna-
done (St. Francis), urge
him to pursue military
career
Saint Francis   SAINT

KNIGHT, THE. See also:
Knight
Prince, The
Unicorn

KNIGHT, THE RED-CROSS.
See: Sir Lancelot

KNIGHTS. See: Black Knights

KNIGHTS, TWO, minions of
Husband (King Mark), spy on
Wife (Iseult) and Lover (Tris-
tram), Picnic at Tintagel
                    PICNI

KODEH. See: Kwahu

KOKLUSH. See: Prince Koklush

KOLIA, Russian schoolboy, Baby
Stork   BABYS

KÖNNYELMÜ (Lighthearted),
shepherd, The Holy Torch
                    HOLYT

KOROLEVICH, BOVA, Russian
knight, saves the Swan Princess from three-headed
dragon, Contes Russes
                    CONTE

KORRIGANES. See: Queen of
the Korriganes

KOSTCHEI, "The Immortal,"
evil magician, killed by
Prince Ivan
Firebird   FIREB
Firebird   FIRED
Firebird   FIREI

KOSTCHEI. See also: Tsarevna,
The Beautiful

KOUM. See: Oksana

KOUM'S WIFE. See: Oksana

KOWALSKI, STANLEY. See:
du Bois, Blanche

KOWALSKI, STELLA. See: du
Bois, Blanche

KOZAKOV, commander of Red
Army Border Patrol; saves
Gayne from her husband;
falls in love with her,
Gayne   GAYNE

KRISTIN, cook for the Count,
father of Miss Julie, Miss
Julie   MISSJ

KRĪVS, THE, Latvian priest,
Le Triomphe de l'Amour
                               TRIOM

KURUC LIEUTENANT, THE,
loves and loved by The
Daughter, Kuruc Fairy
Tale   KURUC

KWAHU (The Eagle), Hopi In-
dian youth, in love with
Kodeh
KODEH, daughter of Hopi
Indian chief
THE OLD CRONE, Hopi
Indian woman
The Feather of the Dawn
                               FEATH

KWANNON, goddess of love and
beauty, unites Princess
Daita and Nao-Shiko, Daita
                               DAITA

KYRAM, BEN, Algerian mer-
chant, The Blood-Red
Flower   BLOOD

KZELKIA, Circassian girl,
falls in love with Rostislav
THE KHAN, her guardian
Prisoner of the Caucasus
                               PRISN
The Prisoner in the Caucasus
                               PRISO

L

LABANC SUITOR, THE, se-
lected as the Daughter's
future husband by her
family, Kuruc Fairy Tale
                               KURUC

LA BIEN-AIMÉE. See:
Poet, The

LA BOLERO. See: Bolero,
La

LABROSSE, scenic artist at the
opera house, The Débutante
                               DEBUT

LA CAPRICCIOSA. See: Capricciosa, La

LA CHASSE. See: Chasse, La

LA CROQUEUSE. See: Cro-
queuse, La

LADIES. See:
Maiden Ladies Out Walking
Waltzing Ladies and Their
Partners

LADIES, HER FOUR. See:
Princess Teaflower

LADIES IN WAITING, to the
Queen
Le Roi Nu   ROINU
Le Roi Nu   ROINV

LADIES IN WAITING. See also:
King, The

LADIES IN WAITING, THE
THE MAIDS, attendants on
the Princess
A Spring Tale   SPRIN

LADIES OF THE TOWN, carouse
with the Rake in a brothel,
The Rake's Progress
                       RAKES

LADIES, TWO. See: Nobleman

LADISLAV. See: Slivovitz,
Ladislav

LADY. See:
Fashionable Lady
Hokinson Lady
Lady, The
Light Lady, The
Society Lady

LADY, A
GENTLEMAN, A, attend gas-
attack precautions course

Perhaps Tomorrow!
                    PERHA

LADY, BEARDED. See:
     Jinx
     Ringmaster

LADY BELERMA, THE. See:
     Durandarte

LADY CAPULET. See:
     Capulet
     Old Capulet

LADY CASTLEREAGH. See:
     Lord Castlereagh

LADY CLARA, maid of honor,
     Betty   BETTY

LADY DULCINEA, THE. See:
     Kitri
     Lorenzo, Aldonza

LADY EMPIRE. See: Lord
     Empire

LADY FRIEND, PERSONAGE'S.
     See: Personage, A

LADY FROM VIENNA. See:
     Young Lady from Vienna,
     A

LADY GAY, THE, sexy dance-
     hall girl, sought by Sur-
     veyor of the Irish Crew
     and Surveyor of the Chi-
     nese Crew, Union Pacific
                         UNION

LADY KNOWN AS LOU, THE.
     See: McGrew, Dan

LADY MONTAGUE. See:
     Montague

LADY OF SHALOTT, THE,
     condemned to watch the
     world only through re-
     flections in her mirror;
     violates her curse when
     she looks at Sir Lancelot;

dies
HER REFLECTION
The Lady of Shalott LADYO

LADY OF SHALOTT, THE. See
     also:
     Lovers, The
     Reapers, The
     Sir Lancelot

LADY OF THE CAMELLIAS,
     THE. See: Gautier, Mar-
     guerite

LADY, OLD. See: Old Man

LADY REWENA. See: Lord
     Rewena

LADY, STRONG. See:
     Jinx
     Ringmaster

LADY, TATTOOED. See:
     Jinx
     Ringmaster

LADY, THE, many times widowed
     bored with her present hus-
     band
     THE HUSBAND, challenges
     the Seducer to a duel, dies
     of fright
     THE SEDUCER, attracted to
     the Lady, insults the Husband,
     accepts challenge to duel
     Deuil en 24 Heures DEUIL
     Young girl, torn between
     Sailor (Stranger) and the
     Husband; marries the latter
     THE HUSBAND, widower,
     kind but stolid
     HUSBAND'S CHILDREN, by
     a former marriage
     SAILOR (STRANGER), former
     lover of the Lady; deserted
     her years before
     Lady From the Sea LADYE
     Lady From the Sea LADYF
     Temporarily taken with the
     Student; demands from him
     a blood-red rose
     Le Rossignol et la Rose

ROSSG
Le Rossignol et la Rose
ROSSI

LADY, THE.   See also:
Comus
Lady
Rose, The
Unicorn

LADY, THE WHITE.   See:
Raymonda

LADY WITH HIM, THE
THE GENTLEMAN WITH
HER, couple at dance,
presumably attracted to
each other; are reminded
of incidents from their
pasts
A REFLECTION, image of
The Lady With Him
ANOTHER REFLECTION,
image of The Gentleman
With Her
Dim Lustre   DIMLU

LADY WITH HIM, THE.   See
also:
He Wore a White Tie
It Was Spring

LADYBIRD, resident of Butterfly Land, Les Papillons
PAPIO

LADY'S TWO BROTHERS, THE.
See: Comus

LAERTES.   See:
Ophelia
Polonius

LA ESMERALDA.   See: Es-
meralda, La

LA FAVORITA.   See: Favorita, La

LAFE.   See: Bundren, Addie

LAGERTHA.   See: Lodbrok,
Regnar, King of Denmark

LA GITANA.   See: Gitana, La

LA GLOIRE.   See:
Aspirant, The
Gloire, La
Ophelia
Tarquinius, Sextus

LAGOON.   See: Venetian Lagoon

LA GOULUE.   See: Goulue, La

LA GUIABLESSE.   See: Guiablesse, La

LA GUIMARD.   See:
Bougainville, Monsieur de
Guimard, La

LAHORE, MAHARAJAH OF.
See: Noureddin

LAIDERETTE, "the Little Ugly
One, " wretched girl from
the streets, attends masked
ball
RICH YOUNG MAN, momen-
tarily attracted by Laiderette
Laiderette   LAIDE

LALANDA, a famous matador,
in love with La Macarena;
wins her with gift of a
shawl
LA MACARENA, dancer,
"the idol of all Seville"
Cuadro Flamenco   CUADR

LALLA ROOKH.   See:
Alaris, King of Bucharia
Emperor Aurungzebe, The,
Emperor of Hindustan

LA MACARENA.   See: Lalanda

LA MALINCHE.   See: Malinche

LAMB, pet animal belonging to
Paris; coveted by Calchas,
Helen of Troy   HELEN

LAMB.   See also: Ajax I

LAMMON, an old shepherd, Daphnis et Chloë   DAPHN

LA MÔME.   See: Fromage, La Môme

LAMPLIGHTER, at Belvedere Gardens, Vienna; attracts the Flirt, Voices of Spring   VOICE

LANCELOT.   See: Angelic Apparition Sir Lancelot

LANCERS.   See: Cornet of Lancers Officer of Lancers

LAND, QUEEN OF BUTTERFLY. See: Imperialis, Vanessa

LANDLADY OF THE TAVERN, proprietress of tavern in small European village, Coppélia   COPPE

LANQUEDEM, ISAAC, owner of a bazaar at Adrianople, Le Corsaire   CORSA

LARA, defeated in combat by Emazor, Alma   ALMAO

LARA.   See also: Laura

LARGO.   See: Allegretto

LARS, servant of Philemon, Vieux Souvenirs   VIEUX

LAS BASTOÑERAS.   See: Niña del Oro, La

LA SYLPHIDE.   See: Sylphide, La

LAUNDRESSES.   See: Young Apprentice

LAURA.   See: Lara Valentine

LAURENCE, FRIAR, churchman, performs marriage ceremony of Romeo and Juliet, Romeo and Juliet   ROMEO

LAURENCE, FRIAR.   See also: Capulet Montague

LAURENCIA, Castilian village girl, raises her fellow-villagers against the Commendatore COMMENDATORE, tyrant, killed in battle by Frondozo FRONDOZO, betrothed to Laurencia Laurencia   LAURE

LAURETTA, loved by Luigi, marries Doctor Omeopatico MATHEA, her mother, postmistress, wishes her daughter to marry for money La Tarentule   TAREN

LAURETTA.   See also: Duke of Medina-Celi, The Mina Omeopatico, Doctor Parembo Sacristan, The Smouroff

LAUVA, LIEUTENANT, Latvian officer, falls in love with Ilga, helps her return to her homeland THE COMMANDANT, his commanding officer Ilga   ILGAA

LAWYER, A, gives Ozaï gift of bouquet, scent and sweets, Ozaï   OZAII

LAWYERS, THREE, represent Mr. Taylor in legal matters, The Prospect Before Us   PROSP

LEADER.   See: Bear-Leader

Enemy Leader, The
Hopak Leader
Traitor

LEADER OF THE BACCHANTES
BACCHANTES, pleasure-
seeking women "who have
not known love"; destroy
Orpheus
Orpheus   ORPHE

LEADER OF THE BAND of
Circassians, holds Bakhmetiev prisoner, The Prisoner
in the Caucasus   PRISR

LEADER OF THE BASMACH.
See: Radzhab

LEADER OF BLACK GROUP.
See: Destiny

LEADER OF BLUE GROUP
BLUE GROUP, personifica-
tions of evil forces
Rouge et Noir   ROUGE

LEADER OF THE CANCAN
GIRLS. See: Dance Master

LEADER OF THE CONVICTS
THE YOUNG CONVICT
THE BLACKSMITH, convict
CONVICTS, escapees from
penal colony
Piège de Lumière PIEGE

LEADER OF THE FURIES
FURIES, inhabitants of the
Underworld
Orpheus   ORPHE
Orpheus and Eurydice
                               ORPHU

LEADER OF THE JUNIOR
CADETS
JUNIOR CADETS, attend
graduation ball at fashion-
able girls' school in Vienna
Graduation Ball   GRADU

LEADER OF THE JUNIOR
CADETS. See also: Old

General, The

LEADER OF THE JUNIOR GIRLS
JUNIOR GIRLS, attend graduation ball at fashionable girls'
school in Vienna
Graduation Ball   GRADU

LEADER OF THE MUSES. See:
Apollo

LEADER OF RED GROUP (TOWN)
RED GROUP, personifica-
tions of evil forces
Rouge et Noir   ROUGE

LEADER OF THE SALAMANDERS.
See: Belphegor

LEADER OF YELLOW GROUP
(COUNTRY)
YELLOW GROUP, personi-
fications of evil forces
Rouge et Noir   ROUGE

LEADER, THE, personification
of dictatorship, The Green
Table   GREEN

LEAF-MAIDENS, THE, seen by
the Princess in her dream,
A Spring Tale   SPRIN

LEAF, THE, personification,
The Leaf and the Wind
                               LEAFA

LEANDRE, elderly suitor to
Colombine; outwitted by
Harlequin, Harlequinade
                               HARLI

LEAR, King of Britain, goes mad
GONERIL
REGAN
CORDELIA, his daughters
THE FOOL, "sinister intro-
ducer to Lear's hallucina-
tions"
Sundered Majesty   SUNDE

LE COQ D'OR. See: Golden
Cockerel, The

LE CORSAIRE. See: Cor-
    saire, Le

LEDA, wooed by Jupiter in
    the form of a swan
    Les Amours de Jupiter
                        AMOUJ
    Performs dance with swan
    Bacchanale   BACCH
    Queen, once knew Jupiter
    as a swan
    CASTOR
    POLLUX, her twin sons,
    protectors of sailors
    Castor et Pollux CASTO

LEDA. See also: Swan

LEE, ANNABEL, young girl,
    dies, buried by the sea
    HER LOVER, rests beside
    her, drowned as he sleeps
    HER HIGHBORN KINSMEN
    Annabel Lee   ANNAB

LEE, ANNABEL. See also:
    Death

LEFORT, minister and confi-
    dant to Peter I, Tsar of
    Russia, Gli Strelizzi
                        STREL

LEGATION. See:
    Dutch Legation
    Tyrolian Legation

LEILA, friend of Farfalla, Le
    Papillon   PAPIL

LEILA. See also:
    Nourmahal
    Pasha, The
    Péri, The

LEILO. See: Blondelaine

LENNY, colored boy, killed
    by white people
    SARIE, white girl, loves
    and loved by Lenny, also
    killed by white people who
    oppose their love

The Path of Thunder
                        PATHO

LENNY. See also: Curley's
    Wife

LEO. See: Young Man, The

LÉON. See: Saint-Léon, Arthur
    Michel

LEONARDO. See:
    Count Leonardo
    Felicita
    Wife, The

LEONORA, loved by Count di
    Luna and by Manrico; in
    love with Manrico, Revanche
                        REVAN

LEOPARD, overcome by Tariel,
    Chota Roustaveli   CHOTA

LEPIDOPTERIST, visits park
    GIRLS, encountered in park
    Promenade   PROMN

LE RENARD. See: Fox, The
    (Le Renard)

LESSAU. See: Louis the Illu-
    sionist

LES SYLPHIDES. See: Syl-
    phides, Les

LETIKA, mate of ship captained
    by Grey
    LETIKA'S FIANCEE
    Red Sails   REDSA

LETO. See:
    Apollo
    Nymphs, Two

L'ETOILE, ballerina, rehearsing
    ballet dance, Foyer de Danse
                        FOYED

LETTS, CHIEF OF THE. See:
    Tautvaldis

LEUCOTHÉA, Queen of the
Nereids, rescues, falls
in love with Nautéos,
Nautéos   NAUTE

LE VIEUX. See: Marcheur,
Le Vieux

LI-SHAN-FU, Chinese adventurer, The Red Poppy
                        REDPO

LIBERTINE, THE. See:
Young Workman

LIBERTY, personification,
Amor   AMORR

LIBERTY OF THE PRESS, THE,
personification, The Press
                         PRESS

LICINIUS. See: Murena, Licinius

LIEUTENANT, flirts with
Flower Vendor in Emerald;
ordered away by Captain
CAPTAIN, rival of Lieuten-
ant for affections of Flower
Vendor in Emerald
GENERAL, outranks Captain
for affections of Flower Ven-
dor in Emerald
Voices of Spring VOICE

LIEUTENANT. See also:
Alva
First Lieutenant
Flower Vendor in Green
Kije, Lieutenant
Kuruc Lieutenant, The
Lauva, Lieutenant
William, Lieutenant

LIEUTENANTS, TWO AMAZON.
See:
Amazon Captain
Fashionable Lady

LIEVEN. See: Princess
Lieven

LIGHT, personification, Excelsior
                         EXCEL

LIGHT. See also: Children of
Light

LIGHT LADY, THE, "bad girl of
the village," attends barn
dance
THE CITY SLICKER, her
beau, also attends the dance
Barn Dance   BARND

LIGHTHEARTED. See: Könnyelmü

LIGNE. See: Prince de Ligne

LILAC FAIRY, THE, fairy god-
mother of the Princess
Aurora
HER PAGE
The Sleeping Beauty SLEEP

LILÈZ, "a player of the biniou,"
rescues Yvonnette from the
korriganes (fairies), La
Korrigane   KORRI

LILIA, dancer, childhood friend
of Count Frédéric; later his
bride
THÉRÉSINE, her mother,
Count Frédéric's old nurse
Le Diable Amoureux DIABE

LILIA. See also:
Bracaccio
Grand Vizier, The

LILIES. See: Hortense, Queen
of the Swamp Lilies

LILITH. See: Adam

LINCOLN, ABRAHAM, President
of the United States
LINCOLN'S VOICE
"A House Divided--" AHOUS

LIND, JENNY, Swedish soprano,
Ghost Town   GHOST

LINDOR, lover of Denise, attracted to Gloriette, Le Marché des Innocents
MARCH

LION, animal
Carnival of Animals
CARNV
One of Ulysses' sailors, transformed by Circe
Circe   CIRCE
Appears at Eiffel Tower
Les Mariés de la Tour Eiffel   MARIE

LIONEL. See: d'Arc, Jeanne

LIONNE, LA, fashionable French beauty dressed in red; escorted to Paris café by the Duke, Gaîte Parisienne   GAITE

LISE, country girl, in love with Luc, sought in marriage by the Marquis
HER FATHER, a farmer
HER MOTHER, favors her marriage with the Marquis
The Magic Flute   MAGIC

LISE (LISETTE). See:
Simone, Mother
Thomas

LISINION. See: Lykanion

LISTENER. See: Teller of the Tale

LITERARY SATYR, "headliner seeking refuse from publicity," visiting 2222 Club, New York City, Café Society   CAFES

LITTLE AMERICAN GIRL, THE, member of troupe of performers, Parade
PARAD

LITTLE DAUGHTERS, THEIR TWO. See: Cordoba, Pedro

LITTLE EMPEROR, young Chinese ruler, ill, cured by singing of Nightingale after failure of singing of Artificial Nightingale, Chinese Nightingale   CHINE

LITTLE EMPEROR. See also:
Nightingale, Artificial

LITTLE GIRL, central figure, Carnival of Animals
CARNV

LITTLE GIRL, A, "wisdom not yet educated and spoiled," The Great American Goof
GREAT

LITTLE HARE, THE FIRST THE SECOND LITTLE HARE, used by Balda to trick the Old Devil and other devils, The Fairy-Tale of the Priest and His Workman Balda
FAIRY

LITTLE JOHNNY IN TOP-BOOTS. See: Csizmás Janko

LITTLE KING, THE, caricature of cartoon character, The New Yorker   NEWYO

LITTLE MERMAID, THE, in love with the Prince
THE PRINCE, loved by Little Mermaid
The Little Mermaid   LITTM

LITTLE PULCINELLAS, FOUR. See: Pulcinella

LITTLE RED RIDING HOOD. See: Red Riding Hood

LITTLE UGLY ONE, THE. See: Laiderette

LIVERS. See: Riotous Livers

LIZZIE BORDEN. See: Accused, The

LODBROK, REGNAR, King of
Denmark, later marries
Thora
LAGERTHA, Norwegian
Amazon, his wife
THEIR TWO SONS
Lagertha   LAGER

LOÏK, tavern-keeper, employer
of Yvonnette, La Korrigane
                      KORRI

LOLA. See: Montez, Lola

LOLLO. See: Don Lollo

LOMBARD, DOCTOR. See:
Silvio

L'OMBRE. See: Ombre, l'

LONDON NEWS. See: Illus-
trated London News, The

LONELY GIRL, images herself
joining the young people
around her but essentially
always remains alone,
Solitaire   SOLIT

LONELY MAN. See: Yara

LONG EARS. See: Personage
With Long Ears

LONGREN, sailor, afterwards
maker of toy boats
ASSOL, his daughter
MARY, his wife, killed by
Old Menners
EGL, Mary's father
Red Sails   REDSA

LOOKOUT, THE, escaped convict, Piège de Lumière
                      PIEGE

LOPEZ. See: Don Lopez de
Mendoza

LORD. See: Old Lord, The

LORD ADRIANI, loses Namouna

to Don Ottavio in game of
chance, Namouna   NAMOU

LORD BURLEIGH, nobleman, The
Lord of Burleigh   LORDO

LORD CAMPBELL, ardent Royal-
ist, follower of King Charles
II of England
SARAH, his only child, res-
cued as child by Stenio, sto-
len by Trousse-Diable
MEG, Sarah's nurse
NARCISSE DE CRAKENTORP,
Lord Campbell's nephew, "a
conceited fool"
La Gypsy   GYPSY

LORD CAMPBELL. See also:
Mab
Stenio

LORD CASTLEREAGH, nobleman
LADY CASTLEREAGH, his
wife
Vienna- 1814   VIENN

LORD EMPIRE
LADY EMPIRE, visiting no-
bility at 2222 Club, New York
City
Café Society   CAFES

LORD OF CREATION, THE. See:
Man

LORD OF EAST GOTHLAND.
See: Thora

LORD OF EVIL. See: Beelzebub

LORD OF THE MANOR, donates
bell to small European vil-
lage
Coppélia   COPPE
Officiates at festival
Javotte   JAVOT

LORD OF THE MOUNTAIN, THE,
guest at the Prince's ball,
Cinderella   CINDR

LORD OF THE VALE, THE,
  guest at the Prince's ball,
  Cinderella   CINDR

LORD REWENA, nobleman
  LADY REWENA, his wife
  OSWALD, his brother
  Nathalie   NATHA

LORD REWENA. See also:
  Bettemberg
  Walther

LORD WILSON, later Ta-Hor,
  smokes opium, has dream
  of ancient Egypt in which
  he loves and is loved by
  Aspicia, La Fille du
  Pharaon   FILLP

LORD WILSON. See also:
  Bull, John
  Keeper of the Pyramids
  Mummy of the Pharaoh's
  Daughter

LORÉDAN, handsome young
  man, attracted to Adélaïde,
  Adélaïde, or The Language
  of the Flowers   ADELA

LORENZO, ALDONZA, peasant
  girl, thought by Don Quixote
  to be the Lady Dulcinea
  Don Quixote   DONQI
  Don Quixote   DONQO
  Don Quixote   DONQT
  Don Quichotte   DONQV
  Don Quixote   DONQX

LORENZO, ALDONZA. See
  also: Kitri

LOST BALL, danced by female
  dancer, Street Games
                      STREE

LOST SOULS, in Limbo,
  Lament   LAMEN

LOU, THE LADY KNOWN AS.
  See: McGrew, Dan

LOUIS. See:
  King Louis II
  King Louis XIV, King of
    France
  King Louis XVI, King of
    France
  Philemon

LOUIS THE ILLUSIONIST (The
  Magician), performs at
  minstrel show, also appears
  as Interlocutor
  MOREAU
  LESSAU, his assistants
  Cakewalk   CAKEW

LOUISELLE. See: Catharina

LOVE, personification
  Amor   AMORR
  The Five Gifts   FIVEG

LOVE. See also:
  Chess-Players, Two
  Prince of Love, The

LOVE AND FERTILITY,
  GODDESS OF. See: Ishtar

LOVE, GOD OF. See:
  Amor
  Cupid
  Cupidon
  Eros

LOVE, GODDESS OF. See:
  Venus

LOVE, HIS ROMANTIC. See:
  Youth, A

LOVE, NEW. See: Young
  Husband

LOVE, PERSONIFICATION OF.
  See: Prince of Love, The

LOVE, PROFANE. See: Poet

LOVE, SACRED. See: Poet

LOVER. See: Young Lover, The

LOVER, DARKLING'S. See:
    Darkling, The

LOVER, GHOST OF CANDELAS'
    FORMER. See: Candelas

LOVER, GHOST OF THE DUCH-
    ESS'. See: Duchess, The

LOVER, HER. See:
    Caroline
    Fifi, Mademoiselle
    Peaches

LOVER, L'OMBRE'S. See:
    Ombre, l'

LOVER, PERSONAGE'S WIFE'S.
    See: Personage, A

LOVER, THE, wishes to marry
    Young Girl, jilted; joins
    League of Light, mission-
    ary group, finds gold in
    Africa
    Bonne-Bouche   BONNE
    Wins hand of Chung-Yang,
    daughter of Mandarin
    DRAGON, impersonated by
    Lover
    L'Épreuve d'Amour
                        EPREU
    Personification
    Letter to the World
                        LETTE

LOVER, THE QUEEN'S. See:
    King, The

LOVER (TRISTRAM). See:
    Husband (King Mark)
    Knights, Two

LOVER, YOUNG GIRL'S. See:
    Young Girl

LOVERS. See:
    Bird Woman
    Lovers, The
    Poor Lovers
    Young Lovers

LOVER'S FATHER, HER. See:

Fifi, Mademoiselle

LOVERS-IN-INNOCENCE
    LOVERS-IN-EXPERIENCE,
    personifications
    Pillar of Fire   PILLA

LOVERS, THE, seen by the Lady
    of Shalott in her mirror
    The Lady of Shalott LADYO
    Residents of the Gorbals,
    slum quarter in Glasgow
    Miracle in the Gorbals
                        MIRAC

LOVERS, THE. See also:
    Lovers

LOVERS, TWO. See: Khadra

LOVING. See: Szerelmes

LOVING CHILDREN, members
    of Paris working class, Le
    Rendez-Vous   RENDE

LOYS. See: Albrecht, Duke of
    Silesia

LUBAVA. See: Sadko

LUC, poor country boy, in love
    with Lise, The Magic Flute
                        MAGIC

LUC. See also:
    Judge, The
    Oberon

LUCA. See: Marquis di Luca,
    The

LUCAR. See: Marquis de San
    Lucar, The

LUCENTIO. See: Fabiani,
    Lucentio

LUCIA, village girl, helps
    Carmelo to win Candelas,
    El Amor Brujo   AMORB

LUCIA. See also: Dlugoszewski,

Lucia

LUCIEN D'HERVILLY. See:
Comte d'Hervilly, The
Paquita

LUCIFER, a devil, Lucifer
LUCIF

LUCIFER. See also: Archangel Lucifer

LUCILE. See: Jourdaine,
Monsieur

LUCILE GRAHN. See: Tag-
lioni, Marie

LUCINE, THE DUCHESS.
See: Isabelle

LUCRETIA. See:
Gloire, La
Tarquinius, Sextus

LUCREZIA. See: Rosina

LUDMILLA. See: Russlan

LUDWIG OF BAVARIA, KING.
See: King Louis II

LUGANO, MARCO, a rich
Venetian merchant
ANNUNZIATA
FLAMINIA
ANGELICA, his daughters
OLIVIA SOLARINO, distant
relative of Marco Lugano
The Blood-Red Flower
BLOOD

LUGANO, MARCO. See also:
del Sato, Orsino
Fabiani, Lucentio
Monster, A
Podesta, Giovanni

LUIGI, young peasant, in
love with Lauretta, La
Tarentule   TAREN

LUIGI. See also:
Omeopatico, Doctor
Sacristan, The

LUKE. See: Luc

LUNA. See: Count di Luna

LUST, PERSONIFICATION OF.
See: Spanish Woman

LUSTFUL VIRGIN. See: Priggish Virgin

LUTINE, MADEMOISELLE, head
pupil at opera house, The
Débutante   DEBUT

LUZY. See: Marquis de Luzy,
The

LYDIA, KING OF. See: Candaules

LYKANION (Lisinion), evil tempt-
ress, tries to seduce Daphnis,
Daphnis et Chloë   DAPHN

LYRIC POETRY, a muse, Sylvia
SYLVA

LYS. See:
Fleur-de-Lys
Prince Fleur-de-Lys

LYSANDER, in love with Hermia
The Dream   DREAM
A Midsummer Night's Dream
MIDSU

LYSISTRATA, conceives plan for
women to end war by refus-
ing themselves to their hus-
bands
Lysistrata   LYSIS
Lysistrata   LYSIT

M

MAB, Queen of the Gypsies,
jealous of Sarah over Stenio's
love, La Gypsy   GYPSY

MAB. See also: Lord Campbell

MAC, filling station attendant,
Filling Station   FILLI

MAC. See also:
Gangster, The
Motorist, The
Ray
Rich Boy, The
State Trooper, The

MACARENA, LA. See: La-
landa

McGREW, DAN, Alaskan miner
THE LADY KNOWN AS
LOU, his sweetheart
THE STRANGER, shoots
Dan McGrew
The Shooting of Dan Mc-
Grew   SHOOT

MADAME. See:
Chrysanthème, Madame
Gertrude, Madame
Navailles, Madame de
Périgord, Madame de
Sagan, Madame de

MADAME ALOISE DE GONDE-
LAURIER. See: Fleur-de-
Lys

MADAME DE BOUGAINVILLE.
See: Bougainville, Mon-
sieur de

MADAME DE SAINT-ANGE.
See: Duc de Vendôme,
The

MADAME DE SÉNANGE. See:
Zoé

MADAME DUVET. See: Duvet,
Mademoiselle Delphine

MADAME NOVERRE. See:
Noverre, Monsieur

MADAME RENONCULE. See:
Chrysanthème, Madame

MADAME ROBINTZEL. See:
Robintzel

MADDALENA. See: Courtesan

MADELEINE. See:
Camargo
Usher, Roderick

MADELEINE, MARQUISE. See:
Armide

MADEMOISELLE, prima ballerina, La Prima Ballerina
                       PRIMA

MADEMOISELLE. See also:
Chartreuse, Mademoiselle
Marianne
d'Avril, Mademoiselle Pluie
Duvet, Mademoiselle Del-
phine
Fifi, Mademoiselle
Florita, Mademoiselle
Lutine, Mademoiselle
Mam'zelle
Théodore, Mademoiselle
Virginie
Wisteria, Mademoiselle

MADEMOISELLE DE BOUGAIN-
VILLE. See:
Bougainville, Monsieur de
Guimard, La

MADEMOISELLE PRUNE. See:
Chrysanthème, Madame

MADEMOISELLE PURETÉ. See:
Chrysanthème, Madame

MADGE. See: Old Madge

MADHAVA, favorite of Dushmata,
King of India, Sakuntala
                       SAKUN

MADMAN, THE
THE WOMAN
THE MAN, visitors at skat-
ing rink; engaged in three-
cornered romance
Skating Rink   SKATI

MADONNA. See: Young Girl

MAGDAVEYA, a fakir, La Bayadère BAYAD

MAGICIAN, THE, leader of troupe of traveling players, Les Forains FORAI

MAGICIAN, THE. See also: Louis the Illusionist

MAGICIAN, THE EVIL. See: St. George

MAGISTRATE, VILLAGE. See: Courasche

MAHARAJAH OF LAHORE. See: Noureddin

MAHARAJAH, THE, potentate FLORENCIJA, the Maharanee, his wife Ilga ILGAA

MAHARAJAH, THE. See also: British Governor, The Master of Ceremonies

MAHARANEE, THE. See: Maharajah, The

MAHOMET, King of Granada HIS WIVES La Révolte au Sérail REVOL

MAHOMET. See also: Zeir

MAIA, celestial star, Electra ELECT

MAID. See: Circassian Maid, The Serving-Maid, The

MAID, BEATRIX'S WAITING. See: Cesarius

MAID (BRANGAENE), maid to Wife (Iseult), Picnic at Tintagel PICNI

MAID (BRANGAENE). See also: Husband (King Mark)

MAID OF HONOR, QUEEN'S. See: Blanche

MAIDEN. See: Snow Maiden, The Tsar-Maiden, The

MAIDEN LADIES OUT WALKING, promenaders, Pillar of Fire PILLA

MAIDEN, THE, overtaken by the shadow of Death "in all her innocent happiness" DEATH, overtakes the Maiden; discovered by her to be gentle Death and the Maiden DEATH

MAIDEN, THE CHOSEN. See: Chosen One, The

MAIDEN, THE ICE. See: Solveig

MAIDEN, THE ICE (FAIRY). See: Bridegroom

MAIDEN, YOUNG. See: Mandarin

MAIDENS. See: Leaf-Maidens, The

MAIDS OF HONOR, HER. See: Princess, The

MAIDS OF HONOR, QUEEN'S. See: Blanche Navailles, Madame de Vert-Vert

MAIDS, THE. See: Ladies in Waiting, The

MAIL. See: Daily Mail, The Male

MAÎTRE DE BALLET, conducts
   ballet rehearsal
   Foyer de Danse   FOYED
   At the ballet
   Gala Performance GALAP

MAÎTRE D'HÔTEL, at 2222
   Club, New York City
   Café Society   CAFES
   Caricature of cartoon
   character
   WAITERS, caricatures of
   cartoon characters
   The New Yorker   NEWYO

MAKAR. See: Bashmirskaya,
   Panni

MAKER. See: Wig-Maker

MALACORDA, an incubus,
   Kalkabrino   KALKA

MALASPINA. See: Marquis
   Obizzo di Malaspina

MALATESTA, GIANCIOTTO.
   See:
   Dwarfs
   Francesca (Francesca da
      Rimini)
   Girolamo

MALATESTA, PAOLO. See:
   Angelic Apparition
   Francesca (Francesca da
      Rimini)

MALDA. See:
   Sauldots
   Sorceress, The
   Tautvaldis

MALE. See also: Mail

MALE DANCER, A. See:
   Female Dancer, A

MALE NURSES, THE, on
   duty at the Logéat Mental Hospital, Les Algues
                      ALGUE

MALE SABIÁ. See: Gavião

MALINCHE (La Malinche),
   beautiful Mexican Indian,
   becomes companion and in-
   terpreter for Cortez; re-
   garded as a traitor by her
   people until she returns to
   aid them in their struggle
   for liberty
   CORTEZ, Spanish conqueror
   of Mexico
   EL INDIO, Indian native
   La Malinche   MALIN

MAM'ZELLE. See:
   Angot, Mam'zelle
   Mademoiselle

MAN, personification
   The Adaptability of Man
                       ADAPT
   "The lord of creation," per-
   sonification
   WOMAN, his companion
   Amor   AMORR
   Personification
   Day on Earth   DAYON
   Returns to his war-ruined
   native village seeking his Be-
   loved; is captured and execu-
   ted
   BELOVED, "dances a lament
   with his dead body"
   Echoes of Trumpets ECHOE
   Discovers that "Hell is an
   eternity of being alone to-
   gether in an ever-lighted
   room"
   TWO WOMEN, make the
   same discovery
   Sonate à Trois   SONAT
   "Scrambles from the Paleoli-
   thic to the penthouse age."
   MAN'S MATE, accompanies
   him
   Story of Mankind   STORY
   "Depicted as prisoner of himself, of a woman, and of
   'the others'"
   WOMAN, with the Man "prisoner of all pressures of mod-

ern life"
Symphonie pour un Homme
Seul   SYMPP

MAN. See also:
    Bearded Old Man
    Blind Old Man
    Bogey Man, The
    Old Man
    Old Man in Prison
    Poor Man, The
    Prometheus
    Property-Man
    Timid Man
    Young Man
    Young Man, A
    Young Man From the House
        Opposite
    Young Man, The

MAN, A WISE. See: Sage

MAN ABOUT TOWN. See:
    Amazon Captain
    Fashionable Lady

MAN IN SPACE, PERSONIFI-
CATION OF MODERN.
See: Icaros

MAN, LONELY. See: Yara

MAN OF THE WORLD, THE,
    introduces "The Sporting
    Times, " The Press
                        PRESS

MAN, OLD. See: Master of
    Ceremonies

MAN ON CRUTCHES, THE,
    passer-by on Paris street,
    La Nuit   NUITT

MAN, PERSONIFICATION OF.
See: Hero, The

MAN, PERSONIFICATION OF
MODERN. See: H. P.

MAN, RICH. See: Hypnotist

MAN, RICH YOUNG. See:

Laiderette

MAN, SEVENTH. See: Salomé

MAN SHE MUST MARRY, THE.
See: Caroline

MAN, THE, personification
    La Création du Monde
                        CREAT
    L'Homme et son Désir
                        HOMME
    "Symbolizing the poetic
    spirit"
    Rouge et Noir   ROUGE
    Personification
    The Seventh Symphony
                        SEVEN

MAN, THE. See also:
    Madman, The
    Woman, The

MAN, THE OTHER. See: Wife,
    The

MAN, THE STRONG. See:
    Athlete, The

MAN, THE YOUNG. See:
    Cat, The
    Shadow, The
    Young Girl, The
    Young Man, The

MAN, WHITE. See: Emperor
    Jones

MAN WHO PUSHES THE WHEEL-
    BARROW, THE, passer-by
    on Paris street, La Nuit
                        NUITT

MAN WITH A SACK, THE,
    passer-by on Paris street,
    La Nuit   NUITT

MAN WITH A VALISE, THE,
    passer-by on Paris street,
    La Nuit   NUITT

MAN, YOUNG. See:
    Death

Destiny
Girl, The

MANAGER FROM NEW YORK,
THE, member of troupe of
performers, Parade
                      PARAD

MANAGER, HIS. See: Champ,
The

MANAGER IN EVENING DRESS,
THE, member of troupe of
performers, Parade
                      PARAD

MANAGER OF THE EIFFEL
TOWER, THE, official,
Les Mariés de la Tour
Eiffel   MARIE

MANAGER ON HORSEBACK,
THE
HIS HORSE, members of
troupe of performers
Parade   PARAD

MANAGER, THE, proprietor
of troupe of dancers including the Street Dancer and
the Athlete
Le Beau Danube BEAUD
Met by Anna I and Anna II
The Seven Deadly Sins
                      SEVED

MANAGER, THE. See also:
Stage-Manager, The

MANASSES, sculptor, creates
statue of Fatma, La Fille
de Marbre   FILLM

MANCENILHA, "intoxicating
flower that changes into a
woman," seduces Caboclo
CABOCLO, Brazilian bandit,
loved by "the most beautiful girl in the region";
poisoned
WITCH, ally of Mancenilha
Mancenilha   MANCE

MANDARIN, offers his daughter
in marriage to the Ambassador
CHUNG-YANG, his daughter,
marries the Lover
L'Épreuve d'Amour EPREU
The Miraculous Mandarin,
absolves the prostitute by
his omnipotence and love
"which conquers violence
and death"
The Miraculous Mandarin
                      MIRAM
Attacked and killed by the
Woman (the Prostitute) and
her associates
The Miraculous Mandarin
                      MIRAR
The Miraculous Mandarin
                      MIRAU
Pursues Young Maiden
YOUNG MAIDEN, attracts
Mandarin
Shadow of the Wind SHADW

MANDARIN. See also:
Butterfly, The
Monkeys

MANDARIN, THE. See: Porcelain Princess, The

MANHOOD. See: Poet, The

MANIAC, A, defendant in murder
case, Hear Ye! Hear Ye!
                      HEARY

MANIJE, loved by Djardje
MOYRAVI, Prince of Eristav,
her father
The Heart of the Hills
                      HEART

MANIJE. See also: Prince
Zaal

MANMATA, a heavenly spirit,
The Talisman   TALIS

MANOLA, THE, Spanish girl,
loves the Torero, jilted by
him for the Duchess, Del

Amor y de la Muerte
<u>AMORY</u>

MANOR. See: Lord of the
Manor

MANOS. See: Duras, Manos

MANRICO. See:
Azucena
Count di Luna
Leonora

MAN'S MATE. See: Man

MANTICORE. See: Poet, The

MANTISES. See: Praying
Mantises, The

MANUEL. See: Don Manuel

MANUELA, gypsy, Don Pedro
Ricco's sweetheart, Gaucho
<u>GAUCH</u>

MARCELLINE, servant at
Madame Gertrude's inn,
<u>La Somnambule</u> SOMNA

MARCH, personification
<u>Letter to the World</u>
LETTE
"First attorney, second
attorney and a snowdrop"
<u>Twelve for the Mail-Coach</u>
TWELV

MARCHESA SAMPIETRI, THE.
See:
Count Pepinelli
Prince Osorio, Governor
of Rome

MARCHEUR, LE VIEUX, visi-
tor at bar of Folies-Bergère,
<u>Bar aux Folies-Bergère</u>
BARAU

MARCO. See:
Lugano, Marco
Spada, Marco

MARE, THE, appears in Stableboy's dream, <u>The Filly</u>
FILLY

MARGARET. See: Princess
Margaret

MARGARITA. See: Peter

MARGHARITA, friend of Ragonda,
daughter of Princess Millefleurs, <u>Fiammetta</u> FIAMM

MARGUERITE, loved by Faust
<u>Abraxas</u>   ABRAX
Seduced by Doctor Faust;
loved by Valentine
BERTA, her mother
<u>Faust</u>   FAUST
Seduced by Faust with the
aid of Mephistopheles (Mephis-
to)
<u>Mephisto Valse</u>   MEPHI
<u>Mephisto Valse</u>   MEPHS
Betrothed to Gaston de Beau-
voir, brother of Clairemonde
<u>The Stars</u>   STARS
Servant of Philemon
<u>Vieux Souvenirs</u>   VIEUX
Seduced by Faust with the
aid of Mephistopheles
(Mephisto)
<u>Vision of Marguerite</u> VISIO

MARGUERITE. See also:
Gautier, Marguerite
Martha

MARIA (MARY). See: Joseph

MARIANNA, DONA. See:
Bridoux
Diavolina

MARIANNE. See:
Chartreuse, Mademoiselle
Marianne
Théodore

MARIE, a Negress and slave,
owned by Dorival; rescued
by Zoé and Théodore

ZOBI, her child
Les Deux Créoles DEUXC
Polish princess, in love
with Vatslav, loved by
Gierey
PRINCE ADAM, her father
The Fountain of Bakhchi-
sarai   FOUNT
Village girl, in love with
Pierre
HEADMAN OF THE VIL-
LAGE, her father
Halte de Cavalerie
                        HALTE

MARIE. See also:
Camargo
Catherine
Taglioni, Marie

MARIE ANTOINETTE, QUEEN.
See: King Louis XVI,
King of France

MARIETTA, a bride
BEPPO, her groom
Gemma   GEMMA
Flower-seller, in love with
Olivier, fascinates Kalka-
brino
RENÉ, her father, an inn-
keeper
Kalkabrino   KALKA

MARIETTA.   See also:
Cigala
Draginiatza
Monk, A
Silvina
Ujel
Vincenetta

MARINETTE, Isabelle's maid,
Ruses d'Amour   RUSES

MARIUCCIA, maid to the
Marquise Silvestra, aunt
of Constanza, Les Femmes
de Bonne Humeur FEMME

MARK ANTONY. See: Antony

MARK, KING. See: Husband

(King Mark)

MARMION, an old colonel
VICTOR, his son, a page
Les Pages du Duc de Ven-
dôme   PAGES

MARQUIS, A, admirer of Ozaï,
Ozaï   OZAII

MARQUIS COSTA DE BEAURE-
GARD, THE, French aristo-
crat
COMTE GEOFFROY, his son,
kills Antoine Mistral
The Flames of Paris FLAME

MARQUIS DAMIS, THE, betrothed
to Isabelle, Ruses d'Amour
                        RUSES

MARQUIS DE BREILLE, aged
nobleman, The Stars   STARS

MARQUIS DE FIERBOIS, magician, host to Vicomte de
Beaugency, Le Pavillon
d'Armide   PAVIL

MARQUIS DE LUZY, THE, nobleman, Vert-Vert   VERTV

MARQUIS DE SAN LUCAR, THE,
nobleman, friend of Don
Bustamente, La Jolie Fille
de Gand   JOLIE

MARQUIS DE SANTA-CROCE,
mesmerist, tries to marry
Countess Gemma by putting
her under hypnotic spell,
Gemma   GEMMA

MARQUIS DE SANTA-CROCE.
See also: Giacomo

MARQUIS DI LUCA, THE,
nobleman, Les Femmes de
Bonne Humeur   FEMME

MARQUIS OBIZZO DI MALASPINA,
elected chief of the Lombard
League, Amor   AMORR

MARQUIS, THE, rich lord,
seeks the hand of Lise
in marriage, The Magic
Flute   MAGIC

MARQUISE MADELEINE. See:
Armide

MARQUISE SILVESTRA, THE.
See:
Constanza
Mariuccia

MARRIAGE, GOD OF. See:
Hymen

MARRIED COUPLE. See:
Older Married Couple, An

MARRIED WOMEN, SEVEN,
members of Eskimo tribe,
Qarrtsiluni   QARRT

MARRY, THE MAN SHE MUST.
See: Caroline

MARS, god of war
The Creatures of Prome-
theus   CREAU
The Loves of Mars and
Venus   LOVEM
Celestial body
HIS RETINUE
The Stars   STARS
God of war
Le Triomphe de l'Amour
                        TRIOP

MARS. See also:
Mortal Born Under Mars
Planet Mars

MARTA. See:
Flik
Van Bett

MARTHA, friend of Marguerite,
Faust   FAUST

MARTHA. See also:
Ben
Father
Myrtha

MARTHE. See: Catherine

MARTIN. See:
Durfort, Sergeant
François

MARTINI, servant to Count
Friedrich Sternhold, Fiammetta   FIAMM

MARTINIÈRE. See: de la
Martinière, Monsieur

MARTYR, THE, burned at the
stake
FOUR CHURCHMEN, offi-
ciate at the burning
Caprichos   CAPRH

MARVIN. See:
Allen, Barbara
Witches, Two Young

MARX, KARL. See: Student
of Karl Marx, A

MARY, Queen of Scots, on her
way to the scaffold, reviews
her lifelong struggle with
Queen Elizabeth I of England
DARNLEY, her second hus-
band
BOTHWELL, her third hus-
band
Episodes   EPISO

MARY. See also:
Chastelard
Hamilton, Mary
Longren
Old Menners
Rizzio, David

MARY (MARIA). See: Joseph

MASETTO, a young peasant,
betrothed to Pachita, La
Gitana   GITAN

MASHA. See:
King of the Mice
Nutcracker
President

Sugarplum Fairy

MASOCH, SACHER, masochist
HIS WIFE
Bacchanale   BACCH

MASSIMO, artist, loves and
loved by Countess Gemma
ANGIOLA, his sister
Gemma   GEMMA

MASTER. See:
Ballet Master
Ballet Master, The
Dance Master
Dancing Master, The
Fencing Master, The

MASTER OF CEREMONIES,
officiates at formal ball
BALLERINA, guest at ball
OLD MAN, also guest at
ball
Assembly Ball   ASSEM
At Prince Charming's
court
Cinderella   CINDL
At the Maharajah's ball
Ilga   ILGAA
Official at Count de Castro's
feast
The Stars   STARS

MASTER OF THE HUNT, offi-
cial, The Stars   STARS

MASTER OF TREGENNIS. See:
Flautist (The Stranger
Player)
Young Tregennis

MATADOR, accepts Death in
the knowledge that there is
someone to replace him
DEATH, claims Matador
Apasionada   APASI

MATCHMAKER, THE, seeks to
arrange marriage between
Yela and the Bridegroom,
The Devil in the Village
                    DEVIV

MATCHMAKERS. See: Bride

MATE, MAN'S. See: Man

MATHEA. See: Lauretta

MATHEUS, DOCTOR, Satan in
disguise, Le Violon du
Diable   VIOLO

MATHURIN, a miller
YVONNE, his daughter, en-
gaged to Herve
PETIT JEAN, his little son
Les Papillons   PAPIO

MATHURIN. See also: Babette

MATO, mercenary, loves Salammbô, Salammbô   SALAO

MATO, DAUGHTERS OF PAI-
DO. See: Zuimaaluti

MATO, PAI-DO. See: Zuimaaluti

MATTEO, young fisherman,
loved by Ondine, betrothed
to Giannina
THERESA, his mother
Ondine   ONDIN

MAY, a young girl, Twelve for
the Mail-Coach   TWELV

MAYENNE. See: Duc de Mayenne

MAYFLIES, residents of Butterfly
Land, Les Papillons PAPIO

MAYFLY, THE, inhabitant of
the insect world, victim of
the Spider
Le Festin de l'Araignée
                    FESTD
Le Festin de l'Araignée
                    FESTI
The Spider's Banquet
                    SPIDE

MAYOR OF SOROCHINSK, town
official, would-be lover of

the witch Khivria, The Fair
at Sorochinsk   FAIRA

MAYOR, THE, official
Nina   NINAO
Paquerette   PAQUE

MAZOURKA, changed by Blind
Old Man into The Countess
for a day
MAZOURKI, her husband,
a basket-maker
Le Diable à Quatre DIABQ

ME-UP. See: Pick-Me-Up

MECHANICAL NIGHTINGALE.
See:
Nightingale, Artificial
Nightingale, Mechanical
Nightingale, The

MEDEA, a colored servant
Loin du Danemark LOIND
Rejected by Jason, re-
venges herself
JASON, her husband, in
love with Creusa
THEIR TWO CHILDREN,
killed by Medea
Medea   MEDEA

MEDEA. See also:
Sorceress
Victim

MÉDÉE, in love with Jason,
jilted by him, Médée et
Jason   MEDEE

MEDERE. See: Ngama

MEDINA-CELI. See: Duke
of Medina-Celi, The

MEDORA, a young Greek girl,
Le Corsaire   CORSA

MEDUSA, murdered by the
Transgressor, Undertow
                       UNDER

MEG. See: Lord Campbell

MEHMENE-BANU. See: Queen
Mehmene-Banu

MEJIAS, IGNACIO SANCHEZ,
bullfighter, killed in the
bullring, Lament for Ig-
nacio Sanchez Mejias
                       LAMEF

MELANCHOLIC VARIATION
SANGUINIC VARIATION
PHLEGMATIC VARIATION
CHOLERIC VARIATION, the
Four Temperaments; psycho-
logical types, portrayed by
dancers
The Four Temperaments
                       FOURT

MELANCHOLY. See: Visions
of Melancholy

MELANIE. See: Princess
Melanie

MELCHOLA. See:
David
King Saul, King of the Is-
raelites
Michal

MELIA, nymph, I Titani TITAN

MELISANDE, young girl found
in forest by Golaud; becomes
his wife, Pelléas et Mélisande   PELLE

MELON HAWKER, THE, me-
chanical toy, performs
routine in toy shop, La
Boutique Fantasque BOUTI

MELUN. See: Comte de Melun

MEN. See:
End Men
Escort Service Men
Fat Men, The Three
Goat Men, Three

MEN, FIVE. See: Woman,
The

MEN, SIX. See: Salomé

MEN, TWENTY. See: Span-
  ish Woman

MEN, TWO. See: Woman
  Who Was Caught, The

MENDOZA. See: Don Lopez
  de Mendoza

MENELAUS. See:
  Helen
  King Menelaus, King of
    Sparta

"MENKEN, THE, " Adah
  Isaacs Menken, American
  actress, one-time wife of
  "Benicia Boy" Heenan,
  Ghost Town   GHOST

MENNERS. See: Old Menners

MENNERS, YOUNG. See:
  Old Menners

MEPHISTOPHELES, the Devil,
  obtains Doctor Faust's
  soul,
  Faust   FAUST
  Mephisto, holds Faust in
  his power, aids the latter
  in the seduction of Marguerite
  Mephisto Valse   MEPHI
  Mephisto Valse   MEPHS
  Vision of Marguerite
                        VISIO

MERCHANT. See:
  Dutch Merchant
  Gay Merchant, The
  Rich Merchant
  Russian Merchant, A

MERCHANT, A, businessman
  in Chinese treaty-port,
  The Red Poppy   REDPO

MERCHANT, THE, rich oriental businessman, temporarily
  loved by Oriane, Oriane et

le Prince d'Amour   ORIAN

MERCURY, god
  Les Amours de Jupiter
                        AMOUJ
  Ballet Comique de la Reine
                        BALLC
  Defense of Paradise DEFEN
  The Descent of Hebe DESCE
  Falls the Shadow Between
                        FALLS
  Fiametta   FIAMM
  Le Jugement de Paris
                        JUGEM
  Spectacle   SPECL

MERCURY. See also:
  Mortal Born Under Mercury
  Planet Mercury

MERCUTIO, friend of Romeo,
  killed by Tybalt
  Romeo and Juliet   ROMEA
  Romeo and Juliet   ROMEJ
  Romeo and Juliet   ROMEO

MERCUTIO. See also:
  Capulet
  Montague
  Old Capulet
  Old Montague

MERLIN (CARETAKER). See:
  Husband (King Mark)

MERMAID. See:
  Fisherman
  Little Mermaid, The

MERMAIDS, RULER OF THE.
  See: Queen of the Nereids

MEROPE, celestial star, Electra
                        ELECT

MERRY WIDOW. See: Cour-
  asche

MERRY WIDOW, THE. See:
  Sonia

MESROUR, grand vizier to the
  Sultan; character in the

ballet "Azalea, or The
Odalisque, " The Débutante
DEBUT

MESSENGER OF DEATH, mes-
senger, Clytemnestra
CLYTE

MESSIAH. See: Indian

MESSIAH, NEW. See: Hermit

METELLUS. See: Pius,
Metellus

METTERNICH. See: Prince
Metternich

MEUHOR, friend and confidant
of Kafur, enemy of Harold,
Sieba   SIEBA

MEXICAN PEON, has dream
fantasy
PEASANT GIRL, figure of
his fantasy, loved by him
TWO WOMEN WITH PLAY
STICKS, figures of his
fantasy
El Salon Mexico   SALON

MEXICAN SWEETHEART, HIS.
See: Billy the Kid

MEXICANS, THE dancers at
the Big Tent, dance hall
and gambling resort,
Union Pacific   UNION

MEZZETINTO, friend of
Blondelaine, Scaramouche
SCARA

MICAELA, rival of Carmen
for the affections of José,
Guns and Castanets GUNSA

MICE, KING OF THE. See:
King of the Mice
President

MICHAEL, SAINT. See:

Archangel St. Michael
Saint Joan

MICHAL. See:
Abigail
Melchola
Saul, King of the Israelites

MICHAUD, MOTHER. See:
Thérèse

MIDAS. See:
King Midas
Signor Midas

MIDDLE KINGDOM, EMPEROR
OF THE. See: Princess
Belle Épine

MIGNONNE, gentleman-in-waiting,
Cinderella   CINDA

MIKADO, THE, ruler of Japan,
intrigued by Yedda
THE PRINCESS, his cousin,
jealous
Yedda   YEDDA

MIKADO, THE. See also: Tô

MIKALIA (GERTRUDE). See:
Gourouli

MILKMAID
THREE MOUNTAINEERS,
engage in yodeling contest
Facade   FACAD

MILLEFLEURS. See: Princess
Millefleurs

MILLER, THE. See:
Dandy, The
Miller's Wife, The

MILLER'S WIFE, THE, in love
with her husband, attracts
the Corregidor
THE MILLER, her husband,
in love with her
Le Tricorne   TRICO

MILLER'S WIFE, THE. See also: Dandy, The

MILLIONAIRESS, THE, American type, seen by the Immigrant, Within the Quota   WITHI

MIME, THE. See: Principal Dancer, The (Adam Zero)

MINA, a gypsy, friend of Lauretta when with gypsies, La Gitana   GITAN
A Negress
La Révolte au Sérail
                                   REVOL

MINERVA, aging entertainer, dances for Paris in boîte de nuit; afterwards picks his pockets, The Judgment of Paris   JUDGM

MINES. See: Queen of the Mines

MINES, EVIL GENIUS OF THE. See: Torbern

MINISTER. See: Bride

MINISTERS, THE THREE, to the King, replaced by the Three Tailors
Le Roi Nu   ROINU
Le Roi Nu   ROINV

MINISTERS, THE THREE. See also: Tailors, The Three

MINOS, King of Crete
PASIPHAE, Queen of Crete, his wife
ARIADNE, their daughter, helps Theseus overcome the Minotaur
THE MINOTAUR, bull-like monster, son of Pasiphae by a white bull; overcome by Theseus
The Minotaur   MINOT

The Minotaur   MINOU

MINOS. See also:
Phaedra
Theseus

MINOS, KING. See: Ariadne

MINOTAUR, THE, monster, conquered by Theseus with the assistance of Ariadne
Labyrinth   LABYR
The Minotaur   MINOT
The Minotaur   MINOU
Spectacle   SPECL

MINOTAUR, THE. See also:
Ariadne
Minos, King of Crete
Theseus

MIRACULOUS MANDARIN, THE. See: Mandarin

MIREILLE. See: Poitiers, Mireille de

MIREWELT. See: Eleonore

MIRKO, village youth, Yela's sweetheart, temporarily possessed by the Devil, The Devil in the Village
                                   DEVIV

MISFORTUNE, personification, La Douairière de Billebahaut   DOUAI

MISS JULIE. See: Julie, Miss

MISSIONARY. See: Mormon Missionary, The

MISTER. See: Puppet, Mister

MISTRAL, ANTOINE, an actor, slain by Comte Geoffroy, son of the Marquis Costa da Beauregard, The Flames of Paris   FLAME

MISTRESS. See:

Head Mistress, The
Wardrobe-Mistress

MISTRESS OF CEREMONIES,
THE, official at court of
the Princess, A Spring
Tale   SPRIN

MISTRESS OF THE COPPER
MOUNTAIN. See: Danila

MISTRESS, THE. See:
Hamilton, Mary

MISTRESS, THE DEVIL'S.
See: Devil, The

MISTRESS, THE WARDROBE.
See: Principal Dancer,
The (Adam Zero)

MITCH. See: du Bois,
Blanche

MNESILLA, a nymph, Cydalise
et le Chèvre-pied   CYDAL

MODEL, HIS PRINCIPAL. See:
Rosa, Salvator

MODELS, TWO. See: Duchic,
Monsieur

MODERN MAN IN SPACE,
PERSONIFICATION OF.
See: Icaros

MODERN MAN, PERSONIFI-
CATION OF. See: H. P.

MOGENS, a nobleman, A
Folk Tale   FOLKT

MOHAMED, tutor to Prince
Djalma, Le Papillon
                     PAPIL

MOLARI, tutor and guardian
to Count Friedrich Stern-
hold, Fiametta   FIAMM

MOLDAVIAN SLAVE, A,
property of Seyd, Le

Corsaire   CORSA

MÔME. See: Fromage, La
Môme

MOMUS, an elf, Les Métamorphoses   METAM

MONARCH OF THE TRUANDS.
See: Trouillefou, Clopin

MONDE. See: Demi-Monde,
The

MONDEGO. See: Nymphs of
Mondego

MONK, A, at first refuses, later
consents to marrying Marietta and Olivier; curses Kalkabrino, Kalkabrino KALKA

MONK, THE, officiates at funeral
of the Woman in Ball Dress,
Apparitions   APPAR

MONKEY, A, imperils Aspicia,
La Fille du Pharaon FILLP

MONKEY TRAINER, circus performer, The Incredible
Flutist   INCRE

MONKEYS, annoy Mandarin, L'
Épreuve d'Amour   EPREU

MONSIEUR. See:
Bougainville, Monsieur de
Comte de N--, le, Monsieur
de la Martinière, Monsieur
Didelot, Monsieur
Duchic, Monsieur
Jourdaine, Monsieur
Noverre, Monsieur
Pirouette, Monsieur
Saint-Rambert, Monsieur de
Vestris, Monsieur

MONSIEUR DE SURVILLE. See:
Bougainville, Monsieur de
Ozaï

MONSIEUR DUVAL. See: Du-

147   MONSIEUR TRÈS-PROPRE

val, Armand

MONSIEUR TRÈS-PROPRE.
See: Chrysanthème,
Madame

MONSTER, abducts Princess
Anastachiuska, afterwards
overcome by Alyosha Popo-
vich, Bogatyri   BOGAT

MONSTER, A, handsome
prince, transformed by
magician; loves Angelica,
daughter of Marco Lugano;
restored, The Blood-Red
Flower   BLOOD

MONTAGU.   See:
Montague
Old Montague
Romeo

MONTAGUE, head of house at
variance with the house of
Capulet
LADY MONTAGUE, his
wife
ROMEO, his son, in love
with, marries, Juliet;
kills Tybalt
BENVOLIO, nephew to
Montague, friend of Romeo
Romeo and Juliet   ROMEO

MONTAGUE.   See also:
Laurence, Friar
Montagu
Old Montague
Rosaline

MONTANO, Otello's predeces-
sor, Otello   OTELL

MONTBAZON. See: Comte de
Montbazon, The

MONTESINOS. See: Durandarte

MONTEZ, LOLA, Irish dancer
and adventuress
Bacchanale   BACCH
Lola Montez   LOLAM

MOON, personification
Prince of the Pagodas
                    PRINO
The Seventh Symphony
                    SEVEN

MOON. See also:
Moon, The
Young Man, The
Young Woman, The

MOON, GODDESS OF THE. See:
Endymion

MOON IN GEMINI. See: Young
Woman, The

MOON, KNIGHT OF THE SILVER.
See: Carrasco, Bachelor
Sampson

MOON, THE, personification
Canticle for Innocent Co-
medians   CANTI
Personification
REFLECTION OF THE MOON
SERVANT OF THE MOON
REFLECTION OF THE SERV-
ANT OF THE MOON
L'Homme et son Désir
                    HOMME
Associated with the Zodiac
Horoscope   HOROS
Queen of the Night
Les Mirages   MIRAG

MOON, THE. See also:
Moon
Shepherd
Wife, The

MOONDOG, a clown, The Lady
and the Fool   LADYA

MOONRISE, personification,
Ardent Song   ARDEN

MOONSET, personification,
Ardent Song   ARDEN

MOONSHINE, representation of
British publication, The
Press   PRESS

MOOR OF VENICE, THE.
  See: Othello

MOOR, THE, victim of plot
  by his friend
  MOOR'S WIFE
  MOOR'S FRIEND
  MOOR'S FRIEND'S WIFE
  Moor's Pavane   MOORP

MOREAU. See: Louis the
  Illusionist

MORGAN, a gypsy, La Source
                   SOURC

MORLAQUE
  GOVINE, squires to Count
  Raoul de Créqui, Raoul de
  Créqui   RAOUL

MORMON MISSIONARY, THE,
  patron at the Big Tent,
  dance hall and gambling
  resort, Union Pacific
                      UNION

MORNING STAR, Venus, loved
  by Count de Castro, The
  Stars   STARS

MORNING STAR, THE, per-
  sonification, La Nuit et le
  Jour   NUITE

MORPHIDES. See: Queen of
  the Morphides, The

MORTAL BORN UNDER MARS,
  The Planets   PLANE

MORTAL BORN UNDER MER-
  CURY, The Planets PLANE

MORTAL BORN UNDER NEP-
  TUNE, The Planets PLANE

MORTALS, TWO, BORN UNDER
  VENUS, The Planets
                      PLANE

MORTE AMOUREUSE, LA, per-
  sonification of Death, loved

by Don Juan, Don Juan
                   DONJA

MORTEN, a Czech, A Folk Tale
                      FOLKT

MOSCATELLO, SERGEANT,
  soldier, in charge of
  Pietro in prison
  ANGULIO
  CARRAOLANA
  CRISTOBAL
  PINIENTO, his soldiers
  Graziosa   GRAZI

MOSES, leader of the Israelites,
  The Man From Midian
                      MANFR

MOSQUITOES, annoy bathers at
  Jones Beach, Jones Beach
                      JONES

MOST BEAUTIFUL GIRL IN THE
  WORLD, THE. See: Young
  Man

MOTHER, "accepts the loss of
  her last son to the sea that
  has taken all the men-folk
  of her family"
  HER TWO DAUGHTERS
  HER TWO SONS
  Threnody   THREN

MOTHER. See also:
  Father
  Judy
  Old Mother, The
  Simone, Mother

MOTHER, A. See: Frickes,
  Mrs.

MOTHER, BABY STORK'S. See:
  Baby Stork
  Vasia

MOTHER, HAMLET'S. See:
  Ophelia

MOTHER, HER. See:
  Accused, The (Lizzie Borden)

Azucena
Betrayed Girl, The
Bride, The
Ilga
Javotte
Lise
Parasha
Solveig
Young Girl
Zoshka

MOTHER, HIS. See:
Armen
Billy the Kid
Bridegroom, The
Tug, Tom
Young Communicant, The

MOTHER-IN-LAW, THE.
See: Bride, The

MOTHER MICHAUD. See:
Thérèse

MOTHER PRINCESS. See:
Prince Siegfried

MOTHER, THE. See:
Anna I
Daughter, The
Father, The

MOTHER, YELA'S. See:
Yela

MOTHERHOOD AND FERTILITY,
GODDESS OF. See: Isis

MOTHERS. See: Children

MOTHS. See: Grey Moths

MOTORIST, THE
HIS WIFE
THEIR CHILD, stop at
Mac's filling station
Filling Station   FILLI

MOUNTAIN. See: Lord of
the Mountain, The

MOUNTAIN ASH. See: Fairy
of the Mountain Ash, The

MOUNTAIN, MISTRESS OF THE
COPPER. See: Danila

MOUNTAINEERS, THREE. See:
Milkmaid

MOUROMETZ, general of the
Bogatyri, Bogatyri   BOGAT

MOUSE, sent by Aphrodite to
tempt the Cat, La Chatte
CHATT

MOVEMENT, personification,
Les Présages   PRESA

MOYRAVL   See:
Djardje
Manije

MOZDOCK. See: Nouredda

MUMMY OF THE PHARAOH'S
DAUGHTER, later Aspicia,
discovered in tomb by Lord
Wilson, La Fille du Pharaon
FILLP

MUMMY OF THE PHARAOH'S
DAUGHTER. See also:
Keeper of the Pyramids

MURAT'S AMBASSADORS, TWO
THEIR WIVES, attending
ball tendered by Prince
Metternich
Vienna-1814   VIENN

MURDERERS, SEVEN, hanged,
Septuor   SEPTU

MURENA, LICINIUS, a consul
DECIUS, his son, friend of
Claudius, La Vestale VESTA

MURI, a witch
DIDERIK
VIDERIK, her sons
A Folk Tale   FOLKT

MUSE, inspires Paganini,
Paganini   PAGAI

MUSE OF SACRED MUSIC.
   See: Polyhymnia

MUSES, LEADER OF THE.
   See: Apollo

MUSES, NINE, goddesses,
   The Creatures of Prometheus   CREAU

MUSIC, MUSE OF SACRED.
   See: Polyhymnia

MUSIC, REPRESENTATION OF
   CLASSICAL. See: Classic

MUSIC, REPRESENTATION OF
   JAZZ. See: Jazz

MUSICIAN. See:
   Agathe
   Strolling Musician
   Young Musician, A

MUSICIAN, STREET. See:
   Young Apprentice

MUSICIANS, TWO, at Grand
   Opera, Paris, Foyer de
   la Danse   FOYER

MUSTAFA, slave dealer,
   character in the ballet
   "Azalea, or The Oda-
   lisque," The Débutante
                 DEBUT

MUSTAPHA, Algerian merchant,
   The Blood-Red Flower
                 BLOOD

MUTCHA, slave
   The Hump-Backed Horse
                 HUMPB
   The Hump-Backed Horse
                 HUMPH

MUTINE, gentleman-in-waiting,
   Cinderella   CINDA

MYRTHA, Queen of the Wilis
   WILIS, restless ghosts of
   unmarried maidens

Giselle   GISEE
Giselle   GISEL
Giselle   GISES

MYRTHA. See also: Martha

MYSSAUF, chief eunuch, La
   Révolte au Sérail   REVOL

MYSTERIOUS GIRL, brings
   spirit of the dance into
   business competition, La
   Concurrence   CONCU

N

N. See: Comte de N--, le,
   Monsieur

NAIADS, TWELVE, supernatural
   beings, Ballet Comique de
   la Reine   BALLC

NAÏLA, the spirit of the spring,
   La Source   SOURC

NAL, betrothed to Nirilya
   KADOOR, his father, an old
   weaver
   The Talisman   TALIS

NAMOUNA, slave, lost by Lord
   Adriani to Don Ottavio in
   game of chance, Namouna
                 NAMOU

NAMOUNA. See also: Andrikès

NAO-SHIKO, young shepherd,
   charms Princess Daïta with
   music of reed pipe, Daïta
                 DAITA

NAO-SHIKO. See also: Kwannon

NAPOLEON. See: Prince Metternich

NARCISINO, character portrayed
   by strolling player, Le
   Marché des Innocents
                 MARCH

NARCISSE DE CRAKENTORP.
   See: Lord Campbell

NARCISSUS, beautiful youth,
   loved by Echo; falls in
   love with his own reflection
   Narcissus and Echo
                 NARCE
   Falls in love with his reflection, pines away
   Narcissus   NARCI

NARKISSOS (Narcissus), falls
   in love with his reflection,
   pines away, Narkissos
                 NARKI

NARRATOR, introduces ballet
   and different musical
   instruments to the audience
   Fanfare   FANFA
   Explains story to the audience
   L'Histoire du Soldat HISTO
   Reads extracts from a
   coroner's report concerning
   the death of Father by starvation
   Inquest   INQUE

NARRATOR. See also: Wood-
   winds

NATHALIE. See: Bettemberg

NATTY. See: Bumppo, Natty

NAUTÉOS, sole survivor of
   shipwreck; loved by
   Leucothéa; falls in love
   with Eurystée, Nautéos
                 NAUTE

NAVAILLES, MADAME DE,
   governess of the Queen's
   maids of honor
   QUEEN'S MAIDS OF HONOR
   Vert-Vert   VERTV

NAVARRE. See: Infanta of
   Navarre, The

NAVY GAZETTE. See: Army
   and Navy Gazette, The

NEARLY DROWNED GIRL, has
   almost fatal accident at
   Jones Beach
   BOY SWIMMER, rescues
   Nearly Drowned Girl
   Jones Beach   JONES

NEGRESS, THE
   HER PICKANINNIES, lost in
   metropolitan railroad terminal
   Terminal   TERMI

NEGRO, A
   HIS WIFE
   THEIR BABY SON, residents
   of tropical jungle, pursued
   by the Planter; saved by
   Baby Stork and jungle ani-
   mals
   Baby Stork   BABYS

NEGRO, A. See also: Gorilla,
   The

NEGRO BOXER, has boxing
   match with White Boxer;
   fouled, loses contest,
   The Golden Age   GOLDE

NEGRO BOXER. See also:
   Referee
   Woman of Soviet Communist
   Youth

NEGRO COUPLE, performs
   dance for Cupid's approval,
   The Whims of Cupid and
   the Ballet Master   WHIMS

NEGRO WAITER, A, witness in
   night-club murder case,
   Hear Ye! Hear Ye! HEARY

NEIGHBOR. See: Rich Old
   Neighbor, A

NELA. See: Don Lollo

NELL. See:
    Eulenspiegel, Til
    Eulenspiegel, Tyl
    Ulenspiegel, Tyl

NELLA. See:
    Flik
    Van Bett

NELLIE, made love to by
    Johnny, for which Frankie
    shoots him, Frankie and
    Johnny   FRANK

NEMESIS, god, friend of
    Aganippe, Undertow UNDER

NEMESIS. See also: Night

NEMESIS FIGURE, personifi-
    cation of fate, Narkissos
                                  NARKI

NEOPHYTE, "strange, mys-
    terious, being," offers
    Tiresias magic wand,
    Tiresias   TIRES

NEPTUNE, God of the Sea
    NEPTUNE'S DAUGHTER,
    marries Tom Tug
    The Triumph of Neptune
                          TRIUM

NEPTUNE. See also:
    Mortal Born Under Neptune
    Planet Neptune

NEPTUNE'S DAUGHTER. See:
    Neptune
    Tug, Tom

NEREIDS, QUEEN OF THE.
    See:
    Leucothéa
    Queen of the Nereids

NEREUS, "a handsome youth,"
    I Titani   TITAN

NESTAN. See: Daredjan,
    Nestan

NEVA, personification of river,
    La Fille du Pharaon FILLP

NEVA, THE, symbolic figure,
    Flik and Flok   FLIKA

NEW LOVE. See: Young
    Husband

NEW MESSIAH. See: Hermit

NEW YORK. See: Manager
    from New York, The

NEW YORKERS, visit 2222 Club,
    New York City, Café So-
    ciety   CAFES

NEWCOMER, THE. See:
    Woman, The

NEWLYWED, MR.
    MRS. NEWLYWED, his
    wife, visitors at 2222 Club,
    New York City
    Café Society   CAFES

NEWS. See:
    Financial News, The
    Illustrated London News, The

NEWSBOY, THE, selling papers
    at metropolitan railroad
    terminal, Terminal TERMI

NEWSBOYS, personifications,
    Le Pas d'Acier   PASDA

NEY, CHARLIE, a rabbit-
    catcher, The Sailor's
    Return   SAILO

NGAMA
    MEDERE
    N'KVA, deities, masters
    of creation
    La Création du Monde
                          CREAT

NICCOLO, waiter at the café,
    Les Femmes de Bonne
    Humeur   FEMME

NICOLETTO, studying dancing
    under Rigadon, Scuola di
    Ballo   SCUOL

NIECE, HER. See: House-
    keeper, The

NIGHT, personification
    The Descent of Hebe
                          DESCE
    Personification
    CALAMITY
    FATE
    DEATH
    NEMESIS
    SIN
    DECEIT
    DISCORD, her children
    I Titani   TITAN

NIGHT. See also:
    Goddess of the Night, The
    Hours of Night, Twelve
    Queen of Night, The
    Watchers of the Night

NIGHT-CLUB HOSTESS, A,
    witness in murder case,
    Hear Ye! Hear Ye!
                          HEARY

NIGHT, DAUGHTERS OF THE.
    See: Shadow, The

NIGHT, QUEEN OF THE.
    See: Moon, The

NIGHT, QUEEN OF THE
    SPIRITS OF. See:
    Sakourada

NIGHT STAR, THE, personi-
    fication, La Nuit et le
    Jour   NUITE

NIGHT WATCHMAN. See:
    Dégas Dancer

NIGHTINGALE
    DOVE
    HEN, participate in "a
    comedy of ornithological
    loves and jealousies"

The Birds   BIRDS
Cures Little Emperor by
    singing
Chinese Nightingale   CHINE

NIGHTINGALE, ARTIFICIAL,
    fails to cure Little Emperor
    by her singing, Chinese
    Nightingale   CHINE

NIGHTINGALE, MECHANICAL,
    gift to Emperor of China
    from Emperor of Japan;
    replaces the Nightingale;
    Song of the Nightingale
                          SONGO

NIGHTINGALE, THE, causes
    rose to bloom at cost of
    her own life
    Le Rossignol et la Rose
                          ROSSG
    Le Rossignol et la Rose
                          ROSSI
    Entertains Emperor of China,
    replaced by Mechanical
    Nightingale, gift of Emperor
    of Japan
    Song of the Nightingale
                          SONGO

NIGHTINGALE, THE. See also:
    Death

NIJNI NOVGOROD, GOVERNOR
    OF. See: Smouroff

NIKIA, a bayadère, loves Solor,
    killed by Gamsatti, daughter
    of the Rajah Dugmanta, La
    Bayadère   BAYAD

NIKITYTCH, DOBRYNA, noted
    Bogatyri hero, Bogatyri
                          BOGAT

NILAS. See: Girl-Reindeer

NILE. See: King of the Nile

NILSSON, host of the inn,
    Electra   ELECT

NINA, loved by and in love
with Germeuil; sought by
Blinval, son of the Gover-
nor of the Province
THE COMTE, her father
Nina   NINAO

NINA. See also:
Arbenin
Elyse
Georges
Princess Nina, The

NIÑA DEL ORO, LA, ballerina
in Spanish dance
THE CAVALIER, her
partner
LOS BASTONEROS, six
Spanish dancers
Madroños   MADRO

NINE. See: Muses, Nine

NINI. See: Patte en l'air,
Nini

NINKA. See: Zoloe

NINTH VARIATION. See:
Theme and First Variation

NIRILYA, betrothed to Nal,
The Talisman   TALIS

NIRITI. See: Amravati

NISIA. See: Candaules, King
of Lydia

N'KVA. See: Ngama

NOBLEMAN, employer of the
Serving-Maid
TWO LADIES, his friends
and guests at picnic;
amused by the Shepherd
The Gods Go A-Begging
                             GODSA
The Gods Go A-Begging
                             GODSG
The Gods Go A-Begging
                             GODSO

NOBLEMAN. See also: Serving-
Maid, The

NOBLEMAN, THE YOUNG. See:
Julien

NORI, Japanese youth, engaged
to Yedda, Yedda   YEDDA

NORWEGIAN COUPLE, performs
Norwegian jumping dance for
Cupid's approval, The Whims
of Cupid and the Ballet Master   WHIMS

NOTARY, A, prepares marriage
contract for Edmond and
Thérèse, La Somnambule
                             SOMNA

NOTARY, THE, releases Georges-
Émile Guérin from the Lo-
géat Mental Hospital
Les Algues   ALGUE
Engaged by Fabrizio to
force Rigadon to return
commission
Scuola di Ballo   SCUOL

NOUREDDA, maiden being sent
to join the Khan's harem
MOZDOCK, her brother
La Source   SOURC

NOUREDDIN, Maharajah of Lahore, betrothed to Damayanti,
The Talisman   TALIS

NOUREDDIN. See also: Djemil

NOURMAHAL, Achmet's "favorite
sultana," replaced in his affections by the Péri (Leila),
La Péri   PERII

NOVEMBER, a man, Twelve for
the Mail-Coach   TWELV

NOVERRE, MONSIEUR, choreographer and ballet master
at the King's Theatre, London

MADAME NOVERRE, his
wife
The Prospect Before Us
                         PROSP

NOVGOROD, GOVERNOR OF
NIJNI. See: Smouroff

NOVICE, THE, newly born,
seeks to destroy men;
kills First Intruder; falls
in love with but later kills
Second Intruder
THE QUEEN, her mother,
ruler of tribe of predatory
females
The Cage   CAGEE

NOZGULLE. See:
Abdurassul, Bey
Bobo-Safar
Zamon

NUBIA. See: King of Nubia,
The

NUMBER. See:
Christmas Number, The
Summer Number, The

NUNES, BLAU, daring and
fearless gaucho, rescues
Santao and Teniguá from
enchanted cave of Sala-
manca do Jaraú; fascinated
by vision of Teniguá
BOI BARROSO, magician,
helps Blau Nunes with the
rescue
Salamanca do Jaraú SALAM

NUNZIATA, innkeeper, confidante of Graziosa, Graziosa
                         GRAZI

NURSE, to Juliet, daughter of
Old Capulet
Romeo and Juliet   ROMEA
To Juliet, daughter of
Capulet
Romeo and Juliet   ROMEJ

NURSE, PRINCESS DAÏTA'S.

See: Jamato

NURSE, THE, to the Daughter,
Kuruc Fairy Tale   KURUC

NURSEMAID. See: Chief Nursemaid, The

NURSEMAIDS. See: Chief
Nursemaid, The

NURSES. See: Male Nurses,
The

NUTCRACKER, toy given Clara
(Masha) by Drosselmeyer as
Christmas present; comes
to life, leads troops against
King of the Mice
The Nutcracker   NUTCA
The Nutcracker   NUTCK
The Nutcracker   NUTCR

NUTCRACKER. See also:
Sugarplum Fairy

NYMPH. See: Chain Store
Nymph

NYMPH OF THE DANUBE, THE,
chosen by the Spirit of the
Danube to watch over Fleur-
des-Champs
UNDINES, her attendants
La Fille du Danube   FILLD

NYMPH, THE
SIX OTHER NYMPHS, en-
counter the Faun; fascinated
with, then frightened by him
The Afternoon of a Faun
                         AFTEN
The Afternoon of a Faun
                         AFTER
Participant in the bacchanale
Bacchanale   BACCH

NYMPHS, supernatural beings,
Defense of Paradise DEFEN

NYMPHS. See also: Governess
of the Nymphs

NYMPHS OF MONDEGO, emerge
    from the Fountain of Tears,
    appear before Doña Ines de
    Castro, Doña Ines de Castro
                                 DONAI

NYMPHS, TWO, handmaidens
    to Leto, mother of Apollo,
    Apollo, Leader of the
    Muses   APOLL

O

O. See: Garatuja, O.

OBEDIENCE, personification,
    Saint Francis   SAINT

OBERON, King of the Fairies
    The Birthday of Oberon
                                BIRTO
    The Dream   DREAM
    Disguised as a hermit,
    gives Luc magic flute
    The Magic Flute   MAGIC
    King of the Fairies
    A Midsummer Night's
    Dream   MIDSU

OBIZZO. See: Marquis Obizzo
    di Malaspina

OBOLA, a Danish pirate,
    Sieba   SIEBA

OCÉANIDE. See: Captain

OCTAVIA. See: Antony

OCTAVIUS. See: Antony

OCTOBER, a huntsman,
    Twelve for the Mail-Coach
                                TWELV

ODALISQUE, AN, chief dancer
    at Shahryar's court,
    Schéhérazade   SCHEH

ODARKA, Russian village girl
    Christmas Eve   CHRIS
    The Pannochka, daughter
    of Polish nobleman, loved

by Andrey, son of Taras
    Bulba
    Taras Bulba   TARAS

ODETTE, Queen of the Swans,
    under Von Rotbart's spell;
    becomes beautiful woman
    between midnight and dawn;
    loved by Prince Siegfried;
    impersonated by Odile
    Swan Lake   SWANA
    Swan Lake   SWANE
    Swan Lake   SWANK
    Swan Lake   SWANL

ODETTE. See also: Cinderella

ODILE. See:
    Odette
    Von Rotbart

ODYSSEUS, legendary Greek
    hero
    PENELOPE, his wife
    I, Odysseus   IODYS
    Legendary Greek hero,
    wanders following the fall
    of Troy, which wanderings
    are seen as "a twentieth
    century journey of the mind"
    Odyssey   ODYSS

ODYSSEUS. See also: Ulysses

OEDIPUS, former King of Thebes,
    conquered by Creon
    JOCASTA, his mother and
    wife
    ANTIGONE, his daughter,
    buries Polynices in defiance
    of Creon's orders
    POLYNICES, her brother,
    killed in battle
    ETIOCLES, her brother,
    killed in battle
    Antigone   ANTIG
    King of Thebes
    JOCASTA, his mother and
    wife
    Night Journey   NIGHJ
    King of Thebes, answers
    riddles put to him by the
    Sphinx; kills her

La Rencontre   RENCO   MIRAC

OEDIPUS. See also: Sphinx,   OGRES. See: King of the Ogres
   The

OENONE, confidante of Phaedra,   OKSANA, Russian village girl,
   Phèdre   PHEDR   loved by Vakula
                                          KOUM, her father
OFFICER, patron of fashionable   KOUM'S WIFE
   café, Offenbach in the Under-   Christmas Eve   CHRIS
   world   OFFEN   Ukrainian peasant girl,
                                          loved by Ostap, son of
OFFICER. See also: Taras Bulba
   Assay Officer   Taras Bulba   TARAS
   Police Officer
                                     OLD AGE. See: Poet, The
OFFICER, AN, accepted by
   Young Girl as her fiance   OLD CAPULET, head of a house
   HIS WIFE, accuses him   at variance with the house
   of attempted bigamy   of Montague
   HIS CHILDREN   JULIET, his daughter, in
   Bonne-Bouche   BONNE   love with Romeo
                                       TYBALT, nephew of Lady
OFFICER OF LANCERS, mem-   Capulet, kills Mercutio,
   ber of troop passing   killed by Romeo
   through small Austrian   Romeo and Juliet   ROMEA
   village, Halte de Cavalerie
                       HALTE   OLD CAPULET. See also:
                                       Capulet
OFFICER, THE, soldier,   Nurse
   spends evening at Paris   Old Montague
   café   Paris
   Gaîte Parisienne   GAITE
   In charge of gas attack   OLD CHARLATAN, THE, magi-
   precautions course   cian, performs at carnival;
   THE GIRL, his sweetheart,   master of the puppets
   places rose in his gas   Petrouchka, the Blackamoor,
   mask   and the Dancer, Petrouchka
   Perhaps Tomorrow!   PETRO
                       PERHA
                                     OLD CHARLATAN, THE. See
OFFICERS, ARMY. See: also:
   Courasche   Blackamoor, The
                                       Dancer, The
OFFICIAL. See: Govern-   Petrouchka
   ment Official, A   Policeman

OFFICIAL, THE, of the Gor-   OLD CHINESE POET, in love
   bals, slum district of   with nature, Shadow of the
   Glasgow; patronizes the   Wind   SHADW
   Prostitute, arranges for
   assassination of the Stran-   OLD CRONE, THE. See: Kwahu
   ger, Miracle in the Gorbals
                                     OLD DEVIL, THE

THE DEVILKIN
THE SHE-DEVIL, over-
come by Balda's cunning
The Fairy-Tale of the
Priest and His Workman
Balda   FAIRY

OLD DEVIL, THE. See also:
Little Hare, The First

OLD FAUN, THE, gives Styrax
and other fauns lesson on
the pan-pipes, Cydalise et
le Chèvre-pied   CYDAL

OLD GENERAL, THE, com-
mander of Junior Cadets,
Graduation Ball   GRADU

OLD GENERAL, THE. See
also: Leader of the Junior
Cadets

OLD KADDISH, THE. See:
Abdurassul, Bey

OLD LADY. See: Old Man

OLD LORD, THE, impoverished,
given financial aid by the
Devil
HIS DAUGHTER, abandons
the Fiance, falls in love
with the Beggar
THE FIANCE, wealthy, be-
trothed to the Old Lord's
daughter
THE BEGGAR, falls in
love with the Old Lord's
daughter
Devil's Holiday   DEVIL

OLD LORD, THE. See also:
Gypsy Girl, The
Hat Seller, The

OLD MADGE, sorceress,
predicts that Effie will
be married, but not to
James Reuben; kills La
Sylphide with magic scarf
La Sylphide   SYLPH
La Sylphide   SYLPL

OLD MAN
OLD LADY, elderly couple
at Belvedere Gardens,
Vienna; watching the passing
scene
Voices of Spring   VOICE

OLD MAN. See also:
Bearded Old Man
Blind Old Man
Master of Ceremonies

OLD MAN IN PRISON, "ignorance,
age and naïveté, " The Great
American Goof   GREAT

OLD MENNERS, dealer, attracted
to Mary, wife of Longren;
kills her in struggle
YOUNG MENNERS, his lout-
ish son
Red Sails   REDSA

OLD MONTAGUE, head of house
at variance with the House
of Capulet
ROMEO, his son, in love
with Juliet
Romeo and Juliet   ROMEA

OLD MONTAGUE. See also:
Capulet
Mercutio
Montagu
Montague
Old Capulet

OLD MOTHER, THE, claimed
by Death, The Green Table
                     GREEN

OLD NEIGHBOR. See: Rich
Old Neighbor, A

OLD PEOPLE, TWO, perform
dance for Cupid's approval,
The Whims of Cupid and the
Ballet Master   WHIMS

OLD PIONEER WOMAN, neighbor
of Young Farmer, Appalachian
Spring   APPAL

OLD POET
   YOUNG WARRIOR, appear
   throughout the ballet, bind
   various episodes together
   Shadow of the Wind SHADW

OLD PROSPECTOR, tells Boy
   Hiker and Girl Hiker
   story of ghost town,
   Ghost Town   GHOST

OLD SHEPHERD, THE, seen
   by Young Musician in his
   dream, Symphonie Fan-
   tastique   SYMPH

OLD SOLDIER, THE. See:
   Young Soldier, The

OLD WOMAN, AN. See:
   Veteran Soldier, A

OLD WOMAN, DYING, "one
   of the living, " The Great
   American Goof   GREAT

OLD WOMAN, THE, carnival
   reveler, Devil's Holiday
                        DEVIL

OLDER MARRIED COUPLE,
   AN, warm marriage bed
   for The Bride and The
   Bridegroom, Les Noces
                        NOCES

OLDER MARRIED COUPLE,
   AN. See also:
   Bride, The
   Bridegroom, The

OLE, a bargeman, Loin du
   Danemark   LOIND

OLIA, Soviet schoolgirl. Baby
   Stork   BABYS

OLIFOUR, chief judge, attracted
   to Zoloe, Le Dieu et la
   Bayadère   DIEUE

OLIFOUR. See also:
   Captain of the Guard

Chief of the Slavs
Olivier
Tchop-Dar, The

OLIVIA SOLARINO. See: Lugano, Marco

OLIVIER, peasant youth, in love
   with Marietta
   Kalkabrino   KALKA
   A trumpeter of musketeers
   and Monsieur de Saint-Rambert's servant
   La Somnambule   SOMNA

OLIVIER. See also:
   Monk, A
   Olifour

OLOVA, a gypsy woman, La
   Gitana   GITAN

OMBRE, L' (The Shade) (The
   Spirit), ghost of murdered
   lady who died by smelling
   bunch of poisoned flowers;
   returns to dance with her
   lover
   L'OMBRE'S LOVER, mourns
   for her
   L'Ombre   OMBRE

OMEOPATICO, DOCTOR, physician
   supposedly widowed, marries
   Lauretta
   SIGNORA CLORINDE, his
   wife, rescued from brigands
   by Luigi
   La Tarentule   TAREN

ONDINE, naiad
   Ondine   ONDIE
   Naiad, lures Palemon from
   Berthe, his betrothed
   Ondine   ONDII
   Naiad
   Ondine   ONDIL
   Naiad, in love with Matteo
   HYDROLA, Queen of the
   Waters, her mother
   Ondine   ONDIN
   Naiad
   Les Ondines   ONDIS

ONDINE. See also:
  Tirrenio, King of the
    Waters
  Undines

ONE. See: Green One, The

ONE, THE CHOSEN. See:
  Chosen One, The
  Sage
  Witch

ONE, THE LITTLE UGLY.
  See: Laiderette

ONE WHO DANCES, THE,
  allegorical figure, Letter
  to the World   LETTE

ONE WHO SPEAKS, THE. See:
  Actress, An

OPERA. See: Director of
  the Opera

OPERETTA STAR
  OPERETTA STAR'S ES-
  CORT, patrons of fashionable café Offenbach in
  the Underworld   OFFEN

OPHELIA, Hamlet's sweetheart
  LAERTES, her brother
  HAMLET, Ophelia's sweet-
  heart, portrayed by La
  Gloire (The Star)
  HAMLET'S MOTHER
  HAMLET'S STEPFATHER
  La Gloire   GLOIR

OPHELIA. See also:
  Gloire, La
  Polonius

OPIUM DEN. See: Proprietor
  of an Opium Den

OPPOSITE. See: Young Man
  From the House Opposite

ORATOR, THE, personification
  Le Pas d'Acier   PASDA
  Discusses wedding guests

with the audience
A Wedding Bouquet   WEDDI

ORCHIDÉE. See: Duchic,
  Monsieur

O'REILLY, MR. , manager of
  the Pantheon Theatre, London; competitor and friend
  of Mr. Taylor, The Prospect
  Before Us   PROSP

ORESTES, attempts to make
  love to Helen of Troy, wife
  of King Menelaus, King of
  Sparta, Helen of Troy
                      HELEN

ORESTES. See also:
  Clytemnestra
  Elektra

ORFEO, singer and musician,
  seeks to bring his wife back
  from the Underworld
  EURYDICE, his late wife
  La Tragedia di Orfeo
                      TRAGO

ORFEO. See also:
  Orphée
  Orpheus

ORIANA, lady, figment of Don
  Quixote's imagination, Don
  Quixote   DONQX

ORIANE, young girl, seeking
  love, falls in love with the
  Prince of Love
  HER FOUR ATTENDANTS
  Oriane et le Prince d'Amour
                      ORIAN

ORIANE. See also:
  Jester, The
  Jongleur, The
  Merchant, The
  Poet, The

ORION, "the robber khan"
  HIS SLAVES
  HIS CONCUBINES

Sylvia   SYLVA
"A giant hunter of the forest," secretly in love with Sylvia
Sylvia   SYLVI

ORLANDO. See:
    Alvarez
    Furioso, Orlando (Roland)

ORO. See: Niña del Oro, La

ORPHÉE (Orpheus), singer and musician, seeks to bring his wife back from the Underworld, depicted wearing blue jeans "in a world full of symbols"
    EURYDICE, his wife, victim of an untimely death
    Orphée   ORPHH

ORPHÉE. See also:
    Orfeo
    Orpheus

ORPHEUS, deity
    The Creatures of Prometheus
                                CREAU
    Singer and musician, seeks to bring his wife back from the Underworld
    EURYDICE, his wife, victim of an untimely death
    Orpheus   ORPHE
    Orpheus in Town   ORPHI
    Orpheus and Eurydice
                                ORPHS
    Orpheus and Eurydice
                                ORPHU

ORPHEUS. See also:
    Amor
    Dark Angel
    Leader of the Bacchantes
    Orfeo
    Orphée

ORRUM, EILLEY. See:
    Orum, Eilley

ORSINO. See: del Sato,
    Orsino

ORSON. See: Hyde, Orson

ORUM, EILLEY (Eilley Orrum), wife of Sandy Bowers, friend of Bonanza King Comstock, Ghost Town
                                GHOST

OSCAR. See: Count Oscar

OSÖD, young shepherd, in love with Buza, The Holy Torch
                                HOLYT

OSÖD. See also: Queen of the Evil Fairies

OSORIO. See: Prince Osorio, Governor of Rome

OSTAP. See:
    Bulba, Taras
    Oksana

OSTRICH, THE, escapes from the Photographer, Les Mariés de la Tour Eiffel
                                MARIE

OSWALD. See:
    Lord Rewena
    Walther

OTELLO, general of the Venetian Republic
    DESDEMONA, his wife
    BRABANZIO, Desdemona's father
    Otello   OTELL

OTELLO. See also:
    Cassio
    Emilia
    Iago
    Montano

OTHELLO, The Moor of Venice, Venetian general
    DESDEMONA, his wife, killed by him as a result of plot by Jago (Iago)
    The Moor of Venice MOORO
    Othello   OTHEL

OTHELLO. See also:
   Iago
   Jago (Iago)

OTHER MAN, THE. See:
   Wife, The

OTHER, THE, circus horse,
   temporarily attracts the
   white mare She from He,
   the black stallion, Idylle
                         IDYLL

OTHER WOMAN, THE, per-
   sonification, L'Homme et
   son Désir   HOMME

OTTAVIO. See: Don Ottavio

OTTO, officer, in love with
   Ragonda, daughter of
   Princess Millefleurs,
   Fiammetta   FIAMM

OUTPOST. See: Commandant
   of the Patrol at the Outpost

OVE, SQUIRE. See: Birthe,
   Miss

OVERSEERS, TWO. See:
   Galley-Slaves

OVERTURE, a captain, Twelve
   for the Mail-Coach TWELV

OWL
   PUSSYCAT, "go to sea in
   a beautiful pea-green
   boat"
   The Owl and the Pussycat
                         OWLAN

OZAÏ, South Seas native girl,
   falls in love with Monsieur
   de Surville, nephew of
   Monsieur de Bougainville,
   Ozaï   OZAII

OZAÏ. See also:
   Financier, A
   Lawyer, A

Marquis, A

P

PACHITA, betrothed to Masetto,
   La Gitana   GITAN

PAGANINI, Italian violinist
   Paganini   PAGAI
   Paganini   PAGAN

PAGANINI. See also:
   Divine Genius, The
   Envy
   Florentine Beauty, A
   Gossip
   Guile
   Muse
   Satan
   Scandal

PAGE, HER. See:
   Carnation Fairy, The
   Cherry Blossom Fairy, The
   Fairy of the Humming Birds,
      The
   Fairy of the Pine Woods, The
   Fairy of the Song-Birds, The
   Lilac Fairy, The

PAGES, HER TWO. See:
   Carabosse

PAI-DO-MATO. See: Zuimaaluti

PAI-DO-MATO, DAUGHTERS OF.
   See: Zuimaaluti

PALEMON, nobleman, lured
   from Berthe by Ondine
   BERTHE, his betrothed
   Ondine   ONDII

PALL BEARERS, FOUR, hooded
   monks, carry Hamlet to his
   grave, Hamlet   HAMLE

PALLAS ATHENA, goddess
   Ballet Comique de la Reine
                         BALLC
   Goddess, competes with
   Aphrodite and Hera in
   beauty contest judged by

Paris
Helen of Troy   HELEN

PALLAS ATHENA. See also:
Athena
King Menelaus, King of
Sparta

PALMERIS OF ENGLAND,
hero of chivalry, figment
of Don Quixote's imagina-
tion, Don Quixote DONQX

PAN, participant in gypsy
carnival
Aleko   ALEKO
God
Ballet Comique de la
Reine   BALLC
Helps reunite Daphnis and
Chloë
Daphnis et Chloë   DAPHN
In love with Admadeya,
appears in ballet at the
Serf's Theatre
Katerina   KATER

PAN. See also:
Pipes of Pan, The
Syrinx

PANDORA, mythological figure,
opens forbidden box
GUIGNOL, her servant
Guignol et Pandore GUIGN
Pandora   PANDO

PANNL See: Bashmirskaya,
Panni

PANNOCHKA, THE. See:
Bulba, Taras
Odarka

PANTALEONE, character por-
trayed by strolling player,
Le Marché des Innocents
MARCH

PANTALON, traditional pantomime figure, Le Carnaval
CARNA

PANTALONE. See: Clarice

PANTOKA, HOUAN, a gypsy,
Zoraiya   ZORAI

PANZA, SANCHO, Don Quixote's
servant and squire
Don Quixote   DONQI
Don Quixote   DONQO
Don Quixote   DONQT
Don Quichotte   DONQU
Don Quichotte   DONQV
Don Quixote   DONQX

PAOLO. See: Rosa

PAOLO MALATESTA. See:
Angelic Apparition
Francesca (Francesca da
Rimini)

PAPERS. See: Society Papers

PAPILLON, young girl, loved by
Pierrot, Le Carnaval
CARNA

PAPIN, inventor, Excelsior
EXCEL

PÂQUERETTE, village girl,
loved by François,
Pâquerette   PAQUE

PAQUITA, young girl, hopes to
become a dancer; flirted
with by Cleophas
Le Diable Boiteux   DIABL
Gypsy dancer, in love with
Lucien d'Hervilly
Paquita   PAQUI
Paquita   PAQUT

PAQUITA. See also: Comte
d'Hervilly, The

PARABHRITICA, friend of Sakuntala, Sakuntala   SAKUN

PARADO. See: Bartolo

PARASHA, Russian girl, in

love with Eugene; dies in
flood
HER MOTHER
The Bronze Horseman
                        BRONZ

PARASSIA. See: Khivria

PARCAE, the Three Fates,
    Les Amours de Jupiter
                        AMOUJ

PAREMBO, Chief of the Gypsies,
    kidnaps Lauretta as child,
    La Gitana   GITAN

PAREMBO. See also: Duke
    of Medina-Celi, The

PARENTS. See: Bride

PARENTS, HER. See: Ida

PARENTS, HIS. See: Karl

PARENTS, THEIR. See:
    Cinderella

PARENTS, YOUNG GIRL'S.
    See: Garatuja, O.

PARIS, kidnaps Helen
    Clytemnestra   CLYTE
    Shepherd, awards golden
    apple to Aphrodite, be-
    comes Helen's lover
    Helen of Troy   HELEN
    Drunken patron of boîte de
    nuit in Paris, France
    The Judgment of Paris
                        JUDGM
    Kidnaps Helen
    The Judgment of Paris
                        JUDGT
    Le Jugement de Paris
                        JUGEM
    Le Jugement de Paris
                        JUGEP
    "Firmly refuses to choose
    between his goddesses"
    Pas des Déesses   PASDS
    Suitor of Juliet, daughter
    of Old Capulet

Romeo and Juliet   ROMEA
Suitor of Juliet, daughter
of Capulet
Romeo and Juliet   ROMEJ
Young nobleman, selected
by Capulet as husband for
his daughter Juliet
Romeo and Juliet   ROMEO
Kidnaps Helen
Spectacle   SPECL

PARIS. See also:
    Ajax I
    Aphrodite
    Calchas
    Helen
    Hera
    Hermes
    Juno
    King Menelaus, King of
        Sparta
    Lamb
    Minerva
    Pallas Athena
    Venus
    Waiter

PARROT, THE. See: Kid, The

PARTNER AND HUSBAND, HER.
    See: Adagio-Bride, The

PARTNER, BALLERINA'S. See:
    Death

PARTNER, HER. See: Gypsy
    Fortune Teller

PARTNERS. See: Waltzing
    Ladies and Their Partners

PARTY-THROWER, THE, host
    to guests at 2222 Club, New
    York City, Café Society
                        CAFES

PASCARILLO, a street-singer,
    Napoli   NAPOL

PASCOU, a hunchback, the town-
    crier, La Korrigane KORRI

PASHA OF THE ISLE OF COS.

See: Seyd

PASHA, THE, oriental po-
tentate, owner of the
runaway slave Leila,
La Péri   PERII

PASHA, THE. See also:
Péri, The

PASIPHAE. See:
Minos, King of Crete
Phaedra

PASQUINA, friend of Constan-
za; betrothed to Battista,
Les Femmes de Bonne
Humeur   FEMME

PASSERS-BY, three girls,
meet Sailors in New York
bar, Fancy Free FANCY

PASSERS-BY. See also:
Sailors, Three

PASSIFONT. See: Bull, John

PASSION, personification, Les
Présages   PRESA

PASSION. See also: Visions
of Passion

PASSOLO, maître de ballet
and premier danseur, La
Prima Ballerina   PRIMA

PAST, AN EPISODE IN HIS.
See: Caroline

PASTOR, friend and spiritual
guide of the Accused (Lizzie Borden); comforts her
at her execution, Fall
River Legend   FALLR

PAT. See: Garrett, Pat

PATHFINDER, allegorical
figure, Wind in the
Mountains   WINDI

PATIMATE, woodcutter in service of the Fairy Hamza, Le
Papillon   PAPIL

PATROL. See:
Captain of the Glow-Worm
Patrol
Commandant of the Patrol
at the Outpost

PATRONESS, THE, opens ball
at Hotel de l'Europe, Buda-
pest
HER HUSBAND
HER THREE DAUGHTERS
HER SON, a lieutenant of
hussars
Carnival at Pest   CARNI

PATTE EN L'AIR, NINI, cancan dancer, Bar aux Folies-
Bergère   BARAU

PAUL, "pleasant, vicious and
quarrelsome," friend of
Josephine
JOHN, "an elder brother,
who regrets the illness of
his father," also a friend
of Josephine
A Wedding Bouquet WEDDI

PAUL. See also: Emperor
Paul I, Emperor of Russia

PAUL, CADET, of the Danish
navy, Loin du Danemark
                           LOIND

PAVANE, Lord Chamberlain,
Cinderella   CINDA

PAWNS. See:
Black Pawns
Red Pawns

PEACE, TEMPLE OF. See:
High Priest of the Temple
of Peace

PEACHES, twentieth century
gold digger

HER LOVER, remains true
to her following 1929 Wall
Street crash
The Creation of the World
                              CREAW

PEARL. See: White Pearl,
The

PEARL FAIRY, THE. See:
Fairy Hamza, The

PEARL, THE YELLOW. See:
White Pearl, The

PEARLS, BLACK. See:
White Pearl, The

PEARLS, PINK. See:
White Pearl, The

PEARSON'S, representation
of British publication,
The Press   PRESS

PEASANT. See also: Pesante

PEASANT GIRL. See: Mexican Peon

PEASANT GIRL, THE, parti-
cipant in festival in small
Spanish town, Capriccio
Espagnol   CAPRI

PEASANT, RICH. See:
Fadette

PEASANT YOUTH, THE,
participant in festival in
small Spanish town,
Capriccio Espagnol CAPRI

PEASANTS, personifications,
Le Pas d'Acier   PASDA

PEASANT'S SON, RICH. See:
Fadette

PECADO, a devil, Pastorela
                              PASTO

PEDDLER, sells cheap jewelry

at fair, driven away by
Three Gypsies
The Fair at Sorochinsk
                              FAIRA
Caricature of cartoon charac-
ter
The New Yorker   NEWYO

PEDRILLO, a miller
HIS WIFE
BABETTE (ROSINE), their
daughter
Les Pages du Duc de Ven-
dôme   PAGES

PEDRO. See: Cordoba, Pedro

PEDRO, DON. See:
Councillor, The
Don Pedro Ricco
Doña Ines de Castro
Infanta of Navarre, The

PEER GYNT. See:
Aase
Anitra
Ingrid
Solveig
Troll King, The

PELLÉAS. See: Goulad

PENDULARS, representations of
machinery, Iron Foundry
                              IRONF

PENELOPE, See: Odysseus

PENNY. See: Golden Penny,
The

PEON. See: Mexican Peon

PEOPLE. See: Old People,
Two

PÉPÉ, Mexican terrier belonging to Julia, A Wedding
Bouquet   WEDDI

PEPINELLI. See: Count Pepinelli

PEPIO, temporarily betrothed
to Gourouli, attracted by
life of gypsies
Les Deux Pigéons   DEUXN
Les Deux Pigéons   DEUXP

PEPIO. See also: Zarifi

PEPPINO, DON. See: Dia-
volina

PEPPO, proprietor of a
lemonade stall, in love
with Teresina, Napoli
                                        NAPOL

PERCUSSION. See: Wood-
winds

PEREGRINA, daughter of local
clergyman, sentenced to
be burned as a witch;
rescued
STUDENT, betrothed to
daughter of burgomaster,
captivated by Peregrina;
attempts suicide by jumping
into fire where Peregrina
being burned; rescued also
The Church Festival at
Delft   CHURC

PEREZ, majordomo of the
Duke of Medina-Celi, La
Gitana   GITAN

PERFUME. See: She Wore a
Perfume

PERFUMED SEDUCTION,
THREE SPIRITS OF.
See: Rose

PÉRI, THE, fairy, stands
guard at the gates of
Paradise, possesses
flower of immortality
ISKENDER, mortal,
takes flower from Péri,
then realizes that he
must die like other
mortals
La Péri   PERIA

Fairy
La Péri   PERIC
La Péri   PERIF
"Imaginary being, like an
elf or fairy," dances and
charms King
KING, takes lotus flower of
immortality from Péri, later
returns it
La Péri   PERID
Oriental fairy, afterwards
Leila, escaped slave, pro-
perty of the Pasha; loved by
Achmet
La Péri   PERII

PÉRI, THE. See also: Nourmahal

PERIGORD, MADAME DE,
Frenchwoman, Vienna- 1814
                                        VIENN

PERLOUSE, appears on beach,
Le Train Bleu   TRAIN

PERRUQUIER, hair dresser at
the opera, The Débutante
                                        DEBUT

PERSEPHONE, Queen of Hades,
abducted by Pluto
PLUTO, her husband, King
of Hades
DEMETER, her mother
ZEUS, god, her father
Falls the Shadow Between
                                        FALLS
Persephone   PERSE
Persephone   PERSF
Persephone   PERSG
Persephone   PERSH
Attends feast of Bacchus
Sylvia   SYLVA

PERSEVERANCE. See: Genii
of Perseverance, The

PERSIA. See: Prince of Persia

PERSIA, PRINCESS OF. See:
Prince of Persia

PERSONAGE, A, attends masked ball with his lady friend; encounters his wife there with her lover
PERSONAGE'S LADY FRIEND
PERSONAGE'S WIFE
PERSONAGE'S WIFE'S LOVER
Les Masques   MASQS

PERSONAGE WITH LONG EARS, personification of animal, Carnival of Animals
                               CARNV

PERSONIFICATION OF DANCE. See:
Bolero
Canzonetta
Tarantella
Tirolese

PERSONIFICATION OF DEATH. See: Morte Amoureuse, La

PERSONIFICATION OF DIC-TATORSHIP. See: Leader, The

PERSONIFICATION OF EVERY-WOMAN. See: Hérodiade

PERSONIFICATION OF EVIL. See: Serpent

PERSONIFICATION OF FALSE-HOOD. See: Duessa

PERSONIFICATION OF FATE. See: Nemesis Figure

PERSONIFICATION OF HOLI-NESS. See: St. George

PERSONIFICATION OF HY-POCRISY. See: Archi-mago

PERSONIFICATION OF LOVE. See: Prince of Love, The

PERSONIFICATION OF LUST. See: Spanish Woman

PERSONIFICATION OF MAN. See: Hero, The

PERSONIFICATION OF MODERN MAN. See: H. P.

PERSONIFICATION OF MODERN MAN IN SPACE. See: Icaros

PERSONIFICATION OF RIVER. See:
Congo
Guadalquivir
Neva
Rhine
Thames
Tiber

PERSONIFICATION OF SENSUAL PLEASURE. See: Volupia

PERSONIFICATION OF TRUTH. See: Una

PERSONIFICATION OF WOMAN. See: Femina

PERSONIFICATIONS OF CAPI-TALISM. See: Fat Men, The Three

PERSONIFICATIONS OF EVIL FORCES. See:
Destiny
Leader of Blue Group
Leader of Red Group (Town)
Leader of Yellow Group (Country)

PERUVIAN, THE, visiting Paris and hoping to have a good time; spends evening at café, Gaîté Parisienne
                               GAITE

PESANTE. See:
Peasant
Signor Pesante

PESTILENCE, personification,
    Job   JOBBB

PETER, young boy, captures
    Wolf with the aid of Bird,
    Duck and Cat
    GRANDFATHER, his grand-
    father, warns Peter against
    Wolf
    Peter and the Wolf   PETER
    Peter and the Wolf   PETEW
    Faithful retainer of Count
    Raoul de Créqui
    MARGARITA, his daughter
    Raoul de Créqui   RAOUL

PETER. See also:
    First Hunter
    Petr
    Pyotr

PETER I, Tsar of Russia
    HIS AIDE-DE-CAMP
    The Bronze Horseman
                          BRONZ
    Tsar of Russia, loved by
    Elizabeth
    PRINCESS SOPHIA, Regent,
    his sister
    Gli Strelizzi   STREL

PETER I. See also: Lefort

PETERS, friend of Valentine,
    Faust   FAUST

PETERSON, a peasant, Flik
    and Flok   FLIKA

PETIT JEAN. See: Mathurin

PETR, an old peasant
    GAVRILO
    DANILO
    IVANOUSHKA, his three
    sons
    The Hump-Backed Horse
                          HUMPB
    The Hump-Backed Horse
                          HUMPH

PETR. See also:
    Hump-Backed Horse, The

Peter
Pyotr
Tsar-Maiden, The

PETROUCHKA, clown-puppet,
    brought to life by the Old
    Charlatan, killed by the
    Blackmoor
    Petrouchka   PETRO

PETRUCIO, chief of the smug-
    glers
    STELLA, his daughter
    JACOPPO BALBI, his nephew
    Stella   STELL

PHAEDRA, portrayed by La
    Gloire (The Star); in love
    with Hippolytus
    HIPPOLYTUS, her stepson
    La Gloire   GLOIR
    Phèdre, in love with Hippo-
    lytus; rejected, falsely ac-
    cuses him of attempting to
    dishonor her, takes poison,
    dies
    THESEUS, her husband
    HIPPOLYTUS, son of Theseus
    and Hippolyte, Queen of the
    Amazons; in love with Aricia
    Phaedra   PHAED
    Phèdre   PHEDR
    MINOS, her father
    PASIPHAË, her mother
    Phèdre   PHEDR

PHAEDRA. See also:
    Aricia
    Oenone
    Poseidon

PHARAOH. See: Aspicia

PHARAOH'S DAUGHTER. See:
    Mummy of the Pharaoh's
    Daughter

PHÈDRE. See: Phaedra

PHILEMON, aged 100 years
    PHILEMON THE YOUNGER,
    his son aged 70 years
    BAUCIS, his wife

LOUIS, a naval officer
JOHN, an army officer
HERMANN, an artist, their
three sons
CAROLINE, Louis' wife
ANN, John's wife
VINCENZO
CLAUDIUS
ANTON
AGLAE
THALIA
EUPHROSINE, the six
grandchildren of Philemon
the Younger
Vieux Souvenirs   VIEUX

PHILEMON. See also:
Lars
Marguerite

PHILIP. See:
Filippo
Philippe
Prince Philip of Spain

PHILIPINO, studying dancing
under Rigadon, Scuola di
Ballo   SCUOL

PHILIPPE, resident of Marseille, French revolutionist
The Flames of Paris
                 FLAME
A page
Les Pages du Duc de Ven-
dôme   PAGES

PHILIPPE. See also:
Filippo
Philip

PHLEGMATIC VARIATION.
See: Melancholic Varia-
tion

PHOEBE, in love with Count
Frédéric; sold by Bracac-
cio to the Grand Vizier,
Le Diable Amoureux
                 DIABE

PHOEBE. See also: Bracaccio

PHOEBUS. See: Chateaupers,
Phoebus de

PHONOGRAPH. See: First
Phonograph

PHONOGRAPH, SECOND. See:
First Phonograph

PHOTOGRAPHER, THE, appears
at Eiffel Tower, Les Mariés
de la Tour Eiffel   MARIE

PHOTOGRAPHER, THE. See
also: Ostrich, The

PHOTOGRAPHERS, taking pic-
tures at metropolitan railroad terminal, Terminal
                 TERMI

PHRYGIA. See: Spartacus

PHRYGIA, KING OF. See:
King Midas

PICK-ME-UP, representation of
British publication, The
Press   PRESS

PICKANINNIES, HER. See:
Negress, The

PICTURE-DEALER, THE, ap-
pears at Eiffel Tower, Les
Mariés de la Tour Eiffel
                 MARIE

PIERRE, peasant, loved by
Marie and Theresa
Halte de Cavalerie   HALTE
A smuggler
Kalkabrino   KALKA
French sailor, enters into
temporary union with Madame
Chrysanthème
YVES, his brother
Madame Chrysanthème
                 MADAM

PIERRE. See also:
Dignitary, A
Gaspard

Gringoire, Pierre

PIERRETTE, traditional panto-
mime character
Harlequinade   HARLI
The Sleeping Beauty
                    SLEEP
Vert-Vert   VERTV

PIERROT, traditional panto-
mime character, portrayed
by girl dancer
Ballade   BALLA
Traditional pantomime
character, in love with
Papillon
Le Carnaval   CARNA
Traditional pantomime
character
Harlequin in April HARLE
Harlequinade   HARLI
Pierrot Lunaire   PIERR
The Sleeping Beauty
                    SLEEP
Vert-Vert   VERTV

PIETRO, a muleteer, in love
with Graziosa; calls in
the Podesta to break up
duel between Don Rodrigo
and Don Manuel; arrested,
Graziosa   GRAZI

PIETRO. See also:
Bernadone, Francesco
Moscatello, Sergeant

PIGEONS. See: Jackdaw

PIGMALION, sculptor, creates
statue, falls in love with
it
GALATEA, statue created
by Pigmalion; comes to
life
Pigmalion   PIGMA

PIGMALION. See also:
Pygmalion

PIGNEROLLE. See: Cava-
lier Pignerolle, The

PIMPINELLA. See: Pulcinella

PINE WOODS. See: Fairy of
the Pine Woods, The

PINEAPPLE POLL, bumboat
woman, loved by Jasper;
in love with Captain Belaye,
Pineapple Poll   PINEA

PINIENTO. See: Moscatello,
Sergeant

PINK. See: Girl in Pink

PINK PEARLS. See: White
Pearl, The

PIONEER WOMAN. See:
American Pioneer Woman
Old Pioneer Woman

PIPES OF PAN, THE, personification, L'Homme et son
Désir   HOMME

PIROUETTE, MONSIEUR, maître
de ballet at the opera house
CELESTINE, his wife, sec-
ond dancer at the opera
ISIDORE, their son, assistant
ballet-master
The Débutante   DEBUT

PISTON RODS, representations
of machinery, Iron Foundry
                    IRONF

PISTONS. See: Principal
Pistons

PIT. See: King of the Snake
Pit

PIUS, METELLUS, high priest,
La Vestale   VESTA

PLANET MARS, personification
The Planets   PLANE
The Planets   PLANT

PLANET MERCURY, personification

PLANET NEPTUNE

The Planets   PLANE
The Planets   PLANT

PLANET NEPTUNE, personi-
fication
The Planets   PLANE
The Planets   PLANT

PLANET VENUS, personifica-
tion
The Planets   PLANE
The Planets   PLANT

PLANTER, A, pursues Negro
and his family; consumed
by Crocodile, Baby Stork
                   BABYS

PLANTS, personifications, The
Seventh Symphony SEVEN

PLAY STICKS, TWO WOMEN
WITH. See: Mexican
Peon

PLAYER. See:
Accordion-Player, An
Bondura Player
Golf Player
Polo Player, The
Tennis Player
Tennis Player, The

PLAYER, STROLLING. See:
Strolling Musician

PLAYER, THE STRANGER.
See: Flautist

PLAYERS. See: Chess-
Players, Two

PLEASURE, personification,
The Five Gifts   FIVEG

PLEASURE, PERSONIFICA-
TION OF SENSUAL. See:
Volupia

PLUIE. See: d'Avril,
Mademoiselle Pluie

PLUTO, God of the Under-

world
Orpheus   ORPHE
Attends feast of Bacchus
Sylvia   SYLVA

PLUTO. See also: Persephone,
Queen of Hades

POCAHONTAS. See: Princess
Pocahontas

PODESTA, GIOVANNI, Marco
Lugano's man of business,
The Blood-Red Flower
                   BLOOD

PODESTA, THE, official, orders
Pietro arrested, Graziosa
                   GRAZI

POET
POET'S BELOVED, creatures
of Aleko's delirious fantasy
Aleko   ALEKO
"Attempts to become part of
the life in which he has
been born"
SACRED LOVE (Beauty),
personification, loved by
Poet
PROFANE LOVE, personifi-
cation, fascinates Poet
DANDY, rival of Poet
KING
QUEEN, crowned by Bishop
at coronation, which Poet
attends
BISHOP, crowns King and
Queen at coronation
Illuminations   ILLUM

POET. See also:
Harold (The Poet)
Old Chinese Poet
Old Poet
Young Poet

POET, THE, seeks poetic
inspiration; falls in
love with the Woman
in Ball Dress, later
kills himself

Apparitions   APPAR
Conjures up memories
through music he plays on
the piano
LA BIEN-AIMÉE, once
loved by him
La Bien-Aimée   BIENA
Guest at the Baron's
masked ball; attracted to
the Sleepwalker, wife of
the Baron; incurs jealousy
of the Coquette, killed by
the Baron
Night Shadow   NIGHT
In love with Oriane;
stabbed
Oriane et le Prince d'Amour
                     ORIAN
Leads Unicorn, Gorgon and
Manticore about the town
UNICORN
GORGON
MANTICORE, "symbols of
Youth, Manhood and Old
Age"
The Unicorn, The Gorgon
and the Manticore   UNICO

POET, THE.   See also:
Hussar, The
Selina
Usher, Roderick

POETIC BELOVED.   See:
Sisters, Three

POETRY, personification,
Anguish Sonata   ANGUI

POETRY.   See also:
Epic Poetry
Erotic Poetry
Lyric Poetry

POET'S BELOVED.   See:
Poet

POITIERS, MIREILLE DE,
an actress and revolu-
tionary, The Flames
of Paris   FLAME

POLAR STAR, celestial body,

The Stars   STARS

POLICE.   See: Chief of Police,
The

POLICE OFFICER, at the bottom of the sea, Flik and
Flok   FLIKA

POLICEMAN, THE, "orderly
idiocy"
The Great American Goof
                     GREAT
Caricature of cartoon char-
acter
The New Yorker   NEWYO
Attempts to arrest the Old
Charlatan
Petrouchka   PETRO
On duty at metropolitan rail-
road terminal
Terminal   TERMI

POLICEMEN, pursue the Thief
on bicycles, The Thief Who
Loved a Ghost   THIEF

POLINSKI.   See: Count Polinski,
The

POLITICS, personification,
Metropolitan Daily   METRO

POLKAN, GENERAL, soldier
serving King Dondon, Le
Coq d'Or   COQDO

POLL.   See: Pineapple Poll

POLLUX, Cybele's lover,
neighborhood boy; friend of
Pudicitia, Undertow UNDER

POLLUX.   See also:
Castor
Leda
Transgressor, The

POLLY.   See: Fishwife

POLO PLAYER, THE, passing
through metropolitan railroad terminal, Terminal

POLONIUS, lord chamberlain
   at court of Denmark
   LAERTES, his son
   OPHELIA, his daughter,
   sweetheart of Hamlet
   Hamlet   HAMLE
   Hamlet   HAMLL
   Hamlet   HAMLS
   Hamlet   HAMLT

POLOVETSIAN GIRL
   POLOVETSIAN WOMAN
   POLOVETSIAN CHIEF,
   perform Tartar dance
   Prince Igor   PRINC

POLYHYMNIA, muse
   Apollon Musagète   APOLN
   Muse of sacred music,
   "emptily pompous hymn-
   singer"
   Undertow   UNDER

POLYMNIA (Polyhymnia), "muse,
   represents mime,"
   Apollo, Leader of the
   Muses   APOLL

POLYNICES. See: Oedipus

POMONA, goddess
   Pomone   POMOE
   Pomona   POMON

PONY. See: Wild Pony

POODLES. See: Dancing
   Poodles

POOR GIRL. See: Hypnotist

POOR GIRL, A, flower seller;
   attracted to Young Man,
   jilted by him for Rich
   Girl, Nocturne   NOCTU

POOR GIRL, A. See also:
   Spectator, A

POOR LOVERS, in public
   garden, Jardin Public

POOR MAN, THE, given alms
   by Francesco Bernadone
   (St. Francis), Saint Francis
                         SAINT

POP, priest, hires Balda as
   his handyman
   POPADIA, his wife
   POPOVNA, his daughter
   POPENOK, his little son
   The Fairy-Tale of the Priest
   and His Workman Balda
                         FAIRY

POPADIA. See: Pop

POPE, THE, madman in London
   madhouse, The Rake's
   Progress   RAKES

POPENOK. See: Pop

POPOFF, BARON. See: Sonia

POPOLONI, ALCHEMIST, assists
   Baron Bluebeard to dispose
   of his first five wives,
   Bluebeard   BLUEB

POPOVICH, ALYOSHA, dashing
   Russian youth, betrothed to
   Princess Anastachiuska,
   rescues her from Monster,
   Bogatyri   BOGAT

POPOVNA. See: Pop

PORCELAIN PRINCESS, THE
   THE MANDARIN, characters
   in a Chinese tale
   The Sleeping Beauty   SLEEP

PORT. See: Chief of the Port

PORTERS, working at metropolitan railroad terminal,
   Terminal   TERMI

PORTUGAL, PRINCESS CATHER-
   INE OF. See: Prince
   Charles

PORTUGAL, THE KING OF.
See: Doña Ines de Castro

PORTUGUESE EXILE, personification, Concerto Brasileiro
                        CONCB

POSEIDON, god of the sea
I, Odysseus   IODYS
King of the sea, kills Hip-
polytus at the request of
Theseus
Phèdre   PHEDR

POSEIDON. See also:
Phaedra

POTEAU, a maître de ballet
and professor of dancing,
Katerina   KATER

POTIPHAR, wealthy Egyptian
official, purchaser of
Joseph
POTIPHAR'S WIFE, at-
tracted to Joseph, spurned
by him; orders him pun-
ished
Joseph the Beautiful
                        JOSEP
La Légende de Joseph
                        LEGEN

POTIPHAR. See also: Sheik

POTIPHAR'S WIFE, Biblical
figure, Billy Sunday BILLS

POTIPHAR'S WIFE. See also:
Joseph
Potiphar

POVERTY, personification, be-
comes mystical bride of
Francesco Bernadone (St.
Francis), Saint Francis
                        SAINT

POWAHATAN, KING. See:
Princess Pocahontas

POWER. See: Young Man

POWERFUL. See: All-Power-
ful Father, The

PRALINE. See: Princess Praline

PRAYING BOY, "a dreamer of
kites and fishes," The Great
American Goof   GREAT

PRAYING MANTISES, THE, in-
habitants of the insect
world, overcome the Spider
Le Festin de l'Araignée
                        FESTD
Le Festin de l'Araignée
                        FESTI
The Spider's Banquet
                        SPIDE

PREMIER DANSEUR at the Grand
Opera, Paris, Foyer de la
Danse   FOYER

PREMIER DANSEUR. See also:
Ballerina, The

PRESIDENT, local official at
whose home Christmas party
is being given
HIS WIFE
FRITZ, their son
DROSSELMEYER, godfather
to Clara (Masha)
THEIR COUSINS
THEIR FRIENDS, guests at
the party
The Nutcracker   NUTCA
The Nutcracker   NUTCK
The Nutcracker   NUTCR
CLARA, daughter of Presi-
dent, given toy nutcracker
by Drosselmeyer
The Nutcracker   NUTCA
The Nutcracker   NUTCR
MASHA, daughter of Presi-
dent, given toy nutcracker
by Drosselmeyer
The Nutcracker   NUTCK

PRESIDENT. See also:
Nutcracker

Sugarplum Fairy

PRESIDENT OF THE UNITED
STATES. See: Lincoln,
Abraham

PRESS. See: Liberty of the
Press, The

PRIAM, KING. See: Cassan-
dra

PRIDE, "as Queen of a corrupt
kingdom," The Quest
                               QUEST

PRIEST, "capitalism," The
Great American Goof
                               GREAT

PRIEST. See also:
High Priest
High Priest of the Temple
High Priest of the Temple
of Peace
High Priest, The

PRIEST, A, friend of Don
Quixote
Don Quixote   DONQX
Performs marriage cere-
mony for Princess Poca-
hontas and John Rolfe
Pocahontas   POCAH

PRIEST, THE, churchman,
Sea Gallows   SEAGA

PRIESTESS. See: Snake
Priestess

PRIGGISH VIRGIN
GREEDY VIRGIN
LUSTFUL VIRGIN, three
virgins, tempted by a
Youth and a Devil; over-
come by the latter
Three Virgins and a
Devil   THREV

PRIGGISH VIRGIN. See also:
Devil, A
Youth, A

PRIMA BALLERINA at the Grand
Opera, Paris, Foyer de la
Danse   FOYER

PRIME MINISTER OF THULE.
See: Kafur

PRINCE, in love with Princess
PRINCESS, bewitched, in
love with Wooden Prince
THE GOOD FAIRY, unites
Prince and Princess
The Wooden Prince WOODE

PRINCE. See also:
Chinese Prince
East Indian Prince
English Prince, The
Genius-Husband
Georgian Prince, The
Indian Prince, The
Italian Prince, The
Prince, The
Spanish Prince, The
Wooden Prince

PRINCE ADAM. See: Marie

PRINCE APHRON. See: King
Dondon

PRINCE CHARLES, afterwards
Charles II, King of England
PRINCESS CATHERINE OF
PORTUGAL, his wife
Betty   BETTY

PRINCE CHARLES. See also:
Edward

PRINCE CHARMING, meets
Cinderella at ball, traces
her through her lost slipper
THE KING, his father
THE QUEEN, his mother
Cinderella   CINDL
Awakens the Princess
Aurora after her 100 year
sleep
The Sleeping Beauty SLEEP

PRINCE CHARMING. See also:
Chamberlain

Gallison
Master of Ceremonies
Prince Fleur-de-Lys
Prince, The
Princess Aurora, The

PRINCE COCOA, found in
pastry-shop, Schlagobers
SCHLA

PRINCE COFFEE, found in
pastry-shop, Schlagobers
SCHLA

PRINCE DANILO. See: Sonia

PRINCE DE LIGNE, nobleman,
Vienna- 1814   VIENN

PRINCE DJALMA, handsome
prince
ISMAIL BEY, Emir, his
uncle
Le Papillon   PAPIL

PRINCE DJALMA. See also:
Farfalla
Mohamed

PRINCE FLEUR-DE-LYS, host
at ball, meets Cinderella,
falls in love with her,
traces her through lost
glass slipper, Cinderella
CINDA

PRINCE FLEUR-DE-LYS.
See also:
Count Dandini, The
Prince Charming
Prince, The

PRINCE GOUDAL, Caucasian
prince, holding festival in
honor of his wife
PRINCE GOUDAL'S WIFE
Prince Goudal's Festival
PRING

PRINCE GUIDON. See: King
Dondon

PRINCE HUGUES DE PRO-

VENCE, in love with Ysaure,
La Filleule des Fées FILLU

PRINCE HUSSEIN, nobleman,
owner of the slave Thea,
Thea   THEAO

PRINCE HUSSEIN. See also:
Flower Fairy, The

PRINCE IVAN (Ivan Tsarevich),
meets Firebird, falls in
love with the Beautiful Tsarevna, kills Kostchei by
breaking egg holding Kostchei's life
Firebird   FIREB
Firebird   FIRED
Kills Kostchei with magic
sword given him by Firebird
Firebird   FIREI

PRINCE KOKLUSH, "whooping
cough"
The Nutcracker   NUTCA
The Nutcracker   NUTCK
The Nutcracker   NUTCR

PRINCE METTERNICH, Austrian
statesman, celebrating the
defeat of Napoleon; falls in
love with Princess Lieven,
Vienna- 1814   VIENN

PRINCE METTERNICH. See also:
Debutantes
Dutch Legation
Murat's Ambassadors, Two
Princess Lieven
Secretaries
Tyrolian Legation

PRINCE OF ARROGANZA, THE,
nobleman
AMBASSADOR OF ARROGAN-
ZA, his representative
The Lady and the Fool
LADYA

PRINCE OF COURLAND, THE,
nobleman
BATHILDE, his daughter,
affianced to Albrecht

Giselle   GISEE
Giselle   GISEL
Giselle   GISES

PRINCE OF DENMARK. See:
Hamlet, Prince of Denmark

PRINCE OF ERISTAV. See:
Djardje
Manije

PRINCE OF LOVE, THE, per-
sonification of love, loved
by Oriane, Oriane et le
Prince d'Amour   ORIAN

PRINCE OF PERSIA, nobleman
PRINCESS OF PERSIA,
noblewoman
The Figure in the Carpet
FIGUR

PRINCE OF VERONA. See:
Escalus

PRINCE OF WALES. See:
Edward, Prince of Wales

PRINCE OSORIO Governor of
Rome
FEDERICI, his nephew
THE MARCHESA SAMPIE-
TRI, his niece
Marco Spada   MARCO

PRINCE OSORIO. See also:
Count Pepinelli

PRINCE PHILIP OF SPAIN,
ruler, commanding officer
of Duke of Alba; invading
Flanders, Tyl Ulenspiegel
TYLUL

PRINCE, SALAMANDER. See
Princess Belle Épine

PRINCE SANTA CLAUS,
marshal of the court,
Schlagobers   SCHLA

PRINCE SAPPHIRE, attracted
to Floretta (Princess Her-

milia), daughter of King
Bobiche, Bluebeard BLUEB

PRINCE SIEGFRIED, 21 years
old, meets, falls in love
with Odette, Queen of the
Swans
PRINCESS MOTHER, his
mother
Swan Lake   SWANA
Swan Lake   SWANE
Swan Lake   SWANK
Swan Lake   SWANL

PRINCE SIEGFRIED. See also:
Benno
Wolfgang

PRINCE, THE, becomes husband
of Snow-White
Blanche-Neige   BLANC
Meets Cinderella at ball,
falls in love with her, traces
her through lost glass slipper
THE PRINCE'S FOUR
FRIENDS
Cinderella   CINDE
Handsome young nobleman,
falls in love with Cinderella
Cinderella   CINDR
Seeks the Princess in mar-
riage
The Hundred Kisses HUNDR
Betrothed to the Princess
Nina; rival of Bakhmetiev
The Prisoner in the Caucasus
PRISR
In search of a bride, meets
the Princess
THE KNIGHT
THE HUNTSMAN, his com-
panions
A Spring Tale   SPRIN
Stabbed by Thamar, Queen
of Georgia
Thamar   THAMA

PRINCE, THE. See also:
Aide-de-Camp
Bird-Catcher, The
Cat, The
Chamberlain, The
Courtesan

Gardener, The
Hermit, The Wondrous
Jester, The
Little Mermaid, The
Lord of the Mountain, The
Lord of the Vale, The
Prince
Prince Charming
Prince Fleur-de-Lys
Swineherd, The

PRINCE TUTTI, young noble-
man
FOUETTÉ, his doll
The Three Fat Men
                        THREE

PRINCE, WOODEN. See:
Prince
Wooden Prince

PRINCE ZAAL, selected as
husband of Manije by her
parents, The Heart of the
Hills   HEART

PRINCE ZVEZDICH. See:
Arbenin

PRINCE'S FOUR FRIENDS,
THE. See: Prince, The

PRINCESS, noblewoman, La
Belle au Bois Dormant
                        BELLA

PRINCESS. See also:
Ballerina
Enchanted Princess, The
Porcelain Princess, The
Prince
Princess, The
Swan Princess, The
Wooden Prince

PRINCESS ANASTACHIUSKA,
beautiful maiden of Kiev,
betrothed to Alyosha Popovich; dreams of Tartar
youth; abducted by Monster,
later rescued by Popovich,
Bogatyri   BOGAT

PRINCESS AURORA, THE, the
Sleeping Beauty, sleeps for
100 years
Aurora's Wedding   AUROR
Aurora's Wedding   AUROW
The Sleeping Beauty, put
under spell by Carabosse;
sleeps for 100 years, awaken-
ed by Prince Charming
KING FLORESTAN XXIV, her
father
THE QUEEN, her mother
The Sleeping Beauty SLEEP

PRINCESS AURORA, THE. See
also:
Carabosse
Carnation Fairy, The
Cherry Blossom Fairy, The
English Prince, The
Fairy of the Mountain Ash,
The
Fairy of the Pine Woods, The
Fairy of the Song-Birds, The
Indian Prince, The
Italian Prince, The
Lilac Fairy, The
Spanish Prince, The

PRINCESS BATHILDE, becomes
betrothed to Albert of Hungary
THE GRAND ELECTOR, her
father
Les Elfes   ELFES

PRINCESS BELLE ÉPINE, tricks
her father and Princess
Belle Rose out of the kingdom
EMPEROR OF THE MIDDLE
KINGDOM, her father
PRINCESS BELLE ROSE,
her sister; favorite daughter
of the Emperor
SALAMANDER PRINCE, be-
witched as a salamander until Belle Rose expresses her
love for him; vanquishes
Belle Épine, restores kingdom to the Emperor
Prince of the Pagodas
                        PRINO

PRINCESS BELLE ROSE. See:
Princess Belle Épine

PRINCESS CATHERINE OF
PORTUGAL. See:
Prince Charles

PRINCESS DAÏTA. See:
Izuna
Jamato
Kwannon

PRINCESS DAÏTA'S NURSE.
See: Jamato

PRINCESS, EAST INDIAN.
See: East Indian Prince

PRINCESS GUNDEMEY OF DA-
HOMEY. See: Tulip

PRINCESS HERMILIA (FLOR-
ETTA). See: King Bobi-
che

PRINCESS LIEVEN, noble-
woman, loved by Prince
Metternich, Vienna- 1814
VIENN

PRINCESS MARGARET, noble-
woman, The Press PRESS

PRINCESS MELANIE, noble-
woman, Vienna- 1814
VIENN

PRINCESS MILLEFLEURS,
noblewoman
RAGONDA, her daughter,
in love with Otto; protected
by Cupid from Count Friedrich Sternhold, Fiammetta
FIAMM

PRINCESS MILLEFLEURS.
See also:
Eolinda
Margharita

PRINCESS MOTHER. See:
Prince Siegfried

PRINCESS NINA, THE, betro-
thed to the Prince, once
loved by Bakhmetiev
THE PRINCESS'S COUSIN
THE PRINCESS'S FATHER,
a general
The Prisoner in the Caucasus
PRISR

PRINCESS OF PERSIA. See:
Prince of Persia

PRINCESS OF THE COURT OF
BUCHARIA, noblewoman,
Lalla Rookh   LALLA

PRINCESS POCAHONTAS, Indian
maiden, falls in love with,
marries John Rolfe
KING POWAHATAN, her
father, Indian chief
INDIANS, members of their
tribe
Pocahontas   POCAH

PRINCESS POCAHONTAS. See
also: Priest, A

PRINCESS PRALINE, found in
pastry-shop, Schlagobers
SCHLA

PRINCESS SOPHIA. See: Peter
I, Tsar of Russia

PRINCESS TEAFLOWER, found
in pastry-shop
HER FOUR LADIES
Schlagobers   SCHLA

PRINCESS, THE, turned into
hind, meets Knight-Errant;
later restored to human
shape
Le Chevalier et la Damoiselle
CHEVA
Shallow and conceited;
sought in marriage by the
Prince
THE KING, her father
HER MAIDS OF HONOR
The Hundred Kisses HUNDR

Meets the Prince, later
falls in love with him
THE QUEEN, her mother
A Spring Tale   SPRIN

PRINCESS, THE. See also:
    Bird-Catcher, The
    Bogey Man, The
    Butler, The
    Gardener, The
    Hermit, The Wondrous
    Joseph
    Ladies in Waiting, The
    Leaf-Maidens, The
    Mikado, The
    Princess
    Snake, The
    Squires, Three
    Storm Witches, The
    Swan, The
    Tô
    Tree-Sprite, The
    Wood-Witches, The

PRINCESS TURANDOT, agrees
    to marry the prince who
    answers her three riddles
    correctly
    KALAF, prince, answers
    riddles, conquers her in-
    difference
    Princess Turandot PRINT

PRINCESS'S COUSIN, THE.
    See: Princess Nina, The

PRINCESS'S FATHER, THE.
    See: Princess Nina, The

PRINCIPAL DANCER, THE
    (Adam Zero), personifies
    various stages of Man's
    life
    THE CHOREOGRAPHER,
    his creator and destroyer
    THE DESIGNER
    THE WARDROBE MISTRESS
    THE DRESSER, his three
    fates
    THE BALLERINA, his first
    love, wife and mistress
    THE UNDERSTUDIES, his
    son and daughter

THE CHARACTER DANCERS,
    his cat and dog
    THE MIME, his spiritual
    adviser
    Adam Zero   ADAMZ

PRINCIPAL DANCER, THE.
    See also:
    Death
    Stage Director, The

PRINCIPAL DYNAMOS, TWO,
    representations of magic
    and might of electricity,
    Iron Foundry   IRONF

PRINCIPAL MODEL, HIS. See:
    Rosa, Salvator

PRINCIPAL PISTONS, represen-
    tations of machinery, Iron
    Foundry   IRONF

PRINTING, THE FATHER OF
    ENGLISH. See: Caxton,
    William

PRISON. See: Old Man in
    Prison

PRIYAMWADA, friend of Sakun-
    tala, Sakuntala   SAKUN

PRODIGAL SON, THE, young
    man, leaves home, seduced
    by the Siren, returns home
    impoverished
    THE FATHER OF THE
    PRODIGAL SON
    THE SISTERS OF THE
    PRODIGAL SON, his two
    devoted sisters
    THE COMPANIONS OF THE
    PRODIGAL SON, two friends,
    induce him to leave home
    The Prodigal Son   PRODA
    The Prodigal Son   PRODG
    The Prodigal Son   PRODI
    The Prodigal Son   PRODL
    The Prodigal Son   PRODO
    The Prodigal Son   PRODS

PRODUCER, THE, passing

through metropolitan railroad terminal, Terminal
                    TERMI

PROFANE LOVE. See: Poet

PROFITEER. See: War
Profiteer, The

PROMETHEUS, brings statues
of Man and Woman to life
with his torch
MAN
WOMAN, his "creatures"
The Creatures of Prome-
theus   CREAU
Les Créatures de Prome-
thée   CREAV
Titan, brings fire to the
world
Prometheus   PROMS
Promethée   PROMT
Prometheus   PROMV
Prometheus   PROMW

PROPERTY-MAN at Grand
Opera, Paris, Foyer de
la Danse   FOYER

PROPHET, THE. See:
Samuel
Spirit of the Prophet
Samuel

PROPRE, MONSIEUR TRÈS.
See: Chrysanthème,
Madame

PROPRIETOR OF AN OPIUM
DEN in treaty-port in
China, The Red Poppy
                    REDPO

PROSECUTING ATTORNEY, A,
prosecutes murder case,
Hear Ye! Hear Ye!
                    HEARY

PROSPECTOR. See: Old
Prospector

PROSPERO, an armorer, The
Three Fat Men   THREE

PROSTITUTE, THE, resident of
the Gorbals, slum district
of Glasgow; reformed by the
Stranger
Miracle in the Gorbals
                    MIRAC
Acts as decoy for gangsters;
"absolved by the omnipotence
and love between her and the
Mandarin which conquers
violence and death"
THREE GANGSTERS, her
associates, rob and murder
their victims
The Miraculous Mandarin
                    MIRAM

PROSTITUTE, THE. See also:
Blind Girl
Mandarin
Official, The
Woman, The

PROTÉE, sea god, able to
change his form at will,
Protée   PROTE

PROUD. See: Dacos

PROVENCE. See: Prince
Hugues de Provence

PROVINCE. See: Governor of
the Province, The

PRUDENCE, hostess at party
Lady of the Camellias
                    LADYB
The Lady of the Camellias
                    LADYC

PRUDENZA, loved by Florindo,
in love with Pulcinella
(Punch)
IL DOTTORE, her father
Pulcinella   PULCI

PRUNE, MADEMOISELLE. See:
Chrysanthème, Madame

PSYCHE, beautiful mortal, falls
in love with Cupid
L'Amour et Son Amour

AMOUT
Cupid and Psyche   CUPID
Psyche   PSYCH

PSYCHE. See also: Zephyrs,
Seven

P'TIT. See: Bleu, P'tit

PUCK, fairy
The Dream   DREAM
A Midsummer Night's
Dream   MIDSU

PUDICITIA, neighborhood girl,
friend of Pollux, Undertow
                     UNDER

PUGILIST, THE. See: Girl,
The

PULCINELLA (Punch), tradi-
tional pantomime figure,
loved by Prudenza and
Rosetta, rejects them both
PIMPINELLA, his wife
FOUR LITTLE PULCIN-
ELLAS
Pulcinella   PULCI
In love with Rosetta
Salade   SALAD

PULCINELLA. See also:
Fourbo

PUNCH, representation of
humorous British magazine
The Press   PRESS
Character in Punch and
Judy show
FATHER of Child, becomes
associated with Punch in
Child's mind
Punch and the Child
                     PUNCH
Traditional comic puppet
figure
Punch and the Judy PUNCJ

PUNCHINELLO, traditional
pantomime figure, Vene-
ziana   VENEZ

PUPIL, THE BAD. See:
Felicita

PUPILS. See: Ballet Master

PUPPET, MISTER, allegorical
figure, speaks long soliloquy
"which expresses his search
for a soul and his own de-
struction"
FEMALE DOLL, in whom
Mister Puppet tries to find
his objectives; stands si-
lently beside him
Mr. Puppet   MRPUP

PUPPETEER, manager of Punch
and Judy show
THE DEVIL, becomes asso-
ciated with Puppeteer in
Child's mind
Punch and the Child PUNCH

PURETÉ, MADEMOISELLE.
See: Chrysanthème, Madame

PURITAN, THE, American type,
seen by the Immigrant,
Within the Quota   WITHI

PUSS IN BOOTS, fairy tale
character, The Sleeping
Beauty   SLEEP

PUSSYCAT. See: Owl

PYGMALION, sculptor, creates
statue, falls in love with it
GALATEA, statue created
by Pygmalion, comes to
life
Pygmalion   PYGMA

PYGMALION. See also:
Pigmalion

PYOTR. See:
Peter
Petr
Zina

PYRAMIDS. See: Keeper of

the Pyramids

PYRAMUS, resident of ancient
    Babylon, in love with
    Thisbe; suicide
THISBE, his sweetheart,
    also a suicide
    Pyramus and Thisbe
                          PYRAM

PYTHIA, oracle, consulted by
    Candaules, King of Lydia,
    Le Roi Candaule   ROICA

Q

QUAKER COUPLE, perform
    dance for Cupid's approval,
    The Whims of Cupid and
    the Ballet Master   WHIMS

QUAKER GIRL, THE.   See:
    Farm Boy, The

QUASIMODO, hunchbacked bell
    ringer of Notre Dame;
    hopelessly loves La Es-
    meralda, saves her life,
    La Esmeralda   ESMER

QUEEN.   See:
    Black Queen, The
    Fairy Queen, The
    Poet
    Red Queen, The

QUEEN BEE, THE, personi-
    fication, La Nuit et le
    Jour   NUITE

QUEEN CLEMENTINE.   See:
    Alvarez
    King Bobiche

QUEEN ELIZABETH I, Queen
    of England, enemy of
    Mary, Queen of Scots,
    Episodes   EPISO

QUEEN ELIZABETH WOOD-
    VILLE, noblewoman, The
    Press   PRESS

QUEEN HÉRODIAS.   See:
    Salomé

QUEEN MARIE ANTOINETTE.
    See: King Louis XVI, King
    of France

QUEEN MEHMENE-BANU, sacri-
    fices her beauty and personal
    happiness to save her sister
    SHIRIENE, her sister
    FERHAD, youth, had loved
    Shiriene, renounces his love
    to sacrifice himself for his
    people
    STRANGER, an unknown
    Legend of Love   LEGEL

QUEEN OF BABYLON, THE,
    poisons Alexander the Great,
    Alexandre le Grand ALEXA

QUEEN OF BUTTERFLY LAND.
    See: Imperialis, Vanessa

QUEEN OF CARTHAGE.   See:
    Dido

QUEEN OF CLUBS, THE
    QUEEN OF HEARTS, THE
    KING OF SPADES, THE
    KING OF DIAMONDS, THE,
    four dolls dressed as court
    cards, perform mazurka in
    toy shop
    La Boutique Fantasque
                          BOUTI

QUEEN OF CRETE.   See:
    Minos, King of Crete

QUEEN OF DENMARK.   See:
    Hamlet, Prince of Denmark

QUEEN OF DIAMONDS, playing
    card, participates in poker
    game, Card Game   CARDG

QUEEN OF EGYPT.   See:
    Cleopatra
    Cléopâtre

185   QUEEN OF ENGLAND

QUEEN OF ENGLAND. See:
  Queen Elizabeth I

QUEEN OF FIRE, THE, alle-
  gorical figure
  HER CONSORT
  Homage to the Queen
               HOMAG

QUEEN OF GEORGIA. See:
  Thamar

QUEEN OF HADES. See:
  Persephone

QUEEN OF HEARTS, playing
  card, participates in poker
  game, Card Game CARDG

QUEEN OF HEARTS, THE.
  See: Queen of Clubs, The

QUEEN OF NIGHT, THE, per-
  sonification, La Nuit et le
  Jour   NUITE

QUEEN OF SCOTS. See:
  Mary, Queen of Scots

QUEEN OF SHEMAKHA,
  daughter of the air, becomes bride of King Dondon, Le Coq d'Or COQDO

QUEEN OF SNOW. See: King
  of Snow

QUEEN OF SPADES, playing
  card, participates in poker
  game, Card Game CARDG

QUEEN OF THE AIR, THE,
  allegorical figure
  HER CONSORT
  Homage to the Queen
               HOMAG

QUEEN OF THE AMAZONS.
  See:
  Hippolyta
  Phaedra

QUEEN OF THE AMAZONS,

THE, tames, later killed by
the White Horse
THE WHITE HORSE
Le Massacre des Amazones
               MASSA

QUEEN OF THE CARRIAGE
  TRADE, patron of fashionable
  café, Offenbach in the Underworld   OFFEN

QUEEN OF THE DANCE (La
  Reine de la Danse), Russian
  ballerina, from Moscow
  GODDESS OF THE DANCE
  (La Déesse de la Danse),
  Italian ballerina, from Milan
  DAUGHTER OF TERPSICHORE
  (La Fille de Terpsichore),
  French ballerina, from Paris
  ATTENDANT CAVALIERS TO
  THE RUSSIAN BALLERINA
  CAVALIER TO THE ITALIAN
  BALLERINA
  CAVALIER TO THE FRENCH
  BALLERINA
  Gala Performance GALAP

QUEEN OF THE DAY, THE,
  personification, La Nuit et
  le Jour   NUITE

QUEEN OF THE DEMONS. See:
  Bambo

QUEEN OF THE EARTH, THE,
  allegorical figure
  HER CONSORT
  Homage to the Queen
               HOMAG

QUEEN OF THE ELFRITS. See:
  Hertha

QUEEN OF THE ELVES. See:
  Adda

QUEEN OF THE EVIL FAIRIES,
  attempts to captivate Osöd,
  The Holy Torch   HOLYT

QUEEN OF THE FAIRIES. See:
  Titania

QUEEN OF THE GYPSIES,
ruler of gypsy tribe
Les Deux Pigéons   DEUXN
Les Deux Pigéons   DEUXP

QUEEN OF THE GYPSIES.
See also: Mab

QUEEN OF THE KORRIGANES,
fairy, La Korrigane
KORRI

QUEEN OF THE MINES, takes
Alman under her protec-
tion, Rosida   ROSID

QUEEN OF THE MORPHIDES,
THE, butterfly, Piège de
Lumière   PLEGE

QUEEN OF THE NEREIDS
ruler of the mermaids
The Hump-Backed Horse
HUMPB
The Hump-Backed Horse
HUMPH

QUEEN OF THE NEREIDS.
See also: Leucothéa

QUEEN OF THE NIGHT.
See: Moon, The

QUEEN OF THE SEA. See:
Amphitrite
Captain

QUEEN OF THE SPIRITS OF
NIGHT. See: Sakourada

QUEEN OF THE STARS, ce-
lestial deity, Electra
ELECT

QUEEN OF THE SWAMP
LILIES. See: Hortense,
Queen of the Swamp Lilies

QUEEN OF THE SWANS.
See: Odette

QUEEN OF THE TRIBES.
See: Femina

QUEEN OF THE WATERS. See:
Ondine

QUEEN OF THE WATERS, THE,
allegorical figure
HER CONSORT
Homage to the Queen
HOMAG

QUEEN OF THE WILIS. See:
Myrtha, Queen of the Wilis

QUEEN TAMARA, loved by
Chota Roustaveli who dedi-
cates his poem to her,
Chota Roustaveli   CHOTA

QUEEN, THE. See:
Huntsman, The
King of the Gnomes, The
King, The
Ladies in Waiting
Novice, The
Prince Charming
Princess Aurora, The
Princess, The
Queen
Snow-White
Zadig

QUEEN'S LOVER, THE. See:
King, The

QUEEN'S MAID OF HONOR.
See: Blanche

QUEEN'S MAIDS OF HONOR.
See:
Blanche
Navailles, Madame de
Vert-Vert

QUIXOTE. See: Don Quixote

R

RACKETS, TWO, toys, Jeux
d'Enfants   JEUXX

RACKOZSKI. See: Count
Rackozski

RADIO ANNOUNCER, interviews

celebrity at metropolitan
railroad terminal, Terminal
                                TERMI

RADZHAB, leader of the Bas-
mach, accomplice of Bey
Abdurassul, The Two
Roses   TWORO

RAFAEL, Antonia's former
lover, still in love with
her
ANTONIA, now in love
with Sebastian
SEBASTIAN, Antonia's cur-
rent lover
Antonia   ANTON

RAFAEL. See also: Baron
Salomon

RAGGED FAIRY GODMOTHER,
THE. See: Cinderella

RAGONDA. See:
    Eolinda
    Margharita
    Otto
    Princess Millefleurs

RAJAH DUGMANTA, THE,
Indian ruler
GAMSATTI, his daughter,
betrothed to Solor, kills
Nikia
La Bayadère   BAYAD

RAKE, THE, young English-
man, inherits fortune, takes
downward path through de-
bauchery to madness and
death, The Rake's Progress
                                RAKES
RAKE, THE. See also:
    Betrayed Girl, The
    Bravo, The
    Fencing Master, The
    Jockey, The
    Ladies of the Town
    Tailor, The

RALSTON, American empire
builder, Ghost Town

GHOST

RAM, friend of Rooster, Le
Renard   RENAR

RAMBERT. See: Saint-Rambert,
Monsieur de

RAMSEYA, Aspicia's favorite
slave, La Fille du Pharaon
                                FILLP

RANCHER'S DAUGHTER, rival
of the Cowgirl; sought by
the Champion Roper and the
Head Wrangler, Rodeo
                                RODEO

RAOUL. See: Count Raoul de
Crêqui

RAOUL DE CRÊQUI. See:
Count Raoul de Crêqui

RAPHAEL. See: Rafael

RASPONI, FEDERIGO. See:
    Beatrice
    Clarice

RASUMOVSKY. See: Count
Rasumovsky

RATS, HER FOUR. See:
Carabosse

RAY
    ROY, truck drivers, "natu-
    ral enemies of the State
    Trooper," stop at Mac's
    filling station
    Filling Station   FILLI

RAYMOND. See: Renoualle,
Ysaure de

RAYMONDA, betrothed to Jean
de Brienne
THE COUNTESS SYBILLE,
her aunt
THE WHITE LADY, her an-
cestress, protectress of the
castle

RENARD, LE. See: Fox,
The (Le Renard)

RENÉ, Armide's lover, Le
Pavillon d'Armide   PAVIL

RENÉ. See also: Marietta

RENONCULE, MADAME. See:
Chrysanthème, Madame

RENOUALLE, YSAURE DE,
loved by Arthur, marries
Bluebeard
ANNE, her sister
RAYMOND, her brother
EBREMARD, her brother,
kills Bluebeard
Barbe-Bleue   BARBE

RENOUALLE, YSAURE DE.
See also:
Arthur
Spirit of Curiosity

RENSHI. See: Knight Renshi,
The

REPRESENTATION OF CLASSI-
CAL MUSIC. See: Clas-
sic

REPRESENTATION OF JAZZ
MUSIC. See: Jazz

RETINUE, HIS. See: Mars

REUBEN, a smuggler, Kalkabrino   KALKA

REUBEN, JAMES, Scotch peasant, betrothed to Effie,
falls in love with La Sylphide
ANNA, his mother
EFFIE, Anna's niece, loved
by Gurn; becomes his wife
GURN, rough Scotch peas-
ant, in love with Effie, becomes her husband
La Sylphide   SYLPH
La Sylphide   SYLPL

REVENUE AGENT, American
type, seen by the Immigrant,
Within the Quota   WITHI

REVEREND. See: Cronk,
Reverend Adrian

REVERIE. See: Visions of
Reverie

REVIVALIST, "stamps on sin"
HIS FOUR FOLLOWERS
Appalachian Spring   APPAL

REWENA. See: Lord Rewena

REWENA, LADY. See: Lord
Rewena

RHINE, personification of river,
La Fille du Pharaon FILLP

RICCO. See: Don Pedro Ricco

RICH BOY, THE
RICH GIRL, THE, "alcoholic
refugees from country club
dance, " stop at Mac's filling
station
Filling Station   FILLI

RICH GIRL, A, wins Young Man
from Poor Girl, Nocturne
                      NOCTU

RICH GIRL, A. See also:
Spectator, A

RICH GIRL, THE. See: Rich
Boy, The

RICH MAN. See: Hypnotist

RICH MERCHANT, rejects
daughters of Seven Clowns,
Chout   CHOUR

RICH OLD NEIGHBOR, A, be-
comes bridegroom of Young
Girl; dies before wedding
HIS BUTLER
Bonne-Bouche   BONNE

RICH PEASANT. See: Fadette

RICH PEASANT'S SON. See:
Fadette

RICH YOUNG MAN. See:
Laiderette

RICHARD, DUKE OF GLOSTER,
nobleman, The Press
PRESS

RICHES, personification, The
Five Gifts   FĪVEG

RIDERS, BAREBACK. See:
Jinx
Ringmaster

RIDING HOOD. See: Red
Riding Hood

RIDOLFO, friend of Rigadon,
Scuola di Ballo   SCUOL

RIGADON, a professor of
dancing, Scuola di Ballo
SCUOL

RIGADON. See also:
Bianca
Carlino
Felicita
Josephina
Nicoletto
Notary, The
Philipino
Ridolfo
Rosalba
Rosina

RIGODON, the court dancing-
master, Cinderella CINDA

RIMINI, FRANCESCA DA.
See: Francesca

RINALDO, chief of the bandits
La Prima Ballerina
PRIMA
A warrior
Rinaldo and Armida
RINAL

RINALDO. See also:
Astolfo
Count Rinaldo, The
Gandolfo

RINGER. See: Bell-Ringer

RINGMASTER, circus performer
Every Soul Is a Circus
EVERY
Circus performer, believes
Jinx brings him bad luck
BEARDED LADY
TATTOOED LADY
STRONG LADY
BAREBACK RIDERS
WIRE WALKERS, circus
performers, also believe
Jinx brings them bad luck
Jinx   JINXX

RINGMASTER. See also: Jinx

RIOTOUS LIVERS, "the dying,"
The Great American Goof
GREAT

RIPSIK. See: Gayne

RIVER, PERSONIFICATION OF.
See:
Congo
Guadalquivir
Neva
Rhine
Thames
Tiber

RIZZIO, DAVID, secretary to
Mary, Queen of Scots,
Episodes   EPISO

ROBBERS
SOLDIERS, engage in fight
Ballet de la Nuit   BALLN

ROBERT, young man, divided
between his loves for two
women
FELICE, about 30, loved by
him
AIMÉE, about 21, also loved
him

Winter Night   WINTE

ROBINTZEL, a burgomaster
MADAME ROBINTZEL,
his wife
La Vivandière   VIVAN

ROCHESTER. See: Duke of
Rochester, The

ROCK. See also: Rocks

ROCK AND RYE, drink served
at 2222 Club, New York
City, Café Society   CAFES

ROCKING HORSES. See:
Wooden Rocking Horses,
The

ROCKS, personifications, The
Seventh Symphony SEVEN

ROCKS. See also: Rock and
Rye

RODERICK. See: Usher,
Roderick

RODRIGO, Venetian nobleman,
Otello   OTELL

RODRIGO. See also: Don Rodrigo

RODS. See: Piston Rods

ROLAND. See: Furioso, Or-
lando (Roland)

ROLFE, JOHN, Virginia colo-
nist, falls in love with,
marries Princess Pocahon-
tas
CAPTAIN JOHN SMITH,
his mentor, also a colo-
nist
Pocahontas   POCAH

ROLFE, JOHN. See also:
Priest, A

ROMANTIC LOVE, HIS. See:
Youth, A

ROME, GOVERNOR OF. See:
Prince Osorio

ROMEO, son of Montagu, head
of house at variance with
the house of Capulet; in love
with Juliet, Romeo and
Juliet   ROMEJ

ROMEO. See also:
Benvolio
Capulet
Laurence, Friar
Mercutio
Montague
Old Capulet
Old Montague
Rosaline

ROOKH, LALLA. See:
Alaris, King of Bucharia
Emperor Aurungzebe, The,
Emperor of Hindustan

ROOSTER, "by his ingenuity gets
the best of the sly and ava-
ricious Fox," Le Renard
                     RENAR

ROOSTER. See also:
Cat
Ram

ROPE. See: Gentleman With a
Rope, The

ROPER. See: Champion Roper,
The

ROSA, loved by Paolo
PAOLO, Rosa's sweetheart,
sharpshooter
Flower Festival at Genzano
                     FLOWE

ROSA, SALVATOR, well-known
painter, captured by Catarina's band of robbers; betrothed to Florida
HIS PRINCIPAL MODEL
Catarina   CATAR

ROSALBA, studying dancing

under Rigadon, Scuola di
Ballo   SCUOL

ROSALINDE. See: Baron
Bluebeard

ROSALINE, friend of Romeo
and Mercutio, Romeo and
Juliet   ROMEO

ROSALINE. See also:
Montague

ROSAMONDE, dancer, Vert-
Vert   VERTV

ROSE
VIOLET
CARNATION, "three spirits
of perfumed seduction, con-
jured up by the Alchemist
to assist the Contessa win
Zenobio Bonaventuri"
Quelques Fleurs   QUELQ

ROSE. See also:
Ben
Blue Rose
Father
Nightingale
Rose, The

ROSE FAIRY, THE, presents
gift to Ysaure, La Filleule
des Fées   FILLU

ROSE, GOLDEN. See: Bobo-
Safar

ROSE, PRINCESS BELLE.
See: Princess Belle
Épine

ROSE SPIRIT (Rose Ghost),
appears to young girl in
her dream
YOUNG GIRL, returns from
ball carrying rose; dreams
Le Spectre de la Rose
                         SPECT

ROSE, THE, given to the Lady
by the Student; cast aside

by her
Le Rossignol et la Rose
                         ROSSG
Le Rossignol et la Rose
                         ROSSI

ROSE, THE. See also:
Nightingale, The
Rose

ROSE, WHITE. See: Bobo-
Safar

ROSETTA, loved by Caviello, in
love with Pulcinella (Punch)
TARTAGLIA, her father
Pulcinella   PULCI
In love with Pulcinella
TARTAGLIA, her father,
wishes her to marry Captain
Cartuccia
Salade   SALAD

ROSETTA. See also: Coviello

ROSIDA, young Sicilian maiden,
in love with Alman, Rosida
                         ROSID

ROSINA, dancer, pupil of Riga-
don
LUCREZIA, her mother
Scuola di Ballo   SCUOL

ROSINANTE, Don Quixote's
horse, Don Quichotte
                         DONQU

ROSINANTE. See also: Rozinante

ROSINE (BABETTE). See:
Pedrillo

ROSITA. See: Fernandez

ROTBART. See: Von Rotbart

ROTISLAV, Russian prisoner of
the Circassians; loved by
Kzelkia
HIS FATHER
HIS BETROTHED

193   ROUCEM

Prisoner of the Caucasus
                         PRISN
The Prisoner in the
Caucasus   PRISO

ROUCEM, chief eunuch of Achmet's harem, La Pêri
                         PERII

ROUCEM.   See also: Slave-
   Dealer, A

ROUSTAVELI, CHOTA,
   Georgian poet, dedicates
   his work to Queen Tamara
   with whom he is in love,
   Chota Roustaveli   CHOTA

ROUSTAVELI, CHOTA.   See
   also:
   Tariel
   Tzetzkly

ROXANE.   See: Bergerac,
   Cyrano de

ROY.   See: Ray

ROZINANTE, Don Quixote's
   "sorry nag, " Don Quixote
                         DONQX

ROZINANTE.   See also:
   Rosinante

RÜBEZAHL, "the Gnome, " rejected by Eoline in favor
   of Edgar; sets fire to her
   oak, Eoline   EOLIN

RUBY, a fairy, The Triumph
   of Neptune   TRIUM

RUDOLPH, squire to Baron
   Willibald; in love with
   Fleur-des-Champs, La
   Fille du Danube   FILLD

RUGGER, danced by two male
   dancers, Street Games
                         STREE

RULER OF JAPAN.   See:

Mikado, The

RULER OF THE MERMAIDS.
   See: Queen of the Nereids

RUSSIA.   See: Spirit of Russia

RUSSIA, CZARINA OF.   See:
   Tsarina Catherine II

RUSSIA, EMPEROR OF.   See:
   Emperor Paul I, Emperor of
   Russia

RUSSIA, TSAR OF.   See: Peter
   I

RUSSIA, TSARINA OF.   See:
   Tsarina Catherine II

RUSSIAN BALLERINA, ATTEN-
   DANT CAVALIERS TO THE.
   See: Queen of the Dance

RUSSIAN MERCHANT, A
   HIS FAMILY, customers at
   toy shop
   La Boutique Fantasque
                         BOUTI

RUSSLAN, Russian knight
   LUDMILLA, sought in mar-
   riage by Russlan
   Russlan and Ludmilla RUSSL

RYE.   See: Rock and Rye

                    S

SABI.   See:
   Danina
   Jeafre

SABIÁ, FEMALE.   See: Gavião

SABIÁ, MALE.   See: Gavião

SABRINA.   See: Comus

SACHER.   See: Masoch, Sacher

SACK.   See: Man With a Sack,
   The

SACOUNTALA. See: Sakuntala

SACRAMENTO. See: Duke of
Sacramento, The

SACRED LOVE. See: Poet

SACRED MUSIC, MUSE OF.
See: Polyhymnia

SACRISTAN, THE, assigned to
officiate at marriage of
Luigi and Lauretta, La
Tarentule   TAREN

SADKO, singer and gousli
player of Novgorod
LUBAVA, his wife
Sadko   SADKO

SAFAR. See: Bobo-Safar

SAGAN, MADAME DE,
Frenchwoman, Vienna-
1814   VIENN

SAGE (A Wise Man), member
of tribe which sacrifices
the Chosen One
Le Sacré du Printemps
                     SACRD
Le Sacré du Printemps
                     SACRE

SAILOR. See:
Amazon Captain
Fashionable Lady
First Sailor

SAILOR, SECOND. See:
First Sailor

SAILOR (STRANGER). See:
Lady, The

SAILOR, THE, visiting London
London Morning   LONDO
Personification
Le Pas d'Acier   PASDA
Madman in London mad-
house
The Rake's Progress
                     RAKES

SAILOR, THIRD. See: First
Sailor

SAILORS. See: Farm Boy, The

SAILORS, THREE, enjoying
shore leave, attempt to pick
up girls in New York bar,
Fancy Free   FANCY

SAILORS, THREE. See also:
Passers-By

SAINT-ANGE, MADAME DE.
See: Duc de Vendôme, The

SAINT FRANCIS. See: Bernadone, Francesco

SAINT GEORGE, personification
of holiness, reunited with
Una after being deceived by
evil magician, The Quest
                     QUEST

SAINT IBARS. See: Baron de
Saint Ibars, The

SAINT JOAN, Joan of Arc, "sees
herself as Maid, Warrior,
and Martyr"
Seraphic Dialogue   SERAP
Triumph of St. Joan TRIUS
SAINT MICHAEL, receives
Joan into the communion of
saints
Seraphic Dialogue   SERAP

SAINT JOAN. See also: d'Arc,
Jeanne

SAINT-LÉON, ARTHUR MICHEL,
French choreographer, dan-
cer and violinist, Pas des
Déesses   PASDS

SAINT MICHAEL. See:
Archangel St. Michael
Saint Joan

SAINT-RAMBERT, MONSIEUR
DE, a young colonel of
musketeers and lord of

the Manor, La Somnambule
SOMNA

SAINT-RAMBERT, MONSIEUR
DE. See also: Olivier

SAKOURADA, queen of the
spirits of night, Yedda
YEDDA

SAKOURADA. See also:
Yedda

SAKUNTALA, Indian maiden,
in love with and loved by
Dushmata, King of India
KANU, a Brahmin, her
father
Sakuntala   SAKUN

SAKUNTALA. See also:
Anusuya
Executioner
Parabhritica
Priyamwada
Tchaturica

SALAMANDER PRINCE. See:
Princess Belle Épine

SALAMANDERS, LEADER OF
THE. See: Belphegor

SALAMMBÔ, Carthagenian
princess, loved by Mato,
Salammbô   SALAO

SALOMÉ, "searches for her
ideal on the roads of the
world but none of the six
men she meets fulfills her
dreams"
SIX MEN, fail to meet
Salomé's requirements
SEVENTH MAN, meets
Salomé's requirements,
conquered by her "only to
feel in his love the taste
of death"
Dancing Tragedy   DANCT
Princess, dances for King
Herod
QUEEN HÉRODIAS, her

mother
KING HEROD, husband of
Queen Hérodias
Salomé   SALOM
La Tragédie de Salomé
TRAGD
La Tragédie de Salomé
TRAGE
La Tragédie de Salomé
TRAGG
La Tragédie de Salomé
TRAGH
La Tragédie de Salomé
TRAGI

SALOMÉ. See also: John the
Baptist

SALOMON. See: Baron Salomon

SALT, JACK, prize fighter,
kills William Targett, The
Sailor's Return   SAILO

SALT, JACK. See also: Tulip

SALVATOR. See: Rosa, Salvator

SAMBO, black page, servant of
Cinderella's family, Cinderella   CINDA

SAMBO. See also: Tulip

SAMPIETRI, THE MARCHESA.
See:
Count Pepinelli
Prince Osorio, Governor of
Rome

SAMSON. See:
Agonistes, Samson
Carrasco, Bachelor Samson
Delilah

SAMUEL, the Prophet, David
DAVID

SAMUEL. See also: Spirit of
the Prophet Samuel

SAN LUCAR. See: Marquis de

San Lucar, The

SAN-SEVERINO, COUNT OF.
See: Countess Gemma

SANCHEZ. See: Mejias, Ig-
nacio Sanchez

SANCHO. See: Panza, Sancho

SANDOVAL. See: Dom Sando-
val

SANDY BOWERS. See: Orum,
Eilley

SANGHINE, betrothed to Zarragulle, daughter of Bobo-
Safar, The Two Roses
                        TWORO

SANGUINIC VARIATION. See:
Melancholic Variation

SANS-SOUS, THE BARON DE.
See: Cinderella

SANSFOY
SANSJOY
SANSLOY, three knights
The Quest   QUEST

SANTA CLAUS. See: Prince
Santa Claus

SANTA-CROCE, MARQUIS DE.
See: Marquis de Santa-
Croce

SANTÃO, heretical sacristan,
prisoner in the enchanted
cavern Salamanca do Jaraú
TENIGUÁ, Moorish prin-
cess, his beloved, also
prisoner in the cavern
Salamanca do Jaraú SALAM

SANTÃO. See also: Nunes,
Blau

SAPPHIRE. See: Prince
Sapphire

SARADUTA, a Brahmin, Sakuntala   SAKUN

SARAH. See:
Lord Campbell
Mab
Stenio

SARIE. See: Lenny

SARNAGRAVA, a Brahmin,
Sakuntala   SAKUN

SATAN, Ballestriga's master
Abraxas   ABRAX
Tests Job's faith
Job   JOBBB
The Devil, appears to exert
malignant influence on Paga-
nini's violin technique
Paganini   PAGAN

SATAN. See also:
Beelzebub
Cadaval
Comforters, Three
Matheus, Doctor

SATANAZ, a devil, Pastorela
                     PASTO

SATO. See: del Sato, Orsino

SATURN, celestial body
The Stars   STARS
God
I Titani   TITAN

SATYR. See: Literary Satyr

SATYRISCI, THREE, "three
boorish adolescent delin-
quents," Undertow   UNDER

SATYRS, EIGHT, supernatural
beings, Ballet Comique de
la Reine   BALLC

SATYRS, TWO, spectators at
the bacchanale, Bacchanale
                     BACCH

SAUL, King of the Israelites
    JONATHAN, his son
    MICHAL, his daughter
    David   DAVID

SAUL. See also: King Saul,
    King of the Israelites

SAULDOTS, young boyard,
    loved by Aina and Malda,
    Le Triomphe de l'Amour
                              TRIOM

SAULDOTS. See also:
    Tautvaldis

SAVING SUSIES, act as Chorus,
    sing verses of song des-
    cribing action, Frankie
    and Johnny   FRANK

SCANDAL, personification,
    spectator at Paganini's
    concert, Paganini   PAGAN

SCARAMOUCHE, wandering
    violinist, fascinates Blond-
    elaine with his music;
    stabbed by her
    A WOMAN
    A BOY, who accompany
    him
    Scaramouche   SCARA

SCHÉHÉRAZADE
    THE SHAH
    HIS BROTHER, characters
    in an Arabian story
    Schêhêrazade   SCHEE
    The Sleeping Beauty
                              SLEEP

SCIENCE. See: Genii of
    Science, The

SCOTCH AND SODA, drink
    served at 2222 Club, New
    York City, Café Society
                              CAFES

SCOTS. See: Mary, Queen of
    Scots

SCOTSMAN, encounters, becomes
    interested in Sylphide,
    Scotch Symphony   SCOTC

SCREEN-STRUCK, boy and girl,
    in love, influenced by lovers
    in motion picture, Street
    Games   STREE

SCRUBWOMEN, working at
    metropolitan railroad termi-
    nal, Terminal   TERMI

SEA. See:
    Gods of the Sea
    Spirit of the Sea, The

SEA, GOD OF THE. See:
    Neptune
    Poseidon

SEA, GODDESS OF THE. See:
    Amphitrite

SEA, KING OF THE. See:
    Poseidon

SEA, QUEEN OF THE. See:
    Amphitrite
    Captain

SEAL HUNTERS, FOUR, mem-
    bers of Eskimo tribe,
    Qarrtsiluni   QARRT

SEBASTIAN. See:
    Courtesan
    Rafael

SECOND BRIDESMAN. See:
    Bride, The

SECOND EUNUCH. See: Chief
    Eunuch

SECOND FAVORITE WIFE. See:
    Gierey

SECOND INTRUDER. See:
    First Intruder

SECOND LITTLE HARE, THE.

See: Little Hare, The
First

SECOND PHONOGRAPH. See:
First Phonograph

SECOND RED KNIGHT. See:
First Red Knight

SECOND SAILOR. See: First
Sailor

SECOND TELEGRAM. See:
First Telegram

SECOND VARIATION. See:
Theme and First Variation

SECRETARIES, attending ball
tendered by Prince Metternich, Vienna- 1814 VIENN

SEDUCER, THE. See:
Delilah
Lady, The

SEDUCTION, THREE SPIRITS
OF PERFUMED. See:
Rose

SEEKERS, BARGAIN. See:
Floorwalker

SEEKS. See: She Who Seeks

SEINE, THE, symbolic figure,
Flik and Flok   FLIKA

SELENE. See:
Endymion
Hyperion

SELF, HIS SPIRITUAL. See:
Job

SELINA, young girl
THE BROTHER, her
brother
THE POET, in love with
Selina
AGNES, incompetent witch,
attempts to cast spells
Selina   SELIN

SELLER. See:
Flower-Seller
Glove-Seller
Hat Seller, The

SELLER OF FRUIT, THE, merchant in Paris market, Mam'-
zelle Angot   MAMZE

SELLER OF VEGETABLES, THE,
merchant in Paris market,
Mam'zelle Angot   MAMZE

SELLERS. See: Flower Sellers

SEMIRAMIS, mythical Assyrian
queen
Semiramis   SEMIR
Spectacle   SPECL

SÉNANGE, MADAME DE. See:
Zoé

SENSUAL PLEASURE, PERSONI-
FICATION OF. See: Volupia

SEPPI, rich peasant youth, rival
of Csizmás Janko for the affections of Ildiko, Little
Johnny in Top-Boots LITTL

SEPTEMBER, a house-painter,
Twelve for the Mail-Coach
                   TWELV

SERAPHINA, DOÑA. See:
Comte d'Hervilly, The

SERGEANT, seeks to arrest
Count Rackozski, The
Hungarian Hut   HUNGA

SERGEANT. See also:
Durfort, Sergeant
Moscatello, Sergeant

SERGEI. See: Alexandrovitch,
Sergei

SERPENT, personification of
evil, The Seventh Symphony
                   SEVEN

SERPENT, THE, summoned
    from Hell by Ballestriga,
    Abraxas   ABRAX

SERPENTS. See: Snakes
    (Serpents), Two

SERVANT, scrub-woman at
    bar of Folies-Bergère, Bar
    aux Folies-Bergère,
                            BARAU

SERVANT, FEMALE. See:
    Una

SERVANT OF THE MOON.
    See: Moon, The

SERVANT OF THE MOON,
    REFLECTION OF THE.
    See: Moon, The

SERVANTS, THE DUKE'S.
    See: Duchess, The

SERVICE MEN. See: Escort
    Service Men

SERVING-MAID, THE, em-
    ployed by Nobleman,
    actually a divinity in
    disguise
    THE SHEPHERD, also a
    divinity
    The Gods Go A-Begging
                            GODSA
    The Gods Go A-Begging
                            GODSG
    The Gods Go A-Begging
                            GODSO

SEVEN. See:
    Clowns, Seven
    Dwarfs, The Seven
    Married Women, Seven
    Murderers, Seven
    Unmarried Women, Seven
    Young Women, Seven
    Zephyrs, Seven

SEVEN DAUGHTERS, THEIR.
    See: Clowns, Seven

SEVEN DEADLY SINS, THE,
    personifications, The Quest
                            QUEST

SEVEN DEADLY SINS, THE.
    See also:
    Seven Sins, The
    Young Girl

SEVEN SINS, THE, personifica-
    tions, The Seven Sins
                            SEVES

SEVEN SINS, THE. See also:
    Seven Deadly Sins, The

SEVEN SOLDIERS. See: Clowns,
    Seven

SEVEN SONS, HIS. See: Job

SEVEN WIVES, THEIR. See:
    Clowns, Seven

SEVENTH MAN. See: Salomé

SEVENTH VARIATION. See:
    Theme and First Variation

SEVERINO, COUNT OF SAN.
    See: Countess Gemma

SEVILLANOS, participate in
    gaiety at Seville café,
    Cuadro Flamenco   CUADR

SEVILLE. See: Governor of
    Seville, The

SEXTON, "aged and sanctimoni-
    ous," flirts with the witch
    Khivria, The Fair at Soro-
    chinsk   FAIRA

SEXTUS. See: Tarquinius,
    Sextus

SEYD, Pasha of the Isle of Cos
    ZULMEA, his favorite sul-
    tana
    Le Corsaire   CORSA

SEYD. See also:
   Chief Eunuch
   English Slave, An
   French Slave, A
   Gulnare
   Italian Slave, An
   Moldavian Slave, A
   Spanish Slave, A

SGANARELLE, servant to Don
   Juan, Don Juan   DONJU

SHADE, THE. See: Ombre,
   l'

SHADOW, THE, attendant upon
   the Young Man
   THE YOUNG MAN, re-
   leases the Daughters of
   the Night
   Les Mirages   MIRAG
   Inhabitant of Hades
   Orphée   ORPHH

SHADOW, THE. See also:
   Youth, A

SHAH, THE. See:
   Schéhérazade

SHAH-ZEMAN. See:
   Shahryar, King of India
   and China

SHAHRYAR, King of India and
   China
   ZOBEIDA, his unfaithful
   wife
   ZOBEIDA'S FAVORITE
   SLAVE, her lover
   SHAH-ZEMAN, Shahryar's
   brother
   Schéhérazade   SCHEH

SHAHRYAR. See also:
   Chief Eunuch
   Odalisque, An

SHAH'S BROTHER, The.
   See: Schéhérazade

SHALOTT, THE LADY OF.
   See:

   Lady of Shalott, The
   Lovers, The
   Reapers, The
   Sir Lancelot

SHAMMAH. See: Jessee

SHAN. See: Li-Shan-Fu

SHAPRUT. See: Hazdai-Ben-
   Shaprut

SHE, white mare, friend of the
   black stallion He; attracted
   to the Other, circus horse,
   Idylle   IDYLL

SHE. See also:
   He
   Who Was She?

SHE-DEVIL, THE. See: Old
   Devil, The

SHE OF THE GROUND, allegorical figure, Dark Meadow
                       DARKM

SHE WHO SEEKS, allegorical
   figure, Dark Meadow
                       DARKM

SHE WORE A PERFUME,
   memory recalled by The
   Gentleman With Her, Dim
   Lustre   DIMLU

SHEIK, sells Joseph to Potiphar,
   La Légende de Joseph
                       LEGEN

SHELL BUTTERFLIES. See:
   Tortoise Shell Butterflies

SHEMAKHA. See: Queen of
   Shemakha

SHEPHERD
   SHEPHERDESS, represent
   the Golden Age to Don
   Quixote
   Don Quixote   DONQX
   Acts as guide for the Moon

on her nightly wanderings
Les Mirages   MIRAG

SHEPHERD. See also:
Old Shepherd, The
Snow Maiden, The
Young Shepherd, The

SHEPHERD, THE, unfaithful
lover of the Dryad, The
Dryad   DRYAD

SHEPHERD, THE. See also:
Nobleman
Serving-Maid, The

SHEPHERDESS. See: Shep-
herd

SHEPHERDESS, THIRD. See:
Shepherdesses, Two

SHEPHERDESSES, TWO, pre-
sented to Third Shepherdess
by Amor
THIRD SHEPHERDESS,
thought by the Two Shep-
herdesses to be a man;
loved by them
Les Petits Riens   PETIT

SHERIFF, American type, seen
by the Immigrant, Within
The Quota   WITHI

SHIKO. See: Nao-Shiko

SHIRIENE. See: Queen
Mehmene-Banu

SHOEMAKER, THE, helps
Cinderella's two ugly step-
sisters prepare for ball,
Cinderella   CINDE

SHOPKEEPER, THE, proprietor
of toy shop
HIS ASSISTANT
La Boutique Fantasque
                     BOUTI

SHOPKEEPERS. See: Cour-
asche

SHORT CAVALIER, HER. See:
Tall Ballerina

SHOWER OF GOLD, form as-
sumed by Jupiter while wooing Danaë, Les Amours de
Jupiter   AMOUJ

SHUKANIN. See: Elizabeth

SHURALE. See: Suimbike

SHUTTLECOCK, A, toy, Jeux
d'Enfants   JEUXX

SIAMESE TWINS, members of
troupe of travling players,
Les Forains   FORAI

SIBILLA, a sorceress, Rinaldo
and Armida   RINAL

SIEBA, a valkyrie, gives Harold
magic sword; falls in love
with him, punished by Wotan,
Sieba   SIEBA

SIEGFRIED. See: Prince Siegfried

SIGNOR MIDAS, a society host,
The Lady and the Fool
                     LADYA

SIGNOR MIDAS. See also:
Capricciosa, La

SIGNOR PESANTE, chef d'
orchestre at the opera
house, The Débutante
                     DEBUT

SIGNORA CLORINDE. See:
Omeopatico, Doctor

SILANUS, JULIUS, a Consul,
La Vestale   VESTA

SILENI, THREE, "customers of
the prostitute Volupia,"
Undertow   UNDER

SILENUS, woodland deity, The

Triumph of Bacchus and
Ariadne   TRIUB

SILESIA, DUKE OF. See:
Albrecht

SILLY COUNTRY GIRL
A YOKEL
AN IRATE SQUIRE, per-
form country dance
Façade   FACAD

SILVER MOON, KNIGHT OF
THE. See: Carrasco,
Bachelor Sampson

SILVESTRA, THE MARQUISE.
See:
Constanza
Mariuccia

SILVIA. See: Tebrick, Mr.

SILVINA, friend of Marietta,
Kalkabrino   KALKA

SILVIO, betrothed to Clarice
DOCTOR LOMBARD, his
father
The False Bridegroom
FALSE

SIMON, fruit vendor, in love
with Gloriette
Le Marché des Innocents
MARCH
Shepherd, in love with
Zoshka
The Nightingale   NIGHI

SIMONE, MOTHER, wealthy
widow, disapproves of her
daughter's interest in Colin
(Colas)
LISETTE (LISE), her
daughter, in love with
Colin (Colas)
La Fille Mal Gardée
FILLE
La Fille Mal Gardée
FILLG

SIMONE, MOTHER. See also:

Thomas

SIMPLICE, Janetta's sweetheart,
Le Diable Amoureux   DIABE

SIN. See: Night

SINDJAR, attendant on the Khan,
La Source   SOURC

SINGER. See: Ballad Singer,
The

SINS. See: Seven Sins, The

SINS, THE SEVEN DEADLY.
See:
Seven Deadly Sins, The
Seven Sins, The
Young Girl

SIR EDWARD ELGAR. See:
Theme and First Variation

SIR HILDEBRAND, of Ringstetten,
knight, attracts attention of
the Duke's adopted daughter
Bertha; falls in love with
and marries Coralia
HIS SQUIRE
Coralia   CORAL

SIR HIPS, commander of treaty-
port in China, The Red
Poppy   REDPO

SIR LANCELOT, the red-cross
knight, seen by the Lady of
Shalott, The Lady of Shalott
LADYO

SIR LANCELOT. See also:
Angelic Apparition

SIREN, personification, H.P.
HPPPP

SIREN, THE, seduces the Prodi-
gal Son
The Prodigal Son   PRODA
The Prodigal Son   PRODG
The Prodigal Son   PRODI
The Prodigal Son   PRODL

The Prodigal Son   PRODO
The Prodigal Son   PRODS

SIREN, THE. See also:
    Vagabond, The

SISTER ANNE. See: Blue-
    beard

SISTER, ELDEST. See: Hagar

SISTER, HER. See: Daughter,
    The

SISTER, YOUNGEST. See:
    Friend, The
    Hagar

SISTERS, BRONTË. See:
    Sisters, Three

SISTERS, HER. See: Swan
    Princess, The

SISTERS OF THE PRODIGAL
    SON. See: Prodigal Son,
    The

SISTERS, THE TWO UGLY.
    See: Cinderella

SISTERS, THREE, allegoric
    representations of the
    Brontë sisters
    POETIC BELOVED
    DARK BELOVED, personi-
    fications
    Deaths and Entrances
                        DEATS

SISYPHUS, King of Corinth,
    condemned in Hades to roll
    a heavy stone up a steep
    hill, only to have it roll
    down again, Sisyphus
                        SISYP

SIX. See: Hours of Day, Six

SIX HUNTERS. See: First
    Hunter

SIX MEN. See: Salomé

SIX OTHER NYMPHS. See:
    Nymph, The

SIXTH VARIATION. See: Theme
    and First Variation

SKATERS, enjoy ice skating on
    secluded pond
    Les Patineurs   PATIN
    Les Plaisirs de l'Hiver
                        PLAIS

SKATERS, TWO, perform skating
    dance, Wind in the Mountains
                        WINDI

SKETCH, THE, representation
    of British newspaper, The
    Press   PRESS

SKIPPING, danced by three fe-
    male dancers, Street Games
                        STREE

SKY, THE, personification, The
    Seventh Symphony   SEVEN

SLAVE. See:
    African Slave
    English Slave, An
    French Slave, A
    Italian Slave, An
    Moldavian Slave, A
    Spanish Slave, A

SLAVE-DEALER, A, sells four
    female slaves to Roucem
    FOUR FEMALE SLAVES,
    sold to Roucem
    La Péri   PERII

SLAVE OF ARMIDE. See:
    Armide

SLAVE, ZOBEIDA'S FAVORITE.
    See: Shahryar, King of
    India and China

SLAVES. See:
    Chief of the Slaves
    Galley-Slaves

SLAVES, FOUR FEMALE. See:

Slave-Dealer, A

SLAVES, HIS. See: Orion

SLEEPER, "visited by three
apparitions of his dreams"
THREE APPARITIONS, of
Sleeper's dream
Night Spell   NIGHP

SLEEPING BEAUTY, THE,
member of troupe of
traveling players, Les
Forains   FORAI

SLEEPING BEAUTY, THE.
See also:
Princess Aurora, The

SLEEPWALKER, THE. See:
Baron, The
Coquette, The
Poet, The

SLICKER, THE CITY. See:
Light Lady, The

SLIVOVITZ, LADISLAV, a
liqueur, Schlagobers
                     SCHLA

SLOPER. See: Alley Sloper

SMALL CARDS, FOUR, play-
ing cards, participate in
poker game, Card Game
                     CARDG

SMALL FRY, caricature of
cartoon characters, The
New Yorker   NEWYO

SMERALDINA, in love with
Truffaldino, The False
Bridegroom   FALSE

SMITH, CAPTAIN JOHN. See:
Rolfe, John

SMOUROFF, Governor of Nijni
Novgorod
IVAN, his son, falls in
love with Lauretta when

she is with gypsies; loved
by her
La Gitana   GITAN

SMOUROFF. See also: Duke of
Medina-Celi, The

SNAKE, creature of Aleko's
delirium
Aleko   ALEKO
One of Ulysses' sailors,
transformed by Circe
Circe   CIRCE

SNAKE. See also: Snake, The

SNAKE DANCER, circus per-
former, The Incredible
Flutist   INCRE

SNAKE PIT. See: King of the
Snake Pit

SNAKE PRIESTESS, pagan church-
woman, The Minotaur
                     MINOU

SNAKE, THE, seen by the
Princess in her dream, A
Spring Tale   SPRIN

SNAKE, THE. See also: Snake

SNAKES (SERPENTS), TWO, one
of which killed by Tiresias,
Tiresias   TIRES

SNOB, THE, mechanical toy,
performs routine in toy
shop, La Boutique Fantasque
                     BOUTI

SNOW, personification, Les
Saisons   SAISO

SNOW. See also: King of Snow

SNOW MAIDEN, THE, super-
natural being, lives only
during the cold of winter,
disappears with the warmth
of spring; falls in love with
Shepherd

SHEPHERD, mortal, loved
by Snow Maiden, loses her
with the coming of Spring
SPRING, personification
The Snow Maiden   SNOWM
The Snow Maiden   SNOWN

SNOW, QUEEN OF.   See:
King of Snow

SNOW-WHITE, princess, incurs
jealousy of the Queen;
adopted by the Seven
Dwarfs
THE QUEEN, her step-
mother, orders her death
Blanche-Neige   BLANC

SNOW-WHITE.   See also:
Dwarfs, The Seven
Fairy, The
Huntsman, The
Prince, The

SNOWBALL, a "blackman,"
destroys magic telescope,
The Triumph of Neptune
                       TRIUM

SOAP BUBBLES, toys, Jeux
d'Enfants   JEUXX

SOCIAL REFORMER, American
type, seen by the Immigrant,
Within the Quota   WITHI

SOCIAL WORKER, active in
the Gorbals, slum district
of Glasgow, Miracle in
the Gorbals   MIRAC

SOCIETY GIRLS, creatures of
Aleko's delirium, Aleko
                       ALEKO

SOCIETY LADY, creature of
Aleko's delirium, Aleko
                       ALEKO

SOCIETY PAPERS, representation of British publications,
The Press   PRESS

SODA.   See: Scotch and Soda

SOLANGE, Urbain's nurse, Le
Violon du Diable   VIOLO

SOLARINO, OLIVIA.   See: Lugano, Marco

SOLAXA, witch, friend of the
Devil, Christmas Eve
                       CHRIS

SOLAXA.   See also:
Choub
Clerk, The
Sverbigouz

SOLDIER, clockwork toy
The Nutcracker   NUTCA
The Nutcracker   NUTCK
The Nutcracker   NUTCR

SOLDIER.   See also:
Hypnotist
Veteran Soldier, A
Young Soldier, The

SOLDIER, THE OLD.   See:
Young Soldier, The

SOLDIERS.   See: Robbers

SOLDIERS, FIVE COSSACK.
See: Cossack Chief, The

SOLDIERS, SEVEN.   See:
Clowns, Seven

SOLIMAN, ABU.   See:
Caliph Abderraman
Hazdai-Ben-Shaprut

SOLLISTE at the Grand Opera,
Paris, Foyer de la Danse
                       FOYER

SOLOIST, female dancer, prepares stage for the Ballerina, Ballet Imperial BALLE

SOLOR, a young warrior, loved
by Nikia and Gamsatti,

daughter of the Rajah Dugmanta, La Bayadère
                          BAYAD

SOLVEIG, the Ice Maiden,
supernatural being, loved
by Asak
HER MOTHER
The Ice Maiden   ICEMA
Waits faithfully for Peer
Gynt, son of Aase
Peer Gynt   PEERG

SON. See:
Father
Prodigal Son, The
Sons
Sun
Sun, The

SON, HER. See: Patroness,
The

SON, HIS. See: Tell, William

SON, RICH PEASANT'S. See:
Fadette

SONG-BIRDS. See: Fairy of
the Song-Birds, The

SONIA, the Merry Widow,
beautiful heiress, native
of Marsovia
PRINCE DANILO, Secretary
to the Marsovian legation;
falls in love with Sonia
BARON POPOFF, Marsovian
ambassador, Prince Dani-
lo's ally
Vilia   VILIA

SONS. See also: Son

SONS, FOUR YOUNGER. See:
Jesse

SONS, HER TWO. See:
Mother

SONS, HIS SEVEN. See: Job

SONS, THEIR TWO. See:

Lodbrok, Regnar, King of
Denmark

SONS, TWO. See: Anna I

SOPHIA, PRINCESS. See:
Peter I, Tsar of Russia

SORCERER. See: Girl-Reindeer

SORCERER'S APPRENTICE, re-
members magic word which
sets Broom to carrying
water for him, forgets word
which will stop the broom
BROOM, carries water at
command of Sorcerer's Ap-
prentice
The Sorcerer's Apprentice
                          SORCE

SORCERESS, representation of
Medea, Cave of the Heart
                          CAVEO

SORCERESS. See also:
Bayadère Sorceress, A
Victim

SORCERESS, THE, consulted by
King Saul, conjures up Spirit
of the Prophet Samuel
David Triomphant   DAVIT
Gives Malda crown with
which she can bewitch Aina,
her stepdaughter
Le Triomphe de l'Amour
                          TRIOM

SORCERESS, THE. See also:
Tautvaldis

SOROCHINSK. See: Mayor of
Sorochinsk

SOUL, FISHERMAN'S. See:
Fisherman

SOULS. See: Lost Souls

SOUS, THE BARON DE SANS.
See: Cinderella

SOVIET COMMUNIST YOUTH.
　　See: Woman of Soviet
　　Communist Youth

SOVIET FOOTBALL TEAM.
　　See: Captain of Soviet
　　Football Team

SOVIET STEAMER.　See:
　　Captain of a Soviet
　　Steamer

SPACE, PERSONIFICATION
OF MODERN MAN IN.
　　See: Icaros

SPADA, MARCO, bandit chief
　　ANGELA, his daughter
　　Marco Spada　　　MARCO

SPADA, MARCO.　See also:
　　Genario

SPADES.　See:
　　Knave of Spades
　　Queen of Spades

SPADES, THE KING OF.　See:
　　Queen of Clubs, The

SPAIN.　See:
　　Infanta of Spain
　　King of Spain, The
　　Prince Philip of Spain

SPANISH ESPADA, attracts
　　Femina as gitana in Anda-
　　lusia; takes her from
　　lover, Femina　　FEMIN

SPANISH PRINCE, THE, seeks
　　hand of the Princess Aurora
　　in marriage, The Sleeping
　　Beauty　　　　SLEEP

SPANISH SLAVE, A, property
　　of Seyd, Le Corsaire,
　　　　　　　　CORSA

SPANISH WOMAN, personifi-
　　cation of Lust, dances to
　　music of Ravel's "Bolero"
　　on table top in café

TWENTY MEN, her com-
　　panions, dance with her
　　Bolero　　　　BOLER

SPARTA, KING OF.　See: King
　　Menelaus

SPARTACUS, gladiator, leader
　　of insurrection
　　PHRYGIA, in love with
　　Spartacus
　　AEGINA, courtesan, en-
　　amored of Harmodius; be-
　　trays Spartacus and his
　　followers
　　HARMODIUS, friend of
　　Spartacus
　　Spartacus　　　　SPART

SPEAKER FOR THE JURY, offi-
　　cial at trial of the Accused
　　(Lizzie Borden), Fall River
　　Legend　　　　FALLR

SPEAKS, THE ONE WHO.　See:
　　Actress, An

SPECTATOR, A, comforts Poor
　　Girl after she deserted by
　　Young Man for Rich Girl,
　　Nocturne　　　　NOCTU

SPHINX, THE, half woman, half
　　cat, killed by Oedipus after
　　he answers her riddle cor-
　　rectly
　　THREE HANDMAIDENS, her
　　attendants
　　Le Rencontre　　RENCO
　　Mythological figure
　　The Sphinx　　　SPHIN

SPIDER, THE, inhabitant of the
　　insect world; catches insects
　　in her web, becomes victim
　　of Praying Mantises
　　Le Festin de l'Araignée
　　　　　　　　FESTD
　　Le Festin de l'Araignée
　　　　　　　　FESTI
　　The Spider's Banquet
　　　　　　　　SPIDE
　　Resident of Butterfly Land

Les Papillons   PAPIO

SPIDER, THE.   See also:
Ants
Butterfly, The
Mayfly, The

SPIES, TWO, enemies of
Svetlana's homeland, cap-
tured by her and her
neighbors, Svetlana
                          SVETL

SPIRIT.   See:
Rose Spirit
Spirit, The

SPIRIT, ATTENDANT.   See:
Comus

SPIRIT OF CREATION, THE,
personification, The Sev-
enth Symphony   SEVEN

SPIRIT OF CURIOSITY, THE,
tempts Ysaure de Renou-
alle to open forbidden
door, Barbe-Bleue BARBE

SPIRIT OF DARKNESS, THE,
personification, Excelsior
                          EXCEL

SPIRIT OF DESTINY, personification, Flik and Flok
                          FLIKA

SPIRIT OF EVIL, THE, supernatural being, Le Triomphe
de l'Amour   TRIOM

SPIRIT OF FIRE, personification, Homage to the Queen
                          HOMAG

SPIRIT OF FORTUNE, personification, Flik and Flok
                          FLIKA

SPIRIT OF RUSSIA, personification, La Nuit et le Jour
                          NUITE

SPIRIT OF THE CORN, personification, Les Saisons SAISO

SPIRIT OF THE DANUBE, THE,
chooses Nymph of the Dan-
ube to watch over Fleur-
des-Champs, La Fille du
Danube   FILLD

SPIRIT OF THE PROPHET
SAMUEL, conjured up by
the Sorceress, David Triomphant   DAVIT

SPIRIT OF THE SEA, THE,
personification
THE FISHER-BOY, in love
with her
The Spirit of the Sea SPIRI

SPIRIT OF THE SPRING, THE,
personification, Cydalise et
le Chèvre-pied   CYDAL

SPIRIT OF THE SPRING, THE.
See also: Naïla

SPIRIT OF TRUTH, personification, Flik and Flok FLIKA

SPIRIT OF VANITY, THE, personification, overcomes
Femina, Femina   FEMIN

SPIRIT OF WOMANKIND, THE,
in the guise of a slave, La
Révolte au Serail   REVOL

SPIRIT, THE.   See:
Ombre, l'
Spirit

SPIRITS, GODDESS OF THE
HEAVENLY. See: Amravati

SPIRITS OF NIGHT, QUEEN OF
THE.   See: Sakourada

SPIRITS OF PERFUMED SEDUC-
TION, THREE. See: Rose

SPIRITS OF THE EARTH, per-

sonifications, The Talisman
TALIS

SPIRITS OF VARIOUS ARTS,
personifications, Amor
AMORR

SPIRITS WHO GOVERN THE
TOYS, THE, animate toys
for the Child, Jeux d'
Enfants   JEUXX

SPIRITUAL SELF, HIS. See:
Job

SPORTING TIMES, THE, rep-
resentation of British newspaper, The Press   PRESS

SPORTING TIMES, THE. See
also: Man of the World,
The

SPORTSMAN, A, attends gas-
attack precautions course,
Perhaps Tomorrow!
PERHA

SPORTSMAN, THE, appears
at Eiffel Tower, Les
Mariés de la Tour Eiffel
MARIE

SPORTSMEN, THREE, athletes,
Jeux d'Enfants   JEUXX

SPREE, THE, symbolic figure,
Flik and Flok   FLIKA

SPRING, personification
Les Quatre Saisons QUATR
Les Saisons   SAISO

SPRING. See also:
Birds
Fairy Spring, The
Flowers
It Was Spring
Snow Maiden, The
Spirit of the Spring, The

SPRING, THE SPIRIT OF THE.
See: Naila

SPRING VALVES, representations of machinery, Iron
Foundry   IRONF

SPRINGINSFELD. See: Cour-
asche

SPRITE, THE, successively appears to Karl as a page, a
rustic coquette, a Will o'
the wisp, a folie, a domino
and a cavalier, Les Métamorphoses   METAM

SPRITE, THE. See also: Tree-
Sprite, The

SQUARE DANCERS. See: Caller

SQUIRE, AN IRATE. See:
Silly Country Girl

SQUIRE, HIS. See: Sir Hildebrand

SQUIRE OVE. See: Birthe,
Miss

SQUIRES, HIS TWO. See:
Knight, The

SQUIRES, THREE, pledge their
love and fealty to the Princess, Le Chevalier et la
Damoiselle   CHEVA

STABLEBOY, falls asleep, has
dream, The Filly   FILLY

STABLEBOY. See also:
Filly, The
Foal, The
Mare, The
Stallion, The

STAG. See also: Stags

STAG BEETLE, "public executioner," resident of Butterfly Land, Les Papillons
PAPIO

STAGE DIRECTOR, THE, at

ballet where Adam Zero is
created and destroyed,
Adam Zero   ADAMZ

STAGE-MANAGER, THE, at
the Theatre Royal, Madrid,
Le Diable Boiteux   DIABL

STAGS. See also: Stag

STAGS, COLLEGE. See:
Debutante

STALLION, THE, appears in
Stableboy's dream, The
Filly   FILLY

STANDARD, THE, representation of British newspaper,
The Press   PRESS

STANLEY KOWALSKI. See:
du Bois, Blanche

STAR. See:
Film Star, The
Morning Star
Morning Star, The
Night Star, The
Operetta Star
Polar Star

STAR, THE, representation of
British newspaper
The Press   PRESS
Motion picture actress,
"eloping for the fifth
time," passing through
metropolitan railroad
terminal
Terminal   TERMI

STAR, THE. See also:
Gloire, La

STARS. See:
Double Stars
Queen of the Stars

STAR'S ESCORT, OPERETTA.
See: Operetta Star

STATE TROOPER, THE, "natu-

ral enemy of Ray and Roy,"
truck drivers; stops at Mac's
filling station, Filling Station
FILLI

STATE TROOPER, THE. See
also: Ray

STATUE. See: Stone Statue, A

STATUES, danced by four female dancers, Street Games
STREE

STEAMER. See: Captain of a
Soviet Steamer

STEFANO, an old servant
Les Deux Pigéons   DEUXN
Les Deux Pigéons   DEUXP

STELLA. See: Petrucio

STELLA KOWALSKI. See: du
Bois, Blanche

STENBOCK, hunter, friend of
Ehrick, Electra   ELECT

STENIO, fugitive Roundhead officer, joins gypsies led by
Trousse-Diable; when Sarah
is child, saves her from
wild beast; later marries
her, La Gypsy   GYPSY

STENIO. See also:
Lord Campbell
Mab

STENOGRAPHERS, passing
through metropolitan railroad terminal, Terminal
TERMI

STEPFATHER, HAMLET'S. See:
Ophelia

STEPMOTHER, HER. See: Accused, The (Lizzie Borden)

STEPSISTERS, HER TWO UGLY.
See: Cinderella

211   STERNHOLD

STERNHOLD. See: Count
   Friedrich Sternhold

STEROPE, celestial star,
   Electra   ELECT

STEWARD, serving on frigate,
   Loin du Danemark LOIND

STICKS, THE DEVIL ON TWO.
   See: Asmodeus

STICKS, TWO WOMEN WITH
   PLAY. See: Mexican
   Peon

STINGO, MR., owner of the
   Sailor's Rest inn, The
   Sailor's Return   SAILO

STONE STATUE, A (Sylvia),
   loved by Count Frederick;
   brought to life during the
   day by Adda, Les Elfes
                          ELFES

STONE STATUE, A. See
   also: Albert of Hungary

STORE NYMPH. See:
   Chain Store Nymph

STORK. See: Baby Stork

STORK'S MOTHER, BABY.
   See:
   Baby Stork
   Vasia

STORM WITCHES, THE, seen
   by the Princess in her
   dream, A Spring Tale
                          SPRIN

STOUT AUNT, THE. See:
   Daughter, The

STRAHL, BARONESS. See:
   Arbenin

STRANGER. See:
   Adam
   Queen Mehmene-Banu

Stranger, The
Young Man

STRANGER PLAYER, THE.
   See: Flautist

STRANGER (SAILOR). See:
   Lady, The

STRANGER, THE, God, visiting
   the Gorbals, slum district
   of Glasgow; reforms the
   Prostitute, murdered by the
   Official and gang of hoodlums, Miracle in the Gorbals
                          MIRAC

STRANGER, THE. See also:
   Ben
   Devil, The
   McGrew, Dan
   Stranger
   Suicide, The
   Young Girl, The

STREAM, THE, personification,
   The Seventh Symphony
                          SEVEN

STREET BOY, A, leader of gang
   of hoodlums in the Gorbals,
   slum district of Glasgow
   HOODLUMS, his followers
   Miracle in the Gorbals
                          MIRAC

STREET CLEANER. See:
   Constable

STREET DANCER, THE, parti-
   pant in gypsy carnival
   Aleko   ALEKO
   Former lover of the Hussar
   Le Beau Danube   BEAUD

STREET DANCER, THE. See
   also:
   Athlete, The
   Manager, The

STREET DANCERS, THE, two
   participants in carnival celebrating Butter Week,

Petrouchka   PETRO

STREET MUSICIAN. See:
Young Apprentice

STREET VENDOR, performs
dance prelude, Contes
Russes   CONTE

STREETS. See: Woman of
the Streets, A

STRINGS. See: Woodwinds

STRIP TEASER, falls in love
with Junior
BIG BOSS, her husband,
racketeer, jealous of
Junior
GANGSTERS, accomplices
of Big Boss, assigned to
assassinate Junior
Slaughter on Tenth Avenue
SLAUG

STRIPS. See: Comic Strips

STROLLING MUSICIAN (Strolling Player), distributes
symbolic balloons, Ballade
BALLA

STROLLING PLAYER. See:
Strolling Musician

STRONG LADY. See:
Jinx
Ringmaster

STRONG MAN, THE. See:
Athlete, The

STRUCK. See: Screen-
Struck

STRUTTER, THE, dancer,
performs before city
workers, Skyscrapers
SKYSC

STUDENT. See:
Peregrina
Young Student

STUDENT, A, attends gas-attack
precautions course, Perhaps
Tomorrow!   PERHA

STUDENT OF KARL MARX, A,
"an opium addict, " The
Great American Goof
GREAT

STUDENT, THE, guest of the
Gardener, in love with the
Lady who demands a blood-
red rose
THE GARDENER, his host
APPRENTICE GARDENERS
Le Rossignol et la Rose
ROSSG
Le Rossignol et la Rose
ROSSI

STUDENT, THE. See also:
Rose, The

STUDENT, TIMOROUS. See:
Amore (Cupid)
Fashionable Lady

STURMEY, MRS. See: Tulip

STYRAX, faun, temporarily at-
tracted to the ballet-dancer
Cydalise, Cydalise et le
Chèvre-Pied   CYDAL

STYRAX. See also: Old Faun,
The

STYRIAN COUPLE, performs
dance for Cupid's approval,
The Whims of Cupid and
the Ballet Master   WHIMS

SUBLIME HYMNS, a muse,
Sylvia   SYLVA

SUGARPLUM FAIRY, welcomes
Clara (Masha) and Nutcracker
to the Kingdom of Sweets
The Nutcracker   NUTCA
The Nutcracker   NUTCK
The Nutcracker   NUTCR

SUGARPLUM FAIRY. See also:

President

SUGURO. See: Don Suguro

SUICIDE, THE, girl in black, brought back to life by the Stranger, Miracle in the Gorbals   MIRAC

SUIMBIKE, bird-girl, falls in love with Ali-Batyr ALI-BATYR, hunter, loved by Suimbike SHURALE, wood sprite, steals Suimbike's wings, thus preventing her from flying away Shurale   SHURA

SUITE, HIS. See: Knight of Death

SUITOR. See: Labanc Suitor, The Surtor Wealthy Widow

SUITOR, THE. See: Hamilton, Mary

SUITORS, TWO, to Cinderella's two ugly stepsisters, Cinderella   CINDE

SULTAN, THE, character in ballet in which Cydalise appears Cydalise et le Chèvre-pied Character in the ballet "Azalea, or The Odalisque" THE SULTANA, his wife, also a character in the ballet The Débutante   DEBUT

SULTAN, THE. See also: Mesrour Zulma

SULTANA, THE. See: Sultan, The Zulma

SUMMER, personification, Les Quatre Saisons   QUATR

SUMMER NUMBER, THE, representation of British publication, The Press   PRESS

SUMMER, THE FAIRY. See: Fairy Spring, The

SUMMONS. See: He Who Summons

SUN, personification, The Seventh Symphony   SEVEN

SUN. See also: Son Sun, The Young Man, The Young Woman, The

SUN IN VIRGO. See: Young Woman, The

SUN KING, THE, allegorical figure, Ballet de la Nuit   BALLN

SUN, THE, personification Canticle for Innocent Comedians   CANTI Representation of British newspaper, The Press   PRESS

SUN, THE. See also: Icare Son Sun

SUNDAY, BILLY, American evangelist, Billy Sunday   BILLS

SUOK, a circus performer, The Three Fat Men   THREE

SUPERVISOR OVER COOLIES. See: Chief Supervisor over Coolies

SURTOR, a demon, rival of
   Wotan, <u>Sieba</u>   SIEBA

SURTOR. See also: Suitor

SURVEYOR OF THE CHINESE
   CREW. See:
   Lady Gay, The
   Surveyor of the Irish Crew

SURVEYOR OF THE IRISH
   CREW
   SURVEYOR OF THE
   CHINESE CREW, workers
   building Union Pacific Railroad, rivals for the affections of the Lady Gay
   <u>Union Pacific</u>   UNION

SURVEYOR OF THE IRISH
   CREW. See also: Lady
   Gay, The

SURVILLE, MONSIEUR DE.
   See:
   Bougainville, Monsieur De
   Ozai

SUSIES. See: Saving Susies

SVEA, peasant, <u>Miss Julie</u>
                          MISSJ

SVERBIGOUZ, a Cossack,
   would-be lover of Solaxa,
   <u>Christmas Eve</u>   CHRIS

SVETLANA, young Russian
   girl, in love with Ilko,
   helps capture enemy spy,
   <u>Svetlana</u>   SVETL

SVETLANA. See also: Spies,
   Two

SWAMP LILIES. See: Hor-
   tense, Queen of the Swamp
   Lilies

SWAN, form assumed by
   Jupiter while wooing
   Leda
   Les Amours de Jupiter

                                AMOUJ
Cygne, dying, depicted in
dance
   <u>The Dying Swan</u>   DYING
   <u>La Mort du Cygne</u>   MORTD

SWAN PRINCESS, THE, saved
   from three-headed dragon by
   Bova Korolevich
   HER SISTERS
   <u>Contes Russes</u>   CONTE

SWAN, THE, helps the Trouba-
   dour save the Princess from
   Tuonela (Hades)
   THE TROUBADOUR, helps
   the Swan save the Princess
   THE PRINCESS, saved from
   Tuonela
   <u>The Swan of Tuonela</u> SWANT

SWANILDA, village girl, in love
   with Frantz, jealous of
   Coppélia
   <u>Coppélia</u>   COPPE
   <u>Coppélia</u>   COPPI

SWANS, QUEEN OF THE. See:
   Odette

SWEETHEART. See: World's
   Sweetheart, The

SWEETHEART, ALVA'S. See:
   Alva

SWEETHEART, HIS MEXICAN.
   See:
   Billy the Kid

SWEETHEARTS, HIS DAUGHTERS'.
   See: Veteran Soldier, A

SWIMMER, BOY. See: Nearly
   Drowned Girl

SWINBURNE, ALGERNON C.,
   English poet and playwright,
   <u>Ghost Town</u>   GHOST

SWINEHERD, THE, exchanges
   musical instrument consist-
   ing of a bowl and a spoon

Le Roi Nu   ROINV

TAILORS, THE THREE. See
  also: Ministers, The
  Three

TAILORS, TWO, business rivals La Concurrence
                    CONCU

TALE. See: Teller of the
  Tale

TALL BALLERINA, tolerantly
  amused by her cavalier
  HER SHORT CAVALIER,
  dancing partner, greatly
  impressed with her techn-
  nique
  Bourrée Fantasque BOURR

TALLEYRAND, French statesman, Vienna- 1814 VIENN

TAMARA, Russian, Pages of
  Life   PAGEL

TAMARA. See also: Queen
  Tamara

TAMARAGUA, Indian warrior,
  smokes opium, dreams of
  beautiful girl who becomes
  his ideal; loved by a
  Bayadère sorceress, The
  Dance Dream   DANCE

TAMARAT. See: Ali-Ben-
  Tamarat

TAMBOURINE DANCER, par-
  ticipates in merrymaking,
  Don Juan   DONJU

TAMMUZ. See: Ishtar

TANCRED, brave Christian
  crusader and warrior,
  falls in love with Clorinda
  CLORINDA, Saracen, pagan
  girl warrior, falls in love
  with Tancred, killed by him
  in duel

The Duel   DUELL

TARANTELLA, personification
  of dance, Soirée Musicale
                    SOIRE

TARANTELLA DANCERS, per-
  form for customers at toy
  shop, La Boutique Fantasque
                    BOUTI

TARAS. See: Bulba, Taras

TARGETT, HARRY. See:
  Tulip

TARGETT, WILLIAM. See:
  Carter, A
  Salt, Jack
  Tulip

TARIEL, hero of Chota Rousta-
  veli's poem, in love with
  Nestan Daredjan, Chota
  Roustaveli   CHOTA

TARIEL. See also:
  Enemy Chief
  Leopard

TARQUINIUS, SEXTUS, Roman
  officer, ravishes Lucretia,
  the latter being portrayed by
  La Gloire (The Star),
  La Gloire   GLOIR

TARTAGLIA. See:
  Captain Cartuccia
  Coviello
  Rosetta

TARTAR YOUTH, seen by Princess Anastachiuska in her
  dream, Bogatyri   BOGAT

TATTERDEMALION (Tramp),
  brings spirit of the dance
  into business competition,
  La Concurrence   CONCU

TATTOOED LADY. See:
  Jinx
  Ringmaster

TAURUS, the Bull, personification assumed by Jupiter
while wooing Europa, Les
Amours de Jupiter AMOUJ

TAUTVALDIS, Chief of the
Letts
AINA, his daughter, in
love with Sauldots
MALDA, Aina's step-
mother, also in love with
Sauldots
Le Triomphe de l'Amour
TRIOM

TAUTVALDIS. See also:
Sorceress, The

TAVERN. See: Landlady of
the Tavern

TAYETA, celestial star,
Electra   ELECT

TAYLOR, MR., manager of
the King's Theatre, London;
competitor and friend of
Mr. O'Reilly, The Prospect
Before Us   PROSP

TAYLOR, MR. See also:
Lawyers, Three

TCHATURICA, friend of
Sakuntala, Sakuntala
SAKUN

TCHOP-DAR, THE, follower
of Olifour, Le Dieu et la
Bayadère   DIEUE

TEAFLOWER. See: Princess
Teaflower

TEAM. See: Captain of So-
viet Football Team

TEASER. See: Strip
Teaser

TEBRICK, MR., British
sportsman, fox hunter
SILVIA, his wife, trans-

formed into a fox
MRS. CORK, Silvia's old
nurse
Lady into Fox   LADYI

TELEGRAM, FIFTH. See:
First Telegram

TELEGRAM, FIRST. See:
First Telegram

TELEGRAM, FOURTH. See:
First Telegram

TELEGRAM, SECOND. See:
First Telegram

TELEGRAM, THIRD. See:
First Telegram

TELEGRAPH. See: Daily
Telegraph, The

TELEGRAPH BOY, elopes with
Film Star, Pastorale
PASTE

TELESCOPE KEEPERS, proprie-
tors of magic telescope
through which fairyland may
be observed, The Triumph
of Neptune   TRIUM

TELL, WILLIAM, legendary
Swiss hero
HIS SON
GESSLER, tyrant
William Tell   WILLI

TELLER. See:
Fortune Teller
Gypsy Fortune Teller

TELLER OF THE TALE, tells
story of Judith
LISTENER, one to whom the
tale is told
Legend of Judith   LEGEJ

TEMPERAMENTS, THE FOUR.
See: Melancholic Variation

TEMPLE. See: High Priest of

the Temple

TEMPLE OF PEACE. See:
High Priest of the Temple
of Peace

TEMPTATION, urges the
Choreographer to renounce
his quest
La Création   CREAI
Personification
Les Présages   PRESA

TEMPTER, THE. See:
Agonistes, Samson

TENIGUÁ. See:
Nunes, Blau
Santão

TENNIS CHAMPION, appears
on beach, Le Train Bleu
                           TRAIN

TENNIS PLAYER, attracted to
two girls, unable to decide
between them; returns to
his game of tennis
TWO GIRLS, attracted to
him
Jeux (Games)   JEUXG

TENNIS PLAYER, THE, fickle
dandy, alternately attracted
to the Girl and the Syl-
phide
THE GIRL, attracts, later
rejected by the Tennis
Player
THE SYLPHIDE, attracts
the Tennis Player, takes
him from the Girl
À la Françaix   FRANI

TENOR, "engaging in an Edwardian romp at a French
plage, " Les Sirènes
                           SIREN

TENTH VARIATION. See:
Theme and First Variation

TEPANCALTZIN, Emperor of

the Toltecs
XOCHITL (The Flower), be-
comes Empress of the Tol-
tecs
THE FATHER OF XOCHITL,
discovers that intoxicant can
be made of the maguey
plant; brings this discovery
to Tepancaltzin
Xochitl   XOCHI

TERESA. See: Theresa

TERESINA, loved by Gennaro,
Giacomo and Peppo; in love
with Gennaro, captured by
Golfo
VERONICA, her mother, "a
watchful widow"
Napoli   NAPOL

TERESINA. See also: Ambrosio,
Fra

TERPSICHORE, muse, "reveals
dancing to the world"
Apollo, Leader of the Muses
                           APOLL
Muse
Apollon Musagète   APOLN
Fiametta   FIAMM

TERPSICHORE, DAUGHTER OF.
See: Queen of the Dance

THALIA. See: Philemon

THAMAR, Queen of Georgia,
stabs the Prince, Thamar
                           THAMA

THAMES, personification of
river, La Fille du Pharaon
                           FILLP

THAMES, THE, symbolic figure,
Flik and Flok   FLIKA

THANATOS, figure of death,
Alcestis   ALCES

THEA, favorite slave of Prince
Hussein, Thea   THEAO

THEA. See also: Flower
    Fairy, The

THEATER, personification,
    Metropolitan Daily METRO

THEBES, KING OF. See:
    Creon
    Oedipus

THEIA. See: Hyperion

THEME, lonely boy, attempts
    to find companionship
    among various people with
    whom he comes in contact
    WOMAN
    WITCH, fail to give Theme
    companionship he wishes
    Variations on a Lonely
    Theme   VARIL

THEME AND FIRST VARIATION
    SECOND VARIATION
    THIRD VARIATION
    FOURTH VARIATION
    FIFTH VARIATION
    SIXTH VARIATION
    SEVENTH VARIATION
    EIGHTH VARIATION
    NINTH VARIATION
    TENTH VARIATION
    ELEVENTH VARIATION
    TWELFTH VARIATION
    THIRTEENTH VARIATION
    FOURTEENTH VARIATION,
    abstract dances interpreting
    Elgar's music
    Enigma Variations ENIGM

THÉODORE, in love with Zoé
    MARIANNE, his mother
    Les Deux Créoles DEUXC

THÉODORE. See also:
    Dominguo
    Marie

THÉODORE, MADEMOISELLE,
    premiere danseuse at the
    King's Theatre, London, The
    Prospect Before Us PROSP

THERESA, village girl, in love
    with Pierre, Halte de
    Cavalerie   HALTE

THERESA. See also: Matteo

THÉRÈSE, French actress and
    revolutionist
    The Flames of Paris
                              FLAME
    Orphan girl, raised by
    Mother Michaud; betrothed
    to Edmond
    MOTHER MICHAUD, her
    foster-mother
    La Somnambule SOMNA

THÉRÈSE. See also: Notary, A

THÉRÉSINE. See: Lilia

THESEUS, Duke of Athens, be-
    trothed to Hippolyta
    The Dream   DREAM
    A Midsummer Night's Dream
                              MIDSU
    Conquers with Minotaur with
    the assistance of Ariadne
    Labyrinth   LABYR
    The Minotaur   MINOT
    The Minotaur   MINOU
    Spectacle   SPECL

THESEUS. See also:
    Ariadne
    Phaedra
    Poseidon

THESSALY, KING OF. See:
    Alcestis

THIEF, A, enters toy shop look-
    ing for loot, La Boutique
    Fantasque   BOUTI

THIEF, THE, inmate of the
    Logéat Mental Hospital
    Les Algues   ALGUE
    Attempts to steal necklace
    The Thief Who Loved a
    Ghost   THIEF

THIEF, THE.   See also:
    Ballerinas, Two Former
    Detective
    Policemen

THIN AUNT, THE.   See:
    Daughter, The

THIRD SAILOR.   See: First
    Sailor

THIRD SHEPHERDESS.   See:
    Shepherdesses, Two

THIRD TELEGRAM.   See:
    First Telegram

THIRD VARIATION.   See:
    Theme and First Variation

THIRTEENTH VARIATION.
    See: Theme and First
    Variation

THOMAS, wealthy vine grower,
    hopes to betroth his son
    to Lisette (Lise), daughter
    of Mother Simone
    ALAIN, his son, interested
    in chasing butterflies
    La Fille Mal Gardée
                   FILLE
    La Fille Mal Gardée
                   FILLG

THORA, becomes bride of
    Regnar Lodbrok, King of
    Denmark
    HEROTH, Lord of East
    Gothland, her father
    Lagertha   LAGER

THREE.   See:
    Bacchantes, Three
    Bandits, Three
    Chefs, Three
    Comforters, Three
    Fat Men, The Three
    Girls With Gloved Hands,
      Three
    Goat Men, Three
    Graces, The Three
    Gypsies, Three

    Jailers, Three
    Lawyers, Three
    Ministers, The Three
    Sailors, Three
    Satyrisci, Three
    Sileni, Three
    Sisters, Three
    Sportsmen, Three
    Squires, Three
    Tailors, The Three
    Visitors, Three

THREE APPARITIONS.   See:
    Sleeper

THREE BOY-FRIENDS, HER.
    See: Debutante

THREE COMPANIONS, HIS.
    See: Bernadone, Francesco

THREE DAUGHTERS, HER.
    See:
    Patroness, The

THREE DAUGHTERS, HIS.   See:
    Job

THREE FATES, THE.   See:
    Parcae

THREE GANGSTERS.   See:
    Prostitute, The

THREE HANDMAIDENS.   See:
    Sphinx, The

THREE MOUNTAINEERS.   See:
    Milkmaid

THREE SPIRITS OF PERFUMED
    SEDUCTION.   See: Rose

THREE THUGS.   See: Girl

THREE VIRGINS.   See: Priggish
    Virgin

THROWER.   See: Party-Throw-
    er, The

THUGS, THREE.   See: Girl

THULE, KING OF. See:
Harold

THULE, PRIME MINISTER OF.
See: Kafur

THUMB. See: Hop o' My
Thumb

TIBER, personification of
river, La Fille du Pharaon
FILLP

TIBUL, a gymnast, The Three
Fat Men   THREE

TID-BITS, representation of
British publication, The
Press   PRESS

TIE. See: He Wore a White
Tie

TIGER, THE, summoned from
Hell by Ballestriga,
Abraxas   ABRAX

TIGHTROPE WALKER, circus
performer
Carte Blanche   CARTE
Performer
Douanes   DOUAN

TIL. See:
Eulenspiegel, Til
Tyl

TILLEY, EUSTACE, caricature
of cartoon character, The
New Yorker   NEWYO

TIME, personification, La
Nuit et le Jour NUITE

TIMES. See:
Father Times
Financial Times, The
Sporting Times, The

TIMID. See: Fêlênk

TIMID MAN, caricature of
cartoon character, The

New Yorker   NEWYO

TIMOROUS STUDENT. See:
Amore (Cupid)
Fashionable Lady

TIRESIAS, blind seer
Night Journey   NIGHJ
Cretan prince, given gift of
prophecy by Zeus, becomes
blind seer; appears as both
man and woman
Tiresias   TIRES

TIRESIAS. See also:
Neophyte
Snakes (Serpents), Two

TIROLESE, personification of
dance, Soirêe Musicale
SOIRE

TIRRENIO, King of the Waters,
Ondine's protector, Ondine
ONDII

TISBAH, faithful companion of
Zoraiya, daughter of Caliph
Abderraman, Zoraiya
ZORAI

TITANIA, Queen of the Fairies
The Dream   DREAM
A Midsummer Night's Dream
MIDSU

TITANS, revolt against Jupiter,
I Titani   TITAN

TITUS, handsome neighbor of
Bilby, in love with Doll
THE TWINS, his sisters
A Mirror for Witches
MIRRO

TÔ, Jester to the Mikado, loves
the Princess, Yedda YEDDA

TOBY, country boy, goes to
big city, becomes infatuated
with Bride; disillusioned,
returns home
FLOWERS, rescue Toby,

return him to the country
Antic Spring   ANTIS

TOKYO, KING OF THE ISLAND
OF. See: Jamato

TOLTECS, EMPEROR OF THE.
See: Tepancaltzin

TOM. See: Tug, Tom

TONIELLO, young Sicilian
villager, betrothed to
Fiorita, loved by Hertha,
Fiorita et la Reine des
Elfrides   FIORI

TONIELLO. See also: Anar

TOP-BOOTS, LITTLE JOHNNY
IN. See: Csizmás Janko

TOP, THE, toy, Jeux d'Enfants
                      JEUXX

TOPAZZA. See: King of the
Gnomes, The

TORBERN, "evil genius of
the mines," Rosida
                      ROSID

TOREADOR, THE (Escamillo),
attracted by Carmen,
Carmen   CARME

TORRERO, THE, lover of the
Manola; fascinated by the
Duchess, stabbed by ser-
vants of the Duke, husband
of the Duchess, Del Amor
y de la Muerte   AMORY

TORTOISE SHELL BUTTERFLIES,
residents of Butterfly Land,
Les Papillons   PAPIO

TORTOISES, TWO, animals,
Carnival of Animals
                      CARNV

TORTONI, visits Paris café,
Gaîté Parisienne   GAITE

TOUCH, danced by three female
dancers, Street Games
                      STREE

TOUPET, a perruquier, Cinderella   CINDA

TOURISTS, sightseeing in London,
London Morning   LONDO

TOWER. See: Manager of the
Eiffel Tower, The

TOWN. See:
Ladies of the Town
Leader of the Red Group
(Town)

TOWN, GIRL OF THE. See:
Flutist

TOWN, MAN ABOUT. See:
Amazon Captain
Fashionable Lady

TOWNSMAN. See: Young
Townsman

TOWNSWOMEN, GOSSIPING.
See: Weidman, Fireman

TOYS. See: Spirits Who
Govern the Toys, The

TRACTOR-DRIVER, A, disguises
himself as a dog, The Bright
Stream   BRIGH

TRADE. See: Queen of the
Carriage Trade

TRAGEDY, a muse, Sylvia
                      SYLVA

TRAINER. See: Monkey Trainer

TRAINER, THE ANIMAL. See:
Young Girl, The

TRAITOR, betrays Leader
LEADER, betrayed by Trai-
tor "as Christ was betrayed
by Judas Iscariot"

The Traitor   TRAIT

TRAMP, Parisian, Le Rendez-
Vous   RENDE

TRAMP. See also: Tatter-
demalion

TRANIO. See: Biondello,
Tranio

TRANSGRESSOR, THE, boy,
driven to murder Medusa
CYBELE, goddess, his
mother; rejects him
Undertow   UNDER

TRANSGRESSOR, THE. See
also:
Aganippe
Ate
Hymen
Medusa
Pollux
Volupia

TRAPEZE ARTISTS, TWO,
circus performers, Carte
Blanche   CARTE

TRAVELER, THE, dances with
the Child, Jeux d'Enfants
JEUXX

TRAVELING. See: Barber,
The Traveling

TRAVELLERS, arrive at
foreign airport, are mis-
treated, brainwashed, and
one is shot, The Travel-
lers   TRÁVE

TREE-SPRITE, THE, seen by
the Princess in her dream,
A Spring Tale   SPRIN

TREGENNIS, MASTER OF.
See:
Flautist (The Stranger
Player)
Young Tregennis

TRÈS-PROPRE, MONSIEUR.
See: Chrysanthème, Madame

TRIBES, QUEEN OF THE. See:
Femina

TRIPPA. See: Franca-Trippa

TRISTAN, Cornish knight, lover
of Isolde, Mad Tristan
MADTR

TRISTRAM (LOVER). See:
Husband (King Mark)
Knights, Two

TRITON. See: Amphitrite

TROISONDIN. See: Coralia

TROLL KING, THE
TROLLS, supernatural beings,
capture Peer Gynt
Peer Gynt   PEERG

TROOPER. See: State Trooper,
The

TROUBADOUR, THE. See:
Swan, The

TROUILLEFOU, CLOPIN, "monarch of the Truands," La
Esmeralda   ESMER

TROUSSE-DIABLE, leader of
band of gypsies, steals
Sarah as child, La Gypsy
GYPSY

TROUSSE-DIABLE. See also:
Lord Campbell
Stenio

TROUVILLE. See: Bathing-
Girl from Trouville, The

TROY, HELEN OF. See:
King Menelaus, King of
Sparta
Orestes

TRUANDS, MONARCH OF THE.
    See: Trouillefou, Clopin

TRUFFALDINO, rascal, in
    love with Smeraldina; be-
    comes servant of Florindo
    and of Beatrice, The False
    Bridegroom   FALSE

TRUTH. See: Spirit of Truth

TRUTH, PERSONIFICATION OF.
    See: Una

TSAR-MAIDEN, THE, sought
    by the Khan, marries
    Ivanoushka, son of Petr
    The Hump-Backed Horse
                        HUMPB
    The Hump-Backed Horse
                        HUMPH

TSAR OF RUSSIA. See:
    Peter I

TSAREVICH, IVAN. See:
    Prince Ivan

TSAREVNA, THE BEAUTIFUL,
    princess, held under spell
    by Kostchei, falls in love
    with Prince Ivan
    Firebird   FIREB
    Firebird   FIRED
    Firebird   FIREI

TSARINA CATHERINE II,
    Tsarina of Russia,
    Christmas Eve   CHRIS

TUG, TOM, sailor, visits
    fairyland, becomes fairy
    prince, marries Neptune's
    daughter
    HIS WIFE, seduced by the
    Dandy
    HIS MOTHER
    The Triumph of Neptune
                        TRIUM

TUG, TOM. See also:
    Journalists, Two

TULIO. See: Bartolo

TULIP, Princess Gundemey of
    Dahomey, African native,
    becomes wife of William
    Targett
    KING OF DAHOMEY, her
    father
    WILLIAM TARGETT, her
    husband, sailor; killed by
    a carter and Jack Salt
    SAMBO, infant son of Tulip
    and William Targett
    HARRY TARGETT, William's
    brother
    MRS. STURMEY, sister of
    William and Harry Targett
    The Sailor's Return   SAILO

TURANDOT. See: Princess
    Turandot

TUTTI. See: Prince Tutti

TWELFTH VARIATION. See:
    Theme and First Variation

TWELVE. See:
    Hours of Night, Twelve
    Naiads, Twelve

TWENTY MEN. See: Spanish
    Woman

TWINS. See: Siamese Twins

TWINS, THE. See: Titus

TWO. See:
    Acrobats, Two
    Angels, Two
    Bacchantes, Two
    Ballerinas, Two Former
    Cadets, Two
    Chess-Players, Two
    Columbines, Two
    Cupids, Two
    Dressmakers, Two
    Girls, Two
    Goats, Two
    Harlequins, Two
    Husband-Hunters, Two

Journalists, Two
Knights, Two
Mortals, Two, Born Under
  Venus
Murat's Ambassadors, Two
Musicians, Two
Nymphs, Two
Old People, Two
Principal Dynamos, Two
Rackets, Two
Satyrs, Two
Shepherdesses, Two
Skaters, Two
Snakes (Serpents), Two
Spies, Two
Suitors, Two
Tailors, Two
Tortoises, Two
Trapeze Artists, Two
Vaudeville Dandies, Two
Witches, Two Young

TWO AMAZON LIEUTENANTS.
  See:
Amazon Captain
Fashionable Lady

TWO BROTHERS, HIS. See:
  Innocent Ivan

TWO BROTHERS, THE LADY'S.
  See: Comus

TWO CHILDREN, THEIR. See:
  Medea

TWO COMPANIONS, HER.
  See: Venus

TWO DAUGHTERS, HER.
  See: Mother

TWO DAUGHTERS, HIS.
  See: Veteran Soldier, A

TWO FLIRTATIOUS COUPLES.
  See: Umbrella

TWO FRIENDS, HER. See:
  Cariné

TWO FRIENDS, HIS. See:
  Ambassador, The

TWO GIRLS. See: Tennis
  Player

TWO LADIES. See: Nobleman

TWO LITTLE DAUGHTERS,
  THEIR. See: Cordoba,
  Pedro

TWO LOVERS. See: Khadra

TWO MEN. See: Woman Who
  Was Caught, The

TWO MODELS. See: Duchic,
  Monsieur

TWO OVERSEERS. See:
  Galley-Slaves

TWO PAGES, HER. See:
  Carabosse

TWO SONS. See: Anna I

TWO SONS, HER. See: Mother

TWO SONS, THEIR. See: Lodbrok, Regnar, King of Denmark

TWO SQUIRES, HIS. See:
  Knight, The

TWO STICKS, THE DEVIL ON.
  See: Asmodeus

TWO UGLY SISTERS, THE.
  See: Cinderella

TWO UGLY STEPSISTERS, HER.
  See: Cinderella

TWO WOMEN. See: Man

TWO WOMEN WITH PLAY
  STICKS. See: Mexican
  Peon

TYBALT. See:
Capulet
Mercutio
Old Capulet

TYCOON, "collapsing and
   bringing everyone else
   down with him as Wall
   Street crashed," Atavisms
                        ATAVI

TYL. See:
   Eulenspiegel, Tyl
   Til
   Ulenspiegel, Tyl

TYRANT, oppressor of the
   people
   TYRANT'S COURTESAN
   Legend of Judith   LEGEJ

TYROLIAN LEGATION, attending ball tendered by Prince
   Metternich, Vienna- 1814
                        VIENN

TZETZKLY, a little bird, attendant upon Chota Roustaveli, Chota Roustaveli
                        CHOTA

U

UGLY INDIAN. See: Uirapurú

UGLY ONE, THE LITTLE.
   See: Laiderette

UGLY SISTERS, THE TWO.
   See: Cinderella

UGLY STEPSISTERS, HER TWO.
   See: Cinderella

UIRAPURÚ, bird of love and
   happiness, transformed
   into Handsome Indian when
   shot by Huntress, transformed again into bird
   when shot by Ugly Indian
   HUNTRESS, shoots Uira-
   purú with arrow
   UGLY INDIAN, jealous of
   Uirapurú, shoots him with
   arrow
   Uirapurú   UIRAP

UJEL, friend of Marietta,

Kalkabrino   KALKA

ULENSPIEGEL, TYL, "merry
   prankster and liberator of
   Flanders from the Spanish
   invaders," appears in several guises
   NELL, his wife
   Tyl Ulenspiegel   TYLUL

ULENSPIEGEL, TYL. See also:
   Death
   Duke of Alba
   Eulenspiegel, Til
   Eulenspiegel, Tyl

ULINKA, engaged to Andrey
   HER FATHER, landowner
   and proprietor of the Serfs'
   Theatre
   Katerina   KATER

ULRICH. See: Coralia

ULYSSES, tempted by Circe,
   rescued by Helmsman
   Circe   CIRCE
   Greek warrior, captive of
   Calypso
   Télémaque dans l'Île de
   Calypso   TELEM

ULYSSES. See also:
   Deer
   Goat
   Lion
   Odysseus
   Snake

UMBRELLA, "changes the lives
   of two flirtatious couples"
   TWO FLIRTATIOUS COUPLES,
   whose lives are changed
   The Umbrella   UMBRE

UNA, personification of truth,
   reunited with St. George
   FEMALE SERVANT, "transformed into Una"
   The Quest   QUEST

UNCERTAINTY, plagues the
   Choreographer, La Création

227 UNCLE REMUS

CREAI

UNCLE REMUS, tells stories
to Child
CHILD, hears stories
Uncle Remus   UNCLE

UNCLE, THE. See:
Daughter, The
Yela

UNDERSTUDIES, THE. See:
Principal Dancer, The
(Adam Zero)

UNDERWORLD, GOD OF THE.
See: Pluto

UNDERWORLD, KING OF THE.
See: King Hades

UNDINES. See:
Nymph of the Danube, The
Ondine

UNICORN, "traditional guardian
of chastity"
Harlequin in April HARLE
Accepts nourishment only
from the hands of a virgin;
dies when he sees that the
Lady has a lover
THE LADY, heartbroken
at death of Unicorn, re-
fuses to see the Knight
further
THE KNIGHT, her lover
The Lady and the Unicorn
LADYU

UNICORN. See also: Poet,
The

UNION. See: Genii of Union,
The

UNITED STATES, PRESIDENT
OF THE. See: Lincoln,
Abraham

UNKNOWN, THE, allegorical
figure
Anguish Sonata   ANGUI

Actually the God Brama in
disguise; rescued by, later
rescues Zoloe
Le Dieu et la Bayadère
DIEUE

UNMARRIED WOMEN, SEVEN,
members of Eskimo tribe,
Qarrtsiluni   QARTT

UP. See:
Dressing-Up
Pick-Me-Up

UPLIFTER, American type,
seen by the Immigrant,
Within the Quota   WITHI

URBAIN, celebrated violinist,
Le Violon du Diable VIOLO

URBAIN. See also: Solange

URGANDA, lady, figment of Don
Quixote's imagination, Don
Quixote   DONQX

URIAH THE HITTITE. See:
Bathsheba

URIELLE, a female demon, sent
by Beelzebub to act as page
to Count Frédéric; falls in
love with him,
Le Diable Amoureux DIABE

URSULA, friend of Young Tregennis; dances with him in
haunted ballroom, The
Haunted Ballroom   HAUNT

URSULE, innkeeper, Le Violon
du Diable   VIOLO

USHER, RODERICK, madman,
last male heir of the House
of Usher
MADELEINE, his twin sister,
dying
THE POET, friend of Usher,
tells story of his end
Usher   USHER

VARIATION, TENTH. See:
Theme and First Variation

VARIATION, THIRD. See:
Theme and First Variation

VARIATION, THIRTEENTH.
See: Theme and First
Variation

VARIATION, TWELFTH. See:
Theme and First Variation

VARIOUS ARTS. See: Spirits
of Various Arts

VASIA, Russian schoolboy,
kills Baby Stork's mother
with a stone, Baby Stork
                            BABYS

VASIA. See also: Baby
Stork

VASIANO. See: Gennaro,
Vasiano

VATSLAV, a young nobleman,
in love with Marie, The
Fountain of Bakhchisarai
                            FOUNT

VAUDEVILLE DANDIES, TWO,
perform "hoofing" act,
Façade   FACAD

VAVASOUR, CAPTAIN, "en-
gaging in an Edwardian
romp at a French plage,"
Les Sirènes   SIREN

VAYOU, god of the wind, The
Talisman   TALIS

VEGETABLES. See: Seller
of Vegetables, The

VENDÔME. See: Duc de
Vendôme, The

VENDOR. See:
Balloon-Vendor
Street-Vendor

VENDOR IN EMERALD, FLOWER.
See:
Flower Vendor in Green
Lieutenant

VENDOR IN GREEN, FLOWER.
See:
Boy in Grey
Flower Vendor in Green
Lieutenant

VENETIAN LAGOON, symbolic
figure, Flik and Flok
                            FLIKA

VENICE, THE MOOR OF. See:
Othello

VENTADOUR, BERNARD DE,
a troubadour, Raymonda
                            RAYMO

VENUS, goddess, in love with
Adonis
Adonis   ADONI
Goddess, "wearing a pale
pink union suit and a blond
wig"
HER TWO COMPANIONS
Bacchanale   BACCH
Goddess of love
Ballet de la Nuit   BALLN
Goddess, appears with the
Three Graces to perform
dance at minstrel show
Cakewalk   CAKEW
Aging entertainer, dances
for Paris at boîte de nuit,
afterwards picks his pockets
The Judgement of Paris
                            JUDGM
Goddess of love
The Loves of Mars and Venus
                            LOVEM
Goddess of love, in love with
Adonis
The Loves of Venus and
Adonis   LOVEV
Goddess of love
La Naissance de Vénus
                            NAISV

VENUS. See also:

Cupid
Morning Star
Mortals, Two, Born Under
   Venus
Planet Venus

VERONA, PRINCE OF. See:
Escalus

VERONICA. See: Teresina

VERONIQUE, a donkey,
Cinderella   CINDA

VERT-VERT, parrot, pet of
the Queen's maids of
honor; dies
CANDIDE, replaces Vert-
Vert as pet
Vert-Vert   VERTV

VERT-VERT. See also:
Blanche
Colombus

VESTRIS, maître de ballet
and dancer to the court,
Camargo   CAMAR

VESTRIS, MONSIEUR, dancer
at the King's Theatre,
London, The Prospect
Before Us   PROSP

VETERAN SOLDIER, A, for-
mer member of Count
Rackozski's command
HIS TWO DAUGHTERS
HIS DAUGHTERS'
   SWEETHEARTS
AN OLD WOMAN, servant
in his household
The Hungarian Hut HUNGA

VICOMTE DE BEAUGENCY,
nobleman, guest of Marquis
de Fierbois, magician;
sees reincarnation of
Armide, Le Pavillon d'
Armide   PAVIL

VICTIM, of blood lust lynching
Atavisims   ATAVI

Of Sorceress' (Medea's)
vengeance following her de-
sertion by Adventurer (Jason)
Cave of the Heart   CAVEO

VICTIM. See also:
Young Man
Zealot

VICTIM, THE. See: Defendant,
A

VICTOR, peasant, in love with
Georgette, daughter of
Georges, Nina   NINAO

VICTOR. See also: Marmion

VIDERIK. See: Muri

VIENNA. See:
Gentlemen from Vienna, A
Young Lady from Vienna, A

VIEUX. See: Marcheur, Le
Vieux

VILLAGE ELDER, tribal
patriarch
VILLAGE ELDER'S DAUGH-
TER, in love with Company
Agent
VILLAGE ELDER'S HEIR,
brother of Village Elder's
daughter, engages in violent
struggle with Company Agent
COMPANY AGENT, Western
engineer, in love with Village
Agent's Daughter
Place in the Desert PLACE

VILLAGE, HEADMAN OF THE.
See: Marie

VILLAGE MAGISTRATE. See:
Courasche

VINCINETTA, friend of Marietta,
Kalkabrino   KALKA

VINCENZO. See: Philemon

VIOLENT. See: Eröszakos

VIOLET, "an aggressive young
lady," pursues Ernest, A
Wedding Bouquet   WEDDI

VIOLET. See also:
Alchemist, The
Rose

VIOLINIST, THE, madman in
London madhouse, The
Rake's Progress   RAKES

VIRGIN, GREEDY. See:
Priggish Virgin

VIRGIN, LUSTFUL. See:
Priggish Virgin

VIRGIN, PRIGGISH. See:
Priggish Virgin

VIRGINIE, Mademoiselle's
maid, La Prima Balle-
rina   PRIMA

VIRGINS. See:
Foolish Virgins, Five
Wise Virgins
Wise Virgins, Five

VIRGINS, FOOLISH. See:
Wise Virgins

VIRGINS, THREE. See:
Priggish Virgin

VIRGO. See: Young Woman,
The

VIRTUES, protect children of
the earth, I Titani TITAN

VIRTUES, FOUR, personifications, Ballet Comique de
la Reine   BALLC

VISCOUNT DE BEAUGENCY.
See: King Hydrao

VISION. See: Infanta of
Spain

VISIONS D'ART, members of a
troupe of traveling players,
Les Forains   FORAI

VISIONS OF GAIETY, seen by
Young Musician in his dream,
Symphonie Fantastique
                     SYMPH

VISIONS OF MELANCHOLY, seen
by Young Musician in his
dream, Symphonie Fantas-
tique   SYMPH

VISIONS OF PASSION, seen by
Young Musician in his dream,
Symphonie Fantastique
                     SYMPH

VISIONS OF REVERIE, seen by
Young Musician in his dream,
Symphonie Fantastique
                     SYMPH

VISITORS, THREE, to London
madhouse, The Rake's
Progress   RAKES

VITELLI, a revenue officer
GENNARO, his son
Stella   STELL

VIVANDIÈRE, clockwork toy
The Nutcracker   NUTCA
The Nutcracker   NUTCK
The Nutcracker   NUTCR

VIZIER. See: Grand Vizier,
The

VLADIMIR, footman and premier
danseur of the Serfs'
Theatre; friend of Katerina,
Katerina   KATER

VODKA, BORIS, a liqueur,
Schlagobers   SCHLA

VOICE, LINCOLN'S. See:
Lincoln, Abraham

VOLTA, Italian physicist, Excelsior   EXCEL

VOLUPIA, prostitute, personification of sensual pleasure,
attracts the Transgressor,
Undertow   UNDER

VOLUPIA. See also: Sileni,
Three

VON GENTZ, FREDERICH,
diplomat, Vienna- 1814
VIENN

VON ROTBART, evil magician,
holds Odette, Queen of the
Swans, in his power
ODILE, his daughter, im-
personates Odette
Swan Lake   SWANA
Swan Lake   SWANE
Swan Lake   SWANK
Swan Lake   SWANL

VZULA. See: Diavolina

W

W. See: Brown, W.

WAGNER. See: Wolger

WAITER in boîte de nuit,
Paris, France; helps pick
Paris' pockets, The Judg-
ment of Paris   JUDGM

WAITER. See also: Negro
Waiter, A

WAITERS, at 2222 Club, New
York City, Café Society
CAFES

WAITERS. See also: Maître
d'Hotel

WAITING. See:
Ladies in Waiting
Ladies in Waiting, The

WAITING-MAID, BEATRIX'S.
See: Cesarius

WALES. See: Edward, Prince

of Wales

WALKER. See: Tightrope
Walker

WALKERS, WIRE. See:
Jinx
Ringmaster

WALKING. See: Maiden Ladies
Out Walking

WALL. See: Writing on the
Wall

WALLFLOWER, THE, character
portrayed at minstrel show,
Cakewalk   CAKEW

WALTHER, confidant of Oswald,
Lord Rewena's brother,
Nathalie   NATHA

WALTZING LADIES AND THEIR
PARTNERS, dancing couples
at ball, Dim Lustre DIMLU

WANDERER, "in his imagination
reliving his experiences of
life, " The Wanderer
WANDE

WAR, personification, Job
JOBBB

WAR CRY, THE, representation
of British newspaper, The
Press   PRESS

WAR, GOD OF. See: Mars

WAR PROFITEER, THE, per-
sonification, The Green
Table   GREEN

WARDER, guards Count Raoul
de Crêqui in prison, Raoul
de Crêqui   RAOUL

WARDROBE MISTRESS at Grand
Opera, Paris, Foyer de la
Danse   FOYER

WARDROBE MISTRESS, THE.
See: Principal Dancer,
The (Adam Zero)

WARRIOR, YOUNG. See:
Old Poet

WATCHERS OF THE NIGHT,
mysterious supernatural
beings, invade wood where
Young Lovers are meeting,
Fantasy   FANTA

WATCHMAN, NIGHT. See:
Dégas Dancer

WATER, personification, The
Seventh Symphony
                                SEVEN

WATER, THE, personification,
Les Éléments   ELEME

WATERS, KING OF THE. See:
Coralia
Tirrenio

WATERS, QUEEN OF THE.
See:
Ondine
Queen of the Waters, The

WEALTHY WIDOW, pursued,
won by Suitor; saved by
Flutist (The Incredible
Flutist)
SUITOR, pursues, even-
tually wins Wealthy Widow
The Incredible Flutist
                                INCRE

WEAVER, THE, Russian vil-
lager, Christmas Eve
                                CHRIS

WEBSTER, maid, A Wedding
Bouquet   WEDDI

WEIDMAN, FIREMAN, rises
from ordinary fireman to
captain of fire department
of the Canal Zone during
the building of the Panama

Canal
GOSSIPING TOWNSWOMEN,
read selections from local
newspapers telling of his
rise
And Daddy Was a Fireman
                                ANDDA

WHEEL. See: Fly Wheel

WHEELBARROW. See:
Man Who Pushes the Wheel-
barrow, The
Woman in the Wheelbarrow,
The

WHITE. See:
Black and White
He Wore a White Tie
Snow-White

WHITE, BILL. See: Duras,
Manos

WHITE BOXER, has boxing
match with Negro Boxer;
fouls his opponent, awarded
decision, The Golden Age
                                GOLDE

WHITE BOXER. See also:
Referee
Woman of Soviet Communist
Youth

WHITE CAT, THE, fairy tale
character, The Sleeping
Beauty   SLEEP

WHITE FAIRY, THE, presents
gift to Ysaure, La Filleule
des Fées   FILLU

WHITE HORSE, THE. See:
Black Horses, The
Queen of the Amazons, The

WHITE HOURS, THE, personifications, L'Homme et son
Désir   HOMME

WHITE LADY, THE. See:
Raymonda

WHITE MAN. See: Emperor
Jones

WHITE PEARL, THE, object
of combat between the
Genii of the Earth and
King of the Corals; won by
the Genii
THE YELLOW PEARL
PINK PEARLS
BLACK PEARLS, her
friends
The Beautiful Pearl
                    BEAUT

WHITE ROSE. See: Bobo-
Safar

WHITE WINGS, street-cleaner,
Skyscrapers   SKYSC

WHITE WITCH, participant in
orgy on Bald Mountain,
The Fair at Sorochinsk
                    FAIRA

WHO DANCES. See: One Who
Dances, The

WHO SPEAKS, THE ONE.
See: Actress, An

WHO WAS SHE?, three young
girls, memories recalled
by the Gentleman With Her,
Dim Lustre   DIMLU

WIDOW. See: Wealthy Widow

WIDOW, MERRY. See:
Courasche

WIDOW, THE MERRY. See:
Sonia

WIDOWER, THE. See: Dead
Girl, The

WIFE, once dumb, has had her
power of speech restored by
an operation; now talks in-
cessantly
HUSBAND, annoyed by wife's

continual chatter, persuades
doctor to perform operation
to take away his hearing
DOCTOR, performs opera-
tions on Wife and Husband
The Mute Wife   MUTEW

WIFE. See also:
Curley's Wife
Genius-Husband
Husband
Miller's Wife, The
Potiphar's Wife
Wife, The
Young Husband
Young Wife, The

WIFE, BUFFOON'S. See: Buffoon, The

WIFE, CHRISTOPHE'S. See:
Christophe

WIFE, FRENCH. See: Young
Student

WIFE, HIS. See:
Commandant
Commandant of the Patrol
at the Outpost
Cordoba, Pedro
Count Rackozski
Crooner, The
Dweller, A
Farmer, A
Hussar, The
Job
Khan, The
Motorist, The
Officer, An
Pedrillo
President
Tug, Tom

WIFE, HIS FAVORITE. See:
Khan, The

WIFE, HUSBAND'S. See:
Husband, The

WIFE (ISEAULT). See:
Husband (King Mark)
Knights, Two

Maid (Brangaene)

WIFE, KOUM'S. See: Oksana

WIFE, MOOR'S. See: Moor,
The

WIFE, MOOR'S FRIEND'S.
See: Moor, The

WIFE, PERSONAGE'S. See:
Personage, A

WIFE, POTIPHAR'S. See:
Joseph
Potiphar

WIFE, PRINCE GOUDAL'S.
See: Prince Goudal

WIFE, SECOND FAVORITE.
See: Gierey

WIFE, THE, elopes with her
lover Leonardo immedi-
ately after her arranged
wedding
THE BRIDEGROOM, de-
serted by his new bride;
kills Leonardo
LEONARDO, killed by the
Bridegroom
THE MOON, betrays the
Wife and Leonardo
Blood Wedding   BLOOW
Sought by the Other Man
THE HUSBAND, of the
Wife
THE OTHER MAN, seeks
the Wife
Eternal Triangle   ETERT

WIFE, THE. See also:
Girl, The
Wife

WIFE, THE CORREGIDOR'S.
See: Corregidor, The

WIFE'S LOVER, PERSONAGE'S.
See: Personage, A

WIG-MAKER at Grand Opera,

Paris, Foyer de la Danse
FOYER

WILD PONY, performs dance at
minstrel show, Cakewalk
CAKEW

WILFRID, attendant to Albrecht,
Duke of Silesia, Giselle
GISEL

WILIS, QUEEN OF THE. See:
Myrtha, Queen of the Wilis

WILLIAM. See:
Caxton, William
Fanny
Tell, William

WILLIAM, LIEUTENANT, of the
Danish navy, Loin du Danemark   LOIND

WILLIAM TARGETT. See:
Carter, A
Salt, Jack
Tulip

WILLIBALD. See: Baron Willibald

WILSON. See: Lord Wilson

WIND, GOD OF THE. See:
Vayou

WIND, THE, personification,
The Leaf and the Wind
LEAFA

WIND, THE. See also: Autumn
Wind, The

WINDMILLS, attacked by Don
Quixote who imagines them
to be giants, Don Quixote
DONQX

WINDOW. See: Woman at the
Window, The

WINE, GOD OF. See: Bacchus

WINGS. See: White Wings

WINTER, personification
Les Quatre Saisons QUATR
Les Saisons   SAISO

WINTER. See also: Bird of
Winter, The

WINTER, THE FAIRY. See:
Fairy Spring, The

WIRE WALKERS. See:
Jinx
Ringmaster

WISE MAN, A. See: Sage

WISE VIRGINS
FOOLISH VIRGINS, attend
wedding
The Wise and Foolish
Virgins   WISEF
Attend wedding of Bride
and Bridegroom
The Wise Virgins   WISEV

WISE VIRGINS, FIVE, attendants of the Bride, care-
fully tend the trimming of
their lamps, Les Vierges
Folles   VIERG

WISTERIA, MADEMOISELLE,
a courtesan, Madame
Chrysanthème   MADAM

WITCH, old woman, 300 years
old, member of tribe which
sacrifices the Chosen One
Le Sacré du Printemps
SACRD
Le Sacré du Printemps
SACRE

WITCH. See also:
Doll
Fisherman
Hanzel
Mancenilha
Theme
White Witch
Witch, The

WITCH BOY, killed by villagers,
immediately reborn
GIRL, falls in love with
Witch Boy
The Witch Boy   WITCB

WITCH-DOCTOR, HIS. See:
Black King

WITCH, THE, "commands a
fantastic series of dance
events"
The Bewitched   BEWIT
Befriends Csizmás Janko,
gives him sword which leads
him to Fairyland
Little Johnny in Top-Boots
LITTL

WITCH, THE. See also:
Witch

WITCHES. See:
Storm Witches, The
Wood-Witches, The

WITCHES, TWO YOUNG, assist
John in his struggle with
Marvin for the love of
Barbara Allen, Barbara
Allen   BARBA

WIVES, HIS. See: Mahomet,
King of Granada

WIVES, HIS FIVE. See: Hyde,
Orson

WIVES, THEIR. See: Murat's
Ambassadors, Two

WIVES, THEIR SEVEN. See:
Clowns, Seven

WOLF, eats Duck, afterwards
captured by Peter and taken
to zoo by First Hunter
Peter and the Wolf PETER
Peter and the Wolf PETEW
A Danish pirate
Sieba   SIEBA

WOLF. See also:

Bird
Cat

WOLF, THE, attacks villagers,
tamed by Francesco Bern-
done (St. Francis), Saint
Francis   SAINT

WOLF, THE. See also:
Red Riding Hood
Young Girl, The

WOLFGANG, Prince Siegfried's
old tutor
Swan Lake   SWANA
Swan Lake   SWANE
Swan Lake   SWANK
Swan Lake   SWANL

WOLGER, pupil of Doctor
Faust, Faust   FAUST

WOMAN, personification
Day on Earth   DAYON
"Sex"
The Great American Goof
                       GREAT
Sits in theater box, looks
back on dreams of her
childhood as they appear
on the stage
Mother Goose Suite
                       MOTHE

WOMAN. See also:
American Pioneer Woman
Beauty
Bird Girl
Bird Woman
Chinese Prince
Creature of Fear
Hop o' My Thumb
Man
Old Pioneer Woman
Old Woman, Dying
Old Woman, The
Other Woman, The
Prometheus
Spanish Woman
Theme
Woman, The
Working Woman
Young Woman, The

WOMAN, A. See: Scaramouche

WOMAN, AN OLD. See: Vet-
eran Soldier, A

WOMAN AT THE WINDOW, THE,
observer of happenings on
Paris street, La Nuit
                       NUITT

WOMAN IN BALL DRESS, THE,
apparition, "idealized version of all women," loved by
the Poet, Apparitions
                       APPAR

WOMAN IN BALL DRESS, THE.
See also:
Hussar, The
Monk, The
Poet, The

WOMAN IN THE WHEELBARROW,
THE, passer-by on Paris
street, La Nuit   NUITT

WOMAN OF SOVIET COMMUNIST
YOUTH, present at boxing
match between Negro Boxer
and White Boxer; slaps face
of Referee, The Golden Age
                       GOLDE

WOMAN OF THE STREETS, A,
attends gas-attack precautions
course, Perhaps Tomorrow!
                       PERHA

WOMAN, PERSONIFICATION OF.
See: Femina

WOMAN, POLOVETSIAN. See:
Polovetsian Girl

WOMAN, THE, personification
La Création du Monde
                       CREAT
On bathing beach, bored and
idling away the time
THE MAN, also bored, flirts
with the Woman
THE NEWCOMER, flirts with
the Woman, attempts to take

her away from the Man
Facsimile   FACSI
"The bright potential"
The Great American Goof
                   GREAT
Personification
L'Homme et son Désir
                 HOMME
The Prostitute, plies her
trade in "city street any-
where in the world"
FIVE MEN, footpads,
thieves, pimps; her asso-
ciates
The Miraculous Mandarin
                 MIRAR
The Miraculous Mandarin
                 MIRAU
"Abstraction of womanhood"
Rouge et Noir   ROUGE
Personification
The Seventh Symphony
                 SEVEN

WOMAN, THE. See also:
Blind Girl
Madman, The
Mandarin (The Miraculous
  Mandarin)
Prostitute, The
Woman

WOMAN WHO WAS CAUGHT,
THE, entices two men
TWO MEN, catch and
ravish her
Caprichos   CAPRH

WOMAN WITH GUITAR. See:
Aged Woman With Guitar

WOMAN, YOUNG. See:
Young Man

WOMANKIND. See: Spirit
of Womankind, The

WOMEN. See:
Married Women, Seven
Unmarried Women, Seven
Young Women, Seven

WOMEN, TWO. See: Man

WOMEN WITH PLAY STICKS,
TWO. See: Mexican Peon

WONDROUS. See: Hermit, The
Wondrous

WOOD-WITCHES, THE, seen by
the Princess in her dream,
A Spring Tale   SPRIN

WOODEN PRINCE, loved by
Princess, The Wooden Prince
                 WOODE

WOODEN PRINCE. See also:
Prince

WOODEN ROCKING HORSES, THE,
toys, Jeux d'Enfants JEUXX

WOODS. See: Fairy of the Pine
Woods, The

WOODS, FATHER OF THE. See:
Zuimaaluti

WOODVILLE. See: Queen Elizabeth Woodville

WOODWINDS
STRINGS
BRASS
PERCUSSION, group of musi-
cal instruments, demonstrate
their various functions in
dance; introduced by Narrator
Fanfare   FANFA

WORKER, personification, Le
Pas d'Acier   PASDA

WORKER. See also: Social
Worker

WORKERS, "misfits," The Great
American Goof   GREAT

WORKING WOMAN, personification, Le Pas d'Acier PASDA

WORKMAN. See: Young Workman

WORLD. See: Man of the
World, The

WORLD, THE MOST BEAUTI-
FUL GIRL IN THE. See:
Young Man

WORLD'S SWEETHEART, THE,
American type, seen by
the Immigrant, Within the
Quota   WITHI

WORM. See: Captain of the
Glow-Worm Patrol

WOTAN, a god, punishes Sieba
for loving Harold, King of
Thule, a mortal, Sieba
                         SIEBA

WRANGLER. See: Head
Wrangler, The

WRESTLER, THE, passing
through metropolitan railroad terminal, Terminal
                         TERMI

WRITING ON THE WALL,
chalked notation that
"Mary loves Bill,"
Street Games   STREE

                X

XOCHITL. See: Tepancaltzin

XOCHITL, THE FATHER OF.
See: Tepancaltzin

                Y

YAGA. See: Baba-Yaga

YANG, CHUNG. See:
Ambassador, The
Mandarin

YARA, supernatural being,
lives at bottom of lake
LONELY MAN, in love
with Yara, waits for her

on shore
The Legend of Impossible
Love   LEGEI
Siren of rivers and ponds
Yara   YARAA

YEDDA, Japanese girl, engaged
to Nori; given magic branch
by Sakourada
HER FATHER, a farmer
Yedda   YEDDA

YEDDA. See also: Mikado, The

YELA, village maiden, Mirko's
sweetheart, betrothed to
The Bridegroom after Mirko
possessed by The Devil
YELA'S MOTHER
THE UNCLE, her relatives,
wish her to marry The Bridegroom
The Devil in the Village
                        DEVIV

YELA. See also: Matchmaker,
The

YELLOW GROUP. See: Leader
of the Yellow Group (Country)

YELLOW PEARL, THE. See:
White Pearl, The

YELVA, maid to the Countess,
wife of the Count Polinski;
betrothed to Yvan, Le Diable
à Quatre   DIABQ

YOKEL, A. See: Silly Country
Girl

YORK. See:
Duke of York, The
Manager from New York,
The

YORKERS. See: New Yorkers

YOUNG. See: Witches, Two
Young

YOUNG APPRENTICE, leaves

his work to follow street
musician
STREET MUSICIAN, clari-
netist, plays for impromptu
street ball
LAUNDRESSES, participate
in street ball with Young
Apprentice
Le Bal des Blanchisseuses
                        BALDE

YOUNG BRIDE, comes to
Western prairie, lonely,
"creeps for comfort into
the old chest containing
her wedding gown, and is
smothered"
HER HUSBAND, pioneer
on the prairie
Shadow on the Prairie
                        SHADP

YOUNG CHATELAINE, THE.
See: Julien

YOUNG COMMUNICANT, THE,
newly confirmed, visits
pastry-shop
HIS MOTHER
HIS GODFATHER
Schlagobers   SCHLA

YOUNG COMMUNICANT, THE.
See also: Doctor, The

YOUNG COMMUNIST GIRL, A,
representing the U.S.S.R.,
The Golden Age   GOLDE

YOUNG COMMUNIST GIRL, A,
representing Western
Europe, The Golden Age
                        GOLDE

YOUNG CONVICT, THE. See:
Leader of the Convicts

YOUNG FARM GIRL, resident
of rural Argentina, Es-
tancia   ESTAN

YOUNG FARMER, has recently
completed building farm-

house in Pennsylvania hills
HIS BRIDE, soon to become
a mother
Appalachian Spring   APPAL

YOUNG FARMER. See also:
Old Pioneer Woman

YOUNG GIRL, fickle, jilts
several lovers, marries
and is eaten by Black King
HER MOTHER, anxious that
her daughter marry wealth
Bonne-Bouche   BONNE
In love
YOUNG GIRL'S LOVER, in
love with her
YOUNG GIRL'S DUENNA
Los Caprichos   CAPRD
Personification
Day on Earth   DAYON
Succumbs to the Seven Dead-
ly Sins; repents
SEVEN DEADLY SINS, over-
come Young Girl
MADONNA, accepts Young
Girl's offering of roses and
her repentance
Fanciulla delle Rose FANCI
Lonely wallflower at pre-
World I resort hotel, dreams
of being irresistible to all
the young men
Souvenirs   SOUVE

YOUNG GIRL. See also:
Ballerinas, Two Former
Chaperones
Garatuja, O.
Lover, The
Officer, An
Rich Old Neighbor, A
Rose Spirit
Young Workman

YOUNG GIRL, A. See: Youth,
A

YOUNG GIRL, THE, bride, falls
in love with the Wolf
THE YOUNG MAN, her hus-
band, falls in love with the
Gypsy Dancer

THE GYPSY DANCER,
falls in love with the
Young Man
THE WOLF, temporarily
given human form, falls
in love with the Young Girl
THE ANIMAL TRAINER,
necromancer, owner of the
Wolf, changes him to hu-
man likeness
Le Loup   LOUPP
Becomes engaged to a
sailor, remains faithful
to him
HER FRIEND
Les Matelots   MATEL
Aristocrat, in love with
the Baker
La Nuit   NUITT
Falls in love with, mar-
ries the Stranger; subse-
quently kills herself and
him
THE STRANGER, murderer
of Young Girl's former
lover
Sea Gallows   SEAGA

YOUNG GIRL, THE. See also:
First Sailor
Young Man, The

YOUNG GIRL'S PARENTS.
See: Garatuja, O.

YOUNG GYPSY, replaces
Aleko as Zemphira's
lover, stabbed by Aleko
Aleko   ALEKO

YOUNG GYPSY. See also:
Fortune Teller

YOUNG HUSBAND, tired of
his wife, abandons her
WIFE, loyal to her hus-
band, thrust aside
NEW LOVE, goes away
with Young Husband
Shadow of the Wind SHADW

YOUNG JUDITH. See: Judith

YOUNG LADY FROM VIENNA, A,
guest at ball, Carnival at
Pest   CARNI

YOUNG LOVER, THE, carnival
reveler, Devil's Holiday
DEVIL

YOUNG LOVERS, three couples
keeping trysts in a wood,
Fantasy   FANTA

YOUNG LOVERS. See also:
Watchers of the Night

YOUNG MAIDEN. See: Man-
darin

YOUNG MAN, in search of love,
finds his ideal, dies
THE MOST BEAUTIFUL
GIRL IN THE WORLD, his
ideal
Le Rendez-Vous   RENDE
Idealist, "in a world where
cruelty is permanent and so
is power and the victim"
Rites   RITES
Prevents Girl from commit-
ting suicide, finds himself
entangled in her emotional
problems
GIRL, attempts suicide, pre-
vented by Young Man
The Web   WEBBB
Lover of Young Woman
YOUNG WOMAN, in love with
him
STRANGER, from the city,
temporarily intrudes on
Young Man and Young Woman
Wind in the Mountains
WINDI

YOUNG MAN. See also:
Death
Destiny
Girl, The

YOUNG MAN, A, loses faith in
God after his brother is
struck and killed by lightning;
restored to faith by Christian

Girl
HIS BROTHER
El Greco   GRECO
Temporarily attracted to
Poor Girl; jilts her for
Rich Girl
Nocturne   NOCTU

YOUNG MAN, A. See also:
Spectator, A

YOUNG MAN FROM THE
HOUSE OPPOSITE, THE,
seduces Hagar, Pillar of
Fire   PILLA

YOUNG MAN, RICH. See:
Laiderette

YOUNG MAN, THE, "whose
life is ruled by the sun
in Leo and the moon in
Gemini"
Horoscope   HOROS
"Sophisticated, momen-
tarily fascinated by the
simplicity of the Young
Girl"
THE YOUNG GIRL, loved
by the Boy
THE BOY, loves the
Young Girl, "seems at
the end to be left with no
one"
THE BATHING BELLE,
wins the Young Man back
Summer Interlude SUMMI

YOUNG MAN, THE. See also:
Cat, The
Shadow, The
Young Girl, The

YOUNG MENNERS. See: Old
Menners

YOUNG MUSICIAN, A, ex-
periences strange dreams
while under the influence
of opium
THE BELOVED, loved by
him
Symphonie Fantastique

SYMPH

YOUNG MUSICIAN, A. See also:
Deer, The
Jailer, The
Old Shepherd, The
Visions of Gaiety
Visions of Melancholy
Visions of Passion
Visions of Reverie
Young Shepherd, The

YOUNG NOBLEMAN, THE.
See: Julien

YOUNG POET, tries in vain to
save Chrysanthemum from
death following uprooting by
Autumn Wind, Autumn
Leaves   AUTUM

YOUNG SHEPHERD, THE, seen
by Young Musician in his
dream, Symphonie Fantas-
tique   SYMPH

YOUNG SOLDIER, THE
THE OLD SOLDIER, pawns
in diplomatic negotiations;
claimed by Death
The Green Table   GREEN

YOUNG STUDENT, in love with
wife of American; misses
last date with her before
she leaves Paris; commits
suicide
AMERICAN, visiting Paris
FRENCH WIFE of the
American
Broken Date   BROKE

YOUNG TOWNSMAN, resident of
rural Argentina, Estancia
ESTÁN

YOUNG TREGENNIS, enters
haunted ballroom in which
his ancestors died
MASTER OF TREGENNIS,
his father, dies in the
haunted ballroom
The Haunted Ballroom

HAUNT

YOUNG TREGENNIS. See also:
Alicia
Beatrice
Flautist (The Stranger Player)
Ursula

YOUNG WARRIOR. See: Old Poet

YOUNG WIFE, THE, pursued by Don Juan, Don Juan
DONJA

YOUNG WOMAN. See:
Young Man

YOUNG WOMAN, THE,
"whose life is ruled by the sun in Virgo and the moon in Gemini, " Horo-scope   HOROS

YOUNG WOMEN, SEVEN,
members of Eskimo tribe,
Qarrtsiluni   QARRT

YOUNG WORKMAN, homeward bound after the day's work
YOUNG GIRL, his sweet-heart, deserts him for the Libertine; disillusioned
THE LIBERTINE, makes conquest of Young Girl
The Big City   BIGCI

YOUNGER, PHILEMON THE.
See: Philemon

YOUNGER SONS, FOUR. See:
Jesse

YOUNGEST SISTER. See:
Friend, The
Hagar

YOUTH
GIRL, resist enemy invasion
Seventh Symphony   SEVEM

YOUTH. See also:
Country Youth, A
Elora
Gypsy Youth, The
Peasant Youth, The
Poet, The
Tartar Youth
Woman of Soviet Communist Youth

YOUTH, A, divided between his affection for two girls
HIS ROMANTIC LOVE, loved by him
A YOUNG GIRL, also loved by him
THE SHADOW, sinister guardian of the Young Girl; actually exists only in the mind of the Youth
The Shadow   SHADO
Tricks the Three Virgins
Three Virgins and a Devil
THREV

YOUTH, A. See also:
Don Lollo
Priggish Virgin

YOUTH, A FLORENTINE. See:
Florentine Beauty, A

YOUTH, THE, becomes enamoured of Aglaë
Aglaë   AGLAE
Offered five gifts by the Fairy
ANOTHER YOUTH, his friend
The Five Gifts   FIVEG
Personification
The Seventh Symphony
SEVEN

YSAURE, god-child of the fairies, loved by Alain and Prince Hugues de Provence
GUILLAUME, her father
ALAIN, her foster-brother
La Filleule des Fées FILLU

YSAURE. See also:

Berthe
Black Fairy, The
Godmother to Ysaure
Renoualle, Ysaure de
Rose Fairy, The
White Fairy, The

YVAN, house-porter at the
Count Polinski's castle;
betrothed to Yelva, Le
Diable à Quatre   DIABQ

YVAN. See also:
Ivan
Yvonne

YVES. See: Pierre

YVONNE. See:
Herve
Mathurin
Yvan

YVONNETTE, first a tavern
maid, servant of Loïk;
later a korrigane (fairy),
rescued by Lilèz, La
Korrigane   KORRI

Z

ZAAL. See: Prince Zaal

ZADIG, young man, puzzled
by the vagaries of his
destiny; marries the Queen
THE QUEEN, becomes
his bride
Zadig   ZADIG

ZAIDÉE, Farfalla's maid, Le
Papillon   PAPIL

ZAIL, a goblin, La Source
                       SOURC

ZAMON, betrothed to Nozgulle,
daughter of Bobo-Safar,
The Two Roses   TWORO

ZAREMA. See: Gierey

ZARIFI, chief of the gypsies,

helps Gourouli regain Pepio
Les Deux Pigéons   DEUXN
Les Deux Pigéons   DEUXP

ZARRAGULLE. See:
Abdurassul, Bey
Bobo-Safar
Sanghine

ZEALOT, draws Victim from
behind protective walls she
has built about herself
VICTIM, discovers new
fears after leaving protective walls
The Antagonists   ANTAG

ZEIR, page to Mahomet, King of
Granada, La Révolte au
Sérail   REVOL

ZEMEN, SHAH. See: Shahryar,
King of India and China

ZEMPHIRA, gypsy girl, once in
love with Aleko, spurns him
for Young Gypsy; stabbed by
Aleko
ZEMPHIRA'S FATHER,
gypsy chief
Aleko   ALEKO

ZENOBIO. See: Bonaventuri,
Zenobio

ZEPHIROS, maître de danse,
La Jolie Fille de Gand
                       JOLIE

ZEPHYR, personification, Les
Saisons   SAISO

ZEPHYR. See also: Zephyrus

ZEPHYRS, SEVEN, carry Psyche
to Olympus, L'Amour et
Son Amour   AMOUT

ZEPHYRUS, in love with Flora
(Chloris), flirts with Cleonisa
Flore et Zéphire   FLORE
Zephyr, in love with Flora
Zephyr and Flora   ZEPHY

ZEPHYRUS. See also: Cupid

ZERO, ADAM. See:
    Death
    Principal Dancer, The
    Stage Director, The

ZEUS, god, carries the dead
    Alexander the Great to
    Olympus
    Alexandre le Grand
                                ALEXA
    God
    I, Odysseus   IODYS
    God, gives Tiresias gift
    of prophecy
    HERA, his wife, strikes
    Tiresias blind
    Tiresias   TIRES

ZEUS. See also:
    Apollo
    Persephone, Queen of
        Hades

ZI'DIMA, hunchback, village
    tinker; temporarily im-
    prisoned inside oil jar
    belonging to Don Lollo,
    La Jarre   JARRE
    La Jarre   JARRR

ZINA, former student of danc-
    ing, old friend of Female
    Dancer
    PYOTR, her husband, an
    agricultural student
    The Bright Stream BRIGH

ZOBEIDA. See: Shahryar,
    King of India and China

ZOBEIDA'S FAVORITE SLAVE.
    See: Shahryar, King of
    India and China

ZOBI. See: Marie

ZODIAC, personification,
    Defense of Paradise
                                DEFEN

ZOÉ, in love with Théodore

MADAME DE SÉNANGE, her
    mother
    Les Deux Créoles   DEUXC

ZOÉ. See also: Marie

ZOLOE, bayadère, rescues,
    later rescued by the Unknown
    NINKA
    FATME, her friends and
    fellow bayadères
    Le Dieu et la Bayadère
                                DIEUE

ZOLOE. See also: Olifour

ZORAIYA. See:
    Caliph Abderraman
    Tisbah

ZOSHKA, in love with Simon
    HER FATHER
    HER MOTHER
    KATUSHA, her sister
    The Nightingale   NIGHI

ZUBILLAGA, chief of the buc-
    caneers, Jovita   JOVIT

ZUG, a goat-herd, Nathalie
                                NATHA

ZUIMAALUTI, Indian girl, "un-
    wittingly joins in the dances
    of the daughters of Pai-do-
    Mato and becomes their com-
    panion forever"
    PAI-DO-MATO, Father of
    the Woods
    DAUGHTERS OF PAI-DO-
    MATO
    Zuimaaluti   ZUMAI

ZULMA, confidante of the Sul-
    tana, wife of the Sultan;
    character in the ballet
    "Azalea, or The Odalisque"
    The Débutante   DEBUT
    Betrothed to Ismaël
    La Révolute au Sérail
                                REVOL

ZULMEA. See: Seyd

ZVEZDICH, PRINCE. See:
   Arbenin

ZYRAB, friend of Djardje,
   The Heart of the Hills
                         HEART

ABRAX Abraxas, ballet (5 scenes). Music, Werner Egk; choroegraphy, Marcel Luipart; book, Egk, based on a ballet scenario by Heinrich Heine; décor, Wolfgang Znamenacek. Munich Staatsoper, June 6, 1948. Later staged for the Berlin Städtische Oper, October 8, 1949, with choreography by Janine Charrat and scenery and costumes by Joseph Fenneker.

ADAMZ Adam Zero, ballet (1 act). Music, Arthur Bliss; choreography, Robert Helpmann; book, Michael Benthall; scenery and costumes, Roger Furse. Royal Opera, Covent Garden, London, April 10, 1946.

ADAPT The Adaptability of Man, solo dance. Music, Serge Prokofiev; choreography and costume, Sybil Shearer. New York Times Hall, New York, May 3, 1946.

ADELA Adélaïde, or The Language of the Flowers, ballet (1 act). Music and book, Maurice Ravel; choreography, Natashe Trouhanova. Théâtre du Châtelet, Paris, April, 1912.

ADONI Adonis, ballet. Music,
Lehman Engel; choreography, Ruth Page. Chicago, Ill., 1944.

AFTEN The Afternoon of a Faun, ballet (1 act). Music, Claude Debussy (Prélude à l'après-midi d'un faune); choreography, Jerome Robbins; décor, Jean Rosenthal; costumes, Irene Sharaff. City Center, New York, May 14, 1953.

AFTER The Afternoon of a Faun (L'Après-midi d'un faune), choreographic tableau (1 act). Music, Claude Debussy (Prélude à l'après-midi d'un faune); choreography and book, Vaslav Nijinsky; décor, Léon Bakst. Théâtre du Châtelet, Paris, May 29, 1912.

AGEOE The Age of Anxiety, dramatic ballet (6 scenes). Music, Leonard Bernstein (Second Symphony, based on the poem, "The Age of Anxiety" by W. H. Auden); choreography, Jerome Robbins; scenery, Oliver Smith; costumes, Irene Sharaff. City Center, New York, February 26, 1950.

AGLAE Aglaë, ou l'Élève de l' Amour (Algaë, or Cupid's Pupil), ballet divertissement (1 act). Music, Keller; choreography and book, Filippo Taglioni. St. Petersburg, January 22, 1841.

AHOUS "A House Divided--, "
group dance. Music, Lio-
nel Nowak; spoken text
selected from speeches of
Abraham Lincoln by Charles
Weidman; choreography,
Weidman and Doris Hum-
phrey; costumes, Weidman.
Needle Trades High School,
New York, November 4,
1945.

ALCES Alcestis, modern
dance work. Music, Vivian
Fine; choreography and
costumes, Martha Graham;
décor, Isamu Noguchi.
54th St. (formerly Adelphi)
Theater, New York, April
29, 1960.

ALEKO Aleko, ballet (4
scenes). Music, Peter
Ilyich Tchaikovsky ("Trio
in A minor"), orchestra-
ted by Erno Rapée; chore-
ography, Leonide Massine;
book, Massine, based on
Pushkin's poem "The Gyp-
sies"; scenery and cos-
tumes, Marc Chagall.
Ballet Theatre, Palacio
de Bellas Artes, Mexico
City, September 8, 1942.

ALEXA Alexandre le Grande
(Alexander the Great),
choreographic epic (pro-
logue, 3 scenes, epilogue).
Music, Philippe Gaubert's
symphonic suite, "Inscrip-
tions pour les Portes de
la Ville"; choreography and
book, Serge Lifar; scenery
and costumes, P. R. Larthe.
Théâtre de l'Opéra, Paris,
June 21, 1937.

ALGUE Les Algues (Seaweed),
ballet (1 act). Music,
electronic score by Guy
Bernard; choreography,
Janine Charrat; scenery

and costumes, Louis-Bertrand
Castelli. Théâtre des
Champs-Élysées, Paris,
April 20, 1953.

ALMAO Alma ou la Fille de
Feu, ballet (4 scenes).
Music, G. Costa; choreography,
Jules Perrot and Fanny Ceri-
to; book, André Jean-
Jacques Deshayes; scenery,
W. Grieve. Her Majesty's
Theatre, London, June 23,
1842.

AMORB El Amor Brujo (L'
Amour Sorcier) (Love the
Magician) (Love the Sor-
cerer), ballet (1 act). Music
Manuel de Falla; choreography,
Pastora Imperio; book, G.
Martinez Sierra, based on
an Andalusian gypsy tale.
Teatro de Lara, Madrid,
April 15, 1915.

AMORR Amor, ballet (2 parts).
Music, Romualdo Marenco;
choreography and book,
Luigi Manzotti; scenery and
costumes, Alfredo Edel.
Teatro alla Scala, Milan,
February 17, 1886.

AMORY Del Amor y de la
Muerte (Of Love and Death),
dramatic ballet (2 scenes
and an interlude). Music,
Enrique Granados, from the
opera "Goyescas," arranged
by Ernest Schelling; choreography, Ana Ricarda;
scenery and costumes,
Cecilia Hubbard. Théâtre
de Monte Carlo, Monte
Carlo, April 29, 1949.

AMOUJ Les Amours de Jupiter,
ballet (5 scenes). Music,
Jacques Ibert; choreography,
Roland Petit; book, Boris
Kochno, based on themes
from Ovid's "Metamorphoses";

scenery and costumes,
Jean Hugo. Théâtre des
Champs-Élysées, Paris,
March 5, 1946.

AMOUR Les Amours d'Antoine
et de Chéopâtre, historical
ballet (3 acts). Music,
Kreutzer; choreography,
Jean Aumer; book, Aumer.
Théâtre de l'Académie
Royale de Musique, Paris,
March 8, 1808.

AMOUT L'Amour et Son Amour
(Cupid and His Love), ballet
(2 scenes). Music, César
Franck ("Psyché"); chore-
ography, Jean Babilée;
scenery and costumes,
Jean Cocteau. Théâtre
des Champs Élysées,
Paris, December 13, 1948.

ANDDA And Daddy Was a
Fireman, modern dance
work. Music, Herbert
Haufrecht, adapting popular
airs (including "Oh, Su-
sanna"); choreography and
costumes, Charles Weid-
man; décor, Harnley Per-
kins. Humphrey-Weidman
Theatre, New York, 1943.

ANGEG L'Ange Gris, ballet
(1 act). Music, Claude
Debussy; choreography,
George Skibine; book,
Marquis de Cuevas; scen-
ery and costumes, Sébire.
Théâtre du Casino, Deau-
ville, France, August 20,
1953.

ANGUI Anguish Sonata, ballet
(3 movements). Music,
Béla Bartók's Sonata for
Two Pianos and Percussion;
choreography and idea,
Aurel Milloss; décor, Darcy
Penteado. Teatro Municipal,
Rio de Janeiro, Brazil, 1954.

ANNAB Annabel Lee, dance
ballad (1 act). Music, Byron Schiffmann; choreography
and book, George Skibine,
after the poem by Edgar Allan Poe; scenery and cos-
tumes, André Delfau.
Théâtre du Casino, Deauville,
France, August 26, 1951.

ANTAG The Antagonists, mod-
ern dance work. Music,
Igor Stravinsky's Concertino
and Three Pieces for String
Quartet; choreography, Ruth
Currier; décor, Thomas de
Gaetani. Connecticut Col-
lege, New London, Conn.,
August 20, 1955.

ANTIG Antigone, ballet (1 act).
Music, Mikis Theodorakis;
choreography, John Cranko;
décor, Rufino Tamayo.
Royal Opera House, Covent
Garden, London, October 19,
1959.

ANTIS Antic Spring, ballet (1
act). Music, Jacques Ibert's
Divertissement and Three
Short Pieces for Wood Wind
Quintet; choreography, Grant
Strate; décor, Mark Negin.
Palace Theatre, Hamilton,
Ontario, October 26, 1960.

ANTON Antonia, ballet (1 act).
Music, Jean Sibelius; chore-
ography and book, Walter
Gore; settings and costumes,
Harry Cordwell. King's
Theatre, Hammersmith,
London, October 17, 1949.

APASI Apasionada, modern
dance work. Music, Carlos
Surinach; choreography and
book, Pearl Lang. Hunter
College Playhouse, New
York, January 5, 1962.

APOLL Apollo, Leader of the

Muses (Apollon Musagète),
ballet (2 scenes). Music,
Igor Stravinsky; chore-
ography, George Balanchine;
décor, André Bauchant.
Théâtre Sarah Bernhardt,
Paris, June 12, 1928.

APOLN Apollon Musagète, ballet (2 scenes). Music and
book, Igor Stravinsky;
choreography, Adolph
Bolm. Library of Con-
gress, Washington, D. C. ,
April 27, 1928.

APPAL Appalachian Spring,
modern dance work. Music,
Aaron Copland; choreography,
Martha Graham, based on a
poem by Hart Crane; set-
tings, Isamu Noguchi; costumes, Edith Guilfond. Library of Congress, Washington, D. C. , October 30,
1944.

APPAR Apparitions, dramatic
ballet (prologue, 3 scenes,
epilogue). Music, Franz
Liszt, orchestrated by
Gordon Jacob; choreography,
Frederick Ashton; book,
Constant Lambert; scenery
and costumes, Cecil Beaton.
Sadler's Wells Theatre,
London, February 11, 1936.

ARCAD Arcade, ballet (1 act).
Music, Igor Stravinsky
(Concerto for Piano and
Wind Instruments); chore-
ography, John Taras; dé-
cor, David Hays; costumes,
Ruth Sobotka. City Center,
New York, March 28, 1963.

ARDEN Ardent Song, modern
dance work. Music, Alan
Hovhaness; choreography
and costumes, Martha Gra-
ham. Saville Theatre,
London, March 18, 1954.

ARTEM Artémis Troublée, ballet. Music, Paray; chore-
ography, Nicola Guerra;
décor, Léon Bakst. Paris
Opéra, Paris, April 28,
1922.

ASILA As I Lay Dying, modern
dance work. Music, Ber-
nardo Segall; choreography,
Valerie Bettis; book based
on the novel by William
Faulkner; costumes, Kim
Swados; properties, Eddie
Light. Hunter College Playhouse, New York, December
19, 1948.

ASSEM Assembly Ball, classic
ballet (1 act). Music,
Georges Bizet ("Symphony
in C"); choreography and
décor, Andrée Howard.
Sadler's Wells Theatre,
London, April 8, 1946.

ATAVI Atavisms, suite of
three modern group dances
(Bargain Counter, Stock Ex-
change and Lynch Town).
Music, Lehman Engel;
choreography, Charles
Weidman. Guild Theatre,
New York, January 26, 1936.

AUBAA Aubade, ballet. Music,
François Poulenc; chore-
ography, George Balanchine;
décor, A. M. Cassandre.
Monte Carlo, April 11, 1936.

AUBAB Aubade, ballet. Music,
François Poulenc: chore-
ography, Serge Lifar. Monte
Carlo, December, 1946.

AUBAC Aubade, ballet. Music,
François Poulenc; chore-
ography, Alexis Dolinoff;
décor, R. Deshays. Phila-
delphia, Pa. , 1936.

AUBAD Aubade, ballet. Music

and book, François Poulenc;
choreography, Bronislava
Nijinska. Paris, 1929.

AUBAE Aubade, ballet. Mu-
sic, François Poulenc;
choreography and book,
George Balanchine; décor,
Ortiz. Paris, January,
1930.

AUROR Aurora's Wedding,
suite of dances from the
last act of "The Sleeping
Princess" with some addi-
tions. Music, Peter Ilyich
Tchaikovsky; choreography,
Marius Petipa; costumes,
from Benois's "Pavillon d'
Armide"; décor, Léon
Bakst. Paris Opéra,
Paris, May 18, 1922. New
York première 1941, with
choreography by Anton Do-
lin, and décor by Michel
Boronoff, after Bakst.

AUROW Aurora's Wedding,
ballet (excerpts from "The
Sleeping Princess"); music,
Peter Ilyich Tchaikovsky;
choreography, Nicholas
Sergeyev, after Marius
Petipa; décor, Léon Bakst.
Paris Opéra, Paris, 1922.

AUTUMN Autumn Leaves,
choreographic poem (1 act).
Music, Frédéric Chopin;
choreography and book,
Anna Pavlova; scenery,
Konstantin Korovin Castro.
Rio de Janiero, Brazil,
1918.

BABYS Baby Stork (The Little
Stork), ballet (3 acts). Mu-
sic, Klebanoff; choreography,
N. Popko, L. Pospekhin and
A. I. Radunsky; book, M. Ya.
Pinchevsky; décor, Zimin.
School performance at Bol-
shoy Theatre, Moscow, June
6, 1937.

BACCH Bacchanale, surrealist
ballet (1 act). Music, Richard Wagner (Tannhäuser);
choreography, Leonide Massine; libretto, scenery and
costumes. Salvador Dali.
Metropolitan Opera House,
New York, November 9,
1939.

BACCU Bacchus and Ariadne,
ballet. Music, Albert Rous-
sel; choreography, Serge
Lifar; décor, Giorgio de
Chirico. Paris Opéra,
Paris, 1931.

BAISE Le Baiser de la Fée,
ballet-allegory (4 scenes).
Music and book, Igor Stra-
vinsky; choreography, George
Balanchine; costumes and
scenery, Alicia Halicka.
Metropolitan Opera House,
New York, April 27, 1937.

BALDE Le Bal des Blanchisseuses, ballet (1 act). Music, Vernon Duke; chore-
ography, Roland Petit; book,
Boris Kochno; décor, Stanislas Lepri. Ballets des
Champs-Élysées, Paris,
December 19, 1946.

BALLA Ballade, dramatic ballet
(1 act). Music, Claude Debussy (flute solo, "Syrinx"
and "Six Antique Epigraphs,"
orchestrated by Ernest Anser-
met); choreography, Jerome
Robbins; scenery and cos-
tumes, Boris Aronson. City
Center, New York, February
14, 1952.

BALLC Ballet Comique de la
Reine, ballet. Music, Sieur
de Beaulieu; choreography,
Balthasar de Beaujoyeux
(Baldassarino de Belgiojoso);

verses, La Chesnaye; scenery and costumes, Jacques Patin. Paris, October 15, 1581.

BALLD Ballad, ballet (1 act). Music, Harry Somers; choreography, Grant Strate; décor, Mark Negin. Capitol Theatre, Ottawa, Canada, November 4, 1959.

BALLE Ballet Imperial, classical ballet (3 movements). Music, Tchaikovsky (Piano Concerto No. 2 in G major); choreography, George Balanchine; scenery and costumes, Mstislav Doboujinsky. Hunter College Playhouse, New York, May 29, 1941.

BALLN Ballet de la Nuit, ballet (3 acts). Music, Jean Baptiste Lully; choreography, unknown. Paris, 1653.

BALLP Ballad in a Popular Style, modern dance solo. Music, Alex North; choreography, Anna Sokolow. Guild Theater, New York, November 14, 1937.

BALLS Ballet School, ballet (1 act). Music, Liadov, Liapunov, Glazounov and Shostakovitch; choreography, Asaf Messerer. Metropolitan Opera House, New York, September 17, 1962.

BALLX Ballerina, ballet. Music, Mushel; choreography, Baranovsky and Litvinova; décor, Ryftina. Tashkent Ballet, 1952.

BARAU Bar aux Folies-Bergère, ballet (1 act). Music, Emmanual Chabrier; chore-

ography and book, Ninette de Valois; scenery and costumes, William Chappell. Mercury Theatre, London, May 15, 1934.

BARBA Barbara Allen, ballet (1 act). Music, Louis Applebaum; choreography, David Adams; décor, Kay Ambrose. Palace Theatre, Hamilton, Ontario, October 26, 1960.

BARBE Barbe-Bleue, ballet (3 acts). Music, Schenck; choreography, Marius Petipa; book, L. Pashkova; scenery, Lambini, Ivanov, Levogt and Perminov. Maryinsky Theatre, St. Petersburg, December 8, 1896.

BARND Barn Dance, ballet (1 act). Music, David Guion, John Powell and Louis Moreau Gottschalk; choreography and book, Catherine Littlefield; scenery and costumes, A. Pinto and S. Pinto. Fox Theater, Philadelphia, April 23, 1937.

BAYAD La Bayadère, ballet (3 acts). Music, Leon Minkus; choreography, Marius Petipa; book, Petipa and Sergei Khudekov. Maryinsky Theatre, St. Petersburg, January 23, 1877.

BEAUB Beauty and the Beast, dramatic ballet (2 scenes). Music, Maurice Ravel (excerpts from "Mother Goose Suite"); choreography, John Cranko; scenery and costumes, Margaret Kaye. Sadler's Wells Theatre, London, December 20, 1949.

BEAUD Le Beau Danube (The Beautiful Danube), character-

ballet (2, later 1 act).
Music, Johann Strauss, ar-
ranged and orchestrated by
Roger Désormière; book
and choreography, Leonide
Massine; scenery by Vladi-
mir Polunin, after Constan-
tin Guys; costumes by Count
Étienne de Beaumont. First
presented in a two-act ver-
sion by Count Étienne de
Beaumont's Soirée de Paris,
Paris, May 17, 1924; first
presented in the final one-
act version by the Ballet
Russe de Monte Carlo,
Théâtre de Monte Carlo,
April 15, 1933.

BEAUT   The Beautiful Pearl,
ballet (1 act). Music, Ric-
cardo Drigo; choreography,
Marius Petipa; setting, P.
B. Lambini, after the de-
sign by M. I. Bocharov.
Bolshoy Theatre, Moscow,
May 17, 1896.

BELLA   La Belle au Bois Dormant, ballet. Music,
Louis J. F. Hérold; choreography, Jean Aumer.
1829.

BELLS   The Bells, ballet (5
episodes). Music, Darius
Milhaud; choreography,
Ruth Page; book, Page,
after the poem by Edgar
Allan Poe; setting and cos-
tumes, Isamu Noguchi.
Mandel Hall, University of
Chicago, April 26, 1946.

BETTY   Betty, pantomimic
ballet (2 acts). Music,
Ambroise Thomas; chore-
ography and book, Joseph
Mazilier; scenery, Cicéri
and Rubé, Desplèchin,
Diéterle and Séchan, Philastre and Cambon. Théâ-
tre de l'Académie Royale

de Musique, Paris, July 10,
1846.

BEWIT   The Bewitched, modern
dance work. Music, Harry
Partch, composed for instruments designed and built by
the composer plus clarinet,
bass clarinet and cello;
choreography, Joyce Trisler;
setting design and production
coordination, Thomas de
Gaetani; costumes, Malcolm
McCormack. Juilliard Con-
cert Hall, New York, April
10, 1959. Previously per-
formed at the University of
Illinois' 1957 Festival of
Contemporary Arts with the
same music but choreography
by Alvin Nikolais.

BIBLI   Bibliska Bilder (The Mes-
sage), ballet (1 act). Music,
Handel and Gluck; chore-
ography, Ivo Cramèr; décor,
Alvar Granström. Concert
Hall, Stockholm, November
16, 1945.

BICHE   Les Biches (The House
Party) (The Gazelles), ballet
(1 act). Music, François
Poulenc; choreography, Bronislava Nijinska; scenery and
costumes, Marie Laurencin.
Théâtre de Monte Carlo,
Monte Carlo, January 6,
1924.

BIENA   La Bien-Aimée (The
Beloved), ballet (1 act). Music, Schubert and Liszt, arranged by Darius Milhaud;
choreography, Bronislava Nijinska; book, scenery and
costumes, Alexandre Benois.
Théâtre National de l'Opéra,
Paris, November 22, 1928.

BIGCI   The Big City, ballet (3
scenes). Music, Alexander
Tansman (Sonatine Transat-

BILLS   254

lantique); choreography and
book, Kurt Jooss. Opera
House, Cologne, November
21, 1932.

BILLS Billy Sunday, or Giving
the Devil His Due, ballet
(4 episodes). Music, Remi
Gassmann; choreography
and book, Ruth Page; spok-
en text, J. Ray Hunt; dé-
cor, Herbert Andrews.
Mandel Hall, Chicago, De-
cember 13, 1946.

BILLY Billy the Kid, charac-
ter-ballet (1 act). Music,
Aaron Copland; chore-
ography, Eugene Loring;
book, Lincoln Kirstein,
scenery and costumes,
Jared French. Chicago
Opera House, Chicago,
October 16, 1938.

BIRDS The Birds, ballet (1
act). Music, Ottorino Respighi; choreography and
libretto, Robert Helpmann;
décor, Chiang Lee. New
Theatre, London, Novem-
ber 24, 1942.

BIRTO The Birthday of Oberon,
ballet. Music, Henry Pur-
cell, orchestrated by Constant Lambert; choreography,
Ninette de Valois; décor,
John Armstrong. Sadler's
Wells Theatre, London,
1933.

BLANC Blanche-Neige, ballet
(3 acts). Music, Maurice
Yvain; choreography, Serge
Lifar; scenery and cos-
tumes, Dmitri Bouchène.
Théâtre National de l'Opéra,
Paris, November 15, 1951.

BLOOD The Blood-Red Flower,
fantastic ballet (6 scenes).
Music, F. A. Hartmann;

choreography, Nicholas Le-
gat; book, Marzhetsky,
adapted from the story by
S. T. Aksakhov; scenery and
costumes, Constantine Koro-
vine. Maryinsky Theatre,
St. Petersburg, December
16, 1907.

BLOOW Blood Wedding, ballet
(1 act). Music, Denis Ap-
Ivor; choreography, Alfred
Rodrigues; book, ApIvor and
Rodrigues, based on the Federico García Lorca play; décor, Isabel Lambert. Sad-
ler's Wells Theatre, London,
June 5, 1953.

BLUEB Bluebeard, comic ballet
(2 prologues, 4 acts, 3 inter-
ludes). Music, Jacques Offenbach, arranged by Antal
Dorati; choreography, Michel
Fokine; book, Fokine, after
the opéra-bouffe by Henri
Meilhac and Ludovic Halévy;
scenery and costumes, Marcel Vertès. Palacio de Bellas Artes, Mexico City,
October 27, 1941.

BLUER A Blue Rose, ballet (1
act). Music, Samuel Barber
(Suite of Six Short Dance
Movements); choreography,
Peter Wright; décor, Yolande
Sonnabend. Royal Opera
House, Covent Garden, Lon-
don, December 26, 1957.

BOGAT Bogatyri, fantasy-ballet
(prologue, 4 movements).
Music, Aleksandr Porfirevich
Borodin; choreography and
libretto, Leonide Massine,
based on old Russian folk
tales; settings and costumes,
Nathalie Gontcharova. Metropolitan Opera House, New
York, October 20, 1938.

BOLER Bolero, ballet (1 scene).

Music, Maurice Ravel;
choreography, Bronislava
Nijinska; décor, Alexandre
Benois. Paris Opéra,
Paris, November 22, 1928.

BONNE Bonne-Bouche (Tidbit),
comic ballet (3 scenes).
Music, Arthur Oldham;
choreography, John Cranko;
book, Cranko; scenery and
costumes, Osbert Lancast-
er. Royal Opera House,
Covent Garden, London,
April 4, 1952.

BOURE Le Bourgeois Gentil-
homme (The Would-Be
Gentleman), ballet. Music,
Jean Baptiste Lully and
André Grétry; choreography,
William Christensen; book,
after Molière's comedy.
San Francisco, Calif.,
1944.

BOURG Le Bourgeois Gentilhomme (The Would-Be
Gentleman), comic ballet
(2 scenes). Music, Rich-
ard Strauss ("Ariadne auf
Naxos"); choreography,
George Balanchine; libretto,
Boris Kochno, after Mo-
lière's comedy; décor,
Alexandre Benois. Théâ-
tre de Monte Carlo, Monte
Carlo, 1932; revived with
décor by Eugene German
at City Center, New York,
1944.

BOURR Bourrée Fantasque,
classical ballet (3 parts).
Music, Emmanuel Chabrier;
choreography, George Bal-
anchine; costumes, Barbara
Karinska; lighting, Jean
Rosenthal. City Center,
New York, December 1,
1949.

BOUTI La Boutique Fantasque

(The Fantastic Toy-Shop),
ballet (1 act). Music, Gioac-
chino Rossini, arranged and
orchestrated by Ottorino
Respighi; choreography,
Leonide Massine; curtain,
scenery and costumes, André
Derain. Diaghilev Ballets
Russes, Alhambra Theatre,
London, June 5, 1919.

BRIGH The Bright Stream,
comedy ballet (3 acts). Music, Dmitri Shostakovich;
choreography and book, F. V.
Lopukhov; scenery, M. P.
Bobyshov. Maly Operny
Theatre, Leningrad, April
4, 1935.

BROKE Broken Date, ballet (3
acts). Music, Michel Magne;
choreography, John Taras
and Don Lurio; book, Fran-
çoise Sagan; décor, Bernard
Buffet; costumes, Franco
Laurenti. Monte Carlo
Opera House, Monte Carlo,
January 3, 1958.

BRONZ The Bronze Horseman,
ballet (4 acts). Music,
Reinhold Glière; choreography
and production, Rotislav Zakharov; book, Pyotr Abolimov,
after the poem by Alexander
Pushkin; scenery and cos-
tumes, Mikhail Bobyshov.
Kirov Theatre, Leningrad,
March 14, 1949.

CAFES Café Society, ballet (1
act). Music, Ferde Grofé;
choreography and book,
Catherine Littlefield; costumes, Carl Schaffer. Civic
Opera House, Chicago, No-
vember 13, 1938.

CAGEE The Cage, ballet (1
scene). Music, Igor Stravinsky ("Concerto Grosso in D
for Strings"); choreography

and book, Jerome Robbins;
costumes, Ruth Sobotka;
décor, Jean Rosenthal.
City Center, New York,
June 14, 1951.

CAINA   Cain and Abel, ballet.
Music, Richard Wagner
(from "Siegfried" and "Die
Götterdämmerung"); chore-
ography, David Lichine;
décor, Miguel Priero.
Palacio de Bellas Artes,
Mexico City, 1946.

CAKEW   Cakewalk, American
ballet (3 parts). Music,
Louis Moreau Gottschalk,
adapted and orchestrated
by Hershy Kay; chore-
ography, Ruthanna Boris;
scenery and costumes,
Robert Drew; lighting,
Jean Rosenthal. City Cen-
ter, New York, June 12,
1951.

CAMAR   Camargo, ballet (3
acts). Music, Leon Min-
kus; choreography, Marius
Petipa; book, Petipa and
Vernoy de Saint-Georges;
scenery, Roller; costumes,
Ponomarev. Maryinsky
Theatre, St. Petersburg,
December 17, 1872.

CAMIL   Camille, ballet. Music, Franz Schubert and
Vittorio Rieti; choreography,
John Taras; book, after
Alexandre Dumas, fils; décor, Cecil Beaton. Pala-
cio de Bellas Artes, Mexico City, 1946.

CANGA   Cangaceira (The Woman Bandit), ballet (1 act).
Music, Camargo Guarnieri;
choreography, Aurel Milloss;
idea and décor, Flavio de
Carvalho. Teatro Municipal,
Rio de Janeiro, Brazil, 1954.

CANTI   Canticle for Innocent
Comedians, modern dance
work. Music, Thomas Rib-
bink; choreography and cos-
tumes, Martha Graham; set,
Frederick Kiesler. Juilliard
Concert Hall, New York,
April 22, 1952.

CAPRD   Los Caprichos, ballet.
Music, traditional Spanish
airs; choreography, Ana
Nevada; décor, Antoni Clavé.
Théâtre des Champs-Élysées,
Paris, 1946.

CAPRH   Caprichos, ballet (4
episodes and epilogue, based
on Francisco Goya's com-
mentaries on his own series
of etchings of the same name).
Music, Béla Bartók ("Con-
trasts for Piano, Clarinet
and Violin"); choreography,
Herbert Ross; costumes,
Helene Pons. Hunter College
Playhouse, New York, January 29, 1950.

CAPRI   Capriccio Espagnole
(Capricio Español), ballet
(1 act). Music, Nicolai
Rimsky-Korsakov ("Capriccio
Espagnole"); choreography,
Leonide Massine in collabora-
tion with Mlle. Argentinita;
book, Massine; scenery and
costumes, Mariano Andreu.
Théâtre de Monte Carlo,
Monte Carlo, May 4, 1939.

CARDG   Card Game (Card Party)
(Jeu de Cartes) (Poker Game),
ballet (3 "deals"). Music,
Igor Stravinsky; choreography,
George Balanchine; book,
Stravinsky, in collaboration
with M. Malaieff; scenery
and costumes, Irene Sharaff;
Metropolitan Opera House,
New York, April 27, 1937.
Revised version with chore-
ography by Janine Charrat

and scenery and costumes by Pierre Roy produced at Théâtre des Champs Élysées, Paris, October 12, 1945.

CARME Carmen, dramatic ballet (5 scenes). Music, Georges Bizet; choreography, Roland Petit; book, Petit, after Henri Meilhac and Ludovic Halévy; scenery and costumes, Antoine Clavé. Prince's Theatre, London, February 21, 1949.

CARNA Le Carnaval, romantic ballet (1 act). Music, Robert Schumann; choreography, Michel Fokine; book, Fokine; scenery and costumes, Léon Bakst. Théâtre National de l'Opéra, Paris, June 4, 1910.

CARNI Carnival at Pest, ballet (1 act). Music, Franz Liszt; choreography, Ede Brada; book, Brada; scenery and costumes, Gusztáv Olah. Royal Hungarian Opera, Budapest, December 6, 1930.

CARNV Carnival of Animals, ballet. Music, Camille Saint-Saëns; choreography and décor, Andrée Howard. Mercury Theatre, London, March 26, 1943.

CARTE Carte Blanche, ballet (1 act). Music, John Addison; choreography, Walter Gor'; décor, Kenneth Rowell. Empire Theatre, Edinburgh, September 10, 1953.

CASAN Casanova, ballet. Music, Rosenberg; choreography, Julian Algo; décor, Jon-And. Stockholm,

1937.

CASSA Cassandre, ballet. Verses, Bensserade. Paris, 1651.

CASTO Castor et Pollux, ballet. Music, Jean Philippe Rameau; choreography, Gaetan Vestris. L'Académie Royale de Danse, Paris, 1772. A ballet with the same title was staged at the Oxford University Opera Club in 1934, with choreography by Antony Tudor.

CASTR Castor and Pollux, ballet. Music, Jean Philippe Rameau; choreography, Nicola Guerra; décor, Drésa. Paris Opéra, Paris, March 21, 1918.

CATAR Catarina ou la Fille du Bandit, ballet (3 acts). Music, Cesare Pugni; choreography and book, Jules Perrot; scenery, Charles Marshall. Her Majesty's Theatre, London, March 3, 1846.

CAVEO Cave of the Heart (originally Serpent's Heart), modern dance work. Music, Samuel Barber; choreography, Martha Graham; décor, Isamu Noguchi; costumes, Edythe Gilford. Ziegfeld Theater, New York, February 27, 1947. Produced as Serpent's Heart at McMillin Theater, New York, May 10, 1946.

CESAR Cesare in Egitto, ballet. Music, unknown; choreography, Gaetano Gioja. La Scala, Milan, 1815.

CHAOK Chao-Kang, ballet. Music, unknown; choreography, Louis X. S. Henri. Théâtre

Nautique, Paris, 1834?.

CHASE The Chase, ballet.
Music, Wolfgang Amadeus
Mozart (Horn Concerto No.
3); choreography, Jacques
d'Amboise; décor, David
Hays; costumes, Barbara
Karinska. City Center,
New York, September 18,
1963.

CHATT La Chatte, ballet (1
act). Music, Henri Sauguet;
choreography, George Bal-
anchine; book, Sobeka (Boris Kochno); scenery and
costumes, Naum Gabo and
Antoine Pevsner. Théâ-
tre de Monte Carlo, Monte
Carlo, April 30, 1927.

CHECK Checkmate, dramatic
or allegorical ballet (pro-
logue, 1 scene). Music,
Arthur Bliss; choreography,
Ninette de Valois; book,
Bliss; scenery and costumes,
E. McKnight Kauffer. Théâ-
tre des Champs-Élysées,
Paris, June 15, 1937.

CHEVA Le Chevalier et la
Damoiselle, ballet (2 acts).
Music, Philippe Gaubert;
choreography and book,
Serge Lifar; scenery and
costumes, A. M. Cassandre.
Théâtre National de l'Opéra,
Paris, July 2, 1941.

CHINE Chinese Nightingale,
ballet (4 scenes). Music,
Werner Egk; choreography,
Tatiana Gsovska; book, Egk,
based on the story by Hans
Christian Andersen; décor,
Helmut Jürgens; costumes,
Rosemarie Jakameit.
Deutsches Museum, Munich,
May 7, 1953.

CHOTA Chota Roustaveli,

Georgian choreographic epic
(4 acts). Music, Arthur
Honegger, Alexander Tcherepnine and Tibor Harsanyi,
after rhymes devised by
Serge Lifar; choreography,
Lifar; book, Lifar and Nico-
las Evreinov, after the poem
"A Hero in a Leopard's
Skin" by Chota Roustaveli;
curtain, settings and costumes
by Prince A. Schervachidze
and C. Nepokoichitsky. Théâtre de Monte Carlo, Monte
Carlo, May 5, 1946.

CHOUT Chout, comic ballet (6
scenes). Music, Sergei
Prokofiev; choreography and
scenario, Tadeo Slavinsky
and Michel Larionov; settings
and costumes, Larionov.
Théâtre de la Gaîté-Lyrique,
Paris, May, 1921.

CHRIS Christmas Eve, ballet (3
acts). Music, B.V. Asafiev;
choreography, V. A. Varkovit-
sky; book, U. E. Slonimsky,
after the story by Nicholas
Gogol; scenery and costumes,
A. A. Kolomoytsev; production,
E. N. Ivanov. Maly Theatre,
Leningrad, June 15, 1938.

CHRON Chronica, dance drama
(prelude, 3 acts). Music,
Bertholde Goldschmidt;
choreography and book, Kurt
Jooss; costumes, Dmitri
Bouchêne. Arts Theatre,
Cambridge, February 14,
1939.

CHURC The Church Festival at
Delft (Die Kirmes von Delft),
ballet (3 scenes). Music,
Hermann Reutter; chore-
ography and book, Sonia
Korty; décor, Ludwig Sievert.
Baden Baden, Germany,
March 20, 1937.

CINDA Cinderella, fairy ballet
    (5 scenes). Music, Sidney
    Jones; choreography, Fred
    Farren and Alexander Genee;
    book, C. Wilhelm, after
    Perrault's fairy tale; cos-
    tumes, Wilhelm; scenery,
    Hawes Craven, Joseph
    Harker, E. Banks and H.
    Brooks. Empire Theatre,
    London, January 6, 1906.

CINDE Cinderella, ballet (3
    acts). Music, Serge Proko-
    fiev; choreography, Fred-
    erick Ashton; book, M. D.
    Volkov, after Perrault's
    fairy tale, adapted by Ash-
    ton; scenery and costumes,
    Jean-Denis Maclès. Royal
    Opera House, Covent Gar-
    den, London, December
    23, 1948.

CINDL Cinderella, fantastic
    ballet (3 acts). Music,
    Baron B. Fitinghof-Schell;
    choreography, Marius
    Petipa, E. Cecchetti and
    L. I. Ivanov; book, Lydia
    Pashkova, after Perrault's
    fairy tale; scenery, G.
    Levogt, M. Shiskov and
    M. Botcharov. Maryinsky
    Theatre, St. Petersburgh,
    December 1, 1893.

CINDR Cinderella (Cendrillon),
    ballet (3 parts). Music,
    Frederic d'Erlanger; chore-
    ography, Michel Fokine;
    book, Fokine, after Per-
    rault's fairy tale; scenery
    and costumes, Nathalie
    Gontcharova. Royal Opera
    House, Covent Garden,
    London, 1938.

CIRCE Circe, modern dance
    work (1 act). Music, Alan
    Hovhaness; choreography,
    Martha Graham; décor, Isa-
    mu Noguchi. Prince of

Wales Theatre, London,
    September 8, 1963.

CLEOP Cléopâtre, ballet (1 act).
    Music, Anton Arensky, with
    additional numbers by S.
    Taneyev, Rimsky-Korsakov,
    Glinka and Glazunov; chore-
    ography and book, Michel
    Fokine; scenery and costumes,
    Léon Bakst. Presented under
    the title Une Nuit d'Égypte,
    Maryinsky Theatre, St.
    Petersburg, March 21, 1908;
    with minor changes under ti-
    tle Cléopâtre, Théâtre du
    Châtelet, Paris, June 2,
    1909.

CLEOR Cleopatra, ballet. Mu-
    sic, ?; choreography, Katti
    Lanner. Empire Theater,
    London, 1897.

CLYTE Clytemnestra, modern
    dance work, based on the
    tragedy by Aeschylus (3 acts).
    Music, Halim El-Dabh;
    choreography and costumes,
    Martha Graham; décor, Isa-
    mu Noguchi. Adelphi Thea-
    tre, London, April 1, 1958.

COAST Coast of Hope, ballet
    (3 acts). Music, Andrei
    Petrov; choreography, Igor
    Belsky; book, Yuri Slonimsky;
    décor, Valery Dorrer.
    Kirov Theatre, Leningrad,
    June 16, 1959.

COBRA The Cobras, ballet. Mu-
    sic, ?; choreography, Ruth
    St. Denis. Hudson Theater,
    New York, March 22, 1906.

COMUS Comus, ballet (2 scenes).
    Music, various theatrical
    works by Henry Purcell, se-
    lected and arranged by Con-
    stant Lambert; choreography,
    Robert Helpmann, after the
    masque by John Milton; dé-

cor, Oliver Messel. New
Theatre, London, January
14, 1942.

CONAM Con Amore, classic
ballet (3 scenes). Music,
Gioacchino Rossini; choreography, Lew Christensen;
libretto, James Graham-
Luhan; scenery and cos-
tumes, James Bodrero.
War Memorial Opera House,
San Francisco, March 10,
1953.

CONCB Concerto Brasileiro,
ballet (3 movements). Mu-
sic, Heckel Tavares's
"Concerto Brasileiro";
choreography, Maryla
Gremo; book, Accioly Net-
to; décor, Fernando Pamp-
lona; costumes, Nelly La-
port. Teatro Municipal,
Rio de Janeiro, Brazil,
1960.

CONCU La Concurrence, ballet
(1 act). Music, Georges
Auric; choreography, George
Balanchine; book, décor and
costumes, André Derain.
Monte Carlo, April 12,
1932.

CONFL Conflicts, ballet (1
act). Music, Ernest Bloch
(Quintet for Piano and
Strings); choreography,
Norman Morrice; realiza-
tion, Ralph Koltai. Sad-
ler's Wells Theatre, Lon-
don, July 23, 1962.

CONTE Contes Russes, ballet
(1 act). Music, Anatole
Liadov; choreography,
Leonide Massine; scenery
and costumes, Michael
Larionov. Théâtre du
Châtelet, Paris, May 11,
1917.

COPPE Coppélia ou la Fille aux
Yeux d'Émail (Coppelia, or
The Girl with Enamel Eyes),
ballet (3 acts). Music, Léo
Delibes; choreography, Arthur Saint-Léon; book, Saint-
Léon and Charles Nuitter
after a story by E. T. A. Hoffmann; scenery, Cambon, Desplêchin, and Lavastre; costumes, Paul Lormier.
Théâtre Impérial de l'Opéra,
Paris, May 25, 1870.

COPPI Coppélia, ballet. Music,
Léo Delibes; choreography,
William Christensen, after
Arthur Saint-Léon; décor,
Charlotte Rider. San Fran-
cisco, Calif., 1939.

COQDO Le Coq d'Or, ballet
(prologue, 3, epilogue).
Music, Rimsky-Korsakoff,
based on the Rimsky-Korsakoff opera with libretto by
Byelsky, suggested by a
poem by Pushkin; choreo-
graphy, Michel Fokine; scenery and costumes, Nathalie
Gontcharova. Ballet Russe
de Monte Carlo, Metropolitan
Opera House, New York,
October 23, 1937. Earlier
productions include opera-
pantomime by Diaghileff,
Paris Opéra, Paris, May 21,
1914 and one by Adolph
Bolm, Metropolitan Opera
House, New York, March 6,
1918.

CORAL Coralia, or The Incon-
stant Knight, ballet (5 scenes).
Music, Cesare Pugni; choreography and book, Paul Taglioni; scenery, Charles
Marshall; costumes, Miss
Bradley and Mr. Whales.
Her Majesty's Theatre, London, February 16, 1847.

CORSA Le Corsaire, panto-
mimic ballet (3 acts). Music, Adolphe Adam; chore-
ography, Joseph Mazilier;
book, Mazilier and H. V.
de Saint-Georges; scenery,
Desplêchin, Cambon, Thierry and Martin; machinery,
Sacrê. Thêâtre Impêrial
de l'Opêra, Paris, January
23, 1856.

CORSI Le Corsaire, ballet.
Music, Bochsa; chore-
ography, Albert; book,
based on Byron's poem.
King's Theatre, London,
June 29, 1837.

CREAI La Crêation, chore-
ographic essay (1 scene).
Music, none; choreography
and book, David Lichine.
Prince's Theatre, London,
September 26, 1948.

CREAT La Crêation du Monde,
ballet (1 act). Music,
Darius Milhaud; chore-
ography, Jean Börlin; book,
Blaise Cendrars; scenery,
curtain and costumes, Fernand Lêger. Thêâtre des
Champs-Élysêes, Paris,
October 25, 1923.

CREAU The Creatures of
Prometheus, ballet (2 acts).
Music, Ludwig van Bee-
thoven; choreography, Salva-
tore Viganò. Imperial
Court Theatre, Vienna,
March 28, 1801.

CREAV Les Crêatures de
Promêthêe, ballet. Music,
Ludwig van Beethoven;
choreography, Serge Lifar;
dêcor, Quelvêe. Paris
Opêra, Paris, December
30, 1929.

CREAW The Creation of the
World, ballet. Music, Dar-
ius Milhaud; choreography,
Todd Bolender; dêcor, David
Hays. City Center, New
York, December 7, 1960.

CROQU La Croqueuse de Dia-
mants (The Diamond Crunch-
er), dramatic ballet (ballet-
review) (4 scenes). Music,
Jean-Michel Damase; chore-
ography and songs, Roland
Petit; book, Petit and Alfred
Adam; lyrics, Raymond
Queneau; scenery and cos-
tumes, Georges Wakhevitch.
Thêâtre Marigny, Paris,
September 25, 1950.

CUADR Cuadro Flamenco, Spanish gypsy dance scene. Music, arranged by Louis
Horst from native MSS;
choreography, Ted Shawn;
costumes designed by Ruth
St. Denis and Ted Shawn,
executed by Pearl Wheeler.
New York, 1915/16.

CUPID Cupid and Psyche, ballet.
Music, Lord Berners; choreography, Frederick Ashton;
dêcor, Sir Francis Rose.
Sadler's Wells Theatre, London, 1939.

CUPIO Cupid Out of His Humor,
17th century ballet. Music,
Henry Purcell; choreography,
Mary Skeaping; dêcor, from
old Swedish ballet designs.
Drottningholm Palace Theatre,
Stockholm, June 14, 1956.

CURLE Curley's Wife, modern
dance work. Music, Marc
Blitzstein; choreography,
Linda Margolies (Linda
Hodes), based on John Stein-
beck's novel, "Of Mice and
Men. " YM-YWHA, New York,
December 9, 1951.

CYDAL Cydalise et le Chèvre-pied (Cydalise and the Faun), ballet (2 acts). Music, Gabriel Pierné; choreography, Léo Staats; book, G. A. de Caillavet and Robert de Flers. Théâtre de l'Opéra, Paris, January 15, 1923.

CYRAN Cyrano de Bergerac, ballet (3 acts). Music, Marius Constant; choreography, Roland Petit, after the play by Edmond Rostand; décor, Basarte; costumes, Yves Saint-Laurent. Alhambra Theatre, Paris, April 17, 1959.

DAITA Daïta, ballet (1 act). Music, G. E. Konius; choreography, Joseph Mendes; book, K. F. Valts. Bolshoy Theatre, Moscow, April 28, 1896.

DANCE The Dance Dream, ballet (7 scenes). Music, Brahms, Glazunov, Tchaikovsky, Luigini and Rubinstein; choreography, Alexander Gorsky; book, Gorsky; scenery, Amable and E. H. Ryan. Alhambra Theatre, London, May 29, 1911.

DANCT Dancing Tragedy, ballet (1 act). Music, Richard Strauss (ballet music from the opera "Salomé"); choreography, Dennis Gray; book, Tiago de Melo; décor, Mario Conde. São Paulo, Brazil, 1957.

DANIN Danina, or Joko the Brazilian Ape (Joko), "grand pantomimic ballet" (4 acts). Music, Peter Joseph von Lindpainter; choreography, Filippo Taglioni, based on an 1825 French melodrama. Stuttgart, Germany, March 12, 1826.

DANSE Danses Concertantes, classic ballet (5 parts). Music, Igor Stravinsky; choreography, George Balanchine; scenery and costumes, Eugène Berman. Ballet Russe de Monte Carlo, City Center, New York, September 10, 1944.

DANTE Dante Sonata, dramatic ballet (1 act). Music, Franz Liszt, orchestrated by Constant Lambert; choreography, Frederick Ashton, based on Dante's "Divine Comedy" as considered by Victor Hugo in his poem "After a Reading of Dante"; scenery and costumes, Sophie Fedorovitch, after John Flaxman. Sadler's Wells Theatre, London, January 23, 1940.

DAPHC Daphnis and Chloë ballet. Music, Maurice Ravel; choreography, Catherine Littlefield, after Michel Fokine; décor, A. Jarin. Philadelphia, Pa., 1936.

DAPHI Daphnis and Chloë, ballet. Music, Maurice Ravel; choreography, Serge Lifar. Paris Opéra, Paris, 1948.

DAPHN Daphnis et Chloë (Daphnis and Chloë), dramatic ballet (1 act and 3 scenes). Music, Maurice Ravel; choreography, Michel Fokine; book, Fokine; scenery and costumes, Léon Bakst. Théâtre du Châtelet, Paris, June 8, 1912.

DAPHS Daphnis and Chloë, ballet. Music, Maurice Ravel; chore-

ography, Frederick Ashton;
décor, John Craxton. Roy-
al Opera House, Covent
Garden, London, April 5,
1951.

DARKE Dark Elegies, dance
of lamentation (cycle of 5
songs). Music, Gustav
Mahler (Kindertotenlieder,
or Songs on the Death of
Children); lyrics selected
by Mahler from a series
of poems by Friedrich
Rückert; choreography,
Antony Tudor; scenery and
costumes, Nadia Benois.
Duchess Theatre, London,
February 19, 1937.

DARKL The Darkling, ballet
(1 act). Music, Benjamin
Britten (Variations on a
Theme by Frank Bridge);
choreography, Brian Mac-
donald; décor, Peter Sym-
cox. Playhouse Theatre,
Winnipeg, October 17, 1958.

DARKM Dark Meadow, group
dance. Music, Carlos
Chavez; choreography, Martha Graham; décor, Isamu
Noguchi; costumes, Edythe
Gilfond. Plymouth Thea-
ter, New York, January
23, 1946.

DAVID David, (6 episodes).
Music, Maurice Jacobson;
choreography, Keith Lester;
book, Poppaea Vanda;
scenery and costumes,
Bernard Meninsky; curtain,
Jacob Epstein. Theatre
Royal, Newcastle-on-Tyne,
November 11, 1935.

DAVIT David Triomphant,
ballet (2 acts). Music,
Debussy and Mussorgsky,
with rhythms by Serge
Lifar, orchestrated by

Vittorio Rieti; choreography
and book, Lifar; scenery
and costumes, Fernand Lé-
ger. Gala d'Inauguration du
Théâtre de la Maison Inter-
nationale des Étudiants,
Paris, December 15, 1936.

DAYIN A Day in a Southern Port,
ballet. Music, Constant
Lambert; choreography,
Frederick Ashton; décor,
Edvard Burra. Sadler's
Wells Theatre, London,
1931. Later revised as
Rio Grande, 1935.

DAYON Day on Earth, modern
dance work. Music, Aaron
Copland (Piano Sonata);
choreography, Doris Humphrey;
costumes, Pauline Lawrence.
City Center, New York, December 21, 1947.

DEATB Death of a Bird, ballet
(1 act). Music, Heitor Villa-
Lobos (Bachiana No. 8);
choreography, Ismael Guiser;
book, Vinicius de Morais;
décor, Emiliano Di Caval-
canti. Teatro Municipal,
Rio de Janeiro, Brazil,
1960.

DEATH Death and the Maiden,
ballet (1 act). Music, Franz
Schubert; choreography and
costumes, Andrée Howard.
Duchess Theatre, London,
February 23, 1937.

DEATS Deaths and Entrances,
modern dance work. Music,
Hunter Johnson; choreography,
Martha Graham; décor, Arch
Lauterer; costumes, Edythe
Gilfond. Bennington College,
Vermont, July 18, 1943.

DEBUT The Débutante, ballet
divertissement (3 scenes).
Music, Cuthbert Clarke and

G. J. M. Glaser; chore-
ography, Fred Farren;
book, scenery and costumes,
C. Wilhelm. Empire Thea-
tre, London, November 14,
1906.

DEFEN Defense of Paradise,
ballet presented by Catherine de' Medici on August
18, 1572.

DEMOI Les Demoiselles de la
Nuit (The Ladies of Mid-
night), dramatic ballet (3
scenes). Music, Jean
Françaix; choreography,
Roland Petit; book, Jean
Anouilh; scenery and cos-
tumes, Léonor Fini. Théâ-
tre Marigny, Paris, May
22, 1948.

DESCE The Descent of Hebe,
ballet (1 act). Music,
Ernest Bloch; choreography
and book, Antony Tudor;
scenery and costumes,
Nadia Benois. Mercury
Theatre, London, April 7,
1935.

DEUIL Deuil en 24 Heures,
(5 scenes). Music, Mau-
rice Thiriet, with his own
arrangements of "Valse
Bleue" and the "Mattchiche";
choreography and book, Roland Petit; scenery and costumes, Antoni Clavé. Théâtre de l'Empire, Paris,
March 17, 1953.

DEUXC Les Deux Créoles,
ballet pantomime (3 acts).
Music, Darondeau; chore-
ography and book, Jean
Aumer. Théâtre de la
Porte Saint-Martin, Paris,
June 28, 1806.

DEUXN Les Deux Pigéons (The
Two Pigeons), ballet (2 acts).

Music, André Messager;
choreography, Frederick
Ashton; décor, Jacques Du-
pont. Royal Opera House,
Covent Garden, London,
February 14, 1961.

DEUXP Les Deux Pigéons (The
Two Pigeons), ballet (3 acts).
Music, André Messager;
choreography, Louis Mérante;
book, Mérante and Henry
Régnier; scenery, Auguste
Rubé, Chaperon and J. B.
Lavastre; costumes, Bian-
chini. Théâtre de l'Opéra,
Paris, October 18, 1886.

DEVIL Devil's Holiday (Le
Diable S' Amuse), ballet
(prologue, 3 scenes, 2 entr'
actes). Music, Vincenzo
Tommasini on themes by
Paganini; choreography,
Frederick Ashton; book,
Tommassini; scenery and
costumes, Eugène Berman.
Metropolitan Opera House,
New York, October 26, 1939.

DEVIV The Devil in the Village,
(3 acts). Music, Fran
Lhotka; choreography, book
and costumes, Pia and Pino
Mlakar; scenery, Roman
Clemens, Stadt-theater,
Zurich, February 18, 1935.

DIABE Le Diable Amoureux,
pantomimic ballet (3 acts).
Music, Benoist and Réber;
choreography, Joseph Mazilier; book, Mazilier and H.
Vernoy de Saint-Georges,
based on a story by Cazotte;
scenery, Philastre and Cambon; costumes, Paul Lormier.
Théâtre de l'Académie Royale
de Musique, Paris, September
23, 1840.

DIABL Le Diable Boiteux (The
Devil on Two Sticks), panto-

265   DIABQ

mimic ballet (3 acts). Music, Casimir Gide; chore-
ography, Jean Coralli;
book, Coralli and Burat de
Gurgy; scenery, Feuchères,
Séchan, J. Dièterle, Philastre and Cambon. Théâtre
de l'Académie Royale de
Musique, Paris, June 1,
1836.

DIABQ Le Diable à Quatre
(The Devil to Pay), pantomimic ballet (2 acts). Music, Adolphe Adam; chore-
ography, Joseph Mazilier;
book, Mazilier and De Leuven, based on C. Coffey's
ballad farce, "The Devil to
Pay; or, The Wives Metam-
orphosed"; scenery, Cicèri,
Desplèchin, Séchan and Dièterle; costumes, Paul Lormier. Théâtre de l'Aca-
démie Royale de Musique,
Paris, August 11, 1845.

DIAVO Diavolina, pantomimic
ballet (1 act). Music,
Cesare Pugni; choreography,
Arthur Saint-Léon; book,
Saint-Léon; scenery, Cam-
bon and Thierry. Théâtre
de l'Opéra, Paris, July 6,
1863.

DIDOO Dido, ballet. Music,
unknown; choreography,
Vincenzo Galeotti. Danish
Royal Theatre, Copenhagen,
1775.

DIEUE Le Dieu et la Bayadère,
opera ballet (2 acts). Music, François Aubert;
choreography, Philippe
Taglioni; book, Eugène
Scribe. Théâtre de l'
Académie Royale de Mu-
sique, Paris, October 13,
1830.

DIMLU Dim Lustre, ballet.

Music, Richard Strauss
(Burlesca); choreography,
Antony Tudor; costumes and
scenery, Motley. Ballet
Theatre, Metropolitan Opera
House, New York, October
20, 1943.

DIONY Dionysus, ballet. Music,
Alexander Glazounov; choreography, Mikhail Mordkin;
décor, Sergei Soudeikine.
New York, 1938.

DONAI Doña Ines de Castro,
ballet (5 scenes). Music,
Joaquin Serra; choreography
and book, Ana Ricarda; setting and costumes, Celia
Hubbard. Théâtre Municipal,
Cannes, March 1, 1952.

DONAL Donald of the Burthens,
dramatic ballet (2 scenes).
Music, Ian Whyte; chore-
ography, Leonide Massine;
book, Massine, after a Scotch
legend; scenery and costumes,
Robert Colquhoun and Robert
MacBryde. Royal Opera
House, Covent Garden, London,
December 12, 1951.

DONJA Don Juan, ballet (1 act).
Music, Richard Strauss;
choreography, Frederick
Ashton, based on Théophile
Gautier's poem "La Morte
Amoureuse" ("The Love That
Caught Strange Light from
Death's Own Eyes"); décor,
Edward Burra. Royal Opera
House, Covent Garden Lon-
don, November 25, 1948.

DONJN Don Juan, ballet. Music,
Christoph Willibald Gluck;
choreography, Eric Allantin
and Michel Fokine; décor,
Mariano Andreù. Alhambra
Theatre, London, June 25,
1936.

DONJU Don Juan, ballet d'ac-
    tion (1 act). Music, Chris-
    tophe Willibald Gluck, writ-
    ten for ballet with a plot
    based on Molière's play,
    "Don Juan, ou le Festin de
    Pierre. " Choreography,
    Gaspare Angiolini. Burg-
    theater, Vienna, 1761. Re-
    done in a new version by
    Eric Allatini and Michel
    Fokine; staging and chore-
    ography, Fokine; curtain,
    scenery and costumes,
    Mariano Andreù. Alhambra
    Theatre, London, June 25,
    1936.

DONQI Don Quixote, ballet (3
    acts, 7 scenes). Music,
    Leon Minkus; choreography,
    Alexander Gorsky, revived
    by Rostislav Zakharov,
    with new mise-en-scène and
    dances; décor, Vadim Ryn-
    din. Bolshoi Theatre,
    Moscow, February 10, 1940.

DONQO Don Quixote, ballet (3
    acts, 5 scenes). Music,
    Nicolas Nabokov; chore-
    ography, George Balan-
    chine; décor and costumes,
    Esteban Francés; costumes
    executed by Barbara Karin-
    ska. New York State Thea-
    ter, New York, May 28,
    1965.

DONQT Don Quixote, ballet.
    Music, Leon Minkus;
    choreography, George Gé
    (Grönfeldt); décor, Nurmi-
    maa; costumes, Platonoff.
    Helsinki, Finland, March
    6, 1958.

DONQU Don Quichotte, ballet
    (4 acts). Music, Leon
    Minkus; choreography,
    Marius Petipa; book,
    Petipa, after the novel
    by Cervantes. Bolshoy

Theatre, Moscow, December
    14, 1869.

DONQV Don Quichotte, ballet.
    Music, Leon Minkus; chore-
    ography, Aurel Milloss.
    Ballet de Champs-Élysées,
    Paris, 1947.

DONQX Don Quixote, ballet (5
    scenes). Music, Roberto
    Gerhard; choreography,
    Ninette de Valois; book, de
    Valois, after the novel by
    Cervantes; scenery and cos-
    tumes, Edward Burra. Roy-
    al Opera House, Covent
    Garden, London, February
    20, 1950.

DOUAI La Douairière de Bille-
    bahaut, "grotesque and fan-
    tastic ballet" given in the
    time of Louis XIII (1626).

DREAM The Dream, ballet (1
    act). Music, Felix Mendel-
    ssohn (overture and incidental
    music for "A Midsummer
    Night's Dream, " arranged by
    John Lanchbery); choreography,
    Frederick Ashton; scenery,
    Henry Bardon; costumes,
    David Walker. Royal Opera
    House, Covent Garden, Lon-
    don, April 2, 1964.

DRYAD The Dryad, pastoral
    fantasy (2 scenes). Music,
    Dora Bright; choreography,
    Alexander Genee; book,
    Bright. Empire Theatre,
    London, September 7, 1908.

DUELL The Duel (The Combat)
    (Le Combat), ballet (1 act).
    Music, Rafaello de Banfield;
    choreography, William Dollar;
    décor, Lauré. Théâtre
    Marigny, Paris, as Le Com-
    bat, June 28, 1949; exten-
    sively revised and presented
    as The Duel, costumes,

Robert Stevenson; lighting, Jean Rosenthal, at City Center, New York, February 24, 1950. Again revised, with décor by Georges Wakhevitch, and presented as The Combat, Royal Opera House, London, 1953.

DUKEO   The Duke of Sacramento or Hobo of the Hills, ballet. Music, Norman Dello Joio; choreography, Eugene Loring; décor, George Bockman. New Hope, Pennsylvania, 1942.

DYING   The Dying Swan (Le Cygne), solo dance. Music, Camille Saint-Saëns; choreography, Michel Fokine; costume, Léon Bakst. First danced by Anna Pavlova, Hall of Noblemen, St. Petersburg, 1905.

EATER   Eaters of Darkness, ballet (1 act). Music, Benjamin Britten (Variations on a Theme of Frank Bridge); choreography and book, Walter Gore; décor, Hein Heckroth. Frankfurt State Opera Ballet, January 29, 1958 (as Die Im Schatten Leben).

ECHOE   Echoes of Trumpets, ballet (1 act). Music, Bohuslav Martinu (Fantaisies Symphoniques); choreography and book, Antony Tudor; décor, Birger Bergling. Royal Theatre, Stockholm, September 20, 1963.

EGYPT   Egypta, ballet. Music, ?; choreography, Ruth St. Denis. New York, 1909.

EIGHT   8 Clear Places, modern dance work. Music, Lucia Dlugoszewski; choreography, Erick Hawkins; designs, Ralph Dorazio. Hunter College Playhouse, New York, October 8, 1960.

ELECT   Electra ou la Pléiade Perdue, ballet (5 scenes). Choreography, Paul Taglioni; book, Taglioni; scenery, Charles Marshall. Her Majesty's Theatre, London, April 19, 1849.

ELEKT   Elektra, ballet (1 act). Music, Malcolm Arnold; choreography, Robert Helpmann; book, after the tragedies of Aeschylus, Sophocles and Euripides; décor, Arthur Boyd. Royal Opera House, Covent Garden, London, March 26, 1963.

ELEME   Les Éléments, divertissement (1 act). Music, Bajetti; choreography, Jules Perrot; book, Perrot. Her Majesty's Theatre, London, June 26, 1847.

ELFES   Les Elfes, fantastic ballet (3 acts). Music, Count Gabrielli; choreography, Joseph Mazilier; book, Mazilier and V. de Saint-Georges; scenery, Despléchin, Nolau, Rubé, Thierry and Martin. Théâtre Impérial de l'Opéra, Paris, August 11, 1856.

EMBAT   Embattled Garden, modern dance work. Music, Carlos Surinach; choreography, Martha Graham; scenery, Isamu Noguchi. Adelphi Theater, New York, April 3, 1958.

EMPER   Emperor Jones, modern

dance work. Music, Heitor
Villa-Lobos; choreography,
José Limón, after the play
by Eugene O'Neill; décor,
Kim Swados; costumes,
Pauline Lawrence. Empire
State Music Festival, El-
lenville, N. Y. , July 12,
1956.

ENDYM Endymion, ballet.
Music, Leguerney; chore-
ography, Serge Lifar; dé-
cor, Dmitri Bouchène.
Paris Opéra, Paris, 1949.

ENIGM Enigma Variations, ab-
stract ballet (1 act). Music, Sir Edward Elgar
("Variations on an Original
Theme for Orchestra");
choreography, Frank Staff;
scenery and costumes,
Guy Sheppard. Arts Thea-
tre, Cambridge, England,
November 26, 1940.

ENTRE Entre Deux Rondes,
ballet. Music, Samuel
Rousseau; choreography,
Serge Lifar; décor, Lan-
dowski, after Edgar Dégas.
Paris Opéra, Paris, April
24, 1940.

EOLIN Eoline ou la Dryade,
ballet (6 scenes). Music,
Cesare Pugni; choreography,
Jules Perrot; book, Perrot.
Her Majesty's Theatre,
London, March 8, 1845.

EPISO Episodes, ballet (2
unrelated parts). Music,
Anton Webern (from his
orchestral works); chore-
ography, Martha Graham
and George Balanchine;
décor and lighting, David
Hayes; costumes, Barbara
Karinska. City Center,
New York, May 14, 1959.

EPREU L'Épreuve d'Amour
(Chung-Yang and the Man-
darin) (The Proof of Love),
ballet (1 act). Music, Mozart; choreography, Michel
Fokine; book, Fokine and
André Derain; scenery and
costumes, Derain. Théâtre
de Monte Carlo, Monte Carlo,
April 4, 1936.

ERRAT Errand into the Maze,
duet. Music, Gian-Carlo
Menotti; choreography, Mar-
tha Graham; costumes,
Edythe Gilfond; décor, Isamu
Noguchi. Ziegfeld Theater,
New York, February 28,
1947.

ESMER La Esmeralda, ballet
(3 acts). Music, Cesare
Pugni; choreography, Jules
Perrot; book, based on Vic-
tor Hugo's "Hunchback of
Notre Dame"; scenery, W.
Grieve; costumes, Mme.
Copère; machinery, D. Slo-
man. Her Majesty's Thea-
tre, London, March 9, 1844.

ESTAN Estancia, ballet (1 act).
Music, Alberto Ginastera;
choreography, Michel Borov-
ski; décor, Dante Ortolani.
Teatro Colón, Buenos Aires,
Argentina, August 19, 1952.

ETERT Eternal Triangle, ballet
(1 act). Music, George Ribal-
owski; choreography and book,
Dennis Gray, inspired by the
Ninth Commandment; décor,
Fernando Pamplona; costumes,
Tomás Santa Rosa. Teatro
Municipal, Rio de Janeiro,
Brazil, 1955.

EVERY Every Soul Is a Circus,
modern dance work. Music,
Paul Nordoff; choreography,
Martha Graham; décor,

Philip Stapp; costumes, Edythe Gilfond. St. James Theater, New York, December 27, 1939.

EXCEL Excelsior, ballet (6 parts). Music, Romualdo Marenco; choreography, Luigi Manzotti; book, Manzotti; scenery and costumes, Alfredo Edel. Teatro alla Scala, Milan, January 11, 1881.

FACAD Façade, ballet (1 act). Music, William Walton; choreography, Frederick Ashton, based on poems by Edith Sitwell; scenery and costumes, John Armstrong. Cambridge Theatre, London, April 26, 1931.

FACSI Facsimile, "choreographic observation" (1 scene). Music, Leonard Bernstein; choreography, Jerome Robbins; scenery, Oliver Smith; costumes, Irene Sharaff. Broadway Theater, New York, October 24, 1946.

FADET Fadetta, ballet (3 acts). Music, Léo Delibes (from his ballet "Sylvia"); choreography, Leonid Lavronsky, based on a chapter of George Sand's novel "La Petite Fadette." Leningrad, 1934.

FAIRA The Fair at Sorochinsk, ballet (4 scenes). Music, Modest Moussorgsky, adapted by Antal Dorati; choreography, David Lichine; book, Lichine, based on stories by Nicholas Gogol; scenery and costumes, Nicolai Remisoff. Metropolitan Opera House, New York, October 14, 1943.

FAIRY The Fairy-Tale of the Priest and His Workman Balda, ballet (4 acts). Music, M. I. Chulaki; choreography, V. A. Varkovitski; book, U. O. Slonimsky, after the fairy tale by Alexander Pushkin; scenery and costumes, A. A. Kolomoitzev. Maly Theatre of Opera and Ballet, Leningrad, November 9, 1940.

FALLR Fall River Legend, American ballet (prologue, 8 scenes). Music, Morton Gould; choreography, Agnes DeMille, based on the true story of Lizzie Borden; scenery, Oliver Smith; costumes, Miles White. Metropolitan Opera House, New York, April 22, 1948.

FALLS Falls the Shadow Between (Persephone), modern dance work. Music, Meyer Kupferman; choreography and costumes, Pearl Lang. Hunter College Playhouse, New York, February 17, 1957.

FALSE The False Bridegroom, ballet (3 acts). Music, M. I. Chulak; choreography, B. A. Fenster; book, after the play by Carlo Goldoni; scenery and costumes, T. G. Brouni. Maly Theatre, Leningrad, March 23, 1946.

FANCI Fanciulla delle Rose, ballet (1 act). Music, Anton Arensky (Variations on a Theme of Tchaikovsky); choreography, Frank Staff; décor, Guy Sheppard. Scala Theatre, London, July 10, 1948.

FANCY Fancy Free, ballet (1 act). Music, Leonard Bernstein; choreography and

book, Jerome Robbins;
scenery, Oliver Smith; costumes, Kermit Love. Met-
ropolitan Opera House, New
York, April 18, 1944.

FANFA Fanfare, classic ballet
(1 act). Music, Benjamin
Britten ("Young Person's
Guide to the Orchestra")
(variations and a fugue on
a theme by Henry Purcell);
choreography, Jerome Rob-
bins; scenery and costumes,
Irene Sharaff; lighting, Jean
Rosenthal. City Center,
New York, June 2, 1953.

FANTA Fantasy, ballet (1 act).
Music, Franz Schubert
(Fantasy Piano Duet, Opus
103), orchestrated by Felix
Mottl; choreography, John
Taras; no décor or cos-
tume credit listed in pro-
gram. City Center, New
York, September 24, 1963.

FARFR Far From Denmark, or
a Costume Ball on Board
Ship (Fjernt Fra Danmark
eller Et Costumebal Onbord),
vaudeville ballet (2 acts).
Music, Hans Christian
Lumbye and Joseph Glaeser;
choreography, August Bournonville. Copenhagen, 1860.

FATES Fate's Revenge, or
Rebellion in the Upper
Rooms, ballet. Music,
Peter Tranchell; choreogra-
phy, David Paltenghi, décor,
Ronald Ferns. 1951.

FAUST Faust, ballet (3 acts).
Music, Panizza, Sir Michael
Costa and N. Bajetti; chore-
ography, Jules Perrot; book,
Perrot, based on tragedy by
Goethe; scenery, Carlo Fon-
tana; machinery, Giuseppe
Ronchi. Teatro alla Scala,

Milan, February 12, 1848.

FEATH The Feather of the
Dawn, "Pueblo pastoral. "
Music, Charles Wakefield
Cadman; choreography, Ted
Shawn; décor, Earle Franke;
costumes, original Hopi Indi-
an pieces. New York, 1915/
16.

FEMIN Femina, grand spectacu-
lar ballet (5 scenes). Music,
George W. Byng and Valverde;
choreography and book, Alfredo Curti; scenery, Amable
and E. H. Ryan. Alhambra
Theatre, London, May 30,
1910.

FEMME Les Femmes de Bonne
Humeur (The Good Humored
Ladies), choreographic comedy
(1 act). Music, Domenico
Scarlatti, arranged by Vincenzo Tommasini; choreography, Leonide Massine, based
on a comedy by Carlo Gol-
doni; scenery and costumes,
Léon Bakst. Teatro Costan-
za, Rome, April 12, 1917.

FESTD Le Festin de l'Araignée
(The Spider's Banquet), ballet.
Music, Albert Roussel;
choreography, Albert Aveline;
décor, Leyritz. Paris Opéra,
Paris, May 1, 1939.

FESTI Le Festin de l'Araignée
(The Spider's Banquet), ballet-pantomime (1 act). Music, Albert Roussel; choreography, Leo Staats; scenario,
Gilbert de Voisins, based on
the "Souvenirs Entomologiques"
of Henri Fabre; scenery and
costumes, Maxime Dethomas.
Théâtre des Arts, Paris,
April 3, 1913.

FETEE La Fête Étrange, ballet
(1 act). Music, Gabriel

Fauré, selected by Ronald Crichton; choreography, Andrée Howard; book, Crighton; scenery and costumes, Sophie Fedorovich. Arts Theatre, London, May 23, 1940.

FIAMM Fiametta (Nemea) (Salamander), fantastic ballet (4 acts). Music, Ludwig Minkus; choreography and book, Arthur Saint-Léon. Bolshoy Theatre, St. Petersburg, February 13, 1864.

FIANC La Fiancée du Diable, ballet. Music, Hubeau; choreography, Roland Petit; décor, Malclès. Théâtre des Champs-Élysées, Paris, December 8, 1945.

FIGUR The Figure in the Carpet, ballet (5 scenes). Music, George Frederic Handel's "Royal Fireworks Music" and "Water Music." Choreography, George Balanchine; scenario, George Lewis; décor, Esteban Francés; costumes executed by Barbara Karinska. City Center, New York, April 13, 1960.

FILLD La Fille du Danube (The Daughter of the Danube), pantomimic ballet (2 acts, 4 scenes). Music, Adolphe Adam; choreography and book, Philippe Taglioni; scenery, Ciceri, Desplêchin, Diéterle, Feuchère and Séchan; costumes, Henri d'Orchevillers. Théâtre de l'Académie Royale de Musique, Paris, September 21, 1836.

FILLE La Fille Mal Gardée (The Unchaperoned Daughter)

(Useless Precautions) (The Wayward Daughter) (Naughty Lisette), ballet (2 acts). Music, Peter Ludwig Hertel; choreography and libretto, Jean Dauberval. Bordeaux, France, 1786 (often called the oldest ballet extant). First performed in America early in the 19th century. Revived in New York by the Mordkin Ballet, 1937; first New York performance, Alvin Theater, New York, November 12, 1938.

FILLG La Fille Mal Gardée, ballet (2 acts). Music, François Joseph Hérold, arranged, re-orchestrated and augmented by John Lanchbery; choreography, Frederick Ashton; décor, Osbert Lancaster. Royal Opera House, Covent Garden, London, January 28, 1960.

FILLI Filling Station, ballet-document (1 act). Music, Virgil Thomson; choreography, Lew Christensen; book, Lincoln Kirstein; scenery and costumes, Paul Cadmus. Avery Memorial Theater, Hartford, Conn., January 6, 1938.

FILLM La Fille de Marbre, pantomimic ballet (2 acts). Music, Cesare Pugni; choreography and book, Arthur Saint-Léon; scenery, Charles Antoine Cambon and J. F. D. Thierry. Théâtre de l' Académie Royale de Musique, Paris, October 20, 1847.

FILLP La Fille du Pharaon (Pharaoh's Daughter), ballet (3 acts, with prologue and epilogue). Music, Cesare Pugni; choreography, Marius Petipa; book, Petipa and

FILLU   Vernoy de Saint-Georges,
based on "Le Roman de la
Momie" by Théophile Gau-
tier.   Maryinsky Theatre,
St. Petersburg, January
18, 1862.

FILLU   La Filleule des Fées
(The Fairies' God-child),
grand fairy ballet (prologue,
2 acts).   Music, Adolphe
Adam and de Saint-Julien;
choreography, Jules Perrot;
book, Perrot and Vernoy de
Saint-Georges; scenery,
Cambon, Desplêchin and
Thierry.   Théâtre de l'
Opéra, Paris, October 8,
1849.

FILLY   The Filly, or A Stableboy's Dream, ballet.   Music, John Colman; chore-
ographer, Todd Bolender;
costumes and décor, Peter
Larkin.   City Center, New
York, May 19, 1953.

FIORI   Fiorita et la Reine des
Elfrides (Fiorita and the
Queen of the Elfrits), ballet (4 scenes).   Music,
Cesare Pugni; choreography
and book, Paul Taglioni;
scenery, Charles Marshall;
costumes, Miss Bradley
and Mr. Whales.   Her
Majesty's Theatre, London,
February 19, 1848.

FIREB   Firebird (L'Oiseau de
Feu), dramatic ballet (1
act and 2 scenes).   Music,
Igor Stravinsky; choreography and book, Michel Fo-
kine; scenery and costumes,
Alexander Golovine and Léon
Bakst.   Théâtre Nationale
de l'Opéra, Paris, June 25,
1910.

FIRED   Firebird, ballet (3 scenes).
Music, Igor Stravinsky;

choreography, Adolph Bolm;
décor, Marc Chagall.   Metropolitan Opera House, New
York, October 24, 1945.

FIREI   Firebird, ballet (3 scenes).
Music, Igor Stravinsky; chore-
ography, George Balanchine;
décor and costumes, Marc
Chagall.   City Center, New
York, November 27, 1949.

FISHE   The Fisherman and His
Soul, ballet (1 act).   Music,
Harry Somers; choreography,
Grant Strate, based on a
fairy tale by Oscar Wilde;
décor, Kay Ambrose.   Palace Theatre, Hamilton, Ontario, November 5, 1956.

FIVEG   The Five Gifts, ballet.
Music, Ernest Dohnanyi
("Variations on a Nursery
Tune"); choreography, Wil-
liam Dollar, based on a
story by Mark Twain; cos-
tumes, Esteban Francês.
City Center, New York,
January 20, 1953.

FLAME   The Flames of Paris,
ballet (4 acts).   Music, Boris V. Asafiev; choreography,
Vasily I. Vainonen; book, Nicolai D. Volkov and Vladimir
V. Dmitriev; scenery, Dmitriev; production, S. E. Radlov.   Kirov Theatre, Leningrad, November 7, 1932.

FLIKA   Flik and Flok, fantastic
ballet (2 acts).   Music, Johann Wilhelm Hertel; choreography and book, Paul Taglioni.   Teatro alla Scala,
Milan, February 13, 1862.

FLORE   Flore et Zéphire, ballet-
divertissement (1 act).   Music, Cesare Bossi; choreography, Charles Didelot; scenery
and machinery, Liparotti.
King's Theatre, London,

273   FLOWE

July 7, 1796.

FLOWE Flower Festival at
Genzano, ballet (1 act).
Music, Edward Helsted and
Holger Simon Paulli; choreography, August Bournon-
ville. Copenhagen, Den-
mark, 1858.

FOLKT A Folk Tale (Et Folk-
esagn), ballet (3 acts).
Music, Gade and Hartmann
(Act II); choreography and
book, August Bournonville;
scenery, Christensen and
Lund; costumes, E. Leh-
mann; machinery, Wedén.
Royal Theatre, Copenhagen,
March 20, 1854.

FORAI Les Forains (The
Traveling Players), ballet
(1 act). Music, Henri
Sauguet; choreography, Ro-
land Petit; book, Boris
Kochno; scenery and cos-
tumes, Christian Bérard.
Théâtre des Champs-
Élysées, Paris, March 2,
1945.

FORTU Fortuna, ballet. Mu-
sic, unknown; choreography,
Antonio Guerra. Imperial
Theatre, Vienna, 184?

FOUNT The Fountain of Bakhchi-
sarai, choreographic poem
(4 acts). Music, Boris
Asafiev; choreography,
Rostislav Zakharov, book,
Nicolai Volkov after the
poem by Pushkin; scenery
and costumes, Valentina
Khodasevich; production,
R. V. Zakharov. Kirov
Theatre, Leningrad, Sep-
tember 28, 1934.

FOURM The Four Marys, ballet (1 act). Music, Scots
ballad ("Ballad of Mary

Hamilton," also called "The
Ballad of the Four Marys"),
adapted and scored by Trude
Rittmann, orchestrated by
Rittmann and Mordechai
Sheinkman; choreography,
Agnes de Mille; décor, Oliver
Smith; costumes, Stanley
Simmons; lighting, Jean Ro-
senthal. New York State
Theater, New York, March
23, 1965.

FOURT The Four Temperaments,
classic ballet (5 parts). Music, Paul Hindemith; choreography, George Balanchine;
scenery and costumes, Kurt
Seligmann; lighting, Jean Rosenthal. Central High School
of Needle Trades, New York,
November 20, 1946.

FOYED Foyer de Danse, ballet
(1 act). Music, Lord Ber-
ners; choreography, Frederick
Ashton; costumes, after Dégas. Mercury Theatre, London, October 9, 1932.

FOYER Foyer de la Danse,
pantomimic ballet (1 act).
Music, Emmanuel Chabrier;
choreography and book,
Adolph Bolm; scenery and
costumes, Nicholas Remisov.
Eighth Street Theater, Chicago, November 27, 1927.

FRANC Francesca da Rimini,
ballet (2 scenes). Music,
Tchaikovsky; choreography,
David Lichine; book, Lichine
and Henry Clifford, partly
from Dante; scenery and costumes, Oliver Messel. Royal Opera House, Covent Garden, London, July 15, 1937.

FRANE Francesca da Rimini,
ballet. Music, Peter Ilyich
Tchaikovsky; choreography,
Michel Fokine. Maryinsky

Theatre, St. Petersburg,
November 28, 1915.

FRANI À La Françaix ballet
(5 parts). Music, Jean
Français (Serenade for
Small Orchestra); chore-
ography, George Balanchine;
lighting, Jean Rosenthal.
City Center, New York,
September 11, 1951.

FRANK Frankie and Johnny,
ballet (1 act). Music,
Jerome Moross; choreogra-
phy, Ruth Page and Bentley
Stone; book, Moross and
Michael Blandford, based
on the song "Frankie and
Johnny"; scenery and cos-
tumes, Paul Dupont.
Great Northern Theater,
Chicago, June 19, 1938.

FRONT Frontier, "An American perspective of the
plains. " Music, Louis
Horst; choreography (solo
dance), Martha Graham;
décor, Isamu Noguchi.
Guild Theater, New York,
April 28, 1935.

GAITE Gaîté Parisienne, ballet
(1 act). Music, Jacques
Offenbach, orchestrated by
Manuel Rosenthal in collaboration with Jacques Brinde-
jonc-Offenbach; choreography,
Léonide Massine; scenery
and costumes, Count Étienne
de Beaumont. Théâtre de
Monte Carlo, Monte Carlo,
April 5, 1938.

GALAP Gala Performance,
comic ballet (2 parts). Music, Serge Prokofiev, or-
chestrated by Paul Baron;
choreography, Antony Tudor;
scenery and costumes, Hugh
Stevenson. Toynbee Hall
Theatre, London, December

5, 1938.

GAMES Games, modern dance
work. Music, traditional
songs, sung by male and
female duet; choreography,
Donald McKayle; décor, Paul
Bertelsen; costumes, Remy
Charlip. Hunter College Playhouse, New York, May 25,
1951.

GAUCH Gaucho, ballet (4 scenes).
Music, Emil Reesen; chore-
ography and book, Harald
Lander; scenery, Svend Gade;
costumes, O. Christian
Pedersen. Royal Theatre,
Copenhagen, December 1,
1931.

GAYNE Gayne (Gayaneh), patri-
otic folk ballet. Music, Aram
Khatchaturian; choreography,
Nina Anisimova; libretto,
Konstantin Derzhavin; scenic
design, Natan Altman. Kirov
Theatre for Opera and Ballet
of the Leningrad State Acad-
emy, Molotov, Russia, De-
cember, 1942.

GAYSW The Gay Swindles of
Courasche (Die Gaunerstreiche
der Courasche), ballet (5
scenes). Music, Richard
Mohaupt; choreography, Rudolf Kölling; décor, Paul
Haferung. Deutsches Opern-
haus, Berlin, 1936, in con-
nection with the XI Olympiad.

GEMMA Gemma, ballet (2 acts).
Music, Count Gabrielli; chore-
ography, Fanny Cerito; book,
Cerito and Théophile Gautier.
Théâtre Impérial de l'Opéra,
Paris, May 31, 1854.

GHOST Ghost Town, American
folk ballet (prologue, 1 scene,
epilogue). Music, Richard
Rodgers, orchestrated by

Hans Spialek; choreography, Marc Platoff; libretto, Rodgers; historical research, Gerald Murphy; scenery and costumes, Raoul Pène du Bois. Metropolitan Opera House, New York, November 12, 1939.

GIFTO Gift of the Magi, ballet (6 scenes). Music, Lukas Foss; choreography, Simon Semenoff; book, Semenoff, based on the short story by O. Henry; décor, Raoul Pène du Bois. Metropolitan Opera House, New York, October 15, 1945.

GISEE Giselle, ballet. Music, Adolphe Adam; choreography, Serge Lifar, after Jean Coralli; décor, Alexandre Benois. Metropolitan Opera House, New York, 1938.

GISEL Giselle ou Les Wilis, fantastic ballet (2 acts). Music, Adolphe Adam; choreography, Jean Coralli and Jules Perrot; book, Coralli, Théophile Gautier and Vernoy de Saint-Georges; scenery, Pierre Ciceri; costumes, Paul Lormier. Théâtre de l'Académie Royale de Musique, Paris, June 28, 1841.

GISER Giselle's Revenge, modern dance satire. Music, Manuel Galea; choreography and costumes, Myra Kinch. Jacob's Pillow Dance Festival, Lee, Mass., 1953.

GISES Giselle, ballet. Music, Adolphe Adam; choreography, Mikhail Mordkin; décor, Sergei Soudeikine. New York, 1937.

GITAA La Gitana, ballet. Music, ?; choreography, Antonio Guerra. Her Majesty's Theatre, London, 1839.

GITAN La Gitana, ballet (prologue, 3 acts). Music, Schmidt and Daniel Aubert; choreography and book, Philippe Taglioni. Bolshoi Theatre, St. Petersburg, November 23, 1838.

GLOIR La Gloire, dramatic ballet (1 act). Music, Ludwig van Beethoven (overtures to "Egmont," "Coriolanus" and "Lenore No. 3"); choreography, Antony Tudor: scenery, Gaston Longchamps; costumes, Barbara Karinska; lighting, Jean Rosenthal. City Center, New York, February 26, 1952.

GODSA The Gods Go A-Begging, or Les Dieux Mendiants, ballet. Music, George Frederick Handel; choreography, David Lichine; décor, Juan Gris, after Léon Bakst. 1937.

GODSG The Gods Go A-Begging, or Les Dieux Mendiants, ballet (1 act). Music, George Frederick Handel; choreography, George Balanchine; book, Sobeka (Boris Kochno); décor, Léon Bakst. His Majesty's Theatre, London, July 16, 1928.

GODSO The Gods Go A-Begging, or Les Dieux Mendiants, ballet (1 act). Music, George Frederick Handel; choreography, Ninette de Valois; décor, Hugh Stevenson. Sadler's Wells Theatre, London, February 21, 1936.

GOLDE The Golden Age (The
Age of Gold), "athletic
ballet" (3 acts, 5 scenes).
Music, Dimitri Shostako-
vich; choreography. E. I.
Kaplan and V. I. Vainonen
with specialty dances by
V. P. Ivanovsky and L. V.
Jacobson; book, A. V. Ivan-
ovsky; scenery and cos-
tumes, V. M. Khodasevich.
Academic Theatre of Opera
and Ballet, Leningrad,
October 26, 1930.

GRADU Graduation Ball, ballet
(1 act). Music, Johann
Strauss, compiled, arranged
and orchestrated by Antal
Dorati; choreography, David
Lichine; scenery and cos-
tumes, Alexandre Benois.
Theatre Royal, Sydney, Australia, February 28, 1940.

GRASS Grasslands, ballet (1
act). Music, Virgil
Thompson (music from the
film "Louisiana Story");
choreography and décor,
Robert Moulton. Playhouse
Theatre, Winnipeg, Man.,
October 18, 1958.

GRAZI Graziosa, pantomimic
ballet (1 act). Music, Théodore Labarre; choreography,
Lucien Petipa; book, Petipa
and J. Derley; scenery;
Charles Antoine Cambon and
J. F. D. Thierry. Théâtre de
l'Opéra, Paris, March 25,
1861.

GREAT The Great American Goof
(A Number of Absurd and Poetic Events in the Life of The
Great American Goof), ballet
play. Music, Henry Brant;
choreography, Eugene Loring;
libretto, William Saroyan;
scenery and costumes, Boris
Aronson. Center Theater,

New York, January 11, 1940.

GRECO El Greco, dance drama
(1 act). Music, D. E. Inghel-
brecht; choreography and
book, Jean Borlin; scenery,
Mouveau; costumes after
paintings by El Greco. Théâtre des Champs-Elysées,
Paris, November 18, 1920.

GREEN The Green Table,
"dance of death" (8 scenes).
Music, Fritz Cohen; choreography and book, Kurt
Jooss; costumes, Hein Heckroth. Théâtre des Champs-
Élysées, Paris, July 3, 1932.

GRISI La Grisi, ballet. Music,
Tomasi and Metra; chore-
ography, Albert Aveline; décor, Dignimont. Paris
Opéra, Paris, June 21, 1935.

GUEST The Guests, classic bal-
let (1 act). Music, Marc
Blitzstein; choreography,
Jerome Robbins; lighting,
Jean Rosenthal. City Center,
New York, January 20, 1949.

GUIAB La Guiablesse, ballet (1
act). Music, William Grant
Still; choreography, Ruth
Page; book, Page, based on
a Creole legend recounted by
Lafcadio Hearn; scenery and
costumes, Nicholas Remisov.
Grand Opera House, Chicago,
June 23, 1933.

GUIGN Guignol et Pandore, bal-
let (1 act). Music, André
Jolivet; choreography, Serge
Lifar; décor, Dignimont.
Paris Opéra, Paris, April
29, 1944.

GUNSA Guns and Castanets,
ballet (1 act). Music,
Georges Bizet, arranged
for small orchestra by

Jerome Moross; songs from the poems of Federico García Lorca, translated by A. L. Lloyd; book, Ruth Page, after the novel "Carmen" by Prosper Mérimée; choreography, Page and Bentley Stone; scenery, Clive Rickenbaugh; costumes, John Pratt. Great Northern Theater, Chicago, February 1, 1939.

GYPSY La Gypsy, pantomimic ballet (3 acts). Music, Benoist, Thomas and Marliani; choreography, Joseph Mazilier; book, Mazilier and H. Vernoy de Saint-Georges, based on Cervantes' "Novelas Examplares"; scenery, Philastre and Cambon; costumes, Paul Lormier. Théâtre de l' Académie Royale de Musique, Paris, January 28, 1839.

HALTE Halte de Cavalerie, character ballet (1 act). Music, Arsheimer; choreography and book, Marius Petipa; scenery, Levogt; costumes, Ponomarev. Maryinsky Theatre, St. Petersburg, January 21, 1896.

HAMLE Hamlet, dramatic ballet (1 act). Music, Peter Ilich Tchaikovsky; choreography, Robert Helpmann; book, Helpmann, after Shakespeare's tragedy; scenery and costumes, Leslie Hurry. New Theatre, London, May 19, 1942.

HAMLL Hamlet, ballet. Music, Franz Liszt; choreography, Bronislava Nijinska; book, after Shakespeare's tragedy; décor, Annenkoff. Paris Opéra,

Paris, 1934.

HAMLS Hamlet, ballet. Music, unknown; choreography, Louis X. S. Henri, after Shakespeare's tragedy. Porte St. Martin Theatre, Paris, 1823?

HAMLT Hamlet, ballet (prologue, 3 scenes). Music, Boris Blacher; choreography, Victor Gsovsky; book, Tatiana Gsovsky, after Shakespeare's tragedy; décor, Helmut Jürgens. Bayerische Staatsoper, Munich, November 19, 1950.

HANSE Hansel and Gretel, ballet. Music, Engelbert Humperdinck; choreography, William Christensen; décor, Jean de Botton. San Francisco, Calif., 1943.

HAPPI Happiness, Armenian ballet (3 acts). Music, Aram Khachaturian; choreography, E. E. Artabov (Gagubian); book, G. A. Ovanesian; scenery and costumes, S. E. Alladzhalov. Armenian Festival of Folk Art, Moscow, August, 1940.

HARLE Harlequin in April, pantomime with divertissemente (2 acts, with prologue, entr'acte and epilogue). Music, Richard Arnell; choreography and book, John Cranko; scenery and costumes, John Piper. Sadler's Wells Theatre, London, May 8, 1951.

HARLI Harlequinade, ballet (2 acts). Music, Riccardo Drigo (Les Millions d'Arlequin); choreography, George Balanchine; décor, costumes and lighting, Rouben Ter-Arutunian. New York State Thea-

ter, New York, February
4, 1965.

HARLJ Harlequinade (Les
Millions d'Arlequin), ballet
(2 acts). Music, Riccardo
Drigo; choreography, Marius
Petipa; décor, Allegri,
costumes, Ponomarov.
Hermitage Theatre, St.
Petersburg, February 10,
1900.

HARLN Harlequinade, ballet.
Music, Riccardo Drigo;
choreography, David Lichine.
Festival Ballet, London,
1950.

HARLQ Harlequin for Presi-
dent (Harlequin), ballet.
Music, Domenico Scarlatti,
orchestrated by Ariadna
Mikeshina; choreography,
Eugene Loring; book, Lin-
coln Kirstein; costumes,
Keith Martin. Bennington,
Vermont, July 17, 1936.

HARLS Harlequin in the
Street, ballet. Music,
François Couperin; chore-
ography, Frederick Ashton;
décor, André Derain.
Arts Theatre, Cambridge,
England, 1937.

HARLX Harlequinade Pas de
Deux, ballet. Music, Ric-
cardo Drigo; choreography,
George Balanchine; cos-
tumes, Barbara Karinska.
City Center, New York,
December 16, 1952.

HAUNT The Haunted Ballroom,
dramatic ballet (1 act and
2 scenes). Music, Geoffrey
Toye; choreography, Ninette
de Valois; book, Toye;
scenery and costumes,
Motley. Sadler's Wells
Theatre, London, April 3,

1934.

HAZAN Hazaña (Achievement),
ballet (1 act). Music, Carlos
Surinach; choreography and
libretto, Norman Morrice;
décor, Ralph Koltai. Sadler's
Wells Theatre, London, May
25, 1959.

HEART The Heart of the Hills,
ballet (5 scenes). Music,
G. Balanchivaidze; chore-
ography, Vakhtang Chabou-
kiani; book, G. Leonidze and
N. Volkov, founded on an
episode in the history of
Georgia; scenery and cos-
tumes, S. Virsaladze. Kirov
State Opera and Ballet Theatre, Leningrad, 1938.

HEARY Hear Ye! Hear Ye!,
ballet (1 act). Music, Aaron
Copland; choreography, Ruth
Page; book, Page and Nicholas
Remisov; scenery and cos-
tumes, Remisov. Chicago
Opera House, Chicago, No-
vember 30, 1934.

HELEN Helen of Troy, comic
ballet (prologue, 3 scenes).
Music, Jacques Offenbach,
arranged and orchestrated by
Antal Dorati; choreography,
David Lichine; book, Dorati
and Lichine; scenery and
costumes, Marcel Vertès.
Ballet Theatre, Mexico City,
September 10, 1942.

HENRY Henry VIII, ballet.
Choreography, Rosella Hightower. New York, 1949.

HEROD Hérodiade, modern
dance work. Music, Paul
Hindemith; choreography,
Martha Graham; décor and
artistic collaboration, Isamu
Noguchi; costumes, Edythe
Gilfond. Library of Congress,

Washington, D. C. , October 28, 1944, as Mirror Before Me.

HIGHL Highland Fling, ballet. Music, Stanley Bate; choreography, William Dollar; costumes and décor, David Ffolkes. Central High School of Needle Trades, New York, March 26, 1947.

HISTO L'Histoire du Soldat (The Soldier's Story), narrative ballet (5 scenes, "to be read, played and danced"). Music, Igor Stravinsky; choreography, Ludmilla Pitoev; words, C. F. Ramuz; scenery and costumes, Renê Auberjonois. Lausanne, Switzerland, September 28, 1918.

HOLYT The Holy Torch (Szent Fakyla), ballet (11 scenes). Music, Erno Dohnanyi; choreography and book, Madame Dohnanyi-Galafres; scenery and costumes, Zoltán Fülöp; direction, Rezsö Brada. Royal Hungarian Opera House, Budapest, December 6, 1934.

HOMAG Homage to the Queen, coronation ballet. Music, Malcolm Arnold; choreography, Frederick Ashton; setting and costumes, Oliver Messel. Royal Opera House, Covent Garden, London, June 2, 1953.

HOMME L'Homme et son Désir, "plastic poem" (1 scene). Music, Darius Milhaud; choreography, Jean Borlin; "plastic poem, " Paul Claudel; scenery and costumes, Andrêe Parr. Thêâtre des Champs-

Élysêes, Paris, June 6, 1921.

HOROS Horoscope, ballet (1 act). Music and book, Constant Lambert; choreography, Frederick Ashton; scenery and costumes, Sophie Fedorovich; Sadler's Wells Theatre, London, January 27, 1938.

HOUSE The House of Birds, ballet (1 act). Music, piano solos by Federico Mompou, orchestrated and arranged by John Lanchbery; choreography, Kenneth MacMillan; libretto, Lanchbery and MacMillan, based on "Jorinda and Joringel" by the Brothers Grimm; décor, Nicholas Georgiadis. Sadler's Wells Theatre, London, May 26, 1955.

HPPPP H. P. , "symbolic ballet" (4 scenes). Music, Carlos Chávez; choreography, Catherine Littlefield; book, scenery and costumes by Chávez and Diego Rivera. Metropolitan Opera House, Philadelphia, November, 1932.

HUMPB The Hump-Backed Horse, ballet (5 acts). Music, Cesare Pugni; choreography, Arthur Saint-Léon; book, Saint-Léon. Bolshoy Theatre, St. Petersburg, December 3, 1864.

HUMPH The Hump-Backed Horse, ballet (3 acts). Music, Rodion Shchedrin; choreography, Alexander Radunsky; book, Vasily Vainonen and Pavel Maliarevsky, based on a fairy tale by P. Yershov; décor, Boris Volkov. Bolshoi Theatre, Moscow,

March 4, 1960.

HUNDR The Hundred Kisses
(Les Cent Baisers), ballet
(1 act). Music, Frederic
d'Erlanger; choreography,
Bronislava Nijinska; libretto,
Boris Kochno, after Hans
Christian Andersen's fairy
tale "The Swineherd";
scenery and costumes,
Jean Hugo. Royal Opera,
Covent Garden, London,
July 18, 1935.

HUNGA The Hungarian Hut,
pantomimic ballet (4 acts,
also 3 act version). Mu-
sic, Benois; choreography
and book, Charles Didelot.
Bolshoy Theatre, St. Petersburg, December 17, 1817.

ICARE Icare, choreographic
legend (1 act). Rhythms,
Serge Lifar, orchestrated
by J. E. Szyfer; choreography and book, Lifar; scenery and costumes, P. R.
Larthe. Théâtre de l'Opéra,
Paris, July 9, 1935.

ICARO Icaros, ballet. Music,
Sven Erik Back; choreography, Birgit Aakesson; dé-
cor, Lage Lindell. Royal
Swedish Ballet, May 24,
1963.

ICEMA The Ice Maiden (Solveig), ballet suite (pro-
logue, 3 acts, epilogue).
Music, Edvard Grieg, ar-
ranged by A. Gauk and F.
Lopukhov, orchestrated by
B. V. Asafiev; choreography,
F. V. Lopukhov; scenery
and costumes, A. Y. Golo-
vin. State Academic Thea-
tre of Opera and Ballet,
Leningrad, April 27, 1927.

IDYLL Idylle, ballet (1 act).

Music, François Serette;
choreography, George Skibine;
book, scenery and costumes,
Alwyn Camble. Théâtre de
l'Empire. Paris, January 2,
1954.

ILGAA Ilga, ballet (4 acts).
Music, Jānis Vitoliņs; choreography, Osvalds Lemanis;
book, Oscars Grosbergs;
scenery and costumes, Nik-
lavs Strunke. National Opera,
Riga, April 27, 1937.

ILLUM Illuminations, dramatic
ballet (1 act). Music, Ben-
jamin Britten; choreography,
Frederick Ashton; words,
poems from Arthur Rimbaud's
"Les Illuminations," set by
Britten; scenery and cos-
tumes, Cecil Beaton; lighting,
Jean Rosenthal. City Center,
New York, March 2, 1950.

INCRE The Incredible Flutist,
ballet (1 act). Music, Walter Piston; choreography,
Hans Wiener. Symphony
Hall, Boston, May, 1938.

INQUE Inquest, modern dance
work. Music, Norman
Lloyd; choreography, Doris
Humphrey, based on a chapter of John Ruskin's "Sesame
and Lilies"; costumes, Pauline Lawrence. Humphrey-
Weidman Studio Theatre,
New York, March 5, 1944.

INVIT The Invitation, ballet (1
act). Music, Matyas Seiber;
choreography, Kenneth Mac-
Millan, based on the novels
"The Ripening Seed" by
Colette and "House of the
Angel" by Beatriz Guido;
décor, Nicholas Georgiadis.
New Theatre, Oxford, Eng-
land, November 10, 1960.

IODYS I, Odysseus, modern dance work (12 episodes). Music, Hugh Aitken; choreography, José Limón; properties, Thomas Watson and William McIver; lighting, Thomas Skelton. New London, Conn., August 18, 1962.

IPHIG Iphigénie en Aulide, tragedy-opera (3 acts). Music, Christoph Willibald Gluck; choreography, Jean Georges Noverre; book, after the tragedy by Euripides. Paris Opéra, Paris, April 12, 1774.

IRONF Iron Foundry (Mechanical Ballet) (Ballet Mécanique), ballet (1 act). Music, A. Mossolov; choreography and book, Adolph Bolm; costumes, Bolm and N. Remisov. Hollywood Bowl, Los Angeles, Calif., August, 1932.

ISHTA Ishtar of the Seven Gates, "mystic dance of Babylon" (3 phases). Music, arranged from the works of Charles T. Griffes; choreography, Ruth St. Denis; décor, Robert Law Studio. New York, 1915/16.

JACKD The Jackdaw and the Pigeons, ballet. Music, Hugh Bradford; choreography, Ninette de Valois; décor, William Chappell. Old Vic, London, 1931.

JARDI Jardin aux Lilas (Lilac Garden), dramatic ballet (1 act). Music, Ernest Chausson (Poème); choreography, Antony Tudor; scenery and costumes, Raymond Sovey, after

sketches by Hugh Stevenson. Mercury Theatre, London, January 26, 1936.

JARDP Jardin Public, ballet (1 act). Music, Vladimir Dukelsky; choreography, Leonide Massine; book, based on a portion of André Gide's "The Counterfeiters"; décor, Halicka, later by Jean Lurçat. Auditorium Theater, Chicago, March 8, 1935.

JARRE La Jarre (The Jar), ballet (1 act). Music, Alfredo Casella; choreography, Jean Borlin; book, Luigi Pirandello; scenery and costumes, Giorgio de Chirico. Théâtre des Champs-Élysees, Paris, November 19, 1924.

JARRR La Jarre (The Jar), ballet (1 act). Music, Alfredo Casella; choreography, Ninette de Valois; book, Luigi Pirandello; décor, William Chappell. Sadler's Wells Theatre, London, October 9, 1934.

JAVOT Javotte, ballet (1 act). Music, Camille Saint-Saëns; choreography, Mariquita; book, J. L. Croze; scenery, Amable; costumes, Marcel Multzer. Grand Theatre, Lyon, December 3, 1896.

JEANN Jeanne d'Arc, ballet (3 acts). Music, Nicolai Peico; choreography, Vladimir Bourmeister; book, Vladimir Pletnev; décor, Vadim Ryndin. Stanislavsky and Nemirovich-Danchenko Lyric Theatre, Moscow, December 29, 1957.

JEUNE Le Jeune Homme et la Mort, ballet (2 scenes). Music

Johann Sebastian Bach;
choreography, Roland Petit,
after suggestions by Jean
Cocteau; book, Cocteau;
scenery and costumes,
George Wakhewitch, after
suggestions by Cocteau.
Théâtre des Champs-Élysées,
Paris, June 25, 1946.

JEUXG   Jeux (Games), ballet
(1 act).   Music, Claude
Debussy; choreography,
Vaslav Nijinsky; book,
Nijinsky; scenery and cos-
tumes, Léon Bakst.   Théâ-
tre des Champs-Élysées,
Paris, May 15, 1913.

JEUXX   Jeux d'Enfants, ballet
(1 act).   Music, Georges
Bizet; choreography, Leo-
nide Massine; book, Boris
Kochno; curtain, scenery
and costumes, Joan Miro.
Théâtre de Monte Carlo,
Monte Carlo, April 14,
1932.

JINXX   Jinx, dramatic ballet
(1 act).   Music, Benjamin
Britten (Variations on a
Theme by Frank Bridge);
choreography, Lew Christ-
ensen; scenery, James
Stewart Morcom; costumes,
Felipe Fiocca.   National
Theater, New York, April
24, 1942.

JOAND   Joan de Zarissa, ballet.
Music, Werner Egk, chore-
ography, Serge Lifar; dé-
cor, Yves Brayer.   Paris
Opéra, Paris, July 10,
1942.

JOANV   Joan von Zarissa (Don
Juan de Zarissa), ballet
(prologue, 4 scenes, epi-
logue).   Music and book,
Werner Egk; choreography,
Lizzie Maudrik; décor,

Josef Fenneker.   Staatsoper,
Berlin, January 20, 1940.

JOBBB   Job, masque for dancing
(8 scenes).   Music, Ralph
Vaughan Williams; choreography, Ninette de Valois; book,
Geoffrey Keynes, based on
William Blake's "Illustra-
tions to the Book of Job";
scenery and costumes, Gwen-
dolen Raverat; wigs and
masks, Hedley Briggs.   Cambridge Theatre, London,
July 5, 1931.

JOLIE   La Jolie Fille de Gand,
pantomimic ballet (3 acts).
Music, Adolphe Adam; chore-
ography, Albert (Ferdinand
Albert Decombe); book, Al-
bert and H. Vernoy de Saint-
Georges, based on the drama
"Victorine, ou la Nuit porte
Conseil" by Dumersan, Gab-
riel and Dupeuty; scenery,
Cicéri, Philastre and Cambon.
Théâtre de l'Académie Royale
de Musique, Paris, June 22,
1842.

JONES   Jones Beach, ballet (4
parts).   Music, Jurriaan
Andriessen (Berkshire Sym-
phonies); choreography,
George Balanchine and Jerome
Robbins; lighting, Jean Rosen-
thal; costumes, Jantzen.
City Center, New York,
March 9, 1950.

JOSEL   Josephslegende (The
Legend of Joseph), ballet.
Music, Richard Strauss;
choreography, Pino Mlakar.
Belgrade, 1934.

JOSEP   Joseph the Beautiful (Joseph the Handsome), ballet
(1 act).   Music, Sergei
Vassilenko; choreography,
Kasian Goleizovsky.   Leningrad, 1924.

JOVIT Jovita ou les Boucaniers, pantomimic ballet (3 scenes). Music, Theodore Labarre; choreography and book, Joseph Mazilier; scenery, Desplêchin, Thierry and Cambon. Thêâtre Impêrial de l'Opêra, Paris, November 11, 1853.

JUAND Juan de Zarissa, ballet. Music, Werner Egk; choreography, Tatiana Gsovska; dêcor, Hector Basaldúa. Teatro Colón, Buenos Aires, Argentina, October 31, 1950.

JUDGM The Judgment of Paris, satiric ballet (1 act). Music, Kurt Weill; choreography, Antony Tudor; scenario, Hugh Laing; scenery and costumes, Lucinda Ballard. Ballet Club, Westminster Theatre, London, June 15, 1938.

JUDGT The Judgment of Paris, ballet. Music, Lennox Berkeley; choreography, Frederick Ashton; dêcor, William Chappell. Sadler's Wells Theatre, London, 1938.

JUGEM Le Jugement de Paris, ballet divertissement (1 act). Music, Cesare Pugni; choreography, Jules Perrot. Her Majesty's Theatre, London, July 23, 1846.

JUGEP Le Jugement de Paris, ballet. Music, unknown; choreography, Pierre Gardel. Paris Opêra, Paris, 178- or later.

KALKA Kalkabrino, fantastic ballet (3 acts). Music, Ludwig Minkus; choreography, Marius Petipa; book,

Modeste Tchaikovsky. Maryinsky Theatre, St. Petersburg, February 13, 1891.

KATER Katerina, ballet (3 acts). Music, Anton Rubinstein, arranged by E. A. Doubrovsky (the music of the "Serf's Ballet" by Adolphe Adam); choreography and book, L. M. Lavronsky; scenery and costumes, V. M. Erbstein. Graduation performance of Leningrad School at Kirov (formerly Maryinsky) Theatre, May 25, 1935.

KERMI The Kermis in Bruges, or The Three Gifts (Kermesse i Brugge Eller de Tre Gaver), romantic ballet (3 acts). Music, Holger Simon Paulli; choreography, August Bournonville. Copenhagen, Denmark, 1851.

KHADR Khadra, ballet (1 act). Music, Jean Sibelius (Belshazzar's Feast); choreography, Celia Franca; scenery and costumes, Honor Frost. Sadler's Wells Theatre, London, May 27, 1946.

KORRI La Korrigane, fantastic ballet (2 acts). Music, C. M. Widor; choreography, Louis Mêrante; book, Mêrante and François Coppée; scenery, J. B. Lavastre, August Rubê and Chaperon; costumes, Eugène Lacoste. Thêâtre National de l'Opêra, Paris, December 1, 1880.

KURUC Kuruc Fairy Tale (Kuruc Mese), ballet (3 acts). Music, Zoltán Kodály; choreography, Aurel Milloss and Rezsö Brada; scenery, Gusztav Oláh. Royal Hungarian Opera House, Budapest,

March 13, 1935.

LABYR Labyrinth, surrealist
ballet (4 tableaux); Music,
Franz Schubert (C major
Symphony); choreography,
Léonide Massine; book,
scenery and costumes,
Salvador Dali. Ballet
Russe de Monte Carlo,
Metropolitan Opera House,
New York, October 8,
1941.

LADYA The Lady and the
Fool, ballet (2 scenes).
Music, Giuseppe Verdi,
arranged by Charles Mac-
kerras; choreography and
book, John Cranko; scenery
and costumes, Richard
Beer. Sadler's Wells
Theatre, London, Febru-
ary 28, 1954; revised
version, Royal Opera,
Covent Garden, London,
June 9, 1955.

LADYB Lady of the Camellias,
ballet (4 acts). Music,
Henri Sauguet; choreography,
Tatiana Gsovska, based on
the novel by Alexandre Du-
mas, fils; décor, Jean
Ponelle. Berliner Theatre,
Berlin, September 29, 1957.

LADYC The Lady of the Camellias, dramatic ballet (4
scenes). Music, Giuseppe
Verdi; choreography, Antony
Tudor, based on the novel
by Alexandre Dumas, fils;
scenery and costumes, Ce-
cil Beaton; lighting, Jean
Rosenthal. City Center,
New York, February 28,
1951.

LADYE Lady From the Sea,
ballet (1 act). Music,
Knudage Riisager; chore-
ography and book, Birgit

Cullberg, based on the play
by Henrik Ibsen; décor,
Kerstin Hedeby. Metropolitan Opera House, New York,
April 20, 1960.

LADYF Lady From the Sea,
ballet (1 act). Music, Saul
Honigman; choreography and
book, Elizabeth Leese, based
on the play by Henrik Ibsen;
décor, Jean de Belleval;
costumes, Kay Ambrose.
Carter Barron Amphitheatre,
Washington, D. C., June 13,
1955.

LADYI Lady into Fox, ballet (1
act). Music, Arthur Honegger, selected by Charles
Lynch; choreography, Andrée
Howard; book, founded on
the novel by David Garnett;
setting and costumes, Nadia
Benois. Mercury Theatre,
London, May 15, 1939.

LADYO The Lady of Shalott,
ballet (1 act). Music, Jean
Sibelius; choreography,
Frederick Ashton; book,
Ashton, based on Tennyson's
poem; costumes, William
Chappell. Mercury Theatre,
London, November 12, 1931.

LADYU The Lady and the Unicorn (La Dame et la Licorne),
ballet (1 act). Music,
Jacques Chailley; choreography, Heinz Rosen; book, décor and costumes, Jean Cocteau. Gärtnerplatztheater,
Munich, May 9, 1953.

LAGER Lagertha, ballet (3
acts). Choreography, Vin-
cenzo Galeotti; book, after
Saxo; scenery, L. Chipart
(Act I) and C. Lerneur
(Act II). Royal Theatre,
Copenhagen, January 30,
1801.

LAIDE Laiderette, ballet (1
act). Music, Frank Mar-
tin's "Petite Symphonie
Concertante"; choreography,
Kenneth MacMillan; décor,
Kenneth Rowell. Sadler's
Wells Theatre, London,
January 24, 1954.

LALLA Lalla Rookh, or The
Rose of Lahore, ballet (4
scenes). Music, Cesare
Pugni; choreography, Jules
Perrot; book, Perrot,
after Thomas Moore's ro-
mance; scenery, Charles
Marshall. Her Majesty's
Theatre, London, June 11,
1846.

LAMEF Lament for Ignacio
Sanchez Mejías, modern
dance work. Music,
Norman Lloyd; choreogra-
phy, Doris Humphrey,
based on the poem by
Federico García Lorca;
décor, Michael Czaja; costumes, Pauline Lawrence.
Belasco Theatre, New
York, January 5, 1947.

LAMEN Lament, modern
dance work. Music, Heitor
Villa-Lobos' "Bachianas
Brasileiros No. 5"; chore-
ography, Louis Johnson.
Central High School of
Needle Trades, New York,
April 12, 1953.

LAMET Lamentation, solo
modern dance. Music,
from Zoltán Kodály's Suite
of 9 pieces for piano;
choreography and costumes,
Martha Graham. Maxine
Elliot Theater, New York,
January 8, 1930.

LAURE Laurencia, ballet (3
acts). Music, Alexander
Krein; choreography, Vakh-

tang Chabukiani; book, Yev-
geny Mandelberg, after Lope
de Vega's drama "Fuente
Ovejuna"; décor, Simon Virsaladze. Kirov Theatre,
Leningrad, March 22, 1939.

LEAFA The Leaf and the Wind,
ballet. Music, Paul Ram-
seier; choreography, William
Dollar. State Fair Auditorium, Dallas, Texas, 1954.

LEGEI The Legend of Impossible
Love, ballet (1 act). Music,
recorded sounds of Brazilian-
Indian folklore and noises of
the forest; choreography,
Aurel Milloss; idea, plot and
décor, Emiliano Di Centen-
ário. Teatro Municipal, Rio
de Janeiro, Brazil, 1954.

LEGEJ Legend of Judith, modern
dance work (1 act). Music,
Mordecai Seter; choreography,
Martha Graham; décor, Dani
Karavan. Habima Theatre,
Tel-Aviv, Israel, October 25,
1962.

LEGEL Legend of Love, ballet
(3 acts). Music, Arif Meli-
kov; choreography, Yuri
Grigorovich; book, Nazym
Hikmet, based on an old
legend; décor, Simon Vir-
saladze. Kirov Theatre,
Leningrad, March 23, 1961.

LEGEN La Légende de Joseph,
ballet (1 act). Music, Richard Strauss; choreography,
Michel Fokine; book, Hugo
von Hofmannsthal and Count
Harry Kessler; scenery,
J. M. Sert; costumes, Léon
Bakst. Théâtre National de
l'Opéra, Paris, May 14, 1914.

LETTE Letter to the World,
modern dance work. Music,
Hunter Johnson; spoken text

LIEUT

from lines of poems by
Emily Dickinson, selected
by Martha Graham; chore-
ography, Graham; décor,
Arch Lauterer; costumes,
Edythe Gilfond. Benning-
ton College, Vermont,
August 11, 1940.

LIEUT Lieutenant Kije, ballet
(1 act). Music, Serge
Prokofiev; choreography,
Alexander Lapauri and Olga
Tarasova; décor, B. A.
Messerer. Bolshoi Thea-
tre, Moscow, February 2,
1963.

LITTL Little Johnny in Top-
Boots, ballet (1 act).
Music, Jenö Kenessey;
choreography, Gyula Harangozó; book, Ervin Clemen-
tis; scenery, Zoltán Fülöp;
costumes, Gusztav Oláh.
Royal Hungarian Opera
House, Budapest, June,
1937.

LITTM The Little Mermaid,
ballet. Music, Henriques;
choreography, Hans Beck;
book, after the story by
Hans Christian Andersen.
Royal Danish Ballet, Copenhagen, 1909.

LOIND Loin du Danemark (Far
from Denmark), vaudeville
ballet (2 acts). Music,
Glaeser, jun. ; choreography
and book, August Bournon-
ville; scenery, Lund and
Christensen; costumes, E.
Lehmann. Royal Theatre,
Copenhagen, April 1, 1860.

LOLAM Lola Montez, ballet.
Music, Fred Witt; chore-
ography, Edward Caton;
décor, Raoul Pène du Bois.
City Center, New York,
1947.

LONDO London Morning, ballet
(1 act). Music, Noel Coward,
orchestrated by Gordon Jacob; choreography, Jack Carter; décor, William Constable;
costumes, Norman MacDowell.
Festival Hall, London, July
14, 1959.

LORDO The Lord of Burleigh,
ballet. Music, Felix Men-
delssohn, arranged by Edwin
Evans; choreography, Frederick Ashton; décor, George
Sheringham. Camargo So-
ciety, London, 1931.

LOUPP Le Loup, ballet (1 act).
Music, Henri Dutilleux; choreography, Roland Petit; book,
Jean Anouilh and Georges
Neveux; scenery and cos-
tumes, Carzou. Théâtre de
l'Empire, Paris, March 17,
1953.

LOVEM The Loves of Mars and
Venus, ballet. Music, un-
known; choreography, John
Weaver. London, 1717.

LOVEV The Loves of Venus and
Adonis, ballet. Music and
choreography, unknown. St.
Petersburg, 1808.

LUCIF Lucifer, ballet. Music,
Delvincourt; choreography,
Serge Lifar; décor, Yves
Brayer. Paris Opéra, Paris,
1949.

LYRIC Lyric Suite, modern
dance work. Music, Alban
Berg's quartet of the same
name; choreography, Anna
Sokolow. Mexico City,
Mexico, 1953.

LYSIS Lysistrata, ballet (3 acts).
Music, Boris Blacher; choreography, Gustav Blank; book,
based on Aristophanes' come-

dy; décor, Ita Maximova. Berlin Festival, September 30, 1951.

LYSIT Lysistrata, ballet. Music, Serge Prokofiev; choreography, Antony Tudor; book, based on Aristophanes' comedy; décor, William Chappell. Marie Rambert Studio, Ladbroke Road, London, 1932.

MADAM Madame Chrysanthème, ballet (1 act). Music, Alan Rawsthorne; choreography, Frederick Ashton; book Ashton and Vera Bowen after the novel by Pierre Loti; scenery and costumes, Isabel Lambert. Royal Opera, Covent Garden, London, April 1, 1955.

MADEM Mademoiselle Fifi, comic ballet (1 act). Music, Theodore Eduard Dufare Lajart, arranged by Samuel Grossman; choreography, Zachary Solov; scenery, Peter Larkin; costumes, Helen Pons. John Hancock Hall, Boston, October 13, 1952.

MADRO Madroños, ballet (1 act, 5 tableaux). Music, Moritz Moskowski, Sebastian Yradier and others, orchestrated by Ivan Boutnikoff; choreography, Antonia Cobos; costumes, Castillo (of Elizabeth Arden). City Center, New York, March 22, 1947.

MADTR Mad Tristan, surrealist ballet. Music, Richard Wagner (Tristan und Isolde, arranged by Ivan Boutnikoff); choreography, Léonide Massine; book, scenery and costumes,

Salvador Dali. Ballet International, International Theater, New York, December 15, 1944.

MAGIC The Magic Flute, ballet (1 act). Music, Riccardo Drigo; choreography and book, Lev Ivanov. Annual pupils' display in Small Theatre of Imperial Ballet School, St. Petersburg, March 10, 1893.

MAIDE The Maiden's Tower, ballet (3 acts). Music, Afrasijab Badal Beili; choreography, Tamara Almas Zade. Akhundov State Opera and Ballet Theatre, Baku, 1940.

MALIN La Malinche, modern dance work (1 scene). Music, Norman Lloyd; choreography, José Limón; costumes, Pauline Lawrence. Ziegfeld Theater, New York, March 31, 1949.

MAMZE Mam'zelle Angot, ballet (3 scenes). Music, Alexandre Charles Lecocq, orchestrated by Gordon Jacob; choreography and book, Léonide Massine; settings and costumes, André Derain. Royal Opera, Covent Garden, London, November 26, 1947.

MANCE Mancenilha, ballet (1 act). Music, Heitor Villa-Lobos; choreography, Madeleine Rosay; décor and costumes, Tomás Santa Rosa. Teatro Municipal, Rio de Janeiro, Brazil, 1953.

MANFR The Man from Midian, ballet. Music, Stephen Wolpe; choreography, Eugene Loring; book, based on a poem by Winthrop Palmer;

décor, James Stewart Morcom; costumes, Felipe Fiocca. New York, Spring, 1942.

MARCH Le Marché des Innocents, ballet-pantomime (1 act). Music, Cesare Pugni; choreography and book, Marius Petipa; scenery, Cambon and Thierry. Maryinsky Theatre, St. Petersburg, April 23, 1859.

MARCO Marco Spada ou la Fille du Bandit, pantomimic ballet (3 acts). Music, François Aubert; choreography and book, Joseph Mazilier, adapted from the comic opera of the same name. Théâtre Impérial de l'Opéra, Paris, April 1, 1857.

MARDI Mardi Gras, ballet (1 act). Music, Leonard Salzedo; choreography, Andrée Howard; décor, Hugh Stevenson. Sadler's Wells Theatre, London, November 26, 1947.

MARIE Les Mariés de la Tour Eiffel, ballet (1 act). Music, Georges Auric, Arthur Honegger, Darius Milhaud, Francis Poulenc and Germaine Tailleferre; choreography, Jean Borlin; book, Jean Cocteau; scenery, Irène Lagut; costumes and masks, Jean Hugo. Théâtre des Champs-Élysées, Paris, June 19, 1921.

MASQE Masquerade, ballet (4 acts). Music, Lev Laputin; choreography and book, Boris Fenster, after the Mikhail Lermontov drama of the same name; décor, Tatiana Bruni. Kirov Theatre, Leningrad, December 29, 1960.

MASQS Les Masques, ballet (1 act). Music, Francis Poulenc's "Trio for Piano, Oboe and Bassoon"; choreography, Frederick Ashton; décor, Sophie Fedorovitch. Mercury Theatre, London, March 5, 1933.

MASSA Le Massacre des Amazones, ballet (1 act). Music, Ivan K. Semenoff; choreography, Janine Charrat; book, Charrat and Maurice Sarrazin; setting and costumes, Jean Bazaine. Théâtre Munipal, Grenoble, December 24, 1952.

MATEL Les Matelots, ballet (5 scenes). Music, Georges Auric; choreography, Léonide Massine; book, Boris Kochno; curtains, scenery and costumes, Pedro Pruna. Théâtre de la Gaîté-Lyrique, Paris, June 17, 1925.

MEDEA Medea, ballet (1 act, 5 scenes). Music, Béla Bartók's piano pieces, arranged by Herbert Sandberg; choreography, Birgit Cullberg; décor, Alvar Grandstrom. Riksteatern, Gaevle, Sweden, October 31, 1950.

MEDEE Médée et Jason, ballet. Music, Rodolphe; choreography, Jean George Noverre. Württemburg Ducal Theatre, Stuttgart, February 11, 1763.

MEPHI Mephisto Valse, ballet (1 act). Music, Franz Liszt's "Mephisto Valse"; choreography, Frederick Ashton; décor, Sophie Fedorovitch. Mercury Theatre,

London, June 13, 1934.

MEPHS Mephisto Valse, ballet
(1 act). Music, Franz
Liszt's "Mephisto Valse";
choreography, Maryla
Gremo; décor and cos-
tumes, Fernando Pamplona.
Teatro Municipal, Rio de
Janeiro, Brazil, 1952.

METAM Les Métamorphoses,
ballet (1 act). Music,
Cesare Pugni; choreography
and book, Paul Taglioni.
Her Majesty's Theatre,
London, March 12, 1850.

METRO Metropolitan Daily,
modern group work. Mu-
sic, Gregory Tucker;
choreography, Hanya Holm.
Television production,
February 19, 1939.

MIDAS Midas (Les Métamor-
phoses), ballet. Music,
Maximilian Steinberg;
choreography, Michel Fo-
kine; décor, Mitislav
Doboujinsky. Paris Opéra,
Paris, 1914.

MIDSU A Midsummer Night's
Dream, ballet (2 acts).
Music, Felix Mendelssohn;
choreography, George
Balanchine, after Shake-
speare; décor, David Hays;
costumes, Barbara Karin-
ska. City Center, New
York, January 17, 1962.

MINOT The Minotaur, ballet
(2 parts). Music, Elliott
Carter; choreography, John
Taras; book, Lincoln Kir-
stein and Joan Junyer;
costumes and décor,
Junyer. Central High
School of Needle Trades,
New York, March 26,
1947.

MINOU The Minotaur, ballet (1
act). Music, Karl-Birger
Blomdahl; choreography, Birgit Aakesson; book, Erik
Lindegren; décor, Tor Hörlin.
Royal Opera Theater, Stockholm, April 5, 1958.

MIRAC Miracle in the Gorbals,
ballet (1 act). Music, Ar-
thur Bliss; choreography,
Robert Helpmann; book,
Michael Benthall; scenery
and costumes, Edward Burra.
Prince's Theatre, London,
October 26, 1944.

MIRAG Les Mirages, chore-
ographic fairy tale (1 act).
Music, Henri Sauguet; choreography, Serge Lifar; book,
Lifar and A. M. Cassandre;
setting and costumes, Cassandre. Théâtre National de l'
Opéra, Paris, December 15,
1947.

MIRAM The Miraculous Mandarin,
dance pantomime (1 act). Music, Béla Bartók; choreography, Hans Strobach; book,
Bartók, after Melchior Leng-
yel. Municipal Stage, Co-
logne, Germany, November
28, 1926.

MIRAR The Miraculous Mandarin,
ballet. Music, Béla Bartók;
choreography, Alfred Rodrigues; décor, Georges Wak-
hevitch. Empire Theatre,
Edinburgh, August 27, 1956.

MIRAU The Miraculous Mandarin,
melodramatic ballet (1 act).
Music, Béla Bartók; choreography, Todd Bolender;
libretto, after Melchior Leng-
yel; scenery and costumes,
Alvin Colt; lighting, Jean Rosenthal. City Center, New
York, September 6, 1951.

MIRRO A Mirror for Witches,
dramatic ballet (prologue,
5 scenes). Music, Denis
ApIvor; choreography, An-
drée Howard; book, Howard,
based on the novel by Es-
ther Forbes; costumes,
Howard; scenery, Norman
Adams. Royal Opera
House, Covent Garden,
London, March 4, 1952.

MISSJ Miss Julie, ballet (4
scenes). Music, Ture
Rangström; choreography,
Birgit Cullberg; book,
after Strindberg's play
"Fröken Julie"; settings
and costumes, Allan Frid-
ericia. Riksteatern,
Vasteros, Sweden, March
1, 1950.

MOHIC Les Mohicans, ballet
(2 acts). Music, Adolphe
Adam; choreography, An-
tonio Guerra; book, after
the novel by James Feni-
more Cooper. Paris Opéra,
Paris, 1837.

MOONR The Moon Reindeer,
ballet (1 act). Music,
Knudage Riisager; chore-
ography, Birgit Cullberg;
décor, Per Falk. Royal
Theatre, Copenhagen,
November 22, 1957.

MOORO The Moor of Venice
(Othello, the Moor of
Venice), ballet (prologue,
8 scenes, epilogue). Mu-
sic, Boris Blacher; chore-
ography, Erika Hanka, after
Shakespeare's "Othello";
décor, Georges Wakhevitch.
Vienna State Opera, Vienna,
November 29, 1955.

MOORP The Moor's Pavane,
modern dance work. Music,
Henry Purcell, arranged by

Simon Sadoff; choreography,
José Limón, based on the
handkerchief episode in
Shakespeare's "Othello"; cos-
tumes, Pauline Lawrence.
Connecticut College, New
London, Conn., August,
1949.

MORTD La Mort du Cygne,
ballet. Music, Frédéric
Chopin; choreography, Serge
Lifar. Paris Opéra, Paris,
1948.

MOTHE Mother Goose Suite,
classic ballet (5 scenes).
Music, Maurice Ravel (Ma
Mère l'Oye); choreography,
Todd Bolender. Central High
School of Needle Trades Au-
ditorium, New York, October
31, 1943; revised and pre-
sented, with costumes by
André Derain, City Center,
New York, November 1, 1948.

MRPUP Mr. Puppet, modern
dance work. Music, spoken
soliloquy; choreography and
costumes, Nina Fonaroff.
YM-YWHA, New York, No-
vember 7, 1948.

MUTEW The Mute Wife, ballet
(1 act). Music, Vittorio
Rieti, ending with his orchestration of Niccolo Paganini's "Moto Perpetuo";
choreography, Antonia Cobos,
based on Anatole France's
"The Man Who Married a
Dumb Wife"; décor, Rico
Lebrun. International Theater, New York, November
22, 1944.

NAISV La Naissance de Vénus,
ballet. Music, J. H. d'
Egville (?), choreography,
d'Egville. King's Theatre,
London, 1826.

NAMOU Namouna, ballet (2 acts). Music, E. Lalo; choreography, Lucien Petipa; book, Petipa and Charles Nuitter; scenery, Rubé, Chaperon and J. B. Lavastre; costumes, Eugène Lacoste. Théâtre de l' Opéra, Paris, March 6, 1882.

NAPOL Napoli, or The Fisherman and His Bride, romantic ballet (3 acts). Music, Paulli, Edvard Helsted, and Svend Gade; choreography, August Bournonville; scenery, Christensen. Theatre Royal, Copenhagen, March 29, 1842.

NARCE Narcissus and Echo, ballet. Music, Arthur Bliss; choreography, Ninette de Valois; décor, William Chappell. Sadler's Wells Theatre, London, 1932.

NARCI Narcissus (Narcisse), ballet (1 act). Music, Maurice Ravel's "Introduction and Allegro for Harp and Strings"; choreography, Nina Verchinina; décor, Henrique Peyceré. Buenos Aires, Argentina, 1950.

NARKI Narkissos, ballet. Music, Robert Prince; choreography, Edward Villella; scenery, costumes and lighting, John Braden. Saratoga Springs Performing Arts Theater, Saratoga Springs, N. Y., July 21, 1966.

NATHA Nathalie ou la Laitière Suisse (Nathalie, or The Swiss Milkmaid), ballet (2 acts). Music, Gyrowitz and Caraffa; choreography and book, Philippe Taglioni; scenery, Ciceri. Théâtre de l'Académie Royale de Musique, Paris, November 7, 1832.

NAUTE Nautéos, ballet (3 acts). Music, Jeanne Leleu; choreography, Serge Lifar; book, René Dumesnil; scenery and costumes, Yves Brayer. Théâtre National de l'Opéra, Paris, July 12, 1954.

NEWYO The New Yorker, ballet (3 scenes). Music, George Gershwin, orchestrated by David Raskin; choreography, Léonide Massine; book, Massine and Rea Irvin; scenery and costumes, Carl Kent, after Irvin and Nathalie Crothers. Fifty-First Street Theater, New York, October 31, 1940.

NIGHI The Nightingale, ballet (3 acts). Music, M. E. Kroshner; choreography, A. N. Yermolayev; book, Yermolayev and J. O. Slonimsky, after the story by Zmitrok Biadulia; scenery and costumes, B. A. Matrunine. Moscow, August, 1940.

NIGHJ Night Journey, modern dance group. Music, William Schuman; choreography, Martha Graham, based on the Oedipus myth; décor and costumes, Isamu Noguchi. Auditorium of the Cambridge and Latin School, Cambridge, Mass., May 3, 1947.

NIGHP Night Spell (original title Quartet No. 1), modern dance work. Music, Priaulx Rainier's "Quartet No. 1"; choreography, Doris Humphrey; costumes, Pauline Lawrence.

Connecticut College, New
London, Conn., August,
1951.

NIGHT Night Shadow (La
Sonnambula), ballet (1 act).
Music, Vittorio Rieti, after Vincenzo Bellini; choreography, George Balanchine;
book, Rieti; scenery and
costumes, Dorothy Tanning.
City Center, New York,
February 27, 1946.

NIGHY The Night City, ballet
(1 act). Music, Béla Bartók's "Miraculous Manda-
rin"; choreography and
book, Leonid Lavrovsky;
décor, Vadim Ryndin.
Bolshoi Theatre, Moscow,
May 21, 1961.

NINAO Nina, ou la Folle par
Amour (Nina, or the Girl
Driven Mad by Love), bal-
let pantomime (2 acts).
Music, Persius; chore-
ography, Louis Milon;
book, Milon. Théâtre de
l'Académie Impériale de
Musique, Paris, November
23, 1813.

NOCEE Les Noces (The Wedding), ballet (1 act). Music, Igor Stravinsky;
choreography, Jerome Rob-
bins; décor, Oliver Smith;
costumes, Patricia Zipprodt.
New York State Theater,
New York, March 30, 1965.

NOCEF Les Noces Fantastiques
(The Fantastic Wedding),
ballet (2 acts). Music,
Marcel Delannoy; choreogra-
phy, Serge Lifar; décor,
Roger Chastel; costumes,
André Levasseur. Paris
Opéra Ballet, February 9,
1955.

NOCES Les Noces (The Wedding),
cantata with dances (4 scenes).
Music, Igor Stravinsky;
choreography, Bronislava Nijinska; words, Stravinsky;
scenery and costumes, Na-
thalie Gontcharova. Théâtre
Gaîté-Lyrique, Paris, June
13, 1923.

NOCTA Noctambules, ballet (1
act). Music, Humphrey
Seale; choreography and
book, Kenneth MacMillan;
décor, Nicholas Georgiadis.
Royal Opera House, Covent
Garden, London, March 1,
1956.

NOCTU Nocturne, ballet (1 act).
Music, Frederick Delius;
choreography, Frederick Ash-
ton; book, Edward Sackville-
West; scenery and costumes,
Sophie Fedorovich. Sadler's
Wells Theatre, London, No-
vember 10, 1936.

NUITD Nuit de Saint-Jean, ballet
(1 act). Music, Hugo Alfvén;
choreography and book, Jean
Borlin; scenery and costumes,
Nils de Dardel. Théâtre des
Champs Élysées, Paris,
October 25, 1920.

NUITE La Nuit et le Jour, ballet (1 act). Music, Leon
Minkus; choreography and
book, Marius Petipa; scenery,
Botcharov and Walz; cos-
tumes, Charlemagne, Baron
Klodt and Grigoriev. Bolshoi Theatre, Moscow, May
18, 1883.

NUITT La Nuit, ballet (1 act).
Music, Henri Sauguet; choreography, Janine Charrat;
book, Boris Kochno; settings
and costumes, Christian
Berard. Théâtre des Champs

Élysées, Paris, April 19, 1949.

NUTCA The Nutcracker, ballet (2 acts). Music, Peter Ilyich Tchaikovsky; choreography, George Balanchine (after Lev Ivanov); décor, Horace Armistead; costumes, Barbara Karinska. City Center, New York, February 2, 1954.

NUTCK The Nutcracker, ballet (3 acts and 6 scenes, with an epilogue). Music, Peter Ilyich Tchaikovsky; choreography and book, V. I. Vynonen; décor, Nicolai Seleznyov. Kirov Theatre, Leningrad, February 18, 1934.

NUTCR The Nutcracker (Casse Noisette), classic ballet (2 acts, 3 scenes). Music, Peter Ilyich Tchaikovsky; choreography, Lev Ivanov, following the projected plan of Marius Petipa; book, Petipa, based on E. T. A. Hoffmann's story "The Nutcracker and the King of Mice"; scenery, M. I. Botcharov and K. M. Ivanov. Maryinsky Theatre, St. Petersburg, December 6, 1892.

ODYSS Odyssey, modern dance work. Music, Ivan Fiedel (percussion, brass and woodwind score); choreography, Murray Louis. Henry Street Playhouse, New York, March 11, 1960.

OEUFA L'Oeuf à la Coque (The Soft-Boiled Egg), fantastic ballet (1 act). Music, Maurice Thiriet; choreography, Roland Petit; scenery and costumes, Stanislas

Lepri. Prince's Theatre, London, February 16, 1949.

OFFEN Offenbach in the Underworld, ballet (1 act). Music, Jacques Offenbach (score for "Gaîté Parisienne" in a different orchestration); choreography, Antony Tudor; décor, Kay Ambrose. Royal Alexandra Theatre, Toronto, Canada, February 1, 1955.

OGARA O. Garatuja, ballet (1 act). Music, Alberto Nepomuceno; choreography, Dennis Gray; story based on a novel by José de Alencar; décor, Nilson Penna. Teatro Municipal, Rio de Janeiro, Brazil, 1960.

OMBRE L'Ombre, ballet (3 acts). Music, L. Wilhelm Maurer; choreography and book, Philippe Taglioni; décor, Fedorov, Serkov, Shenian and Roller; costumes, Mathieu. Bolshoi Theatre, St. Petersburg, December 10, 1839.

ONDIE Ondine, ballet. Music, Antonio Vivaldi (Violin Concertos); choreography, William Dollar; costumes and décor, Horace Armistead. City Center, New York, December 9, 1949.

ONDII Ondine, ballet (3 acts). Music, Hans Werner Henze; choreography, Frederick Ashton; décor, Lisa de Nobili. Royal Opera House, Covent Garden, London, October 27, 1958.

ONDIL Ondine, ballet. Music, Hans Werner Henze; choreography, Alan Carter; décor, von Gugel. Opera House, Munich, January 25, 1959.

ONDIN Ondine ou la Naïade,
  ballet (6 scenes). Music,
  Cesare Pugni; choreography,
  Jules Perrot and Fanny
  Cerito; book, Perrot and
  Cerito; scenery, W. Griève.
  Her Majesty's Theatre,
  London, June 22, 1843.

ONDIS Les Ondines, ballet.
  Music, unknown; chore-
  ography, Louis X. S. Henri.
  Théâtre Nautique, Paris,
  1834?

ONEIN One in Five, ballet (1
  act). Music, an arrangement of polkas and waltzes
  by Josef and Johann Strauss;
  choreography, Ray Powell;
  décor, Derek Rencher.
  Sunday Ballet Club, London, June 12, 1960.

ONSTA On Stage!, ballet (1
  act). Music, Norman
  Dello Joio; choreography,
  Michael Kidd; book, Mi-
  chael and Mary Kidd; décor, Oliver Smith; cos-
  tumes, Alvin Colt. Boston Opera House, Boston,
  October 4, 1945.

ORIAN Oriane et le Prince d'
  Amour, ballet drama (2
  acts). Music, Florent
  Schmitt; choreography,
  Serge Lifar; book, Mme.
  Claude Seran (nom-de-
  plume of Mme. Fauchier-
  Magnan); scenery and cos-
  tumes, Pedro Pruna. Théâ-
  tre National de l'Opéra,
  Paris, January 7, 1938.

ORPHE Orpheus, ballet (3
  scenes). Music, Igor
  Stravinsky; choreography,
  George Balanchine; scen-
  ery and costumes, Isamu
  Noguchi; lighting, Jean
  Rosenthal. City Center,

New York, April 28, 1948.

ORPHH Orphée, choreographic
  drama (1 act). Electronic
  music, Pierre Henry; choreography, Maurice Béjart; décor, Rudolf Kufner. Liège
  Opera, Belgium, September
  17, 1958.

ORPHI Orpheus in Town, ballet.
  Music, Rosenberg; chore-
  ography, Julian Algo; décor,
  Jon-And. Stockholm, 1938.

ORPHS Orpheus and Eurydice,
  ballet (2 acts). Music,
  Christoph Willibald von
  Gluck; choreography, George
  Balanchine; costumes and dé-
  cor, Paul Tchelitchew.
  Metropolitan Opera House,
  New York, May 22, 1936.

ORPHU Orpheus and Eurydice,
  ballet (2 acts). Music,
  Christoph Willibald Gluck,
  from the opera; choreography, Ninette de Valois; book,
  after Ranieri di Calzabigi's
  libretto for the Gluck opera;
  décor, Sophie Fedorovitch.
  New Theatre, London, May
  28, 1941.

OTELL Otello, ballet (5 acts).
  Music, Salvatore Viganò,
  based on airs of other composers; choreography, Viganò;
  book, Viganò, based on Shakespeare's tragedy; scenery,
  Alessandro Sanquirico. Teatro alla Scala, Milan, February 6, 1818.

OTHEL Othello, ballet (4 acts).
  Music, Alexei Machavariani;
  choreography and book, Vakh-
  tang Chabukiani, based on
  Shakespeare's tragedy; décor,
  Simon Virsaladze. Paliash-
  vili Theatre of Opera and
  Ballet, Tbilisi, Georgia,

November 29, 1957.

OWLAN The Owl and the
Pussycat, ballet (1 act).
Music, Dudley Moore;
choreography, Gillian Lynn,
based on the poem of the
same name by Edward
Lear; décor, Kenneth
Rowell. Sunday Ballet
Club, London, June 17,
1962.

OZAII Ozai, ballet (2 acts).
Music, Casimir Gide;
choreography, Jean Coralli;
scenery, Ciceri. Théâtre
de l'Académie Royale de
Musique, Paris, April 26,
1847.

PAGAI Paganini, ballet (1 act);
music, Sergei Rachmani-
noff's "Rhapsody on a Theme
of Paganini"; choreography
and book, Leonid Lavrovsky;
décor, Vadim Ryndin. Bol-
shoi Theatre, Moscow,
April 7, 1960.

PAGAN Paganini, fantastic bal-
let (3 scenes). Music,
Sergei Rachmaninoff's
"Rhapsody on a Theme of
Paganini"; choreography,
Michel Fokine; scenery
and costumes, Sergei Soudei-
kine. Royal Opera House,
Covent Garden, London,
June 30, 1939.

PAGEL Pages of Life, ballet
(1 act). Music, Andrei
Balanchivadze; choreogra-
phy and book, Leonid Lav-
rovsky; décor, Valery
Dorrer. Bolshoi Theatre,
Moscow, November 19,
1961.

PAGES Les Pages du Duc de
Vendôme, ballet (1 act).
Music, Gyrowitz; choreogra-

phy, Jean Aumer; book,
Aumer. Kaernthner Thor
Theatre, Vienna, October
16, 1815.

PANDO Pandora, ballet (2 parts,
6 movements). Music, Ro-
berto Gerhardt; choreography,
Kurt Jooss; décor, Hein
Heckroth. Arts Theatre,
Cambridge, England, Janu-
ary 26, 1944.

PAPAG Papagaio do Moleque
(The Kid's Parrot), ballet
(1 act). Music, Heitor
Villa-Lobos; choreography,
Vaslav Veltcheck; book and
costumes, Gilberto Trompow-
sky; décor, Fernando Pamplona. Teatro Municipal, Rio
de Janeiro, Brazil, 1952.

PAPIL Le Papillon, pantomime-
ballet (2 acts). Music,
Jacques Offenbach; chore-
ography, Marie Taglioni;
book, Taglioni and V. de
Saint-Georges; scenery, Cam-
bon, Thierry, Desplêchin,
Nolau, Rubé and Martin.
Théâtre Impérial de l'Opéra,
Paris, November 26, 1860.

PAPIO Les Papillons, fantastic
ballet divertissement (2
scenes). Music, Leopold
Wenzel; choreography, Katti
Lanner; book and costumes,
C. Wilhelm; scenery, Joseph
Harker. Empire Theatre,
London, March 18, 1901.

PAQUE Pâquerette, pantomimic
ballet (3 acts). Music,
Benoist; choreography, Arthur Saint-Léon; book, Saint-
Léon and Théophile Gautier;
scenery, Desplêchin, Cam-
bon and Thierry. Théâtre de
l'Académie Nationale de
Musique, Paris, January 15,
1851.

PAQUI Paquita, pantomimic
ballet (2 acts). Music,
Edward Deldevez; chore-
ography, Joseph Mazilier;
book, Mazilier and Paul
Foucher; décor, Philastre,
Cambon, Diêterle, Séchan
and Desplêchin. Thêâtre
de l'Académie Royale de
Musique, Paris, April 1,
1846.

PAQUT Paquita, pantomimic
ballet (2 acts). Music,
Leon Minkus, with inter-
polations by Edward Delde-
vez; choreography, Joseph
Mazilier, revisions by
Marius Petipa. Bolshoi
Theatre, St. Petersburg,
September, 1847.

PARAD Parade, realistic ballet (1 act). Music, Eric
Satie; choreography, Léo
nide Massine; book, Jean
Cocteau; curtain, scenery
and costumes, Pablo Pi-
casso. Thêâtre du Chate-
let, Paris, May 18, 1917.

PASDA Le Pas d'Acier (The
March of Steel), ballet (12
sections). Music, Sergei
Prokofiev; choreography,
Léonide Massine; stage de-
sign, Georges Jakouloff.
Paris Opéra, Paris, June
8, 1927.

PASDE Pas de Quatre, diver-
tissement. Music, Cesare
Pugni; choreography, Jules
Perrot. Her Majesty's
Theatre, London, July 12,
1845.

PASDF Pas de Quatre, ballet.
Music, Cesare Pugni, ar-
ranged and orchestrated by
Lucas Leighton; choreography,
Keith Lester (a reconstruc-
tion of Perrot's "Le Pas de

Quatre"); costumes, after
Chalon. Markova-Dolin Com-
pany, 1936; English première,
Royal Opera House, Covent
Garden, London, August 26,
1946.

PASDG Le Pas de Quatre, ballet.
Music, Cesare Pugni, trans-
cribed by Lucas Leighton,
orchestrated by Paul Bowles,
inspired by the lithograph of
A. E. Chalon; choreography,
Anton Dolin (a reconstruction
of Perrot's "Le Pas de
Quatre"). Majestic Theater,
New York, February 16,
1941.

PASDS Pas des Déesses, ballet
(1 act). Music, John Field,
arranged by H. Hardy; choreography, Robert Joffrey.
YM-YWHA, New York, May
29, 1954.

PASTE Pastorale, ballet. Music,
Georges Auric; choreography,
George Balanchine; décor,
Pedro Pruna. Gaîtê-Lyrique,
Paris, 1925.

PASTO Pastorela, opera ballet
(1 act). Music, Paul Bowles,
orchestrated by Blas Galindo;
choreography, Lew Christensen and José Fernandez;
book, José Martinez, based
on "El Concilio de los Siete
Diablos" ("The Council of
Seven Devils"); words, Rafael Alvarez; costumes, Alvin Colt, based on original
sources. Teatro Municipal,
Rio de Janeiro, Brazil,
June 27, 1941.

PATHO The Path of Thunder,
ballet (3 acts). Music,
Kara Karayev; choreography,
Konstantin Sergeyev; book,
Yuri Slonimsky, after the
novel by the South African

author Peter Abrahams; décor, Valery Dorrer. Kirov Theatre, Leningrad, December 31, 1957.

PATIN Les Patineurs (The Skaters), ballet (1 act). Music, Giacomo Meyerbeer ("L'Etoile du Nord" and "Le Prophète"), arranged by Constant Lambert; choreography, Frederick Ashton; scenery and costumes, William Chappell. Sadler's Wells Theatre, London, February 16, 1937.

PAVIL Le Pavillon d'Armide (Armide's Pavilion) (The Animated Goblins), ballet (1 act). Music, Nicholas Tcherepnine; choreography, Michel Fokine; book and décor, Alexandre Benois. Maryinsky Theatre, St. Petersburg, November 25, 1907.

PEERG Peer Gynt, ballet (3 acts, 10 scenes). Music, Edvard Grieg; choreography, Vaslav Orlikovsky; book, from the play "Peer Gynt" by Henrik Ibsen; décor, Edward Delaney; costumes, Yvonne Lloyd. Opera House, Monte Carlo, April 13, 1963.

PELLE Pelléas et Mélisande, choreographic study (1 scene). Music, Gabriel Fauré; choreography, Jean Jacques Etchevery; book, Etchevery, after Maeterlinck's play. Festival International, Enghien-les-Bains, France, June 13, 1953.

PERHA Perhaps Tomorrow!, ballet (1 act). Music, Jenö

Kenessey; choreography, Gyula Harangozó; book, István Juhász; scenery, Aladár Olgyay; costumes, Klára Szunyogh-Tüdös and Tivadar Márk. Metropolitan Art Theatre, Budapest, May 9, 1937.

PERIA La Péri, ballet (1 act). Music, Paul Dukas' tone poem of the same name; choreography, Frederick Ashton; décor, Ivor Hitchens; costumes, André Levasseur. Royal Opera House, Covent Garden, London, February 15, 1956. Earlier version produced at Mercury Theatre, London, February 16, 1931 with costumes by William Chappell.

PERIC La Péri, ballet. Music, Paul Dukas; choreography, Ivan Clustine. Paris Opéra, Paris, 1912.

PERID La Péri, dance drama. Music, Paul Dukas; choreography, Leo Staats. Paris Opéra, Paris, 1921.

PERIF La Péri, ballet. Music, Paul Dukas; choreography, Frank Staff; décor, Alexandre Benois. 1938.

PERII La Péri, fantastic ballet (2 acts). Music, Burgmüller; choreography, Jean Coralli; book, Coralli, and Théophile Gautier; scenery for Act I, Séchan, Diéterle and Despléchin; for Act II, Philastre and Cambon; costumes, Marilhat and Paul Lormier. Théâtre de l'Académie Royale de Musique, Paris, July 17, 1843.

PERSE Persephone, "melodrame" (6 scenes). Music, Igor

Stravinsky; choreography, Frederick Ashton; book, Stravinsky and André Gide; décor, Nico Ghika. Royal Opera House, Covent Garden, London, December 12, 1962.

PERSF Persephone, ballet. Music, F. A. Cohen; choreography, Kurt Jooss. Paris Opéra, Paris, 1934.

PERSG Persephone, ballet. Music, Robert Schumann; choreography, Robert Joffrey. Ballet Rambert, London, 1955.

PERSH Persephone, ballet. Music, Robert Schumann; choreography, John Taras; décor, Lila de Nobili. Théâtre de Monte Carlo, Monte Carlo, 1950.

PETER Peter and the Wolf, ballet for children (1 act). Music, Serge Prokofiev; choreography, Adolph Bolm; story, Prokofiev; scenery and costumes, Lucinda Ballard. Center Theater, New York, January 13, 1940.

PETEW Peter and the Wolf, ballet for children (1 act). Music and book, Serge Prokofiev; choreography, Frank Staff; décor and costumes, Guy Sheppard. Arts Theatre, Cambridge, May 1, 1940.

PETIA Les Petits Riens, ballet. Music, Wolfgang Amadeus Mozart; choreography, Frederick Ashton; décor, William Chappell. Mercury Theatre, London, March 10, 1928.

PETID Les Petits Riens, bal-

let. Music, Wolfgang Amadeus Mozart; choreography, Ninette de Valois; décor, Smyth. Old Vic, London, December 13, 1928.

PETIR Les Petits Riens, ballet. Music, Wolfgang Amadeus Mozart; choreography, Ruth Page; décor, Robert Davison. Chicago, Ill. , 1946.

PETIT Les Petits Riens, ballet-pantomime (3 scenes). Music, Wolfgang Amadeus Mozart; choreography, Jean Georges Noverre. Académie Royale (Opéra), Paris, June 11, 1778.

PETRO Petrouchka, ballet burlesque (4 acts). Music, Igor Stravinsky; choreography, Michel Fokine; book, Stravinsky and Alexandre Benois; scenery and costumes, Benois. Théâtre du Châtelet, Paris, June 13, 1911.

PHAED Phaedra, modern dance work. Music, Robert Starer; choreography and costumes, Martha Graham; décor, Isamu Noguchi. Broadway Theater, New York, March 4, 1962.

PHEDR Phèdre, tragedy in choreography. Music, Georges Auric; choreography, Serge Lifar; book, Jean Cocteau, after Greek legend; scenery and costumes, Cocteau. Théâtre National de l'Opéra, Paris, June 14, 1950.

PICNI Picnic at Tintagel, dramatic ballet (3 scenes). Music, Sir Arnold Bax (The Garden of Fand); choreography, Frederick Ashton; scenery and costumes, Cecil Beaton; costumes executed by Helene Pons; lighting, Jean Rosenthal. City Center, New York, February 28, 1952.

PIEDP The Pied Piper, dance ballet (2 parts). Music, Aaron Copland (Concerto for Clarinet and String Orchestra); choreography, Jerome Robbins; lighting, Jean Rosenthal. City Center, New York, December 4, 1951.

PIEGE Piège de Lumière, ballet (3 scenes). Music, Jean-Michel Damase; choreography, John Taras; book, Philippe Hériat; scenery, Felix Labisse; costumes, André Levasseur; butterfly masks, Marie Molotkoff. Théâtre de l' Empire, Paris, December 23, 1952.

PIERR Pierrot Lunaire, ballet. Music, Arnold Schoenberg; choreography, Adolph Bolm; décor, Nicolai Remisoff. Chicago, 1926.

PIGMA Pigmalion, ballet. Music, J. H. d'Egville (?); choreography, d'Egville. King's Theatre, London, 1808.

PILLA Pillar of Fire, ballet (1 act). Music, Arnold Schönberg ("Verklärte Nacht"); choreography and book, Antony Tudor; scenery and costumes, Jo Mielziner. Metropolitan Opera House, New York, April 8, 1942.

PINEA Pineapple Poll, comic ballet (3 scenes). Music: Sir Arthur Sullivan, arranged by Charles Mackerras; choreography, John Cranko, based on W. S.

Gilbert's Bab Ballad, "The Bumboat Woman's Story"; scenery and costumes, Osbert Lancaster. Sadler's Wells Theatre, London, March 13, 1951.

PLACE Place in the Desert, ballet (1 act). Music, Carlos Surinach's "David and Bathsheba"; choreography and book, Norman Morrice; décor, Ralph Koltai. Sadler's Wells Theatre, London, July 25, 1961.

PLAIS Les Plaisirs de l'Hiver, ou Les Patineurs, ballet divertissement (1 act, 2 scenes). Music, Cesare Pugni; choreography and book, Paul Taglioni. Her Majesty's Theatre, London, July 10, 1849.

PLANE The Planets, ballet (1 act). Music, Gustav Holst's score of the same name; choreography, Antony Tudor; décor, Hugh Stevenson. Mercury Theatre, London, October 28, 1934.

PLANT The Planets, ballet (7 scenes). Music, Gustav Holst's score of the same name; choreography, Erich Walter; décor, Heinrich Wendel; costumes, Xenia Chris. Vienna State Opera, Vienna, November 22, 1961.

POCAH Pocahontas, ballet legend (1 act). Music, Elliott Carter, Jr.; choreography, Lew Christensen; book, Lincoln Kirstein; costumes, Karl Free. Colonial Theater, Keene, N. H., August 17, 1936.

POMOE Pomone, ballet. Music, Robert Cambert; choreography,

Beauchamp. L'Académie
Royale de Musique, Paris,
1669.

POMON Pomona, ballet. Mu-
sic, Constant Lambert;
choreography, Frederick
Ashton; décor, Vanessa
Bell and J. Banting. Cam-
bridge Theatre, London,
October 19, 1930.

PRESA Les Présages (Destiny),
choreographic symphony (4
parts). Music, Tchaikovsky
(Fifth Symphony); chore-
ography and book, Léonide
Massine; scenery and cos-
tumes, André Masson.
Théâtre de Monte Carlo,
Monte Carlo, April 13,
1933.

PRESS The Press, ballet (3
scenes). Music, Leopold
Wenzel; choreography,
Katti Lanner; book, C.
Wilhelm; costumes, Wil-
helm. Empire Theatre,
London, February 14, 1898.

PRIMA La Prima Ballerina,
ou l'Embuscade (The
Principal Dancer, or The
Ambush), ballet divertissement (1 act). Music, Ce-
sare Pugni; choreography
and book, Paul Taglioni.
Her Majesty's Theatre,
London, June 16, 1849.

PRINC Prince Igor, ballet (1
act). Music, Alexander
Borodin; choreography,
Michel Fokine; décor,
Nicholas Roerich; Théâ-
tre du Châtelet, Paris,
May 18, 1909.

PRING Prince Goudal's
Festival, ballet (1 act).
Music, Anton Rubinstein;
choreography, Boris Ro-

manov; décor, Mitislav
Doboujinsky. International
Theater, New York, Novem-
ber 16, 1944.

PRINO Prince of the Pagodas,
ballet (3 acts). Music, Benjamin Britten; choreography
and book, John Cranko; décor, John Piper; costumes,
Desmond Heeley; lighting,
William Bundy. Royal Opera
House, Covent Garden, London, January 1, 1957.

PRINT Princess Turandot, ballet (2 acts). Music, Gott-
fried von Einem; choreography, Tatiana Gsovska; book
and décor, Luigi Malipiero.
State Opera, Dresden, February 5, 1944.

PRISN Prisoner of the Caucasus,
ballet (1 act, 3 scenes). Music, Aram Khachaturian;
choreography, George Ski-
bine; book based on Alexander
Pushkin's poem; décor, Mitislav Doboujinsky. Théâtre de
l'Empire, Paris, December
4, 1951.

PRISO The Prisoner in the Caucasus, ballet (4 acts). Music, Cavos; choreography,
Charles Didelot; book, Didelot, after the poem by Alexander Pushkin. Bolshoy
Theatre, St. Petersburg,
January 15, 1823.

PRISR The Prisoner in the Caucasus, ballet (prologue, 3
acts, 7 scenes). Music,
B. V. Assafiev; choreography,
L. M. Lavrovsky; book, Lavrovsky, N. D. Volkov and
E. S. Zilberstein, after
Alexander Pushkin's poem;
scenery, B. M. Khodasevich;
production, P. E. Feldt.
Maly Theatre, Leningrad,

end of 1938.

PRISS The Prisoners, ballet
(1 act). Music, Béla Bar-
tók; choreography, Peter
Darrell; décor, Barry Kay.
Dartington Hall, Devon,
England, June 24, 1957.

PRODA The Prodigal Son, ballet. Music, F. A. Cohen;
choreography, Kurt Jooss;
décor, Bouchène. Prince's
Theatre, Bristol, England,
October, 1939.

PRODG The Prodigal Son (Le
Fils Prodigue), ballet (3
scenes). Music, Serge
Prokofiev; choreography,
George Balanchine; book,
Sobeka (Boris Kochno);
scenery and costumes,
Georges Rouault. Théâ-
tre Sarah Bernhardt,
Paris, May 21, 1929.

PRODI The Prodigal Son, bal-
let (2 acts, 6 scenes).
Music, F. A. Cohen; chore-
ography and book, Kurt
Jooss; décor and costumes,
Hein Heckroth. Folkwang
Tanzbühne, Amsterdam,
Holland, October 6, 1933.

PRODL The Prodigal Son,
ballet (4 scenes). Music,
Hugo Alfvén; choreography,
Ivo Cramér; décor, Rune
Linstrom. Royal Swedish
Ballet, 1957.

PRODO The Prodigal Son,
ballet. Music, César
Franck; choreography,
Catherine Littlefield.
Philadelphia Ballet Com-
pany, Philadelphia, Pa.,
1936.

PRODS The Prodigal Son,
ballet (3 scenes). Music,

Serge Prokofiev; choreography,
David Lichine; décor, Georges
Rouault. Sydney, Australia,
December 30, 1938.

PROMN Promenade, ballet (1
act). Music, Josef Haydn,
selected by Edwin Evans from
various symphonies and piano
sonatas and orchestrated by
Gordon Jacob; choreography,
Ninette de Valois; décor,
Hugh Stevenson. King's
Theatre, Edinburgh, Scotland,
October 25, 1943.

PROMS Prometheus (The Crea-
tions of Prometheus), ballet
(2 acts). Music, Ludwig van
Beethoven, composed at the
suggestion of the choreographer and to his libretto;
choreography and book, Salvatore Vigano. Vienna,
Austria, March 28, 1801,
under the German title Die
Geschöpfe des Prometheus.

PROMT Promethée, ballet (1
act). Music, Maurica Ohana;
choreography, Maurice Bé-
jart; book, Pierre Rhallys;
décor, Bernard Daydé. Ballet 1956 of Milorad Misko-
vitch for Lyon Festival, June,
1956.

PROMV Prometheus, ballet.
Music, Ludwig van Beethoven,
orchestrated by Constant Lambert; choreography, Ninette
de Valois; décor, John Banting. Sadler's Wells Theatre,
London, 1936.

PROMW Prometheus, ballet.
Music, Ludwig van Beethoven;
choreography, Pino Mlakar.
Zurich, 1935.

PROSP The Prospect Before Us,
ballet (7 scenes). Music,
William Boyce, arranged by

Constant Lambert; choreography, Ninette de Valois, based on Thomas Rowland's caricature, "The Prospect Before Us, " and an incident related in John Eber's "History of the King's Theatre"; scenery and costumes, Roger Furse. Sadler's Wells Theatre, London, July 4, 1940.

PROTE Protée, ballet (1 act). Music, Claude Debussy's "Danse Sacrée et Danse Profane"; choreography, David Lichine; book, Lichine and Henry Clifford; décor, Giorgio de Chirico. Covent Garden Royal Opera House, London, July 5, 1938.

PSYCH Psyche, ballet. Music, unknown; choreography, Pierre Gardel; décor, Jean Baptiste Martin. Paris Opéra, Paris, 1790.

PULCI Pulcinella, dramatic ballet (1 act). Music, Igor Stravinsky, based on scores by Giambattista Pergolesi; choreography, Léonide Massine; curtain, scenery and costumes, Pablo Picasso. Théâtre National de l'Opéra, Paris, May 15, 1920.

PUNCH Punch and the Child, ballet (3 scenes). Music, Richard Arnell; choreography, Fred Danieli; décor, costumes and masks, Horace Armistead. City Center, New York, November 12, 1947.

PUNCJ Punch and the Judy, modern group dance. Music, Robert McBride; choreography, Martha Graham;

spoken text selected by Graham; décor, Arch Lauterer; costumes, Charlotte Trowbridge. Bennington College, Vermont, August 10, 1941.

PUPPE Die Puppenfee (The Fairy Doll), ballet (1 act). Music, Josef Bayer; choreography, Josef Hassreiter; book, Hassreiter and Franz Gaul; décor, Anton Brioschi. Vienna Hofoper, Vienna, April 10 or October 4, 1888.

PYGMA Pygmalion, ballet. Music, ?; choreography, Marie Sallé. Covent Garden, London, February 14, 1734.

PYRAM Pyramus and Thisbe, ballet. Music, Georges Enesco; choreography, William Christensen; décor, Russel Hartley. San Francisco, Calif. , 1945.

QARRT Qarrtsiluni, ballet (1 act). Music, Knudåge Riisager; choreography, Harald Lander; book, Riisager and Lander; scenery and costumes, Svend Johansen. Royal Theatre, Copenhagen, February 21, 1942.

QUATR Les Quatre Saisons, ballet (1 act). Choreography, Jules Perrot; book, Perrot. Her Majesty's Theatre, London, June 13, 1848.

QUELQ Quelques Fleurs, ballet (1 act). Music, Daniel François Auber, compiled by Harry G. Schumer; choreography and book, Ruthanna Boris; scenery and costumes, Robert Davison. Metropolitan Opera House, New York, September, 1948.

QUEST The Quest, ballet (5

scenes). Music, William Walton; choreography, Frederick Ashton; book, Doris Langley, after Spenser's "Faerie Queene"; décor, John Piper. New Theatre, London, April 6, 1943.

RAKES The Rake's Progress, dramatic ballet (6 scenes). Music, Gavin Gordon; choreography, Ninette de Valois; book, Gordon, based on the series of paintings by William Hogarth; scenery and costumes, Rex Whistler. Sadler's Wells Theatre, London, May 20, 1935.

RAOUL Raoul de Créqui, or The Return from the Crusades, grand pantomimic ballet (5 acts). Music, Cavos and Sushkov; choreography and book, Charles Didelot; scenery, Kondrateyev and Dranchet; costumes, Babini; machinery, Burser. Bolshoi Theatre, St. Petersburg, either May 5 or October 3, 1819.

RAYMO Raymonda, ballet (3 acts). Music, Alexandre Glazunov; choreography, Marius Petipa; book, Petipa and Lydia Pashkova; scenery, Allegri, Ivanov and Lambini. Maryinsky Theatre, St. Petersburg, January 7, 1898.

REDPO The Red Poppy, ballet (3 acts). Music, R. M. Glière; choreography, V. Tikhomirov and L. Lashchilin; book, M. Kurilko and V. Tikhomirov; scenery, M. Kurilko. Bolshoi Theatre, Moscow, June 14, 1927. Later retitled The

Red Flower.

REDSA Red Sails, ballet (prologue, 3 acts). Music, V. M. Yurovsky; choreography, N. Popko, L. Pospekhin and A. Radunsky; book, A. V. Talanov, after the story by A. Green; scenery and costumes, P. Williams. Kuibyshev, Russia, December 30, 1942.

RENAR Le Renard (The Fox), ballet-burlesque (1 act). Music and book, Igor Stravinsky, English language version, Harvey Officer; choreography, George Balanchine; décor, Esteban Francés. First American production Hunter College Playhouse, New York, January 13, 1947; previously produced with other choreography elsewhere.

RENCO La Rencontre (Oedipus and the Sphinx), ballet (1 act). Music, Henri Sauguet; choreography, David Lichine; book, Boris Kochno; décor, Christian Bérard. Théâtre des Champs-Élysées, Paris, November 8, 1948.

RENDE Le Rendez-Vous, ballet (1 act). Music, Kosma; choreography, Roland Petit; book, Jacques Prevert; scenery, Brassai; costumes, Mayo. Théâtre Sarah Bernhardt, Paris, June 15, 1945.

REVAN Revanche (Revenge), dramatic ballet (prologue, 4 scenes). Music, Giuseppe Verdi, from "Il Trovatore," arranged by Isaac van Grove; choreography, Ruth Page; book, Page and Nicholas Remisov; décor, Antoni Clavé. Théâtre de l'Empire, Paris, October 17, 1951.

REVOL La Révolte au Serail
(The Revolt in the Harem),
ballet (3 acts). Music, T.
Labarre; choreography and
book, Philippe Taglioni;
scenery, Ciceri, Léger,
Feuchère, and Desplèchin;
costumes, Duponchel.
Théâtre de l'Académie
Royale de Musique, Paris,
December 4, 1833.

RHAPS Rhapsody in Blue, ballet (1 act). Music, George
Gershwin; choreography
and book, Anton Dolin;
scenery and costumes,
Gladys Spencer-Curling.
Théâtre des Champs.
Élysées, Paris, April 16,
1928.

RINAL Rinaldo and Armida,
ballet (1 act). Music, Malcolm Arnold; choreography,
Frederick Ashton; scenery
and costumes, Peter Rice.
Royal Opera, Covent Gar-
den, London, January 6,
1955.

RITES Rites, ballet (1 act).
Music, Ingvar Lidholm;
choreography, Birgit
Aakesson; book, Erik Linde-
gren; décor and costumes,
Lennart Rhode. Royal
Swedish Ballet, March 26,
1960.

RODEO Rodeo, or The Court-
ing at Burnt Ranch, American ballet (2 scenes). Music, Aaron Copland; choreography, Agnes De Mille;
scenery, Oliver Smith;
costumes, Kermit Love.
Ballet Russe de Monte
Carlo, Metropolitan Opera
House, New York, October
16, 1942.

ROICA Le Roi Candaule, ballet

(4 acts). Music, Cesare
Pugni; choreography, Marius
Petipa; book, Petipa and
Vernoy de Saint-Georges;
scenery, David. Maryinsky
Theatre, St. Petersburg,
October 17, 1868.

ROINU Le Roi Nu, ballet (1
act). Music, Jean Françaix;
choreography, Serge Lifar;
book, Lifar, after the story
by Hans Christian Andersen;
scenery and costumes, Pedro
Pruna. Théâtre National de
l'Opéra, Paris, June 15,
1936.

ROINV Le Roi Nu, ballet (1
act). Music, Jean Françaix;
choreography, Ninette de
Valois; book, after the story
by Hans Christian Andersen;
décor, Hedley Briggs. Sadler's Wells Theatre, London,
April 7, 1938.

ROMAN Romantic Age, divertissement (1 act). Music, Vincenzo Bellini, arranged by
Antal Dorati; choreography,
Anton Dolin; book based on
the ballet "Aglaë, or Cupid's
Pupil," by Filippo Taglioni;
décor, Carlos Mérida.
Metropolitan Opera House,
New York, October 23,
1942.

ROMEA Romeo and Juliet, bal-
let (3 acts). Music, Sergei
Prokofiev, arranged by S.
Radlov; choreography, L.
Lavronsky; book, adapted
from the play by William
Shakespeare; scenery and
costumes, P. Williams.
Kirov State Theatre of Opera
and Ballet, Leningrad, 1940.

ROMEJ Romeo and Juliet, dance
poem (1 act). Music, Tchaikovsky; choreography, Gyula

Harangozó; book, adapted
from the play by William
Shakespeare; scenery and
costumes, Gustave Oláh,
Junior. Royal Hungarian
Opera House, Budapest,
April 19, 1939.

ROMEO Romeo and Juliet,
narrative ballet (1 act).
Music, Frederic Delius,
arranged by Antal Dorati;
choreography, Antony Tu-
dor; book, Tudor, based
on Shakespeare's tragedy;
scenery and costumes, Eu-
gene Berman. Metropoli-
tan Opera House, New York,
April 6, 1942 (partial performance); presented in its
entirety, same theater,
April 10, 1942.

ROSID Rosida ou les Mines de
Syracuse, ballet (5 scenes).
Music, Cesare Pugni;
choreography, Fanny Cerito;
scenery, Charles Marshall.
Her Majesty's Theatre,
London, May 29, 1845.

ROSSG Le Rossignol et la
Rose (The Nightingale and
the Rose), ballet. Music,
Robert Schumann; chore-
ography, Roland Petit;
book, after the story by
Oscar Wilde. Théâtre des
Champs-Élysées, Paris,
1945.

ROSSI Le Rossignol et la
Rose, ballet (1 act). Mu-
sic, Jānis Kalninš; choreography, Osvalds Lēmanis;
book, adapted from the
story by Oscar Wilde;
scenery and costumes,
Peter Rožlapa. National
Opera, Riga, October 21,
1938.

ROUGE Rouge et Noir (Red

and Black), also called L'
Étrange Farandole (Strange
Farandole), ballet (4 move-
ments, one scene). Music,
Dmitri Shostakovich; chore-
ography and book, Léonide
Massine; scenery and cos-
tumes, Henri Matisse. Théâ-
tre de Monte Carlo, Monte
Carlo, May 11, 1939.

RUSES Ruses d'Amour (also
called The Trial of Damis),
ballet (1 act). Music, Alexandre Glazunov; choreography
and book, Marius Petipa.
Hermitage Theatre, St.
Petersburg, January 17,
1900.

RUSSI Russian Soldier, ballet
(4 scenes). Music, Sergei
Prokofiev; choreography,
Michel Fokine; décor and
costumes, Mitislav Doboujinsky. Metropolitan Opera
House, New York, April 6,
1942.

RUSSL Russlan and Ludmilla,
ballet. Music, ?; chore-
ography, Adam Glouzhkovsky.
Moscow School, Moscow,
1811?

SACRD Le Sacré du Printemps,
ballet. Music, Igor Stra-
vinsky; choreography, Léonide Massine. 1920.

SACRE Le Sacré du Printemps
(The Rite of Spring), "a picture of ancient Russia" (2
acts). Music, Igor Stravinsky; choreography, Vaslav
Nijinsky; book, Stravinsky
and Nicholas Roehrich; scenery and costumes, Roehrich.
Théâtre des Champs-Élysées,
Paris, May 29, 1913.

SADKO Sadko, ballet. Music,
Nicolai Rimsky-Korsakov

(Under-sea act from the
opera "Sadko"); choreogra-
phy, Adolph Bolm; décor,
Natalia Gontcharova.
Maryinsky Theatre, St.
Petersburg, 1915.

SAILO The Sailor's Return,
ballet (6 scenes). Music,
Arthur Oldham; choreogra-
phy, Andrée Howard;
book, Howard, after the
novel by David Garnett;
scenery and costumes,
Howard. Sadler's Wells
Theatre, London, June 2,
1947.

SAINT Saint Francis (Nobilis-
sima Visione), choreographic legend (1 act, 5 scenes),
Music, Paul Hindemith;
choreography, Léonide
Massine; book, Hindemith
and Massine; scenery and
costumes, Pavel Tchelichev.
Theatre Royal, Drury Lane,
London, July 21, 1938.

SAISO Les Saisons (The Sea-
sons), ballet (1 act). Music, Alexandre Glazunov;
choreography and book,
Marius Petipa; scenery,
Lambini; costumes, Pono-
marev. Hermitage Theatre,
St. Petersburg, February
7, 1900.

SAKUN Sakuntala, pantomimic
ballet (2 acts). Music,
Ernest Reyer; choreography,
Lucien Petipa; book, Théo-
phile Gautier; scenery,
Martin, Nolan and Rubé.
Théâtre Impérial de l'
Opéra, Paris, July 14,
1858.

SALAD Salade, choreographic
counterpoint (2 acts). Music, Darius Milhaud; choreography, Léonide Massine;

book, Albert Flament; scen-
ery and costumes, Georges
Braque. Théâtre de la
Cigale, Paris, May 17, 1924.

SALAM Salamanca do Jaraú,
ballet (7 scenes). Music,
Luiz Cosme; choreography,
Tatiana Leskova; book,
Cosme, based on a folk
tale by Simões Lopes Neto;
décor and costumes, Tomás
Santa Rosa. Porto Alegre,
Brazil, 1945.

SALAO Salammbô, ballet. Music, Andrei Arends; choreography, Igor Moiseyev;
book, after the novel by
Gustave Flaubert. 1932;
previously choreographed by
Alexander Gorsky, 1910.

SALOM Salomé, ballet. Music,
Richard Strauss; choreography, Rosella Hightower; décor, Celia Hubbard. Théâtre des Champs-Élysées,
Paris, 1950.

SALON El Salon Mexico, ballet
(1 act). Music, Aaron Copland; choreography, Doris
Humphrey; costumes and
lighting, Elizabeth Parsons.
Studio Theatre, New York,
March 11, 1943.

SAMSO Samson Agonistes, modern dance work. Music,
Robert Starer; choreography
and costumes, Martha Gra-
ham; décor, Rouben Ter-
Arutunian. 54th Street Theater, New York, April 16,
1961, under its original title Visionary Recital.

SCARA Scaramouche, ballet (2
scenes). Music, Jan Sibelius; choreography, Osvalds
Lemanis; book, Paul Knudsen;
scenery and costumes, Nik-

lavs Strunke. National
Opera, Riga, December
10, 1936.

SCARE The Scarecrow, sym-
bolic ballet (2 scenes).
Music, Francisco Mignone;
choreography, Tatiana Leskova; book, Vera Pacheco
Jordão; décor and cos-
tumes, Tomás Santa Rosa.
Teatro Municipal, Rio de
Janeiro, Brazil, 1954.

SCHEE Schéhérazade, ballet.
Music, Nicholas Rimsky-
Korsakoff; choreography,
Vladimir Bourmeister;
book, after "The Arabian
Nights. " 195?

SCHEH Schéhérazade, dramatic ballet (1 act). Music,
N. Rimsky-Korsakoff;
choreography, Michel Fo-
kine; book, Alexandre
Benois, based on the first
story of "The Arabian
Nights"; scenery and cos-
tumes, Léon Bakst. Théâ-
tre National de l'Opéra,
Paris, June 4, 1910.

SCHLA Schlagobers, ballet
(2 acts). Music, Richard
Strauss; choreography,
Heinrich Kröller; book,
Strauss; scenery and cos-
tumes, Ada Nigrin. Opern-
theater, Vienna, May 9,
1924.

SCOTC Scotch Symphony,
classic ballet (3 parts).
Music, Felix Mendelssohn;
choreography, George
Balanchine; scenery,
Horace Armistead; cos-
tumes, Barbara Karinska
and David Ffolkes; light-
ing, Jean Rosenthal. City
Center, New York, No-
vember 11, 1952.

SCUOL Scuola di Ballo (The
Dancing School), ballet (1
act). Music, Boccherine,
arranged by J. Français;
choreography, Léonide Massine; book, Massine, based
on Goldoni's comedy; scenery and costumes, Comte
Étienne de Beaumont. Théâtre de Monte Carlo, Monte
Carlo, April 25, 1933.

SEAGA Sea Gallows, ballet (1
act). Music, Michel Per-
rault; choreography, Eric
Hyrst; décor, Alexis Chi-
riaeff; costumes, Claudette
Picard. Comédie Canadienne
Theatre, Montreal, Canada,
April 16, 1959.

SEBAS Sebastian, melodramatic
ballet (3 scenes). Music and
story, Gian-Carlo Menotti;
choreography, Edward Caton;
scenery, Oliver Smith; costumes, Milena. International
Theater, New York, October
31, 1944.

SELIN Selina, ballet (1 act).
Music, arranged by Guy War-
rack from several Rossini
operas; choreography, Andrée
Howard; décor and libretto,
Peter Williams. Sadler's
Wells Theatre, London,
November 16, 1948.

SEMIR Semiramis, ballet. Music, Christoph Willibald
Gluck; choreography, Gas-
paro Angiolini. Vienna,
1765.

SEPTU Septuor, ballet (1 act).
Music, Jean Lutèce; chore-
ography, Serge Lifar; décor,
Yves Bonnat. Paris Opéra,
Paris, January 29, 1950.

SERAP Seraphic Dialogue (originally Triumph of St. Joan),

modern dance work. Music, Norman Dello Joio; choreography, Martha Graham; décor, Isamu Noguchi. ANTA Theater, New York, May 8, 1955.

SEVED   The Seven Deadly Sins (De syv Dodssyndet), ballet (prologue, 7 scenes, epilogue). Music, Kurt Weill; choreography, Harald Lander; book, Bertolt Brecht; scenery and costumes, Svend Johansen. Royal Theatre, Copenhagen, November 12, 1936.

SEVEM   Seventh Symphony, ballet (1 act, 2 scenes). Music, Dmitri Shostakovich; choreography, Igor Belsky; décor, Mikhail Gordon. Kirov Theatre, Leningrad, April 14, 1961.

SEVEN   The Seventh Symphony, choreographic symphony (4 movements). Music, Beethoven's Seventh Symphony; choreography and book, Léonide Massine; scenery and costumes, Christian Bérard. Théâtre de Monte Carlo, Monte Carlo, May 5, 1938.

SEVES   The Seven Sins, ballet (1 act). Music, Maurice Ravel ("La Valse"); choreography, Tatiana Leskova; book, décor and costumes, Thamar de Letay. Teatro Municipal, Rio de Janeiro, Brazil, 1954.

SHADO   The Shadow, ballet (1 scene). Music, Erno von Dohnányi; choreography and book, John Cranko; scenery and costumes, John Piper. Royal Opera House, Covent Garden,

London, March 3, 1953.

SHADP   Shadow on the Prairie, ballet (1 act). Music, Robert Fleming, adapted from the old English song "The Mistletoe Bough"; choreography and book, Gweneth Lloyd; décor, John Graham; costumes, Stewart McKay. The Playhouse, Winnipeg, Man., October 30, 1952.

SHADW   Shadow of the Wind, ballet (6 episodes). Music, Gustav Mahler's song cycle "Das Lied von der Erde" ("The Song of the Earth"); choreography and book, Antony Tudor, based on poems of the eighth century Chinese poet Li Po; décor, Jo Mielziner. Metropolitan Opera House, New York, April 14, 1948.

SHOOT   The Shooting of Dan McGrew, ballet (1 act). Music, Eric Wild, an arrangement of traditional drinking songs; choreography and book, Gweneth Lloyd, based on the poem by Robert Service; décor, Joseph Chrabas; costumes, David Yeddeau. The Playhouse, Winnipeg, Man., May 2, 1950.

SHURA   Shurale, ballet (3 acts, 4 scenes). Music, Farid Yarullin; choreography and book, Leonid Yacobson, from the Tartar folk tales by the Tartar writer Faizie; décor, A. Ptushko, L. Milchin and I. Vano. Kirov Theatre, Leningrad, June 28, 1950.

SIEBA   Sieba, ballet (6 acts). Music, Romualdo Marenco; choreography and book, Luigi Manzotti; scenery,

Alfredo Edel.   Turin,
1876.

SIREN   Les Sirènes, ballet (1
act).   Music, Lord Ber-
ners; choreography, Fred-
erick Ashton; décor, Cecil
Beaton.   Royal Opera
House, Covent Garden,
London, November 12,
1946.

SISYP   Sisyphus, ballet (1 act).
Music, Karl-Birger Blom-
dahl; choreography, Birgit
Aakesson and Kaare Gun-
dersen; décor and costumes
Tor Horlin.   Royal Swedish
Ballet, 1957.

SKATI   Skating-Rink, ballet (1
act).   Music, Arthur
Honegger; choreography,
Jean Borlin; book, Riciotto
Canudo; scenery and cos-
tumes, Fernand Léger.
Théâtre des Champs-
Élysées, Paris, January
20, 1922.

SKYSC   Skyscrapers, ballet of
modern city life (1 act).
Music, John Alden Car-
penter; choreography,
Sammy Lee; settings and
costumes, Robert Edmond
Jones.   Metropolitan
Opera House, New York,
February, 1926.

SLAUG   Slaughter on Tenth
Avenue, dramatic ballet
within a musical revue
("On Your Toes" [Richard
Rodgers, George Abbott
and Lorenz Hart]).   Music,
Rodgers; choreography,
George Balanchine; scen-
ery, Jo Mielziner; cos-
tumes, Irene Sharaff.
Imperial Theater, New
York, April 11, 1936.

SLEEP   The Sleeping Beauty (The
Sleeping Princess) (La Belle
au Bois Dormant), classic
ballet (prologue, 3 acts).
Music, Tchaikovsky; choreography, Marius Petipa;
book, Petipa and Ivan Vsevolojsky, after tales by Charles
Perrault; scenery and costumes, Vsevolojsky.   Maryinsky Theatre, St. Petersburg, January 15, 1890.
Produced as The Sleeping
Princess in a revised version at Alhambra Theatre,
London, November 2, 1921.

SNOWM   The Snow Maiden, ballet (3 acts).   Music, Peter
Ilich Tchaikovsky; chore-
ography, Vladimir Bour-
meister; décor, Yuri Pi-
menov and Gennady Epishin.
Festival Hall, London, July
17, 1961.

SNOWN   The Snow Maiden, ballet.
Music, Alexander Glazunov;
choreography, Bronislava
Nijinska; libretto, Sergei J.
Denham; décor, Boris Aaron-
son.   Metropolitan Opera
House, New York, October
12, 1942.

SOIRE   Soirée Musicale, ballet
(1 act).   Music, Rossini-
Benjamin Britten suite
"Soirées Musicales"; choreography, Antony Tudor; décor, Hugh Stevenson.   Pal-
ladium, London, November
26, 1938.

SOLIT   Solitaire, ballet (1 act).
Music, Malcolm Arnold;
choreography, Kenneth Mac-
Millan; décor, Desmond
Heeley.   Sadler's Wells
Theatre, London, June 7,
1956.

SOMNA La Somnambule ou l'
Arrivée d'un Nouveau
Seigneur (The Sleepwalker,
or The Arrival of a New
Lord of the Manor), pan-
tomimic ballet (3 acts).
Music, composed and ar-
ranged by Hérold; chore-
ography, Jean Aumer;
book, Aumer and Scribe.
Théâtre de l'Académie
Royale de Musique, Paris,
September 19, 1827.

SONAT Sonate à Trois, ballet
(1 act). Béla Bartók;
choreography, Maurice
Béjart; book, based on
Jean-Paul Sartre's play
"Huis Clos" ("No Exit");
décor, Bert. Originally
titled after the play.
Théâtre Marigny, Paris,
June 19, 1957.

SONGO The Song of the Nightingale (Le Chant du Rossignol), dramatic ballet (2
scenes), based on Hans
Christian Andersen's story
"The Nightingale." Music,
Igor Stravinsky; chore-
ography, Léonide Massine;
scenery and costumes,
Henri Matisse. Théâtre
de l'Opéra, Paris, Febru-
ary 2, 1920.

SORCE The Sorcerer's Ap-
prentice, ballet (1 act).
Music, Paul Dukas; chore-
ography, Maryla Gremo;
book, based on the ballad
by Goethe; décor, Fernando
Pamplona. Teatro Muni-
cipal, Rio de Janeiro,
Brazil, 1959.

SOURC La Source, ballet (3
acts). Music, Leon Min-
kus and L. Delibes; choreography, Arthur Saint-Léon;
book, Saint-Léon and Charles

Nuitter; scenery, Despléchin
and Lavastre, and Rubé and
Chaperon. Théâtre Impérial
de l'Opéra, Paris, Novem-
ber 12, 1866.

SOUVE Souvenirs, ballet (1 act).
Music, Samuel Barber;
choreography, Todd Bolender;
décor, Rouben Ter-Arutunian.
City Center, New York, November 15, 1955.

SPART Spartacus, ballet (4 acts).
Music, Aram Khachaturian;
choreography, Leonide Yacobson; book, Nicolai Volkov;
décor, Valentina Khodasevich.
Kirov Theatre, Leningrad,
December 27, 1956.

SPECL Spectacle, arranged by
Bergonzio di Botta on the
occasion of the marriage of
the Duke of Milan and Isabella of Aragon (1459),
where each dish at the wedding banquet was presented
with appropriate dances.

SPECT Le Spectre de la Rose
(The Spirit of the Rose),
ballet (1 act). Music, Carl
Maria von Weber; chore-
ography, Michel Fokine;
book, J. L. Vaudoyer; scenery and costumes, Léon
Bakst. Théâtre de Monte
Carlo, April 19, 1911.

SPELL The Spellbound Child (L'
Enfant et les Sortilèges),
opera-ballet (2 parts). Music, Maurice Ravel (L'Enfant
et les Sortilèges"); choreography, George Balanchine;
poem, Colette (Mme. Colette
Willy); décor and costumes,
Aline Bernstein. Central
High School of Needle Trades,
New York, November 20,
1946.

SPHIN   The Sphinx, ballet.
Music, Henri Sauguet;
choreography, David Li-
chine; décor, Christian
Bérard.   Metropolitan
Opera House, New York,
1955.

SPIDE   The Spider's Banquet
(Le Festin de l'Araignée),
ballet (1 act).   Music, Albert Roussel, composed
for the original work, "Le
Festin de l'Araignée");
choreography, Andrée How-
ard; book, Gilbert de
Voisins; scenery and cos-
tumes, Michael Ayrton.
New Theatre, London,
June 20, 1944.

SPIRI   The Spirit of the Sea,
dance fantasy.   Music,
R. S. Stoughton; choreogra-
phy, Ruth St. Denis; décor,
Robert Law Studio.   New
York, 1915/16.

SPRIN   A Spring Tale, romantic
ballet (4 parts).   Music,
F. A. Cohen; choreography
and book, Kurt Jooss; costumes, Hein Heckroth.
Shakespeare Memorial
Theatre, Stratford-on-
Avon, England, February
2, 1939.

SQUAR   Square Dance, ballet
(1 act).   Music, excerpts
from Arcangelo Corelli's
Suite for Strings and from
several concerti grossi by
Antonio Vivaldi; choreography, George Balanchine.
City Center, New York,
November 21, 1957.

STARS   The Stars, fantastic
ballet (4 acts).   Music,
A. J. Simon; choreography,
Ivan Clustine; book, K.
Valts.   Bolshoi Theatre,

Moscow, January 25, 1898.

STELL   Stella ou les Contre-
bandiers, pantomimic ballet
(2 acts).   Music, Cesare
Pugni; choreography and
book, Arthur Saint-Léon;
scenery, Cambon and Thierry.
Théâtre de l'Opéra, Paris,
February 22, 1850.

STONE   The Stone Flower, ballet
(3 acts).   Music, Sergei
Prokofiev; choreography,
Leonid Lavrovsky; libretto,
Lavrovsky and Mira Mendel-
ssohn-Prokofieva, inspired
by the story "The Malachite
Casket" by Pavel Bazhov,
based on Ural Mountain folk
tales.   Bolshoi Theatre,
Moscow, 1954.

STORY   Story of Mankind, modern dance work.   Music,
Lionel Nowak; choreography,
Doris Humphrey; story,
based on a "New Yorker"
cartoon by Carl Rose; costumes, Pauline Lawrence.
Belasco Theater, New York,
January 5, 1947.

STREE   Street Games, ballet (1
act).   Music, Jacques Ibert;
choreography and book, Walter Gore; scenery and costumes, Ronald Wilson.
Wimbledon Theatre, London,
November 11, 1952.

STREL   Gli Strelizzi (The Streletsy), mimodrama (6 acts).
Music, Salvatore Viganò,
based on airs of other composers; choreography and
book, Viganò; scenery,
Alessandro Sanquirico.
Teatro La Fenice, Venice,
1809.

STRET   A Streetcar Named Desire, dramatic ballet (1 act).

Music, Alex North, orchestrated by Rayburn Wright;
choreography, Valerie Bettis, based on the play by
Tennessee Williams; scen-
ery, Peter Larkin; cos-
tumes, Saul Bolasni. Her
Majesty's Theatre, Mon-
treal, October 9, 1952.

SUMMI Summer Interlude,
ballet (1 act). Music,
Ottorio Respighi's arrangement of "Ancient Airs and
Dances"; choreography,
Michael Somes; décor,
Sophie Fedorovitch. Sad-
ler's Wells Theatre, Lon-
don, March 28, 1950.

SUNDE Sundered Majesty, mod-
ern dance work. Music,
Manuel Galea; choreography,
Myra Kinch; book, after
Shakespeare's "King Lear";
décor, John Christian.
Jacob's Pillow Dance Fes-
tival, Lee, Mass., 1955.

SVETL Svetlana, ballet. Mu-
sic, Klebanov; choreography,
Popko, Possekhine and
Radunsky; book, Zhiger.
Affiliated Bolshoi Theatre,
Moscow, 1939.

SWANA Swan Lake, ballet.
Music, Peter Ilich Tchai-
kovsky; choreography,
George Balanchine, after
Lev Ivanov; costumes
and décor, Cecil Beaton.
City Center, New York,
November 20, 1951.

SWANE Swan Lake, ballet
(prologue, 4 acts). Mu-
sic, Peter Ilich Tchai-
kovsky, arranged by Ric-
cardo Drigo; choreography,
Vladimir Bourmeister (1st,
3rd and 4th acts), and
after Lev Ivanov (2nd act);

book, V. P. Begitcheff and
Vasily Geltzer; décor,
Anatole Lushkin. Stanislavsky and Nemirovich-Dan-
chenko Lyric Theatre, Moscow, April 24, 1953.

SWANK Swan Lake, ballet (prologue, 3 acts, today often
described as ballet in 4
acts). Music, Peter Ilich
Tchaikovsky; choreography,
Julius Reisinger; book, V. P.
Begitcheff and Vasily Geltzer;
décor, Shangin, Valtz and
Groppius. Bolshoi Theatre,
Moscow, February 20, 1877
(old style) and March 4, 1877
(new style).

SWANL Swan Lake (Le Lac des
Cygnes), dramatic ballet (4
acts). Music, Peter Ilich
Tchaikovsky; choreography,
Marius Petipa and Lev Ivanov; book, V. P. Begitcheff
and Vasily Geltzer; scenery,
Botcharov and Levogt. Maryinsky Theatre, St. Petersburg, January 15, 1895.

SWANT The Swan of Tuonela,
ballet (1 act). Music, Jean
Sibelius; choreography, Dennis Gray; book, Gray, based
on the Finnish epic "Kalevala";
décor and costumes, Mario
Conde. Teatro Municipal,
Rio de Janeiro, Brazil,
1956.

SYLPH La Sylphide, ballet (2
acts). Music, Jean Schneitz-
hoeffer; choreography, Phil-
ippe Taglioni; book, Adolphe
Nourrit; scenery, Pierre
Ciceri; costumes, Eugène
Lami. Théâtre de l'Académie
Royale de Musique, Paris,
March 12, 1832.

SYLPI Les Sylphides (original
title Chopiniana), classic

ballet (1 act). Music,
Frédéric Chopin, orches-
trated by Alexander Glaz-
ounov; choreography, Mi-
chel Fokine; scenery and
costumes, Alexandre
Benois. Théâtre du
Chatelet, Paris, June 2,
1909

SYLPL La Sylphide (Sylfiden)
(The Sylphide), romantic
ballet (2 acts). Music,
Hermann von Løvenskjold;
choreography, August
Bournonville. Copenhagen,
Denmark, 1836.

SYLVA Sylvia, ballet (3 acts).
Music, Léo Delibes; choreography, Frederick Ash-
ton; book, Jules Barbier
and Baron de Reinach after
Tasso's "Aminta"; settings
and costumes, Robin and
Christopher Ironside.
Royal Opera, Covent Gar-
den, London, September
4, 1952.

SYLVI Sylvia or, The Nymph
of Diana (La Nymphe de
Diane), ballet (3 acts, 4
scenes). Music, Léo
Delibes; choreography,
Louis Mérante; book,
Jules Barbier and Baron
de Reinach; scenery,
Chéret, Rubé and Chaper-
on; costumes, Lacoste.
Théâtre de l'Opéra, Paris,
June 14, 1876.

SYMPH Symphonie Fantastique
(An Episode in the Life of
an Artist), symphonic ballet or choreographic sym-
phony (5 movements or
scenes). Music, Hector
Berlioz; choreography,
Léonide Massine; book,
Berlioz; scenery and cos-
tumes, Christian Bérard.

Royal Opera, Covent Garden,
London, July 24, 1936.

SYMPP Symphonie pour un
Homme Seul (Symphony for
a Lonely Man), ballet (1 act).
Music, an electronic score
by Pierre Schaeffer and
Pierre Henry; choreography,
Maurice Béjart. Théâtre de
l'Étoile, Paris, August 3,
1955.

TALIS The Talisman, fantastic
ballet (3 acts). Music, Riccardo Drigo; choreography,
Marius Petipa; book, Petipa
and K. A. Tarnovsky. Mar-
yinsky Theatre, St. Petersburg, January 25, 1889.

TALLY Tally-Ho, or The Frail
Quarry, ballet (1 act). Music, from Felix Mottl's ballet suite of music by Christoph Wilibald Gluck, ar-
ranged by Paul Nordoff;
choreography, Agnes de
Mille; décor, Motley. Ballet
Theater, Los Angeles, Calif.,
February 25, 1944.

TARAS Taras Bulba, ballet (3
acts). Music, V. Soloviev-
Sedoy; choreography, F. V.
Lopukhov; book, based on
the novel by Nicholas Gogol.
Kirov State Theatre of Opera
and Ballet, Leningrad, 1940.

TAREN La Tarentule, pantomimic
ballet (2 acts). Music, Casimir Gide; choreography, Jean
Coralli; theme, Coralli and
Scribe. Théâtre de l'Aca-
démie Royale de Musique,
Paris, June 24, 1839.

TELEM Télémaque dans l'Ile
de Calypso, ballet. Music,
unknown; choreography,
Pierre Gardel. Paris
Opéra, Paris, 1791.

TERMI Terminal, ballet (1
act). Music, Herbert Kings-
ley, orchestrated by Albert
Boss; choreography and
book, Catherine Littlefield;
scenery and costumes, A.
Pinto. Théâtre des Champs
Élysées, Paris, June 1,
1937.

THAMA Thamar, ballet (1 act).
Music, Balakirev; chore-
ography, Michel Fokine;
book, Léon Bakst; scen-
ery and costumes, Bakst.
Théâtre du Chatelet, Paris,
May 20, 1912.

THEAO Théa ou la Fée aux
Fleurs, ballet (1 act).
Music, Cesare Pugni;
choreography and book,
Paul Taglioni; scenery,
Charles Marshall; costumes,
Miss Bradley and Mr.
Whales. Her Majesty's
Theatre, London, March
17, 1847.

THIEF The Thief Who Loved
a Ghost, story ballet or
entertainment (1 act). Music, Carl Maria von Weber,
arranged by Hershy Kay;
choreography, Herbert
Ross and John Ward; scen-
ery and costumes, Ward.
Young Men's Hebrew As-
sociation, New York, Oc-
tober 14, 1950.

THREE The Three Fat Men,
ballet (4 acts). Music,
V. A. Oransky; choreography,
I. A. Moiseyev; book, I.
Olecha; scenery, B. A.
Matrunine. Bolshoy Thea-
tre, Moscow, March 1,
1935.

THREN Threnody, modern dance
work. Music, Benjamin
Britten's "Sinfonia da Re-

quiem"; choreography, Mary
Anthony; book, based on
J. M. Synge's one-act play,
"Riders to the Sea"; décor,
William Sherman. Benning-
ton College, Vermont, Spring,
1956.

THREV Three Virgins and a
Devil, comedy ballet (1 act).
Music, Ottorino Respighi
("Antiche Danze ed Arie");
choreography, Agnes De
Mille; scenario, Ramon Reed;
scenery, Arne Lundborg
after sketches by Sophie
Harris; costumes, Motley.
Majestic Theater, New York,
February 11, 1941. A pre-
vious version using music
by Walford Hyden was pre-
sented in the review "Why
Not Tonight" at the Palace
Theatre, London, 1934.

TILEU Til Eulenspiegel, ballet.
Music, Richard Strauss ("Til
Eulenspiegel's Merry Pranks");
choreography, Jean Babilée;
scenery and costumes, Tom
Keogh. Théâtre des Champs
Élysées, Paris, November 9,
1949.

TIRES Tiresias, dramatic ballet
(3 scenes). Music, Constant
Lambert; choreography, Frederick Ashton; book, Constant
Lambert; scenery and cos-
tumes, Isabel Lambert.
Royal Opera House, Covent
Garden, London, July 19,
1951.

TITAN I Titani, ballet (6 acts).
Music, Salvatore Viganò,
based on airs of other composers; choreography and
book, Viganò; scenery, Alessandro Sanquirico. Teatro
alla Scala, Milan, October
11, 1819.

TRAGD La Tragède de Salomé,
ballet. Music, Florent
Schmitt; choreography,
Nicola Guerra; décor, Piot.
Paris Opéra, Paris, April
1, 1919.

TRAGE La Tragédie de Salomé,
ballet (1 act, 3 parts).
Music, Florent Schmitt;
choreography, Boris Roman-
off; scenario based on a
poem by Robert d'Humières.
Paris Opéra, Paris, July,
1913.

TRAGF A Tragedy of Fashion
(or The Scarlet Scissors),
ballet (1 act). Music, from
Eugene Goossen's "Kalei-
doscope"; choreography,
Frederick Ashton; décor,
Sophie Fedorovitch. Lyric
Theatre, Hammersmith,
England, June 15, 1926.

TRAGG La Tragédie de Salomé,
ballet. Music, Florent
Schmitt; choreography, Loie
Fuller. Théâtre des Arts,
Paris, 1907.

TRAGH La Tragédie de Salomé,
ballet. Music, Florent
Schmitt; choreography, Albert Aveline; décor, Brayer.
Paris Opéra, Paris, July 7,
1944.

TRAGI La Tragédie de Salomé,
ballet. Music, Florent
Schmitt; choreography,
Nenad Lhotka. Zagreb,
1953.

TRAGO La Tragedia di Orfeo,
ballet (6 scenes). Music,
Wilhelm Killmayer; chore-
ography, Heinz Rosen;
book, Angelo Poliziano;
décor, Helmut Jürgens;
costumes, Charlotte Flem-
ming. State Opera, Munich,

June 9, 1961.

TRAIN Le Train Bleu, ballet
(1 act). Music, Darius Milhaud; choreography, Bronislava Nijinska; book, Jean
Cocteau; scenery, Henri
Laurens; costumes, Chanel;
curtain, Pablo Picasso.
Théâtre des Champs-Élysées,
Paris, June 20, 1924.

TRAIT The Traitor, modern
dance work. Music, Gunther
Schuller's "Symphony for
Brasses"; choreography,
José Limón; décor, Paul
Trautvetter; costumes, Paul-
ine Lawrence. Connecticut
College, New London, Conn.,
August 19, 1954.

TRAVE The Travellers, ballet
(1 act). Music, Leonard
Salzedo; choreography, Norman Morrice; décor and
lighting, Ralph Koltai.
Spoleto, Italy, June 27, 1963.

TRICO Le Tricorne (The Three
Cornered Hat). dramatic
ballet (1 act). Music, Manuel
de Falla; choreography, Léonide Massine; book, Martinez
Sierra; scenery and costumes,
Pablo Picasso. Alhambra
Theatre, London, July 22,
1919.

TRIOM Le Triomphe de l'Amour,
ballet (3 acts). Music,
Jānis Mediņš; choreography,
Osvalds Lēmanis; book,
Voldemars Komisars; scen-
ery and costumes, Ludolfs
Liberts. National Opera,
Riga, May 9, 1935.

TRIOP Le Triomphe de L'Amour,
ballet (25 entrées). Music,
Jean-Baptiste Lully; dances
arranged by Charles L.
Beauchamps and Louis

Pécour (Pécourt); décor,
Jean Bérain; libretto,
Isaac de Bensserade and
Philippe Quinault.   French
Court, St. Germain-en-Laye,
January 21, 1681.

TRIUB   The Triumph of Bacchus
and Ariadne, ballet-cantata.
Music, Vittorio Rieti; choreography, George Balanchine;
décor and costumes, Cotrado
Cagli.   City Center, New
York, February 9, 1948.

TRIUH   The Triumph of Hope,
ballet.   Music, César
Franck; choreography, William Christensen; décor,
Jean de Botton.   San Francisco Ballet, San Fran-
cisco, Calif. , 1944.

TRIUM   The Triumph of Neptune, pantomimic ballet
(2 acts).   Music, Lord
Berners; choreography,
George Balanchine; book,
Sacheverell Sitwell; scenery and costumes, adapted
from scenes and costumes
for the Juvenile Drama,
as published by B. Pollock
and H. J. Webb.   Lyceum
Theatre, London, Decem-
ber 3, 1926.

TRIUS   Triumph of St. Joan,
later titled Seraphic Dialogue, modern dance solo.
Music, Norman Dello Joio;
choreography, Martha Gra-
ham.   Columbia Auditorium,
Louisville, Ky. , December
5, 1951.

TWELV   Twelve for the Mail-
Coach (Tolv med Posten),
ballet (1 act).   Music,
Knudage Riisager; chore-
ography, Borge Ralov; book,
Riisager, after the tale by
Hans Christian Andersen;

scenery and costumes, Svend
Johansen.   Royal Theatre,
Copenhagen, February 21,
1942.

TWOBR   Two Brothers, ballet
(1 act).   Music, Ernst von
Dohnanyi's "String Quartet
No. 2 in D flat, Op. 15";
choreography, Norman Mor-
rice; décor, Ralph Koltai.
Marlowe Theatre, Canterbury,
England, August 14, 1958.

TWORO   The Two Roses, Tadjik
ballet (3 acts).   Music, A.
Lensky; choreography, G.
Vallamat-Zoda, A. Islamova
and A. Prostenko; book,
Mukhamed Rabiyev; scenery
and costumes, V. Ryndine.
Tadjikistan Festival of Art,
Moscow, April, 1941.

TYLEU   Tyl Eulenspiegel, ballet
(1 act).   Music, Richard
Strauss' "Tyl Eulenspiegel's
Merry Pranks"; choreography,
Vaslav Nijinsky; décor, Ro-
bert Edmond Jones.   Metro-
politan Opera House, New
York, October 23, 1916.

TYLUL   Tyl Ulenspiegel, dramatic ballet (2 scenes).   Music,
Richard Strauss; choreography,
George Balanchine; scenery
and costumes, Esteban Fran-
ces; Lighting, Jean Rosenthal.
City Center, New York, November 14, 1951.

UIRAP   Uirapurú, ballet (1 act).
Music and book, Heitor Mil-
loss; choreography, Aurel
Milloss; décor, Clovis
Graciano.   Teatro Municipal,
Rio de Janeiro, Brazil, 1954.

UMBRE   The Umbrella, ballet
(1 act).   Music, Francisco
Mignone; choreography,
Aurel Milloss; book, Oswald

317 UNCLE

de Andrade, Jr. ; décor,
Heitor dos Prazeres.
Teatro Municipal, Rio de
Janeiro, Brazil, 1954.

UNCLE Uncle Remus, ballet.
Music, Gordon Jacob;
choreography, Sara Patrick;
book, based on stories by
Joel Chandler Harris; dé-
cor, Hugh Stevenson. Old
Vic, London, 1934.

UNDER Undertow, contemporary
dramatic ballet (prologue,
1 act, epilogue). Music,
William Schuman; chore-
ography, Antony Tudor;
libretto, Tudor, after a
suggestion by John van
Druten; scenery and cos-
tumes, Raymond Breinin.
Metropolitan Opera House,
New York, April 10, 1945.

UNETU Un et Un Font Deux
(One and One Make Two),
ballet (1 act). Music and
choreography, Michel
Conte; décor, Jacques de
Montjoye. Montreal,
Canada, March, 1957.

UNICO The Unicorn, The
Gorgon and the Manticore,
ballet fable. Music and
libretto, Gian-Carlo Menotti (twelve madrigals with
orchestral interlude); choreography, John Butler; dé-
cor, Jean Rosenthal; cos-
tumes, Robert Fletcher.
Coolidge Auditorium,
Washington, D. C. , October
21, 1956.

UNION Union Pacific, American ballet (1 act and 4
scenes). Music, Nicholas
Nabokov; choreography,
Léonide Massine; book,
Archibald MacLeish;
scenery, Albert Johnson;

costumes, Irene Sharaff.
Forrest Theater, Philadelphia, April 6, 1934.

USHER Usher, ballet (3 scenes).
Music, Roberto Garcia Mo-
rillo; choreography, Léonide
Massine; book, Morillo and
Massine, adapted from Edgar
Allen Poe's "The Fall of
the House of Usher"; décor,
Armando Chiesa; costumes,
Alvaro Duranona y Vedia.
Teatro Colón, Buenos Aires,
Argentina, July 1, 1955.

VALSE La Valse, choreographic
poem (1 act). Music, Maurice Ravel; choreography and
book, Bronislava Nijinska;
setting and costumes, Alexandre Benois. Théâtre de
l'Opéra, Paris, 1929.

VALSS La Valse, ballet (2
parts). Music, Maurice
Ravel; choreography, George
Balanchine; costumes, Bar-
bara Karinska; lighting, Jean
Rosenthal. City Center, New
York, February 20, 1951.

VARIL Variations on a Lonely
Theme, ballet (1 act). Mu-
sic, Johannes Brahms'
"Variations on a Theme by
Haydn"; choreography, Mi-
chel Conte; décor, Claude
Jasmin; costumes, Jacques
de Montjoye. Playhouse
Theatre, Winnipeg, Man. ,
March 18, 1960.

VENEZ Veneziana, ballet (1 act).
Music, Gaetano Donizetti,
arranged and orchestrated
by Denis Aplvor; chore-
ography, Andrée Howard;
scenery and costumes,
Sophie Fedorovich. Royal
Opera, Covent Garden, London, April 9, 1953.

VERTV Vert-Vert, pantomimic ballet (3 acts). Music, Deldevez and Tolbecque; choreography, Joseph Mazilier; book, Mazilier and De Leuven; scenery, Cambon and Thierry; costumes, Paul Lormier. Théâtre de l'Académie Nationale de Musique, Paris, November 24, 1851.

VESTA La Vestale, tragedy ballet (5 acts). Music, Salvatore Viganò, based on airs of other composers; choreography and book, Viganò; scenery, Alessandro Sanquirico. Teatro alla Scala, Milan, June 9, 1818.

VIENN Vienna- 1814, ballet (1 act). Music, Carl von Weber, orchestrated by Russell Bennett; choreography and book, Léonide Massine; scenery and costumes, Stewart Chaney. Fifty-First Street Theater, New York, October 28, 1940.

VIERG Les Vierges Folles, ballet pantomime (1 act). Music, Kurt Atterberg; choreography, Jean Borlin; book, Atterberg and Einar Nerman; scenery and costumes, Nerman. Théâtre des Champs-Élysées, Paris, November 18, 1920.

VIEUX Vieux Souvenirs ou La Lanterne Magique (Old Memories, or The Magic Lantern), ballet (1 act). Music, various composers, arranged by Edvard Helsted; choreography and book, August Bournonville. Royal Theatre, Copenhagen, December 18, 1848.

VILIA Vilia, operetta dansée. Music, Franz Lehár's "The Merry Widow," arranged and orchestrated by Isaac van Grove; choreography, Ruth Page; décor, Georges Wakhevitch. Palace Theatre, Manchester, April 30, 1953.

VIOLO Le Violon du Diable, fantastic ballet (2 acts). Music, Cesare Pugni; choreography and book, Arthur Saint-Léon; scenery, Desplêchin and Thierry. Théâtre de l'Opéra, Paris, January 19, 1849.

VISIO Vision of Marguerite, ballet (1 act). Music, Franz Liszt's "Mephisto Valse"; Choreography, Frederick Ashton; décor, James Bailey. Festival Hall, London, April 3, 1952.

VIVAN La Vivandière, pantomime ballet (1 act). Music, Cesare Pugni; choreography and book, Arthur Saint-Léon; scenery, Desplêchin, Séchan and Dièterle. Her Majesty's Theatre, London, May 23, 1844.

VOICE Voices of Spring, ballet. Music, Johann Strauss, arranged by Mois Zlatkin; choreography and book, Mikhail Mordkin; scenery and costumes, Lee Simonson. Alvin Theater, New York, November 10, 1938.

WANDE The Wanderer, ballet (4 movements). Music, Franz Schubert's "Wanderer" Fantasie; choreography and

book, Frederick Ashton;
décor, Graham Sutherland.
New Theatre, London,
January 27, 1941.

WARBE   The War Between
Men and Women, modern
dance work.   Music, Peter
Ilich Tchaikovsky's "Sym-
phony No. 6 in B minor"
(the "Pathétique"); choreography, Charles Weidman;
book, suggested by James
Thurber's cartoons.   YM-
YWHA, New York, April
25, 1954.

WEBBB   The Web, ballet (1
act).   Music, Anton von
Webern's "String Quartet,
Opus 5"; choreography,
Laverne Meyer; décor,
Diana Dewes.   Elmhurst
Studio Theatre, Camber-
ley, Surrey, England,
September 4, 1962.

WEDDI   A Wedding Bouquet,
comic ballet (1 act).   Mu-
sic, scenery and costumes,
Lord Berners; choreography,
Frederick Ashton; words,
Gertrude Stein.   Sadler's
Wells Theatre, London,
April 27, 1937.

WHIMS   The Whims of Cupid
and the Ballet Master
(Amors of Balletmesterens
Luner), comedy ballet (1
act).   Music, Jens Lolle;
choreography and book,
Vincenzo Galeotti.   Royal
Theatre, Copenhagen,
October 31, 1786.

WHITE   The White Rose, ballet
(2 scenes).   Music, Wolfgang Fortner; choreography,
Jens Keith; book, Oscar
Wilde's "The Birthday of
the Infanta"; décor, Paul
Seltenhammer.   Municipal

Opera, Berlin, April 28,
1951.

WIDOW   The Widow in the Mirror (Enken i Spejlet), ballet
(3 scenes).   Music, Bern-
hard Christensen; choreography, Borge Ralov; book,
scenery and costumes, Kjeld
Abell.   Royal Theatre, Copenhagen, November 20, 1934.

WILLI   William Tell, ballet.
Music, unknown; choreography,
Louis X. S. Henri; book, af-
ter the drama by Schiller.
Théâtre Nautique, Paris,
1834?

WINDI   Wind in the Mountains,
or A Country Calendar, bal-
let (1 act).   Music, Laurence
Rosenthal, based largely on
American songs and folk
tunes; choreography, Agnes
de Mille; décor and lighting,
Jean Rosenthal; costumes,
Stanley Simmons.   New York
State Theater, New York,
March 17, 1965.

WINTE   Winter Night, ballet (1
act).   Music, Sergei Rach-
maninov; choreography and
book, Walter Gore; scenery
and costumes, Kenneth Rowell.
Princess Theatre, Melbourne,
Australia, November 19,
1948.

WISEF   The Wise and Foolish
Virgins, ballet.   Music, Kurt
Atterberg; choreography,
Ninette de Valois; décor,
William Chappell.   Sadler's
Wells Theatre, London,
1933.

WISEV   The Wise Virgins, fantasy-ballet (1 scene).   Music,
Johann Sebastian Bach, selected and arranged by William Walton; choreography,

Frederick Ashton; scenery
and costumes, Rex Whistler.
Sadler's Wells Theatre,
London, April, 1940.

WITCB The Witch Boy, ballet
(1 act, 3 scenes). Music,
Leonard Salzedo; chore-
ography, Jack Carter;
book, based on the "Ballad
of Barbara Allen"; décor,
Norman McDowell. Am-
sterdam, May 24, 1956.

WITHI Within the Quota, bal-
let (1 act). Music, Cole
Porter; choreography,
Jean Borlin; book, scenery
and costumes, Gerald
Murphy. Théatre des
Champs-Élysées, Paris,
October 25, 1923.

WOODE The Wooden Prince,
ballet (1 act). Music,
Béla Bartók; choreography,
Otto Zöblich; book, Béla
Balazs, based on an old
Hungarian fairy tale; dé-
cor, Count Bánffy. Royal
Opera House, Budapest,
May 12, 1917.

XOCHI Xochitl, dance drama
(2 scenes). Music, Homer
Grunn; choreography, Ted
Shawn; scenery, Francisco
Cornejo; costumes, Shawn
and Cornejo. New York,
1915/16.

YANKE Yankee Clipper, ballet-
voyage (1 act). Music,
Paul Bowles; choreography,
Eugene Loring; book, Lin-
coln Kirstein; costumes,
Charles Rain. Town Hall,
Saybrook, Conn., July 12,
1937.

YARAA Yara, ballet (3 scenes).
Music, Heitor Villa-Lobos

("Bachianas," No. 4 and
No. 7); choreography, Har-
ald Lander; idea and argu-
ment, Circe Amado; décor,
Fernando Pamplona; cos-
tumes, Kalma Murtinho.
Teatro Municipal, Rio de
Janeiro, Brazil, 1960.

YEDDA Yedda, ballet (3 acts).
Music, Olivier Métra; choreography, Louis Mérante;
book, Mérante, Philippe
Gille and Arnold Mortier;
scenery, J. B. Lavastre,
Lavastre Senior and Carpé-
zat; costumes, Eugène La-
coste. Théâtre de l'Opéra,
Paris, January 17, 1879.

ZADIG Zadig, ballet. Music,
Pierre Petit; choreography,
Serge Lifar; décor, Labisse.
Paris Opéra, Paris, 1948.

ZEPHY Zephyr and Flora (Zé-
phire et Flore), ballet (1 act).
Music, Vladimir Dukelsky
(Vernon Duke); choreography,
Léonide Massine; décor,
Georges Braque. Théâtre
de Monte Carlo, Monte Carlo,
April 28, 1925.

ZORAI Zoraiya, or The Moorish
Woman in Spain, ballet (4
acts). Music, Leon Minkus;
choreography, Marius Petipa;
book, S. N. Khudekov. Maryinsky Theatre, St. Petersburg, February 1, 1881.

ZUIMA Zuimaaluti, ballet (1 act).
Music, Cláudio Santoro's
"Fifth Symphony"; choreography, Nina Verchinina; book,
Manuel Bandeira, inspired
by the poem "Toada do Pai-
do-Mato" by Mário de An-
drade; décor, Roberto Burle-
Marx. Teatro Municipal, Rio
de Janeiro, Brazil, 1960.